DEBT'S DOMINION

A HISTORY OF BANKRUPTCY LAW
IN AMERICA

DAVID A. SKEEL, JR.

PRINCETON UNIVERSITY PRESS

PRINCETON AND OXFORD

Library of Congress Cataloging-in-Publication Data

Skeel, David A. Jr. 1961-
Debts dominion: a history of backruptcy law in America / David A. Skeel, Jr.
Includes bibliographical references and index.
ISBN 0-691-08810-1 (CL : alk. paper)
1. Bankruptcy—United States—History. 2. Backruptcy—Political aspects—
United States—History. I. Title.
KF1526 .S59 2001
346.7307′8′9—dc21   2001021464

This book has been composed in Electra

www.pup.princeton.edu

Printed in the United States of America

10 9 8 7 6 5 4 3 2 1

DEBT'S DOMINION

For Sharon
and for my parents

CONTENTS

PREFACE

This book is the culmination of a scholarly and professional journey that began well over a decade ago, with a bankruptcy class I took in my final year of law school. Like most literature majors who wind up in law school, I knew little about business and finance, and even less about bankruptcy, when I arrived. I signed up for the bankruptcy class only because of my admiration for the gifts of the professor who would be teaching it. Despite this unenthusiastic beginning, I, like many of the other students in our very large class, found the travails of financially troubled individuals and corporations riveting. It also became clear that American bankruptcy law touches on all aspects of American life. Within a few years, I found myself writing a law school paper on bankruptcy, practicing in a law firm's bankruptcy department, and then continuing to pursue the interest in academia.

In those days (the mid 1980s), bankruptcy law had achieved a new prominence. Although bankruptcy had previously been obscure and faintly unsavory, Congress had completely rewritten the bankruptcy laws only a few years before. In that bankruptcy class, and among bankruptcy professionals, the new law (the "Code") was portrayed in the most exalted of terms. The Code was sweetness and light, and everything good, whereas the old law (the "Act") had been archaic, cumbersome, and ineffective. Bankruptcy practice, if not bankruptcy itself, had become almost "cool."

Shortly after I left law school, I learned that the history of American bankruptcy laws actually was more complicated (and even more interesting) than I had initially realized. The old law may have been archaic and cumbersome, but it had a rather remarkable pedigree. The last major reform had been passed by Congress during the Great Depression. Many of its most important provisions had been drafted by William Douglas, who was appointed to the United States Supreme Court by President Roosevelt shortly thereafter, and went on to serve longer than any other justice in history. (William Brennan described Douglas as one of the two geniuses he had known in his life.) Douglas had worked on the project with a variety of other prominent New Deal reformers. In its own time, Douglas's handiwork had itself been seen as a milestone in progressive, up-to-date legislation for resolving the age-old problem of financial distress.

The puzzle of how a law with such an impressive lineage came to seem so misguided was only the first of many puzzles I encountered along the way. The enigmas are hardly surprising, given the conflicting reactions bankruptcy has always evoked in Americans. We think that honest but unfortunate debtors are entitled to a fresh start, but we also believe that debtors should repay their creditors if they can. This tension, and others like it, has projected bankruptcy onto center stage in every generation of the nation's history.

As this book goes to press, bankruptcy has once again captured lawmakers' attention in Washington. Congress is poised to pass the most significant bankruptcy reforms in over twenty years. The legislation, much of which focuses on consumer bankruptcy, is designed to require more debtors to repay at least some of their debts. Scarcely a day goes by without a major newspaper story either praising (because too many debtors take advantage of the system) or vilifying (because it's simply a sop to heartless credit card companies) the proposed reforms. At the same time, a souring economy has led to a spate of new, high-profile corporate bankruptcies, ranging from TWA to Pacific Gas & Electric, one of California's two major utilities. The shock of financial distress is not a new story, and it never grows old.

Like most books, this one has benefitted from the comments and suggestions of a wide range of individuals. I am especially grateful to Douglas Baird and Howard Rosenthal, each of whom served as a referee for the book, and to Brad Hansen. All three provided extensive written commentary on the entire book. Steve Burbank, Eric Posner, and Bob Rasmussen also provided extremely helpful comments on the entire manuscript. I received valuable comments on individual chapters of the manuscript from Patrick BoHon, Nicholas Georgakopoulos, Melissa Jacoby, Richard Levin, Chuck Mooney, Frank Partnoy, Joseph Pompykala, Tom Smith, Emerson Tiller, Todd Zywicki, Howard Rosenthal's Politics and Finance class at Princeton University, and the participants at faculty workshops at Princeton University and the University of San Diego School of Law. Michael Berman of the Securities and Exchange Commission was an invaluable source of information about the SEC's role in bankruptcy; and Harvey Miller and Ron Trost provided helpful information about the 1978 Code and current bankruptcy practice.

I owe special thanks to Peter Dougherty, my editor at Princeton University Press, who was a constant source of encouragement and insight, from his e-mail messages before the book was accepted for publication (telling me to "keep the faith") to his editorial suggestions on the book. Thanks also to Richard Isomaki for meticulous copyediting and to Bill Laznovsky for his work at the production stage.

Several libraries and librarians also proved invaluable during the course of the project. I am especially grateful to Bill Draper of the Biddle Law Library of the University of Pennsylvania Law School. Bill helped with the research, handled my sometimes onerous requests with unfailing good cheer, and provided a variety of helpful suggestions. I also owe thanks to Ron Day of the Biddle Law Library, John Necci and Larry Reilly of the Temple University School of Law Library, and to the librarians of the Library of Congress.

As I worked on the book, I wrote a number of articles for legal periodicals that touched on the research in one way or another. Although I wrote the book from scratch, some aspects of the analysis and occasional passages are drawn from the articles. The editors of the following pieces have kindly permitted me to reprint passages from the articles: "Public Choice and the Future of Public Choice Influenced Legal Scholarship," 50 *Vanderbilt Law Review* 647 (1997); "The Genius of the 1898 Bankruptcy Act," 15 *Bankruptcy Developments Journal* 321 (1999); "Vern Countryman and the Path of Progressive (and Populist) Bankruptcy Scholarship," 113 *Harvard Law Review* 1075 (2000); and "What's So Bad About Delaware," 54 *Vanderbilt Law Review* (2001). I have cited several other articles in the relevant endnotes.

Finally, my biggest debt of all is to my family. My wife Sharon has been a loving companion for thirteen years now, and has often put her own research on hold during the life of this project. My parents have been a continual support from my earliest years. And my sons, Carter and Stephen, are a continual blessing.

DEBT'S DOMINION

INTRODUCTION

BANKRUPTCY LAW in the United States is unique in the world. Perhaps most startling to outsiders is that individuals and businesses in the United States do not seem to view bankruptcy as the absolute last resort, as an outcome to be avoided at all costs. No one wants to wind up in bankruptcy, of course, but many U.S. debtors treat it as a means to another, healthier end, not as the End.

Consider a few of the high-flying visitors to the nation's bankruptcy courts. In 1987, Texaco filed for bankruptcy, at a time when it had a net worth in the neighborhood of $25 billion. Two years earlier, Texaco had been slapped with the largest jury verdict ever, a $10.53 billion judgment to Pennzoil for interfering with Pennzoil's informal agreement to purchase Getty Oil. When Texaco filed for bankruptcy, no one thought for a moment that the giant oil company would be shut down and its assets scattered to the winds. Texaco filed for bankruptcy preemptively, to halt efforts by Pennzoil to collect on the judgment and to force Pennzoil to negotiate a settlement. The strategy worked, and Texaco emerged from bankruptcy two years later.

Numerous famous and near famous individuals have also made use of the bankruptcy laws. Each year when I teach a course in bankruptcy law, as a diversion from the more technical details I keep a running list of celebrities who have filed for bankruptcy. Tia Carrere filed for bankruptcy in the 1980s in an unsuccessful effort to escape her contract with *General Hospital* and join the cast of *A Team*. Burt Reynolds, Kim Basinger, and James Taylor of the musical group Kool and the Gang all have filed for bankruptcy, as have Eddie Murphy and the famous Colts quarterback Johnny Unitas.

In recent years, the sheer number of bankruptcy filings has proven more newsworthy than even the most glamorous celebrity cases. In 1996, for the first time in the nation's history, more than one million individuals filed for bankruptcy in a single year. The number of businesses in bankruptcy has also been unprecedented, with tens of thousands invoking the bankruptcy laws each year. No one is quite sure why personal bankruptcy filings are so high: creditors contend that the "stigma" of filing for bankruptcy has disappeared, while debtors claim that creditors have been too free in extending credit. What is clear, however, is that U.S. bankruptcy law is far more sympathetic to debtors than are the laws of other nations.

An important benefit of U.S. law for debtors—in addition to generally favorable treatment—is control. An individual who files for bankruptcy has the option to turn her assets over the court and have her obligations immediately discharged (that is, voided), or to keep her assets and make payments to her creditors under a three-to-five-year rehabilitation plan. Although neither option is ideal, the debtor is the one who gets to choose. When a business files for bankruptcy, its managers are given analogous choices. The managers determine whether to file for liquidation or reorganization; and, if they opt for reorganization, the managers are the only party who can propose a reorganization plan for at least the first four months of the case.

In addition to the benefits for debtors, a second distinctive characteristic of U.S. bankruptcy law is the central role of lawyers. In most other countries, bankruptcy is an administrative process. Decisions are made by an administrator or other official, and debtors often are not represented by counsel. In the United States, by contrast, bankruptcy debtors almost always hire a lawyer, as do creditors, and the bankruptcy process unfolds before a bankruptcy judge. In the United States, bankruptcy is pervasively judicial in character.

The contrast with England is particularly revealing. Like the United States, England has a market-based economy, with vibrant capital markets and a wide range of private sources of credit. The two nations also share close historical ties. When the first U.S. bankruptcy law was enacted in 1800, for instance, Congress borrowed nearly the entire legislation from England. Despite the similarities between the two countries, however, their bankruptcy laws now look remarkably different.[1] When an individual debtor files for bankruptcy in England, she faces close scrutiny from an official receiver, generally without the benefit of counsel. The official receiver rather than the debtor is the one who determines the debtor's treatment, and debtors rarely are given an immediate discharge. Far more often, the court, at the recommendation of the official receiver, temporarily delays the discharge or requires the debtor to make additional payments to her creditors.

As with individuals, the managers of English businesses lose control if the firm files for bankruptcy. Creditors and their representative, the trustee, take over, and bankrupt firms are usually liquidated. Although English bankruptcy cases do take place before a judge, as in the United States, the process is pervasively administrative in character. Accountants, rather than lawyers, are the leading private bankruptcy professionals in England.

For anyone with even the faintest interest in U.S. bankruptcy law, its distinctive features raise a question that cries out for an answer: How did we get here? Why does U.S. bankruptcy look so different from the approach in other countries? Although a great deal has been written about the U.S. bankruptcy law, nowhere in the literature can one find a complete account of the political factors that produced modern American bankruptcy law over the course of the last century. In this book, I attempt to fill this gap with the first full-length treatment of the political economy of U.S. bankruptcy. I show that a small assortment of political factors—including the rise of organized creditor groups and the countervailing influence of populism, together with the emergence of the bankruptcy bar—set a pattern that has characterized U.S. bankruptcy law for over a century and shows no signs of decline.

The Three Eras of U.S. Bankruptcy Law

The distinctive features of U.S. bankruptcy law date back to the final decades of the nineteenth century, and we will focus most extensively on the hundred or so years from that era to the present. But the tone for the debates that would fill the nineteenth-century congressional records was first set in the earliest years of the Republic. In the late eighteenth century, bankruptcy lay at the heart of an ideological struggle over the future of the nation. Alexander Hamilton and other Federalists believed that commerce was the key to America's future. As one historian has recounted, bankruptcy was central to the Federalist vision, "both to protect non-fraudulent debtors and creditors and to encourage the speculative extension of credit that fueled commercial growth."[2] On this view, bankruptcy assured that creditors would have access to, and share equally in, the assets of an insolvent debtor, and it facilitated the pattern of failure and renewal that was necessary to a market-based economy. In sharp contrast to the Federalists, Jeffersonian Republicans called for a more agrarian future and questioned whether the United States was ready for a federal bankruptcy law. "Is Commerce so much the basis of the existence of the U.S. as to call for a bankrupt law?" Jefferson asked in 1792. "On the contrary, are we not almost [entirely] agricultural?"[3] Jeffersonian Republicans feared that a federal bankruptcy law would jeopardize farmers' property and shift power away from the states and into the federal courts.

These general concerns would continue to animate lawmakers' debates throughout the nineteenth century. The sympathy of commercial interests and hostility of farmers endured, as did their shared view that one's position on bankruptcy had enormous implications for the U.S. economy as a whole. By the end of the century, the debates over bankruptcy and the battle as to whether silver or gold should be the basis for monetary exchange were treated as flip sides of the same coin. For agrarian populists, both the proposed bankruptcy legislation and restrictions on the use of silver were anathema. "There have been constant efforts on the part of the creditor class to adhere to the single gold standard and bring down prices," Senator Stewart of Nevada complained during the hearings that led to the 1898 act, and the same creditor class sought to regulate commerce through federal bankruptcy legislation.[4]

As the century went on, the debates became more rather than less complicated. In addition to those who either favored or opposed bankruptcy legislation, some lawmakers called for a bankruptcy law that provided only for voluntary bankruptcy—that is, a law that debtors could invoke, but the debtor's creditors could not. Lawmakers also argued over whether any bankruptcy law should include corporations, or limit its reach to natural persons. The debates proved inconclusive for much of the nineteenth century, with Congress enacting bankruptcy laws in 1800, 1841, and 1867, but repealing each of the laws shortly after its enactment. Not until 1898 did Congress finally enact a federal bankruptcy law with staying power.

As lawmakers wrestled over federal bankruptcy legislation, another insolvency drama unfolded entirely outside of Congress. During the course of the nineteenth century, the railroads emerged as the nation's first large-scale corporations. The early growth of the railroads was fraught with problems. Due both to overexpansion and to a series of devastating depressions, or panics, numerous railroads defaulted on their obligations—at times, as much as 20 percent of the nation's track was held by insolvent railroads. Rather than look to Congress, the railroads and their creditors invoked the state and federal courts. By the final decades of the nineteenth century the courts had developed a judicial reorganization technique known as the equity receivership. It was this technique, rather than the Bankruptcy Act of 1898, that became the basis for modern corporate reorganization.

Rather than providing a simple answer to our overarching question—How did we get here?—the early history of U.S. bankruptcy requires us to address a series of additional questions. Why did the Bankruptcy Act of 1898 endure, while each of the earlier acts failed? Why did it take the form it did? Why did large-scale reorganization develop on a different track, in the courts rather than Congress?

With the twentieth century come new questions, and additional drama. At the cusp of the New Deal, lawmakers proposed sweeping changes to the 1898 act—changes that would have given U.S. law a more administrative orientation inspired by the English bankruptcy system. As with welfare and social security, a governmental agency might have taken center stage in the bankruptcy process. The reforms that were eventually adopted were far more modest. In corporate bankruptcy, by contrast, William Douglas and the New Deal reformers completely revamped the reorganization framework, leaving little role for the Wall Street banks and lawyers who had long dominated the process.

The next forty years, from the Chandler Act of 1938, which implemented the New Deal reforms, to the next major overhaul in 1978, were in many respects the dark ages of U.S. bankruptcy law. The number of prominent corporate bankruptcy cases dwindled; and the reputation of bankruptcy practice, which had long been less than ideal, if anything got worse. As the number of personal bankruptcy cases skyrocketed in the 1960s, lawmakers heard increasing calls, especially from the consumer credit industry, for reform. At the same time, a group of prominent bankruptcy lawyers affiliated with the National Bankruptcy Conference began a campaign to address many of the problems that had undermined the reputation of the bankruptcy bar. These efforts eventually led to the enactment of the 1978 Bankruptcy Code, which has produced a complete revitalization and expansion of U.S. bankruptcy law. Law students now flock to bankruptcy classes, the nation's elite law firms have rediscovered bankruptcy practice, and the number and range of personal and business bankruptcies have reached unprecedented levels.

As this brief chronology suggests, the history of U.S. bankruptcy law can be divided into three general eras. The first era culminates in the enactment of the 1898 act, and the perfection of the equity receivership technique for large-scale reorganizations. The first age of U.S. bankruptcy law can be seen as the birth of U.S. insolvency law, the age of rudiments and foundations. It is this era in which the general parameters, and the political dynamic, of U.S. bankruptcy law finally coalesced. The Great Depression and the New Deal ushered in a second era of U.S. bankruptcy. The bankruptcy reforms of this era would reinforce and expand general bankruptcy practice and completely reshape the landscape of large-scale corporate reorganization. The final era includes the 1978 Bankruptcy Code and the complete revitalization of bankruptcy practice (including a repudiation of the New Deal vision for reorganizing large corporations) that has taken place in its wake.

The approach I will use to explore the three eras of U.S. bankruptcy law is public choice, with a particular emphasis on institutions. By identifying the key interest groups and ideological currents, the book will develop a political explanation of the development of U.S. bankruptcy law that is both simple and textured. In a moment, I will briefly describe my approach and its insights into the three eras of U.S. bankruptcy law. To provide the context both for this introductory overview and for the book as a whole, however, two tasks remain. The first is to describe the key attributes of personal and corporate bankruptcy; we then will briefly consider the literature on U.S. bankruptcy prior to this book.

A BRIEF BANKRUPTCY PRIMER

In the popular imagination, bankruptcy laws seem hopelessly complex and arcane. In reality, bankruptcy is not nearly so complicated as it is often made to appear (though the perception of complexity will be important to our story, as one of the reasons the bankruptcy bar has proven so influential). Better still for readers who might otherwise shy away from a discussion of bankruptcy, a very simple overview will supply nearly all of the information we need to understand the political economy of the U.S. bankruptcy laws. We will encounter esoteric terms at various points, but each is related to the basic principles described below. It is these basic principles that motivate the political and legal struggles that have produced the remarkable U.S. approach to financial failure.

Readers who are generally familiar with U.S. bankruptcy law can safely move on to the next section. But for those who are not, the brief primer that follows will provide more than enough background to appreciate how the U.S. bankruptcy laws function. A brief note on terminology before we begin. Until

1978, the federal bankruptcy law was referred to as the *Bankruptcy Act*, or the *1898 act*. Courts and commentators generally refer to the current bankruptcy law, which was originally enacted in 1978, as the *Bankruptcy Code*.

Personal Bankruptcy

The U.S. bankruptcy laws actually address two different kinds of bankruptcy, the bankruptcy of individual debtors and the financial distress of corporations. (Here and throughout the book, the analysis of corporations can also be extended to other business entities, such as limited and general partnerships.) Although personal and corporate bankruptcy overlap in crucial respects, they raise somewhat different policy issues, as will quickly become clear.

The central concept in personal bankruptcy in the U.S. framework is the discharge. The dictionary tells us that *discharge* means "to relieve of a burden" or "to set aside; dismiss, annul"; and this is exactly what the discharge does in bankruptcy. When a debtor receives a discharge, her existing obligations are voided. Creditors can no longer attempt to collect the discharged obligation.

Although the origins of bankruptcy date back several thousand years, the concept of a discharge is relatively recent.[5] Early bankruptcy laws generally functioned as creditor collection devices. Bankruptcy laws authorized a court to take control of a debtor's assets and to use the assets to repay creditors. Even after the seizure of his assets, the debtor was still responsible for any amounts that remained unpaid. While American bankruptcy law has long provided for a discharge, Congress has never offered the discharge to every debtor. A debtor who has engaged in fraud is not entitled to discharge any of his debts, for instance. In addition to precluding discharge altogether in some cases (referred to as *exceptions to the discharge*), bankruptcy law also includes a list of specific debts (*partial exceptions to the discharge*) that cannot be discharged even if a debtor is entitled to discharge his other obligations. Student loans are a particularly controversial illustration. If an individual who has outstanding student loans files for bankruptcy, she can discharge her other obligations, but not her student loans. Debts based on willful and malicious torts also cannot be discharged. This ultimately was why O. J. Simpson could not use bankruptcy to solve his financial problems after the family of Nicole Brown Simpson won their $33.5 million civil judgment against him.[6]

Under current bankruptcy law, debtors have two different alternatives for obtaining a discharge. The first is straight liquidation, currently contained in Chapter 7 of the Bankruptcy Code. In a straight liquidation, the debtor turns all of his assets over to the bankruptcy court. In theory, the assets are then sold by a trustee, and the proceeds are distributed to the debtors' creditors. First in line are secured creditors—that is, creditors who hold a mortgage or security interest in property of the debtor as collateral. After secured and other priority creditors are paid, the other, unsecured creditors are entitled to a pro rata share of any proceeds that remain.

In reality, individual debtors who file for bankruptcy often have no assets that are available for paying their creditors. In these cases—referred to, appropriately enough, as "no asset" cases—there is no need to conduct a sale, and the debtor receives a discharge very quickly. (I will call this an *immediate discharge*, though the debtor actually must wait a week or two until the judge actually signs a discharge order.) In recent years, roughly 75 percent of individual bankruptcies have been no-asset cases.

A debtor's second alternative is to propose a rehabilitation plan under Chapter 13 of the Bankruptcy Code. In a Chapter 13 rehabilitation case, the debtor retains her assets rather than turning them over to the court, and the debtor proposes to repay a portion of her debts over a three-to-five-year period. Originally designed for "wage earners" but now available to any debtor with a "regular income," the rehabilitation option was first offered in 1933 and codified in more developed form in 1938. For debtors, Chapter 13 is attractive if the debtor has property that she wishes to retain. This approach also has long been seen as less "stigmatizing" than straight liquidation. A debtor who tries to repay some of her debts rather than seeking an immediate discharge, Congress believed, would not see herself or be seen by creditors as simply abandoning her obligations. Congress even used different terms to distinguish among debtors. Until the most recent bankruptcy reform in 1978, individuals who chose straight liquidation were called *bankrupts*, whereas those who opted for rehabilitation received the less pejorative term of *debtor*. (Current law uses *debtor* in all cases.)

The essence of personal bankruptcy lies in the three concepts we have seen—straight liquidation, the rehabilitation plan, and the discharge offered under both—plus one more: exemptions. Exempt property is property that the debtor is entitled to keep—it is not available for creditors even if the debtor opts for an immediate discharge under Chapter 7. Included in a debtor's exemptions are items such as professional tools, household goods, and a portion of the equity a debtor has in her house. Everyone needs a few basic items to live and make a living, and exemptions are designed to protect enough of a debtor's assets for the debtor to get back on her feet—to achieve a "fresh start" after bankruptcy. Under the Bankruptcy Code, a debtor's exemptions include up to twenty-four hundred dollars in her car, up to eight thousand dollars in household furnishings, and up to fifteen thousand dollars in her house.[7]

As we will see throughout the book, exemptions have long been a source of tension between state and federal lawmaking. Under the old Bankruptcy Act, Congress simply incorporated state exemptions into bankruptcy. Thus, a Pennsylvania debtor would be entitled to the exemptions supplied by Pennsylvania law, whereas a Texas debtor would receive Texas exemptions. Current bankruptcy law permits a debtor to choose between her state exemptions and a set of federal exemptions unless the debtor's state requires all debtors to use the state alternative. The most important point for the moment, however, is simply that a debtor's exemptions assure that she does not have to give up everything in bankruptcy.

As a practical matter, exemptions figure prominently in a debtor's choice between Chapter 7 liquidation and Chapter 13 rehabilitation. A large percentage of debtors have only a few assets, and most or all of them (such as a sofa or CD player) fit within exemptions. For these debtors—again, the no-asset cases—the debtor can simply file for Chapter 7 and get an immediate discharge. If a debtor has substantial assets that she does not want to lose—such as an interest in a house that exceeds the allowable exemption—the debtor may choose Chapter 13 in order to protect her interest in the house. A debtor's choice may also be influenced by other factors, ranging from stigma, as noted above, to the norms of the bankruptcy practice in the debtor's district (often referred to as local legal culture). But the nature of the debtor's assets is the single most important consideration for most debtors.

Already we have most of the details we need for a general portrait of personal bankruptcy law. To complete the picture we should add one more brushstroke—the choice between voluntary and involuntary bankruptcy. Under current law, the vast majority of debtors file for bankruptcy voluntarily. Although creditors can push a debtor into bankruptcy by filing an involuntary bankruptcy petition, they have little incentive to do so. Because current bankruptcy law is quite generous to debtors (in large part because it offers an immediate discharge), creditors are better off trying to collect outside of bankruptcy. In the nineteenth century, by contrast, involuntary bankruptcy figured quite prominently. Creditors worried that state laws were too generous to local debtors, and they saw a uniform, federal bankruptcy law as the best way to assure that everyone to whom a debtor owed money would be treated equally. For several decades after the Bankruptcy Act was enacted in 1898, roughly half of all bankruptcies were filed by creditors rather than the debtor. Only later did creditors lose their enthusiasm for involuntary petitions.

To summarize, a debtor who files for bankruptcy has two options, straight liquidation (Chapter 7) and rehabilitation (Chapter 13). U.S. bankruptcy law provides a fresh start both by permitting debtors to retain some of their assets, and by discharging the debtor's debts. Although either a debtor or his creditors may invoke the bankruptcy laws, nearly all current bankruptcy petitions are voluntary.

Corporate Bankruptcy

Like individual debtors, the managers of a business that files for bankruptcy can file for either liquidation or reorganization. The liquidation option is governed by the same provisions, Chapter 7 of the current Bankruptcy Code, that regulate straight liquidation for individuals. As with individuals, the business turns all of its assets over to a trustee, who then sells the assets and distributes any proceeds to creditors. (The trustee generally is chosen by an official known, confusingly enough, as the U.S. Trustee, but creditors have the right to make the choice themselves if at least 20 percent of the firm's unsecured creditors ask to select a trustee.) Unlike individual debtors, corporate debtors who file for Chapter 7 do not exempt any property and do not receive a discharge. Because most firms have at least a few assets, corporate liquidations involve an actual sale (or sales) of assets by the trustee.

As an alternative to straight liquidation, corporate debtors can propose to reorganize the firm. Currently housed in Chapter 11 of the Code, the reorganization provisions are melded together from two very different sources. Large-scale reorganization was developed in the courts during the railroad receivership era and relied on negotiations with each class of creditors. The Bankruptcy Act of 1898, which was used by small and medium-sized firms, included a simplified reorganization process (known as *composition* and after 1938 as *arrangement*) that permitted firms to reduce their unsecured debts but not their secured obligations or the interests of their shareholders.

Under current law, the managers of a firm remain in place after the firm files for bankruptcy, at least initially, and the managers continue to run the business. The managers are given a breathing space during which they are the only ones who can propose a reorganization plan. Managers' monopoly over the process is called the "exclusivity period" and lasts for at least four months. In large cases, the bankruptcy court often extends the exclusivity period for as long as the case goes on. As noted earlier, managers' control over the process makes bankruptcy a far more attractive option than would otherwise be the case. No other bankruptcy system in the world gives the managers of a troubled firm so much influence.

Much of a reorganization case consists of negotiations between the debtor's managers and its creditors over the terms of a reorganization plan. Unsecured creditors are represented by an unsecured creditors committee consisting of the seven largest unsecured creditors, and bankruptcy courts sometimes appoint other committees as well in relatively complicated cases. In the Johns Manville bankruptcy, for instance, the court appointed several committees to represent different classes of creditors, and a committee to represent shareholders.

The goal of the parties' negotiations is to develop a reorganization plan that commands widespread support among creditors. The reorganization plan must divide the firm's creditors into classes of similarly situated claims and must specify the treatment that each class will be given under the plan. Each of the firm's creditors and shareholders then is entitled to vote on the proposed plan. If a majority in number and two-thirds in amount of the creditors in a class vote in favor of the proposal, the entire class is treated as having accepted the plan. (A simple two-thirds in amount does the trick for shareholders.) If each class approves the plan, the court can confirm the reorganization, and the business goes back out into the world. This is the usual course of events in large reorganization cases, though the road is often long (several years is the norm), with many a winding place.

If one or more classes vote against the plan, the court still can confirm the plan under the Bankruptcy Code's so-called "cramdown" provisions. (This delicate term refers to the fact that such reorganizations are crammed down the throat of the disgruntled class of creditors.) To be confirmed, a cramdown plan must satisfy the absolute priority rule with respect to the dissenting class. The absolute priority rule, which has a long and colorful history in U.S. bankruptcy law, as we shall see, requires that each class of senior creditors be paid in full before any lower-priority creditors or shareholders are entitled to receive anything. To illustrate, imagine a firm has one senior creditor owed one hundred dollars, one junior creditor owed fifty dollars, and one shareholder. If the junior creditor objects, the reorganization cannot give anything to the shareholder (including a continuing interest in the firm's stock) unless it promises to pay the junior creditor her full fifty dollars. Thus, a proposal to give one hundred dollars to the senior creditor, thirty dollars to the junior creditor, and the stock to the shareholder would fail. Even if the senior creditor wished to give up value for the benefit of the shareholder (for example, under a proposal to sell the firm and give ninety dollars of the proceeds to the senior, thirty dollars to the junior, and ten dollars to the shareholder), the plan could not be confirmed if the junior creditor objected. If the junior creditor is promised less than fifty dollars and objects, all lower-priority claims or interests (here, the shareholder) must be cut off.

The key attributes of corporate reorganization, then, are its emphasis on negotiations among all the firm's managers, creditors, and shareholders, and the use of a firmwide vote to approve or disapprove each proposed reorganization plan. If every class votes in favor, the plan is confirmed. If not, the plan can still be confirmed if it satisfies the absolute priority rule. One participant we do not see in most cases is a trustee. Prior to 1978, the managers of a large corporation were replaced by a trustee if the firm filed for bankruptcy under the provisions designed for publicly held corporations. Under current law, trustees are appointed only under extraordinary circumstances. The assumption is that the corporation's current managers will continue to run the show.

When we think of corporate bankruptcy, we usually have Chapter 11 in mind, and the reorganization provisions will take center stage in nearly all of our discussions of business bankruptcy. But a variety of other provisions affect the overall process, and we should briefly consider two. The first is the automatic stay. The automatic stay is a global injunction that requires creditors to refrain from any further efforts to collect the amounts that the debtor owes them. Creditors cannot bring litigation against the debtor or take any step to "obtain possession . . . or . . . control" of the debtor's property after the debtor files for bankruptcy. Even a letter asking the debtor to repay would violate the automatic stay. It is difficult to overstate the stay's importance to the bankruptcy process. Firms that encounter financial distress are usually besieged by creditors. Even firms that are worth preserving may be dismembered unless the parties can call a truce and reach an orderly decision as to what should be done with the firm's assets. The automatic stay provides the breathing space that the parties need. Newspaper articles nearly always describe a corporation that has filed for Chapter 11 as having sought "relief from its creditors." The relief that these articles have in mind, and one of the most important benefits of filing for bankruptcy, is the automatic stay.

Similarly central to bankruptcy is the trustee's power to avoid preferential transfers. The intuition behind the trustee's avoidance powers is that the debtor should not be permitted to pay some creditors rather than others shortly before it files for bankruptcy. Not only do eve-of-bankruptcy transfers seem unfair to creditors who are not lucky enough to receive a preference, but they also deplete the assets of a firm—assets that could otherwise be used to pay all creditors or reorganize the firm. Under current law, the trustee can retrieve (subject to a variety of exceptions) any transfer to an unsecured creditor that takes place within ninety days of bankruptcy. If the creditor is an insider, the preference period is expanded to a full year on the theory that insiders are the first ones to know that the firm is in trouble, and therefore may be preferring themselves over other creditors with payments that are made more than ninety days before bankruptcy.

Although we will often distinguish between corporate and personal bankruptcy, a substantial majority of the Bankruptcy Code applies to all debtors—both individuals and businesses. Both the automatic stay and preference law, for instance, are designed for both contexts. (Interestingly, preference law was a burning issue in the early debates over personal bankruptcy, but it now figures much more prominently in corporate cases.) The principal distinctions come in the rehabilitation chapters—Chapter 11 for corporate reorganization and Chapter 13 for individual rehabilitation. And even here the lines have blurred in recent years, with individuals occasionally filing for Chapter 11, and a few small businesses invoking Chapter 13.

SOME BOOKS ON U.S. BANKRUPTCY

Although the literature on American bankruptcy law and policy is voluminous, the number of significant *books* exploring bankruptcy policy, theory, or history is surprisingly small. In the space of a page or two, we can easily survey the most important books on bankruptcy issues. (For the benefit of readers who would like a more complete list, I provide additional references in the endnotes.)[8]

The classic work on American bankruptcy law is a book published by Charles Warren in 1935, *Bankruptcy in United States History*.[9] Warren's great contribution was to read all of the congressional debates on bankruptcy from the late eighteenth to early twentieth century, and to assimilate them into a short, textured history of prior American bankruptcy legislation. Warren's chronology is structured around several loose themes. Warren emphasizes the long-standing geographical split between northeastern lawmakers who tended to favor federal bankruptcy legislation and the southern and western lawmakers who opposed it, for instance; and he suggests that U.S. law evolved through creditor-centered and debtor-centered stages to a more balanced approach. But much of book consists of excerpts of speeches made by lawmakers during the debates and synopses of the competing positions. Rather than sustained analysis, an unsympathetic reviewer (and prominent bankruptcy scholar) complained, "Mr. Warren gives a myriad of quotations from little noisy men who have repeated misinformation and appeals to passion at short intervals for nearly a century and a half."[10] Although the book has proven enormously influential and still is the single best general resource, its offers little careful explanation of bankruptcy or of the political dynamics of bankruptcy legislation.[11]

The next significant treatment of U.S. bankruptcy law came several decades later, with the publication of Peter Coleman's *Debtors and Creditors in America*.[12] (Like *Debtors and Creditors in America*, an important empirical study by the Brookings Institution also appeared in the early 1970s—I allude to the study below.) *Debtors and Creditors in America* serves as a useful complement to Warren's earlier analysis. Unlike Warren, who focuses heavily on developments at the federal level, Coleman provides a careful history of state lawmaking on insolvency-related issues. *Debtors and Creditors in America* is the single best treatment of state insolvency law in the United States, and it provides a useful, though brief, overview of developments at the federal level. As with Warren, Coleman offers a relatively traditional overview of bankruptcy and insolvency history—one that predates many of the most important recent developments in political and historical analysis.

For the first time since the 1930s, bankruptcy recaptured the scholarly imagination in the late 1970s and early 1980s, due in large part to the sweeping reforms enacted in 1978 and the conditions that inspired them. At the heart of the debate were sharply divergent views of the nature and purpose of bankruptcy, with law-and-economics scholars adopting a radically new, economics-oriented perspective and progressive scholars defending a more traditional approach. Thomas Jackson, who, along with his frequent coauthor Douglas Baird, was the leading law-and-economics scholar, published *The Logic and Limits of Bankruptcy* in 1986.[13] A reworking and elaboration of Jackson's earlier law review articles, *The Logic and Limits* argues that the principal purpose of bankruptcy law is to provide a collective response to financial distress, and that bankruptcy rules should not otherwise alter the parties' rights under non-bankruptcy law. A more expansive bankruptcy law, Jackson insists, would lead to costly, inefficient struggles between parties who prefer nonbankruptcy law and those who fare better in bankruptcy.

In 1989, two of the leading traditional scholars, Elizabeth Warren and Jay Westbrook, along with demographer Theresa Sullivan, published an extensive empirical analysis of personal bankruptcy entitled *As We Forgive Our Debtors*.[14] (*As We Forgive Our Debtors* was in some respects a follow-up to an influential Brookings Institution study from the early 1970s.)[15] Basing their presentation on an examination of 1,547 case files, Sullivan, Warren, and Westbrook provide a detailed profile of individuals who file for bankruptcy, emphasizing factors such as their high debt load and comparatively low income, and the role of income disruption. Much of Sullivan, Warren, and Westbrook's analysis is designed to refute claims made by law-and-economics scholars. *As We Forgive Our Debtors*, like a follow-up study published in 2000, *The Fragile Middle Class*,[16] challenges assumptions such as the suggestion that debtors will adjust their behavior in response to changes that make the bankruptcy laws stricter or more lenient.

Although *The Logic and Limits of Bankruptcy Law* and *As We Forgive Our Debtors* could not be more different in perspective or approach, both focus almost exclusively on how current bankruptcy law should and does function. The goal of each is to defend a normative vision of bankruptcy law, rather than to explain *how* and *why* American bankruptcy law has taken its distinctive shape.[17] The political forces that have shaped the U.S. bankruptcy system play very little role in either analysis. The earlier books do consider the history and political economy of U.S. bankruptcy but explain these factors only in loose and general terms. What the existing literature lacks is a fully theorized explanation of the remarkable system we have, and how it arose.

In recent years, a few scholars have begun to notice the need for a more compelling and complete explanation of the political economy of U.S. bankruptcy. At the outset of an article on the 1978 Code, Eric Posner notes that a careful analysis of "the political determinants of . . . so significant a piece of legislation . . . is long overdue."[18] A pair of sociologists has recently published an extensive study of the legislative history of the corporate bankruptcy components of the same legislation, the 1978 Code, together with corporate law reforms made in England in 1986. In *Rescuing Business*,[19] Bruce Carruthers and Terence Halliday explore the influence of bankruptcy professionals and large creditors on the corporate bankruptcy changes in 1978. The book is a valuable contribution to the literature, and their findings on the 1978 Bankruptcy Code overlap with my discussion of this period in many respects. Because Carruthers and Halliday focus solely on the process that led to the 1978 reforms, however, they cannot provide a full explanation why the 1978 Code so thoroughly repudiated the existing approach to corporate reorganization. The seeds to this transformation, which dramatically increased the flexibility of corporate reorganization for large firms, were planted quite accidentally in the structure of the New Deal amendments to the prior act in 1938. To understand how and why the earlier vision of corporate reorganization gave way to current law, we must consider the New Deal origins of the prior law.

To make sense of other distinctive features of the U.S. framework, such as lawyers' role as the principal bankruptcy professionals (which stands in striking contrast to the accountant-centered English system), we must go back still further, to the birth of modern U.S. bankruptcy law at the end of the nineteenth century. This book marks the first effort to undertake each of these tasks, to provide a political history of U.S. bankruptcy law that explains where the distinctive features of the U.S. framework came from (as well as a few speculations on where U.S. bankruptcy may and should be headed). As noted earlier, the book does not offer an exhaustive account of every era of bankruptcy history. Although we will start in the beginning, for instance, our tour of the first half of the nineteenth century will be relatively brief. The heart of the story begins with the emergence of modern U.S. bankruptcy law in the final decades of the nineteenth century. Our brief survey of early developments, and the remarkable coalescence later of large-scale reorganization in the courts and general bankruptcy in Congress, will provide the plot-lines for a story that has never before been told.

The Political Story

The political history developed in this book will require us to traverse several different disciplines. Bankruptcy is inescapably legal in nature, and congressional debates over legal issues, together with judicial decisions, will occupy much of the discussion. But the analysis also will draw liberally from recent insights in political science and economics—not least because the theoretical approach I will use was developed in these disciplines. Our analysis also will be steeped in historical perspective and reflects extensive research in primary historical sources. Although the analysis is scholarly and interdisciplinary in nature, I have attempted to make it accessible to the interested nonspecialist.

The public choice literature that will animate much of the analysis is characterized by the "use of economic tools to deal with the traditional problems of political science,"[20] and it has influenced each of these disciplines, as well as law and history. The most familiar branch of public choice analysis is interest group theory. (The other branch of public choice theory is known as social choice, and it plays an important role in chapter 1.) Starting from the assumption that individuals act rationally and in their own self-interest, interest group theory suggests, among other things, that concentrated interest groups often benefit at the expense of more widely scattered groups, even if the diffuse group has more at stake overall. A variety of interest groups have figured prominently in the evolution of U.S. bankruptcy law, including a wide range of creditors and, most importantly for much of this century—bankruptcy lawyers and bankruptcy judges. Each of these groups has coordinated its efforts through lobbying organizations that have had a significant influence on the shape of U.S. bankruptcy. During the course of the analysis, we will witness the growth of creditor organizations such as chambers of commerce and boards of trade in the nineteenth century, the emergence of the National Bankruptcy Conference as the preeminent voice for reform-minded bankruptcy lawyers in the 1930s, and the rise of the consumer credit industry in recent decades.

In addition to interest groups, recent public choice literature has provided a wealth of new insights into structural issues such as the role of committees in congressional deliberations, and the devices lawmakers can use to alter or protect the influence of existing interest groups. These factors, too, will figure in our story, particularly as we consider the rise and fall of the New Deal vision for corporate reorganization.

As Mark Roe has noted in his important recent book on the emergence of the so-called Berle-Means corporation in U.S. corporate law, public choice analysis often emphasizes interest groups and devotes relatively little attention to the role of ideology in political decision making.[21] In some areas, ideology has an undeniable influence. Bankruptcy is one of those areas, as will become clear from the very outset. Bankruptcy lay at the heart of the early struggle between Federalists and Jeffersonian Republicans, and populist and progressive ideologies have figured prominently, and at times decisively, for more than a century.

Nor will our story consist solely of faceless forces such as interest groups and the currents of ideology. At times, particular individuals have provided the inspiration or public face of an interest group or ideology. In the late nineteenth century, one man, Jay Torrey, waged a decade-long campaign for federal bankruptcy legislation on behalf of the creditors' groups that had hired him. Torrey's relentless but cheerful efforts to spur Congress into action drew the admiration of supporters and opponents alike. Bankruptcy law probably would have passed even without Torrey's efforts, but he served as the symbol, namesake, and most visible proponent of the bill that eventually became the nation's first permanent bankruptcy law. The New Deal brought William Douglas, a Yale Law professor, Securities and Exchange Commission chairman, and then Supreme Court justice. Together with a small band of associates at the Securities and Exchange Commission, Douglas drafted reforms that would completely alter the shape of large-scale corporate reorganization. With the most recent bankruptcy reforms in 1978, a small group of prominent bankruptcy lawyers and academics, including George Triester and Professors

Frank Kennedy and Larry King, played an important role; and Harvard Law professor Elizabeth Warren has been a focal point of more recent battles between the consumer credit industry and bankruptcy professionals over personal bankruptcy law.

The heart of the political story of U.S. bankruptcy law is both new and startlingly simple. American bankruptcy law is the product of three forces. The basic parameters of bankruptcy reflect a compromise between organized creditor groups and the countervailing pressures of populism and other prodebtor movements. Within the loose boundaries of this compromise, bankruptcy professionals have spearheaded a relentless expansion of both the scope of the bankruptcy laws and their own prominence. Although large-scale corporate reorganization developed somewhat differently, the political story is analogous in important respects. Since the 1930s, moreover, when all of bankruptcy was brought within a single statute, many of the earlier distinctions have disappeared.

Partisan politics have also figured prominently in bankruptcy history. Much of creditors' influence has been in the Republican party, whereas most prodebtor lawmakers have been Democrats. The political divide was especially pronounced in the nineteenth century, but the interaction of the three principal forces in U.S. bankruptcy law and the two political parties continues to be an important theme, even today.

The political determinants of U.S. bankruptcy law—creditor groups, prodebtor interests, and bankruptcy professionals—have never been static. Quite to the contrary. Periodic price shocks have destabilized the balance of power, increasing the strength of some interests and diminishing others. In the twentieth century, the most dramatic example of this was the Great Depression, which sharply diminished the power of the Wall Street banks and lawyers who had previously dominated large-scale corporate reorganization, and which unleashed a wave of populism. In addition to price shocks, changes in the credit markets also have had a significant impact. At the beginning of the twentieth century, suppliers and other merchants were the principal creditor interests in the bankruptcy debates. With the rise of consumer credit since World War II, the consumer credit industry has played an increasingly prominent role, while suppliers and merchants have receded in importance.

As this description suggests, an important goal of my analysis is to capture both the general pattern of U.S. bankruptcy politics and some of its nuance, with particular emphasis on the past century. The book is divided into four parts. The first and second parts correspond to the first two general eras of U.S. bankruptcy law, and the last two parts take us through the third and most recent era.

Part 1, "The Birth of U.S. Insolvency Law," comprises chapters 1 and 2. Chapter 1 focuses on the legislative efforts to pass federal bankruptcy legislation in the nineteenth century. On three different occasions, lawmakers passed bankruptcy laws in the wake of widespread economic distress, then quickly repealed the legislation. Drawing on the insights of social choice theory, the chapter shows that the principal reason for the instability was lawmakers' multiple, inconsistent perspectives on the desirability of federal bankruptcy law. The chapter then asks why the instability suddenly ended in 1898, when Congress enacted the nation's first permanent bankruptcy law. The answer lies in the three factors that have continued to define the politics of U.S. bankruptcy law: creditors, prodebtor ideology, and bankruptcy professionals. The rise of organized creditor groups created a demand for bankruptcy legislation; populists and other prodebtor lawmakers shaped its contours in important respects, including the 1898 act's scaled-down administrative apparatus. During the decade of Republican control that following the 1898 act, a bankruptcy bar then emerged to fill the void left by the absence of a substantial administrative structure, and the bar reinforced the coalition that fought to protect the new law against repeal.

The legislative battles over bankruptcy in the nineteenth century focused on the insolvencies of individuals and small businesses. Chapter 2 explores the very different process that led to the nation's first large-scale corporate reorganizations. The story of corporate reorganization begins with railroads, and the large number of nineteenth-century railroad failures. When a large railroad failed, both the public interest in an effective transportation system and the economic interests of the relevant parties dictated that the firm be reorganized rather than liquidated. Although the most obvious response might have been for legislators to rescue the railroads, both federal and state lawmakers were constrained by significant constitutional limitations. Rather than a legislative solution, railroad rescue took place in the courts. In a remarkable display of common-law ingenuity, the courts created a reorganization device called equity receivership out of traditional receivership and foreclosure law. The principal players in an equity receivership were the managers of the insolvent firm and the banks that had served as underwriters when the firm sold stock and debt securities to the public. The banks set up committees that purported to represent the interests of the firm's scattered investors—an equity committee representing shareholders, a bondholders' committee for bondholders, and so on—and the committees negotiated with the firm's managers over the terms of the reorganization. By the end of the nineteenth century, J. P. Morgan and a small group of other Wall Street banks, together with an elite Wall Street reorganization bar, figured prominently in nearly every large reorganization case.

In part 2, the scene shifts to the next major era in U.S. bankruptcy law, the tumult of the Great Depression and the New Deal reforms that followed. Until the early New Deal, the framework for addressing individual and small-business bankruptcy remained entirely separate from the receivership process used for large-scale reorganization, and chapters 3 and 4 continue to track this distinction. Chapter 3 focuses on personal and small-business bankruptcy under the Bankruptcy Act of 1898 and explores the influence of bankruptcy professionals and various other interest groups. At the outset of the depression, a pair of large governmental investigations portrayed the bankruptcy bar in an extraordinarily unfavorable light and proposed reforms to inject a much larger governmental presence into U.S. bankruptcy. Yet the bar's effective, nationwide organization and its enormous stake enabled it to prevent substantial reform. Rather than altering the existing approach, the New Deal reforms ultimately preserved and reinforced it. In an era that saw Congress undertake administrative programs for closely related issues such as welfare and social security, bankruptcy remained resolutely judicial. In addition to recounting this history, chapter 3 gives a brief theoretical overview of interest group influence in bankruptcy, with a particular emphasis on bankruptcy professionals.

As chapter 4 will show, the effect of the New Deal on large-scale corporate reorganization could not have been more different. The turmoil of the Great Depression dramatically altered the relative power of the interest groups that had the most at stake in equity receivership. Most importantly, the depression produced widespread, populist hostility toward Wall Street—especially toward the Wall Street "Money Trust" banks, whom many populists blamed for the depression. Much as other New Deal reformers harnessed the anti–Wall Street sentiment to enact sweeping financial reforms such as the (now repealed) Glass-Steagall Act, William Douglas and his peers at the Securities and Exchange Commission used these sentiments to transform large-scale corporate reorganization, which had recently been added to the Bankruptcy Act. Wall Street banks and the elite reorganization bar were ushered out of corporate reorganization almost entirely. One of the great ironies of these developments was the fact that the faintly unsavory, general bankruptcy bar survived the New Deal, whereas the elite Wall Street bar disappeared.

The Chandler Act reforms of 1938 that broke the grip of the Wall Street banks and bar were an enormous success for William Douglas and the SEC and altered the course of U.S. bankruptcy for decades. As we will see, the victory proved, ironically, to be *too* complete. Hidden in the structure of the Chandler Act were the seeds that would lead to the demise of the New Deal vision of corporate bankruptcy.

The two chapters of part 3, "The Revitalization of Bankruptcy," explore the origins of, and changes brought by, the 1978 Bankruptcy Code. The sweeping reforms of the 1978 Code have inaugurated the third and most recent era of U.S. bankruptcy law. Chapter 5 explores the most important consumer and structural reforms of the 1978 Code. The initial push for bankruptcy reform was inspired by a variety of factors, including a meteoric rise in personal bankruptcy filings and the conviction on the part of a number of prominent bankruptcy attorneys—most associated with the National Bankruptcy Conference—that the bankruptcy system needed to be fixed. Congress responded by appointing a National Bankruptcy Commission to develop proposed reforms; the commission's report in 1973 would serve as the template for the legislation that finally passed in 1978. Chapter 5 divides the commission's proposals for personal bankruptcy into four categories, the structural reforms—which proposed, as in the 1930s, to establish a bankruptcy agency; the scope-expanding proposals designed to expand the reach of bankruptcy law; a call for uniform federal exemptions; and a group of proposals that had the effect of altering the balance of power between creditors and debtors. The first two categories reflected the influence of bankruptcy professionals, who played the leading role in stymieing administrative change and promoting the expansion of bankruptcy. The third and fourth categories illustrated the continuing relevance of the political bargain between creditor and prodebtor interests that was first struck eighty years earlier, as well as several revealing changes.

Chapter 6 recounts the dramatic repudiation in the 1978 Code of the New Deal vision for corporate reorganization. Crucial to the demise of the SEC were several factors dating back to the Chandler Act itself: by completely destroying the role of the Wall Street banks and bar, the SEC unintentionally stacked the interest group deck against itself; and the structure of the Chandler Act assured that any future legislative battles would start in a congressional committee, the Judiciary Committee, that was much less sympathetic to the SEC than to the bankruptcy professionals that opposed it. The SEC's stature in bankruptcy had steadily weakened in the years leading up to the 1978 Code. Although the SEC took its case to the Judiciary Committee, to Justice Douglas, and finally to President Carter, the 1978 Code almost completely repudiated both the SEC and the New Deal vision of bankruptcy.

Part 4, which includes chapters 7 and 8, brings our bankruptcy story up to the present. Chapter 7 focuses on consumer bankruptcy and the fierce battle between the consumer credit industry, on the one hand, and the consumer bankruptcy bar and other prodebtor interests, on the other. The biggest puzzle of recent bankruptcy politics is the surprising failure of the most recent National Bankruptcy Review Commission, which was authorized by Congress in 1994 and completed its work in 1997. Whereas its predecessor, the 1973 report, had seemed ideologically neutral to most observers, the 1997 report was viewed as highly partisan. In the words of its critics, the report was "dead on arrival" when its drafters submitted the report to Congress. The explanation for the failure of the 1997 report, as well as the ideologically charged atmosphere of the recent debates, lies in the fact that a dramatic shift in congressional politics—the "Gingrich Revolution"—took place after the commission was authorized but before it completed its report. Rather than the relatively prodebtor proposals of the commission, the Republican Congress considered and nearly enacted a set of reforms that were promoted by the consumer credit industry and backed by an extraordinary lobbying campaign. After considering the creditors' proposals and why the campaign unraveled, the chapter concludes by exploring the principal problem with the existing framework: the moral incoherence of debtors' choice between Chapter 7 and Chapter 13.

Chapter 8 returns to corporate bankruptcy and describes the role that the 1978 Code has played in the resurgence of large-scale corporate reorganization. Most importantly, Chapter 11, the Code's reorganization chapter, has proven far more attractive to troubled firms than prior law because it permits a debtor's current managers to continue running the firm in bankruptcy. This change, and the expanded scope of bankruptcy, have also facilitated the use of bankruptcy to address the mass tort problems of otherwise healthy firms such as Johns Manville, A. H. Robins, and Dow Corning. The resurgence of large-scale reorganization has brought the nation's elite law firms back into bankruptcy practice. The practice is no longer concentrated on Wall Street alone, however, and is much less susceptible to the kinds of populist attack that destroyed the practice in the 1930s. The chapter concludes that the existing approach seems to be here to stay and considers four of the most crucial current issues: efforts to opt out of bankruptcy, the increasing number of large firm filings in Delaware; the new value exception to the absolute priority rule; and international insolvency.

Having pursued U.S. bankruptcy law up to the present, the book concludes with a brief epilogue. In addition to summarizing the political determinants of U.S. bankruptcy, the epilogue considers the effects of globalization on the American bankruptcy framework. In theory, globalization might alter the political factors that have produced the unique U.S. approach to financial relief. In reality, the converse seems to be true. American bankruptcy law has retained its distinctive characteristics, whereas globalization is pressuring other nations to adopt a more U.S.-style approach. Germany has now adopted much of the Chapter 11 framework for corporate insolvency, for instance, and many nations are moving toward an American-style discharge for personal debtors. The epilogue considers why this is so and concludes that, whatever else may happen, the unique U.S. approach to financial distress is here to stay.

PART ONE

THE BIRTH OF U.S. INSOLVENCY LAW

Chapter One

THE PATH TO PERMANENCE IN 1898

CONGRESS'S AUTHORITY to regulate bankruptcy derives quite explicitly from the Constitution, which states in Article I, section 8 that Congress may pass "uniform laws on the subject of bankruptcies." The Founding Fathers included the provision almost as an afterthought. Charles Pinckney of Rhode Island proposed the Bankruptcy Clause late in the constitutional convention of 1787, and it was approved with little debate.[1] Almost the only contemporary evidence of the meaning or importance of "uniform bankruptcy" comes in the Federalist No. 42. Written by James Madison, Federalist No. 42 describes federal bankruptcy legislation as "intimately connected with the regulation of commerce," and necessary to prevent debtors from fleeing to another state to evade local enforcement of their obligations.[2]

Despite its inauspicious beginning, bankruptcy became one of the great legislative battlegrounds of the nineteenth century. The most famous lawmakers of the century, from Thomas Jefferson early on, to Daniel Webster and Henry Clay for many years thereafter, all weighed in on bankruptcy. Bankruptcy pitted farm interests and states' rights advocates against those who favored a more national economy, and it was repeatedly proposed as a remedy for economic depression. For all the discussion, the debates never seemed to reach a stable conclusion. Prior to 1898, Congress passed a series of bankruptcy laws, each of which quickly unraveled and led inexorably to repeal. In the absence of federal regulation, state insolvency laws filled the gap. But state laws suffered from serious jurisdictional limitations, and each new crisis brought calls for federal legislation. With the Bankruptcy Act of 1898, the instability suddenly came to an end. Although lawmakers often amended this act, most dramatically in the 1930s, and it was replaced altogether in 1978, federal bankruptcy has been a permanent fixture ever since. For individual and small-business debtors, then, the first age of bankruptcy consisted of a century of instability that finally led to a permanent federal law in 1898.

The dramatic transition from episodic bankruptcy to a permanent law in 1898 poses an obvious puzzle: what was the magic of the 1898 act? Why did the instability finally stop? To answer this question, we must briefly go back to the beginning, to the decades of debate that preceded the act. A common theme running through the bankruptcy debates was party politics. Throughout the nineteenth century, Democrats and their predecessors often resisted federal bankruptcy legislation, whereas Republicans and their predecessors were its most fervent advocates.[3] Viewing the debates as a conflict between Democrats and Republicans only begins to explain why Congress could not reach a stable resolution, however. Within each party, for instance, lawmakers often held strikingly different views of bankruptcy—Republicans in the commercial Northeast were far more enthusiastic about bankruptcy legislation than their southern and western colleagues, and roughly the reverse held true for the Democratic opposition. Adding to the confusion was the fact that the legislators faced a series of options on the bankruptcy issue. Rather than just favoring or opposing bankruptcy, lawmakers divided into at least three separate camps and sometimes more.

To more fully explain the early instability, I will borrow several basic concepts from the political science literature known as social choice. I will argue in particular that legislators held inconsistent and possibly "cyclical" preferences, no one of which commanded a stable majority: some lawmakers did not want a federal bankruptcy law, some (including both Democrats and Republicans) wanted only voluntary bankruptcy, and some wanted a law that provided for both voluntary and involuntary bankruptcy. We will then go on to consider how this instability was overcome, and how the Republican support for bankruptcy finally won out. The most important development was the emergence of organized creditor groups throughout the country at the end of the nineteenth century. To secure a federal bankruptcy law, creditors were forced to make numerous adjustments to pacify prodebtor lawmakers in the South and West. One of these adjustments, the adoption of a minimalist administrative structure, together with an unusually long period of Republican control, would inspire the rise of the bankruptcy bar. The unique American mix of creditors, prodebtor forces such as populism, and bankruptcy professionals has provided the recipe for every U.S. bankruptcy law that has followed.

We will focus throughout the chapter, as did nineteenth-century lawmakers, on individual and small-business debtors. Chapter 2 will explore the very different approach that emerged for reorganizing railroads and other large, corporate debtors.

THE BUST-AND-BOOM PATTERN OF NINETEENTH-CENTURY BANKRUPTCY LEGISLATION

The nineteenth-century bankruptcy debates have long been seen as fitting a loose, bust-and-boom pattern. In times of economic crisis, Congress rushed to pass bankruptcy legislation to alleviate widespread financial turmoil.[4] Once the crisis passed, so too did the need for a federal bankruptcy law. Like Penelope and her weaving, Congress quickly undid its handiwork on each occasion, only to start all over again when hard times returned. The traditional account is inaccurate in some respects and, as we will see, it does not explain why bankruptcy suddenly became permanent in 1898. But it provides a convenient framework for describing the first century of bankruptcy debate.

Agitation for bankruptcy legislation rose to a fever pitch at roughly twenty-year intervals throughout the nineteenth century. A depression starting in 1793 led to the first federal bankruptcy law in 1800—an act that Congress repealed three years later.[5] Congress went back to the drawing board in the 1820s, when financial crisis and the controversy over the Bank of the United States prompted calls for another bankruptcy law. The debates never came to fruition, however, and it was not until 1841, following the Panic of 1837, that Congress passed its second bankruptcy law. The 1841 act lasted only two years, when defections from the party that had won its passage, the Whigs, led to repeal. The cycle came around once more on the eve of the Civil War, with the Panic of 1857 putting bankruptcy back on the agenda, and setting the stage for the 1867 act. The 1867 act lasted longer than its predecessors, with a movement for repeal leading to amendment instead in 1874. But by 1878, the nation was once again without a federal bankruptcy law.

All told, then, Congress passed three federal bankruptcy laws prior to 1898: the Bankruptcy Acts of 1800, 1841, and 1867. Together, the acts lasted a total of sixteen years. The absence of a federal bankruptcy law did not leave a complete vacuum in debtor-creditor relations, of course. Most states had insolvency laws on the books.[6] Some of them, like Massachusetts's, predated the Revolution. In times of financial panic, states also responded by passing stay laws imposing moratoria on creditor collection. Proponents of federal bankruptcy legislation emphasized both the wide variation in these laws and their serious constitutional limitations, such as the inability of state law to bind out-of-state debtors.[7]

To recite the dates of passage and repeal of the nineteenth-century bankruptcy laws cannot even begin to suggest the urgency and importance that attended lawmakers' deliberations on bankruptcy—especially for a generation like ours that can scarcely remember the last depression. Here is Ralph Waldo Emerson's account of the desperate conditions of 1837. "Society has played out its last stake; it is checkmated. Young men have no hope. Adults stand like day-laborers idle in the streets. None calleth us to labor. . . . The present generation is bankrupt of principles and hope, as of property."[8]

In the early decades of the nineteenth century, commentators characterized the nation's periodic financial panics as acts of God. As recently recounted by a business historian, the Reverend Joel Parker "provided a brief history lesson" for his congregation in 1837 "to illustrate how the financial panic was a direct reproof for the 'peculiar sin' of greed, just as the flood had been a reproof for violence, famine for pride, captivity for sabbath breaking, the destruction of the temple for the rejection of Christ and, more recently, cholera for intemperance." Twenty years later, with the Panic of 1857, commentators looked less to God than to "metaphors of floods, typhoons, tide and hurricanes."[9]

Panics increasingly were seen in naturalistic terms, but they remained both devastating and unpredictable.

Ever mindful of their constituents' trauma, some of the finest lawmakers to walk the halls of Congress turned their attention to bankruptcy at regular intervals. Even in the most dire years, one group viewed federal bankruptcy with deep suspicion and fought hard to preserve the status quo. John Calhoun, the great senator from South Carolina, insisted that "[t]he distress of the country consists in its indebtedness and can only be relieved by the payment of its debts."[10] Not just concern for the repayment of debts, but a belief that local debtors were better served by state regulation of insolvency fueled the ongoing opposition to federal bankruptcy legislation.

On the other side, Daniel Webster, senator from Massachusetts, argued strenuously for federal regulation as necessary for both creditors and debtors.

> I believe the interest of creditors would be greatly benefitted [by passing bankruptcy legislation] . . . and I am quite confident that the public good would be promoted. . . . I verily believe that the power of perpetuating debts against debtors, for no substantial good to the creditor himself, and the power of imprisonment for debt . . . have imposed more restraint on personal liberty than the law of debtor and creditor imposes in any other Christian and commercial country.[11]

(A century later, Harvard Law School Professor James McLaughlin referred to Webster's speech as one of the great moments of American political oratory.)[12]

The two senators just quoted, Calhoun from South Carolina and Webster from Massachusetts, illustrate the geographical lines along which the debates tended to divide. Because southerners feared that northern creditors would use bankruptcy law as a collection device to displace southern farmers from their homesteads, the strongest opposition to federal bankruptcy came from the South. Many western lawmakers opposed bankruptcy legislation for similar reasons. Lawmakers from the commercial northeastern states, by contrast, were much more likely to view federal bankruptcy legislation as essential to the promotion of commercial enterprise.[13]

In addition to geography, lawmakers' views on bankruptcy also tended to divide along party lines. The Federalists (later Whigs, and then Republicans) promoted bankruptcy as essential to the nation's commercial development. Jeffersonian Republicans (later Democratic Republicans, and then Democrats), on the other hand, sought a more agrarian destiny and insisted that bankruptcy legislation would encourage destructive speculation by traders. Northeastern Federalists were the leading cheerleaders for federal bankruptcy legislation, and southern and western Jeffersonians were the staunchest opponents.

As we shall see, the conservative campaign for a permanent bankruptcy law was underwritten by increasingly well organized creditors groups by the end of the nineteenth century. Although rural interests lobbied in a relatively organized fashion on some issues—such as railroad rate legislation—opposition to bankruptcy came less from organized lobbying than from lawmakers who viewed themselves as representing agrarian interests, together with a few ideological entrepreneurs (such as Representative Bailey of Texas, who figured prominently in the 1890s).

Early in the century, constitutional issues figured especially prominently in the bankruptcy debates. Because the Constitution uses the term *bankruptcy* without further elaboration, some lawmakers insisted that the drafters intended to preserve the distinction in earlier English law between "bankruptcy" laws and "insolvency" laws. As distinguished from insolvency laws, which were designed to help debtors, they argued, bankruptcy laws only applied to traders and could not permit voluntary bankruptcy—that is, Congress could not give debtors the right to invoke the bankruptcy laws on their own behalf. Bankruptcy, on this view, was designed solely to help creditors round up a debtor's assets and use them for repayment. These lawmakers insisted that Congress simply did not have the authority to enact more sweeping bankruptcy legislation. Lawmakers who supported a broader bankruptcy law rejected this distinction, arguing that the Bankruptcy Clause used the term *bankruptcy* as a shorthand that referred to any legislation designed to deal with financial distress.

As the nineteenth century wore on, the Supreme Court rejected several of the arguments for a narrow reading of the Bankruptcy Clause.[14] In an important early case, the Supreme Court cast cold water on the claim that Constitution permitted "bankruptcy" but not "insolvency" laws. "Th[e] difficulty of discriminating with any accuracy between insolvent and bankruptcy laws," wrote Chief Justice Marshall, makes clear that "a bankrupt law may contain . . . insolvent laws; and that an insolvent law may contain [provisions] which are common to a bankrupt law."[15] By 1867, it was evident that Congress could enact both voluntary and involuntary laws, and that its powers were not limited to traders. As in other areas, an increasingly conservative and federally minded Supreme Court paved the way for an expansive bankruptcy law.[16] In Congress, however, deep divisions remained as to whether the nation needed a permanent bankruptcy law.

The obstacles for proponents of bankruptcy were not just philosophical, but also practical. The 1800, 1841, and 1867 bankruptcy acts all were administered through the federal district courts. Unlike state courts, which could be found in every county, federal courts were generally located in urban areas. The federal courts were especially inconvenient for potential debtors, many of whom lived far from the nearest city.[17] The problems were compounded by the costliness of the administrative process itself. After a debtor paid fees to the clerk of court, the official who administered his assets, and various others as well, the debtor's creditors often wound up with little or nothing.

The administrative difficulties of the first three bankruptcy acts made each deeply unpopular, not just with opponents but often with the very lawmakers who had most energetically supported them. With continuous opposition, especially from the South and West, and these prickly practical difficulties, the cycle of enactment and repeal continued throughout the nineteenth century. Even as of 1898, it was not obvious that anything had changed.

THE BANKRUPTCY DEBATES AS LEGISLATIVE CYCLING

I have suggested thus far that the nineteenth-century debates pitted opponents of bankruptcy against bankruptcy advocates. In actuality, the debates were much more subtle. Rather than two positions, lawmakers divided into at least three camps, and sometimes more—and these camps crossed party lines. By considering the competing views in slightly more detail, and by analogizing these views to a voting irregularity that political scientists call *cycling*, we can begin to see how deeply unstable bankruptcy was for over a hundred years.

We have already seen proponents of two of the views. Daniel Webster, like the famous Supreme Court justice Joseph Story, argued for an expansive and permanent federal bankruptcy framework. John Calhoun embodied the opposing view that federal bankruptcy legislation would be a serious mistake. Not coincidentally, Webster was a Whig from a commercial state, Massachusetts, whereas Calhoun was a states' rights advocate from the agrarian South.

Senator Henry Clay of Kentucky, a Whig and member along with Webster and Calhoun of the "Great Triumvirate" of famous senators, represented a third, and similarly influential, view of bankruptcy. Clay was willing to support bankruptcy legislation, but only if the law was limited to voluntary bankruptcy.[18] Clay shared the fear of many bankruptcy opponents that northern creditors would use bankruptcy to displace southern farmers from their homesteads, but he believed voluntary bankruptcy would minimize this risk while enabling financially strapped debtors to obtain relief.

Still other lawmakers adopted variations of these views. Democrat Thomas Hart Benton, another prominent senator and grandfather of the twentieth-century artist with the same name, was a vocal opponent of bankruptcy. Here, as elsewhere, he frequently found himself allied with John Calhoun. But Benton also insisted that, if Congress did pass a bankruptcy law, it needed to include corporations as well as individuals. Bankruptcy, in his view, might be one way to reign in the excesses of the nation's growing corporate sector.

A vexing problem when lawmakers (or decision makers of any kind, for that matter) hold a multiplicity of views on a single subject is that their voting may lead to irrational or unstable outcomes. At its extreme, the competing views can lead to the phenomenon of cycling. In a pathbreaking book, the economist Kenneth Arrow demonstrated that no voting institution based on democratic principles can guarantee that voting irregularities of this sort will not arise. If everyone has an equal vote, and every option is available, the voting process may lead to chronically unstable results.[19]

The views of nineteenth-century lawmakers on bankruptcy legislation provide a convenient illustration of the voting problems I have just described. Although the views will be described in stylized form, the overall pattern is not simply hypothetical. The senators I will use for purposes of illustration held views very close to the positions I will attribute to them, and Congress's ever-shifting stances on bankruptcy law in the nineteenth century may well have reflected the kinds of uncertainties we are about to explore.

Assume that three senators, Benton, Webster and Clay, must choose among three options: not passing any bankruptcy law (No Bankruptcy); passing a complete bankruptcy law, including both voluntary and involuntary bankruptcy (Complete Bankruptcy); or passing a law that permits only voluntary bankruptcy (Voluntary Only). As the careful reader will note, I have omitted a fourth option: providing for involuntary but not voluntary bankruptcy. As it turns out, the 1800 act adopted precisely this approach. Both for simplicity and because involuntary-only disappeared as a viable option by the middle of the nineteenth century, however, I will banish it from our discussion.

Of the three options we are considering, Benton would prefer not to pass any bankruptcy law (No Bankruptcy). If a bankruptcy law must pass, his next choice would be a complete bankruptcy law that included involuntary bankruptcy and brought corporations within its sweep (Complete Bankruptcy). His least favorite alternative is Voluntary Only.

As a fervent nationalist, Daniel Webster strongly favors an expansive bankruptcy law that provides for both voluntary and involuntary bankruptcy (Complete Bankruptcy). So strongly does he believe in the importance of bankruptcy to the health of the national economy that he would accept Voluntary Only bankruptcy as a second choice. His least favorite option is No Bankruptcy.

Henry Clay sees voluntary bankruptcy as an opportunity to alleviate the dire financial straits of many of his constituents. But he strongly opposes involuntary bankruptcy, fearing that many debtors who might otherwise recover from their financial distress would be hauled into bankruptcy court by their creditors. Clay's first choice is thus Voluntary Only, his second choice No Bankruptcy, and his last choice Complete Bankruptcy.

The senators' views are illustrated in table 1.1. The problem here is that the senators hold unstable preferences. To see this, consider what would happen if they held a series of votes on the three options and each voted in accordance with his preferences. In a vote between No Bankruptcy and Complete Bankruptcy, the winner would be No Bankruptcy, since both Benton and Clay prefer No Bankruptcy over Complete Bankruptcy. If the Senators then pitted the winner, No Bankruptcy, against Voluntary Only, Voluntary Only would emerge victorious on the strength of votes from Webster and Clay. At this point, Voluntary Only appears to be the winner. But if the senators held a vote

TABLE 1.1
Cycling among Bankruptcy Options in the Nineteenth Century

Senator	First Choice	Second Choice	Third Choice
Benton	No Bankruptcy	Complete Bankruptcy	Voluntary Only
Webster	Complete Bankruptcy	Voluntary Only	No Bankruptcy
Clay	Voluntary Only	No Bankruptcy	Complete Bankruptcy

between Voluntary Only and Complete Bankruptcy in order to complete the comparisons, both Benton and Webster would vote for Complete Bankruptcy. The senators prefer Complete Bankruptcy over Voluntary Only, but they like Complete Bankruptcy less than another option (No Bankruptcy) that Voluntary Only defeats.

If we were to study the alternatives a bit more closely, we would quickly see that Benton, Webster, and Clay could never choose a stable winner among the three alternatives. A familiar line from an old song, "Anything you can do, I can do better," neatly describes their dilemma. For each option that two of the senators favor, there is always a choice that two of the senators like better. If the senators continued to vote and voted in accordance with their preferences, the votes would go around and around forever—that is, they would cycle.

This kind of voting irregularity can arise in either of two ways. If a group of existing voters hold inconsistent views, cycling can occur at the time of a particular vote, as in the illustration we have just considered. But cycling can also take place intertemporally. Even if a clear majority of legislators held Benton's views today, next year's majority might hold the views I have attributed to Webster; and two years down the road might be a Clay year.

I should emphasize—as several readers of this book emphasized to me—that true cycling only occurs under the restrictive conditions defined in Arrow's Theorem. If lawmakers agreed that one option belongs on the left, one in the center, and one on the right, for instance, their preferences would not be cyclical even if they sharply disagreed about the best choice.[20] In view of this, let me emphasize that the principal point of this section is simply that the multiplicity of views contributed to Congress's inability to reach a stable outcome on federal bankruptcy legislation throughout the nineteenth century. Whether lawmakers' inconstancy reflected true cycling, or merely a garden-variety case of shifting legislative outcomes, the point remains the same.

Moreover, it is quite possible that the bankruptcy debates did indeed reflect true legislative cycling. If legislators hold consistent preferences, they will ordinarily gravitate toward a stable outcome even if there are sharply divergent views on what the outcome should be. Yet no such outcome emerged in the bankruptcy debates until late in the century. One is hard-pressed to think of another legislative issue on which Congress flip-flopped so continuously and for so long. (The closest analogue may be the debates whether to base the currency on gold alone, or to include silver as well; but these debates involved fewer shifts and moved more quickly to a relatively stable outcome.)

Rather than receding, the instability of the bankruptcy debates actually got worse as the century wore on. Ironically, as lawmakers came to see the Bankruptcy Clause as an expansive source of authority, and as this was vindicated by the Supreme Court, Congress's broad powers tended to complicate the debate rather than to simplify it.[21] Although the debates prior to the 1800 act were extremely controversial, most lawmakers viewed themselves as having only two options. They could pass a bill that provided only for involuntary bankruptcy, or not pass any bill at all. Because it put more options at lawmakers' disposal—most importantly, the possibility of a Voluntary Only bill—the expanding view of Congress's powers exacerbated the existing instabilities.

From the 1830s on, lawmakers' views were repeatedly splintered among the options we have considered—Complete Bankruptcy, Voluntary Only, and No Bankrupty—along with variations on these themes. In the twentieth century, Congress has developed institutional structures that can assure stability even in the face of inconsistent preferences.[22] One of these, delegation of gatekeeping authority to a committee, dates back to the early nineteenth century. Because the relevant oversight committee determines whether existing legislation is reconsidered, committees have the power to prevent a new Congress from promptly reversing the enactments of its predecessor. In theory, the Judiciary Committee, which has overseen bankruptcy issues since 1821, could have served this purpose. But committees played a less prominent role in the nineteenth century, in part because both Congress and congressional committees operated on a part-time basis. Neither the Judiciary Committee nor any stable block of lawmakers in Congress was in a position to act as agenda setter and provide the kind of stable outcome we see in other contexts where lawmakers hold inconsistent preferences.

Even a brief overview of the debates that led to the 1841 and 1867 acts gives a flavor of the instability that came from the multiplicity of views. The 1841 act was the brainchild of the Whig party, which had made bankruptcy law a crucial plank in the platform that brought them the presidency and control of the Senate the year before. In the face of strong opposition, the Whigs secured the necessary votes for enactment through a controversial logrolling campaign that obtained votes for bankruptcy in return for votes on a land distribution bill. (Logrolling is another possible solution to cyclical preferences. Rather than voting their true preferences, lawmakers permit one bill to pass in return for a favorable vote on other legislation.)

Even before the bill took effect, a vote to repeal passed the House when a small group of southern Whigs reversed their earlier support for the legislation, and a similar proposal fell only one vote short in the Senate.[23] The defection of several more Whigs, this time from the Midwest, brought the coalition tumbling down. Less than two years after it went into effect, President Tyler (who had assumed the presidency after President Harrison died) signed the repeal legislation and the 1841 act was gone. Just as the initial vote papered over a variety of strident dissenting views, the repeal illustrated just how quickly a majority coalition can collapse when lawmakers' underlying preferences are unstable.

The debates on the 1867 bankruptcy act, which dated back to the early 1860s, were complicated by the onset of the Civil War. When the war finally ended, the Republicans held large majorities in the House and Senate, which strengthened the support for a bankruptcy bill that included involuntary as well as voluntary bankruptcy. Northern lawmakers were particularly concerned that creditors would find it impossible to collect from southern debtors in the southern state courts.[24] Yet a sizable group of lawmakers continued either to resist any bankruptcy legislation, or to insist that only voluntary bankruptcy be included. Involuntary bankruptcy, argued Representative Dalbert Paine of Wisconsin in a representative though particularly colorful complaint,

[is] a preposterous and revolting thing. . . . [To force it on debtors] is an intolerable, indefensible wrong. It is peculiarly offensive to the free and easy but honest men of the West whom it will squeeze into the strait jacket so befitting the madmen of Wall Street. The farmers and mechanics of the West will rise against it. . . . No new National collection law is needed.[25]

Although it lasted longer than either of its predecessors, the 1867 act was deeply unstable from the moment it was enacted. In both 1868 and 1872, lawmakers amended the law to soften its effects on debtors, and a move to repeal it led to further concessions to debtors in 1874. By 1878, the act had few defenders, and it was repealed by large majorities of both parties in both houses.

The 1898 act would bring these instabilities to an end, but each of the competing views remained very much in evidence throughout the deliberations that preceded it. Introducing the House bill that would provide the framework for the 1898 act, Representative Henderson of Iowa summed up the "three lines of thought" on bankruptcy in terms that should by now sound extremely familiar.

First come those who [like himself] favor a law providing for both voluntary and involuntary bankruptcy. . . . There is another school who believe in a law which provides only for voluntary bankruptcy, cutting off all right on the part of the creditor to move in bankruptcy proceedings and giving that right only to the debtor. . . .

There is still a third class, namely those who are opposed to any bankruptcy law and are in favor of remitting all remedies of creditors against debtors to the State laws. . . . These are the three schools.[26]

As described in more detail below, in debates that began in 1881 and spanned almost two decades, the Senate voted for the first of these views, Complete Bankruptcy in 1884, as did the House in 1890 and 1896, and Complete Bankruptcy finally prevailed in 1898 in the form of the 1898 act. Proponents of Voluntary Only bankruptcy, the second "school," also had their moments, as the House passed a Voluntary Only bill in 1894, and the Senate passed a somewhat similar bill before agreeing to Complete Bankruptcy in 1898.[27] Throughout this time, opponents of bankruptcy managed (sometimes on the merits, sometimes because Congress ran out of time to act) to preserve the No Bankruptcy status quo.

The reports that the Judiciary Committee sent to Congress during the early 1890s offer a particularly vivid map of the shifts among coalitions at the end of the nineteenth century. In October 1893, a majority of the House Judiciary Committee forwarded a bill that provided for Complete Bankruptcy. The majority's report prompted a dissent from a coalition that included both Voluntary Only advocates and lawmakers who opposed bankruptcy altogether (No Bankruptcy). "The undersigned members of the Judiciary," the minority wrote, "while differing among themselves as to the necessity for any bankruptcy law . . . unite in opposing so much of the bill reported by the committee as provides for involuntary bankruptcy for any cause except actual fraud.[28]

Just two months later, the coalitions suddenly changed. Rather than a Complete bill, the Judiciary Committee now forwarded a Voluntary Only bill that brought together some members who preferred Voluntary Only bankruptcy and others who preferred Complete Bankruptcy. The new coalition admitted that they were "somewhat divided in the reasons which induce them to favor a purely voluntary bankruptcy law":

> A minority of the majority favor it because they think that some law ought be passed, and they believe the passage of a bill embracing an involuntary feature impossible, and that to insist upon such a measure will defeat all legislation on the subject. . . . A majority of the majority are opposed to any law providing for involuntary bankruptcy. . . . [I]t appears to them sufficient to say that a law including an involuntary provision has been tried three different times in our history, and each time has proved unsuccessful.[29]

With the emergence of a Voluntary Only proposal, advocates of Voluntary Only bankruptcy suddenly went from minority to majority status. It was as if the committee preferred Complete Bankruptcy over No Bankruptcy, but Voluntary Bankruptcy over Complete Bankruptcy.[30] This Voluntary Only bill eventually passed the House, after speeches by lawmakers holding the complete range of views reflected in the committee report, but the bill was never brought up for consideration in the Senate.

NINETEENTH-CENTURY ANCESTRY OF THE TWENTIETH-CENTURY BANKRUPTCY BAR

By the end of our discussion in this chapter, lawyers will emerge as a central factor in the political economy of U.S. bankruptcy law, and they will retain center stage for the remainder of the book. It may therefore be useful to pause for a moment to describe the predecessors of the twentieth-century bankruptcy bar. We then can put all of the pieces together and develop an explanation why bankruptcy suddenly came to maturity in the final years of the nineteenth century.

Throughout the nineteenth century, the vast majority of lawyers practiced by themselves and handled a wide range of matters. Central to the practice of most was the collection of debts for their creditor clients. Speaking of western lawyers, the preeminent historian of American law notes,

> Another staple of the lawyer's practice [in addition to real estate] was collection work. Lawyers dunned and sued, both for local people and for Easterners who held debts in the form of promissory notes. The lawyer usually paid himself from the proceeds—if he collected. Indiana attorney Rowland, collecting two notes in 1820 for E. Pollard, one "for 100 dollars in land-office money," the other for $100.37, "payable in leather to be delivered four miles from Bloomington," was to receive the customary fees when the money is collected, and if it is never collected then a reasonable fee for [his] trouble.[31]

The short-lived federal bankruptcy acts therefore served, as another legal historian, Edward Balleisen, has noted in his work on the 1841 act, as "an extension of their most basic stock-in-trade."[32] Bankruptcy provided a wealth of opportunity for attorney involvement. Debtors generally retained counsel to prepare their lists of assets and liabilities, to file the bankruptcy petition, and to represent the debtor on any issues disputed by his creditors. Creditors also needed an attorney when they chose to contest or otherwise participate in the debtor's bankruptcy.

A few attorneys seem to have developed a particular expertise in bankruptcy during the brief periods when federal bankruptcy legislation was in place. In the early 1840s, during the brief life of the 1841 act, several New York attorneys even "went so far as to advertise their services in newspapers," a strategy that proved surprisingly successful.[33] Specialization was relatively unusual, however. For thousands of attorneys, the bankruptcy acts provided one or a small number of new cases. When the acts were repealed, the attorneys simply plugged along with their usual assortment of state law collection cases and other matters. Although the 1867 act lasted over ten years, long enough for somewhat more specialization to occur, bankruptcy remained a limited, peripheral practice for all but a few attorneys. The raw materials for a bankruptcy bar were in place, but a true bar could not emerge in the absence of a permanent federal bankruptcy law.

THE RISE OF ORGANIZED CREDITORS AND THE COUNTERVAILING INFLUENCE OF POPULISM

Most of us have childhood memories of a game called musical chairs. In musical chairs, children walk around a circle of chairs as long as the music continues to play. When the music stops, they scramble to sit in the chairs. There are enough chairs for all but one child. With each round of music, the child who fails to grab a seat is eliminated, until finally, when only two children and one seat remain, one child emerges as the winner.

By now, the similarity between musical chairs and the nineteenth-century bankruptcy debates should be obvious. The principal difference was that, rather than one game of musical chairs, the debates became an endless series of such games. The winning alternative one year might give rise to a new approach the next. When the music stopped in 1898, there was no obvious reason to believe the circling was over—that Complete Bankruptcy had won out for good. But it had.

Why, after a century of legislative turmoil, did Congress finally enact a permanent bankruptcy law in 1898? And why did the first permanent U.S. bankruptcy law look so different from the English bankruptcy law that emerged in the same era under apparently similar circumstances? To answer these questions, we first must consider the role of business organizations and the prodebtor interests that opposed them in the years leading up to the 1898 act; and the role of the bankruptcy bar once the act was in place. The backdrop against which the interest group dramas played out was the general Republican support for, and Democratic hostility to, federal bankruptcy legislation.

The most important development in the years before the 1898 act was the emergence of commercial trade groups throughout the country. As Bradley Hansen has shown in his recent work on the 1898 act, prior to the late 1870s, local chambers of commerce and other business organizations were quite rare.[34] Thereafter, numerous commercial organizations arose, both locally and on a more national scale. Based on a study of 129 commercial organizations for which formation information is available, Hansen found that seventy-four were first formed in the 1880s or 1890s. Thirty-four dated to the 1870s, eleven

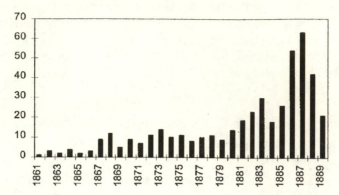

Source: *Report of the Internal Commerce of the U.S.*, 1st sess., 1890, H. Doc. 6 and National Industrial Conference Board, *Trade Associations: Their Economic Significance and Legal Status* (New York 1925)

Fig. 1.1. Business associations formed, 1861–1889. (From Bradley Hansen, "Commercial Associations and the Creation of a National Economy: The Demand for Federal Bankruptcy Law," 72 *Business History Review* 86, 111 (1998). Used by permission.)

to the 1860, and only eight predated 1860 (see fig. 1.1). The emergence of these trade groups was dramatic evidence of the increasingly commercial nature of the nation, and these organizations would be the driving force behind the 1898 act.

Merchants who engaged in interstate commerce complained bitterly and repeatedly that debtors played favorites when they ran into financial trouble. The favorites were family members and local creditors, not the out-of-state merchants. Sometimes a debtor would simply pay the lucky creditors directly; other debtors would assign their assets to a court-appointed receiver with instructions to use the assets to pay specified creditors. (By contrast, some southern lawmakers defended preferences to family members and other favored creditors. According to one senator, these were "debts of honor," and debtors had every right to pay them first.)[35]

In 1880, representatives of many of the creditor groups came together in St. Louis to form the National Organization of Members of Commercial Bodies, for the express purpose of promoting federal bankruptcy legislation. The merchants had commissioned John Lowell, a federal judge from Massachusetts, to draft a proposed bankruptcy bill. Drawing liberally from the English Bankruptcy Act of 1869, which gave extensive control to creditors, Lowell presented draft legislation the following year. The merchants enthusiastically endorsed Lowell's creation, which became known as the Lowell bill and served as the legislative template for their lobbying throughout the 1880s.

The legislative history of the 1898 act was an eighteen-year odyssey of shifts and near misses. The Senate passed the creditors' Lowell bill in 1884, but the bill failed in House. The bill went nowhere the following year and languished for several years thereafter, prompting the creditors groups to commission Jay Torrey, a St. Louis attorney, to produce a revised bill. The Torrey bill passed the House in 1890, but it too bogged down thereafter. In the mid-1890s, a surge of populist support led the House to reject the Torrey bill and to pass the Voluntary Only Bailey bill in 1894. The final push begin in 1896. In 1897, the House passed a version of the Torrey bill known as the Henderson bill, and the Senate passed a much more debtor-friendly bill known as the Nelson bill. For four months, House and Senate conferees sought to resolve their differences. This they finally did, and President McKinley signed the legislation in July 1898.[36]

A useful yardstick for measuring the role of creditors' groups throughout the legislative process is the letters, known as "memorials," that interested parties sent to Congress to support or oppose federal bankruptcy legislation. Memorials were nineteenth-century interest groups' principal mechanism for weighing in on proposed legislation in the absence of (or in addition to) legislative hearings. For most of the nineteenth century, the missives concerning bankruptcy almost always came from states or cities. By the 1890s, the authorship of the memorials looked entirely different. Rather than states and other governmental bodies, it was chambers of commerce, boards of trade, and other commercial organizations who filled lawmakers' mailboxes with their views.[37]

If memorials reflected the grassroots work of commercial organizations, their public face throughout the 1890s was a single individual: Jay Torrey. After revising the Lowell bill in the late 1880s, Torrey spent the next decade tirelessly campaigning for the bill in the corridors of Congress. Both supporters and opponents of the legislation made frequent reference to Torrey's role. In 1893, Republican congressman Oates of Alabama, the floor manager of the bill, noted that the Judiciary Committee had frequently invited Torrey to come and answer questions about the proposed legislation. Although Democrat William Jennings Bryan of Nebraska opposed the legislation, he had effusive praise for Torrey. "I have never known of any person interested in the passage of a bill," Bryan said on the floor of the House, "who seems to be so fair in the presentation of a case."[38] (The year 1898 proved to be an eventful one for Torrey. In addition to seeing the bankruptcy legislation finally enacted, Torrey achieved a small measure of fame as one of the Rough Riders who was in Cuba when Theodore Roosevelt stormed San Juan Hill.)

The 1898 act was thus a testament to the growing influence of national commercial interest groups and their representatives.[39] To say that these creditors organizations were the principal movers behind the 1898 act is not, however, to say that they got everything they wanted with the act. The best way to appreciate the limits of the creditors' influence is to cast a quick glance at developments in England during roughly the same period.[40] The legislation enacted in England in 1869 had called for creditor control of key issues such as the appointment of the assignee who would oversee the bankruptcy process. When this approach proved disappointing, English lawmakers turned to "officialism"—an administratively run system—with the 1883 act. The Bankruptcy Act of 1883 authorized the Board of Trade to appoint an official receiver to conduct most of the administrative functions of the bankruptcy case. This approach established what still are the basic parameters of English bankruptcy law. Under the English approach, an official receiver exercises wide-ranging authority to investigate each debtor (generally without debtors' counsel present), to oversee the appointment of a trustee, and to make recommendations to the court. These powers give the English system a pervasively governmental and administrative character. English bankruptcy is also quite tough on debtors. A debtor who files for bankruptcy in England is subject to searching scrutiny, and courts routinely delay the debtor's discharge for periods up to several years.

U.S. commercial organizations would have been more than happy to see a similar approach in America. But commercial hopes were not to be met. Not only did it take nearly twenty years for creditor groups and their allies to persuade Congress and the president to push bankruptcy legislation through; but creditors also were forced to make important concessions along the way. The opposition to a creditor-inspired bankruptcy law came from a cluster of prodebtor forces that had a crucial restraining effect on the creditors' bankruptcy proposals—much as their predecessors had had since the early decades of the nineteenth century. A unique product of American politics, these forces derived much of their influence from the nation's federalist political structure.

At the heart of this resistance to a creditor-oriented bankruptcy law in the 1880s and 1890s were the agrarian and populist movements that emerged in the last half of the nineteenth century, and which overlapped with the states' rights movement that remained influential in the South.[41] These prodebtor forces faced substantial obstacles in the legislative domain. They were not nearly as well organized as the business organizations were, and by the late nineteenth century they were swimming against the tide of history: the trend of the nation was commercial rather than agricultural, and urban rather than rural. Despite the obstacles, these movements had widespread popular support in many southern and western states. On some issues, such as railroad rate regulation, farmers themselves engaged in coordinated lobbying. Historian Gerald Berk recounts that, although rural "merchants sent representatives to state assemblies throughout the Midwest, where they introduced no fewer than a dozen bills outlawing rate discrimination," this effort failed until midwestern farmers joined the effort. "It was not until the fabulous growth of the Grange[, an agrarian movement] in 1872 and 1873, he concludes, "that legislative initiatives were successful."[42]

With bankruptcy, farm interests were represented less directly. Unlike creditor organizations, farmers and other rural constituencies did not send memorials to Congress or develop specific legislative proposals. Yet bankruptcy was an extraordinarily prominent issue, and lawmakers from farm states actively promoted the ideological views of their rural constituents. Ideological entre- preneurs such as Representative Bailey of Texas, who spearheaded the cam- paign for a voluntary-only bankruptcy bill in the mid-1890s, and Senator Stew- art of Nevada, provided a public face for the prodebtor perspective.

The American political system (i.e., federalism), with its peculiar division of authority between Congress and the states, magnified the influence of the agrarian and populist movements. Because every state had the same number of senators, the less populous states of the South and West had every bit as much authority in the Senate as New York or Massachusetts.[43] The local orien- tation of the Senate was reinforced by the fact that, in the nineteenth century, the senators of each state were selected by the state legislature. Although the rural bias was less pronounced in the House, rural interests also enjoyed dis- proportionate influence in this chamber due to subtle factors such as delays in redistricting.[44]

By the 1890s, populist lawmakers were the standard bearers for the prodebtor perspective, and the debates that led to the 1898 act were full of their exchanges with proponents of a federal bankruptcy law. In the populist imagination, bank- ruptcy law was often linked with the gold standard as the two greatest scourges of the common laborer. Creditors preferred that America yoke its currency solely to gold in order to minimize inflationary pressures and promote ex- change. Populist lawmakers complained that this "sound money" strategy would hurt farmers. In the words of Senator Stewart of Nevada, the gold stan- dard would "depreciate the property and increase the burden of debt" on the common man.[45] (Populists were not worried about the possibility of inflation under a "bimetallist" approach that included silver as well as gold, because inflation would increase property values and decrease the burden on debtors of previously contracted debt.) In the wake of one such populist diatribe, Con- gressman Sibley, a bankruptcy proponent, summed up the populist lament in particularly colorful terms: "If I understand the gentleman's argument, it is this: That the silver legislation [restricting the use of silver as legal tender] is the seed which was sown to the great crop of ruin, and this bankruptcy bill follows as a harvester and thrasher to enable Shylock to gather in his crop."

Creditors exerted most of their influence within the Republican party, of course, and most agrarians and populists were Democrats. But the Republi- cans who promoted bankruptcy had to make concessions to prodebtor inter- ests to minimize defections (especially of southern and western Republicans) and to pick up a few Democrat votes. In short, it was the rise of creditor organizations and countervailing influence of prodebtor forces, working within the structure of the two political parties, that produced both the 1898 act and the shape of U.S. bankruptcy law for the century to come.[46]

SHRINKING THE BANKRUPTCY FRAMEWORK AND CLOSING THE DEAL ON THE 1898 ACT

Other than the imperative somehow to balance the interests of creditors and debtors, the most pressing issue in the debates on the 1898 act was costs. As we saw earlier, the 1867 act had been a disaster in this regard. An assignee commanded the largest fee for managing the overall process. There also had been fees for the clerk who received the debtor's petition and then sent notices to creditors; and a marshal took his cut for administering particular assets. In the vast majority of cases, these officials seemed to make out like bandits, and little or nothing was left over for creditors.[47]

Prodebtor lawmakers tended to view the cost of the bankruptcy apparatus as a fatal problem. The prospect of an expanding federal bureaucracy made matters still worse. "In my judgment," a Texan congressman concluded in 1890, "the people do not want any more Federal officials over them."[48] Hostility to federalization was, of course, a familiar theme from southern and western lawmakers in the annals of nineteenth-century lawmaking, dating back to Jefferson's vision for an agrarian nation and the states' rights movement often associated with Senator John Calhoun. By the late nineteenth century, the states' rights perspective was somewhat nuanced. Southern and western lawmakers actively supported federal railroad rate regulation and intervention by the Interstate Commerce Commission, for instance.[49] With bankruptcy, however, they had much less sympathy, since federal bankruptcy legislation seemed to favor northeastern commercial interests. The cost and inconvenience of the federal courts exacerbated this concern.

Even lawmakers sympathetic to creditors' interests were worried as to whether a cost-effective administrative framework could be devised. Given these concerns, and the sorry legacy of the earlier bankruptcy bills, it was clear from the outset that the creditors' only hope was to propose a bill that pared back the administrative structure to an absolute minimum. The minimalist administrative structure that emerged and the bankruptcy bar it inspired were a crucial legacy of the decades-long battle between creditor groups and their prodebtor opposition.

In the earliest version of the Lowell bill, the creditors groups thought they had preempted these concerns and found an ideal solution—an approach that would assure adequate supervision, and thus protect creditors, while keeping administrative costs at a minimum. Bankruptcy would be administered by the U.S. district courts, but a new set of officials—called "commissioners"—would handle each case on a day-to-day basis. In addition, a group of "supervisors" would oversee the process on a broader, regional level. The Lowell bill proposed that the commissioners and supervisors receive a modest salary for their troubles—three thousand dollars for supervisors and two thousand dollars for commissioners.[50]

As it turned out, even this was not limited enough. When Senator Hoar first introduced the Lowell bill, he extolled its salary approach as an enormous improvement over previous law.[51] Salaried officials, he contended, would have an incentive to move the process along, rather than dragging things out as in a fee-based system. But the opposition to a permanent coterie of bankruptcy officials was immediate and strong. The new officials, Senator Ingalls of Kansas complained in the earliest debate, would be "permanent additions to the already excessive civil service of the government."[52] Complaints about the bureaucracy and its costs (which, as opponents noted, would be far higher than in more geographically centralized England) continued through the entire sixteen years of debate. The early opposition forced bankruptcy advocates to jettison salaries and revert to a fee-based approach. By the time the act finally passed, the proposed supervisors also were long gone. At the heart of the bankruptcy process would be a part-time official—the bankruptcy referee—who was paid a fixed percentage of the assets he distributed in the bankruptcy cases that came before him. Not until 1946 would Congress finally put bankruptcy referees on a salary basis (and only in 1973 would they receive the more flattering title of "bankruptcy judge").

In addition to reducing the cost and administrative structure, which concerned both creditors and prodebtor lawmakers, procreditor lawmakers had to make (or retain) crucial compromises on two other issues: exemptions and the grounds for involuntary bankruptcy. Exempt property is the property that a debtor does not have to turn over to his creditors if he files for bankruptcy. Permitting a debtor to keep a few of his things, the reasoning goes, will help him to make a "fresh start" once his debts have been discharged in bankruptcy. In the nineteenth century, state laws often protected items like a debtor's bed, Bible, and work tools. But many southern and western states also provided a generous exemption for the debtor's homestead, which often was his only asset with real value.

In recent years, the television news programs have aired breathless stories about well-heeled debtors who moved to Florida or Texas to take advantage of enormous homestead exemptions when they file for bankruptcy. A favorite example is Bowie Kuhn, the former commissioner of baseball, who bought a $2 million house in Florida. Kuhn's creditors got only pennies on the dollar when he subsequently filed for bankruptcy, while Kuhn himself kept the house and his enviable lifestyle. The exemption that made all this possible dates back to the nineteenth century, as does the general astonishment that a debtor has so much protection against his creditors.

Not surprisingly, creditors would have preferred to pass a bankruptcy law that made exemptions a matter of federal law. The 1867 act had deferred to state exemptions, and creditors complained bitterly about the results. Not only were the exemptions in some states remarkably generous, but several southern states had the audacity to expand their exemptions after the 1867 act was enacted. A single set of federal exemptions would have eliminated the confusion of dealing with laws that varied from state to state, and limited debtors to a more modest safety net. But bankruptcy advocates knew there was no hope of securing enough votes for bankruptcy unless they conceded to prodebtor lawmakers on this issue. The exemptions issue had generated enormous debate before the 1867 act, and incorporating state exemptions was the only way to assure that the legislation would pass. (It also was probably not incidental that the Republican president who signed the legislation, Andrew Johnson, was a southerner.) By the 1890s, lawmakers treated state regulation of exemptions as nonnegotiable.[53] Until 1902, it was not even clear whether deferring to state exemptions satisfied the constitutional requirement that Congress enact only "uniform" bankruptcy laws. Incorporating state law meant that debtors' exemptions would vary from one state to the next, which might easily have been construed as making the bankruptcy framework nonuniform. Nevertheless, constitutional doubts or not, state control of exemptions was a settled policy in each of the bankruptcy bills proposed in the 1880s and 1890s.

On the second set of issues, involuntary bankruptcy and the related issue of grounds for refusing to discharge the debtor's obligations, creditors dug in their heels much more. As against opponents' claims that malicious creditors would use the involuntary provision to throw struggling but financially viable debtors into bankruptcy, the commercial groups and their advocates insisted that creditors had no incentive to wrongfully invoke bankruptcy. And only with involuntary bankruptcy, they insisted, would creditors be assured a fair share of debtors' assets.

Over the course of the debates, creditors agreed to a series of protections to ward off creditor misbehavior. As early as 1882, lawmakers added a provision giving debtors the right to a state court jury trial if creditors filed an involuntary bankruptcy petition. For a rural debtor, this assured a jury of his peers, in the nearby state court rather than the federal court in a distant city. A provision permitting courts to detain a potential debtor was weakened in response to protests by prodebtor lawmakers, and creditors would be required to post a bond in connection with an involuntary petition. On the crucial issue of which "acts of bankruptcy" would justify an involuntary petition, however, creditors were much more grudging. The list of bases for involuntary bankruptcy was distilled by the 1890s to nine "acts of bankruptcy," which generated fierce, ongoing debate. While proponents of Voluntary Only bankruptcy wanted to eliminate the section altogether, or at the most limit it to cases of actual fraud, the creditor groups that supported Complete Bankruptcy refused to scale back.

Not until late in the debates did procreditor lawmakers make any important concessions. The ninth act of bankruptcy, which made failure for more than thirty days to make payments on commercial paper an act of bankruptcy, was removed in 1896. This is where things stood as of 1898.

For four months in 1898, a group composed of representatives from the House and Senate attempted to hammer out a compromise bill that would reconcile the creditor-supported Henderson bill passed by the House and the much more debtor-friendly Nelson bill that had emerged from the Senate.[54] The key issue in the negotiations was the eight acts of bankruptcy. The House team, lead by Senator Henderson, fought to preserve all eight of the acts of bankruptcy in order to protect creditors' right to invoke the bankruptcy laws. Nelson and the Senate team, by contrast, chaffed at any basis for involuntary bankruptcy other than fraud. In the end, the two men reached an eleventh-hour compromise that eliminated three more acts of bankruptcy, reducing the final list to five. The compromise also reduced the grounds for denying a debtor's discharge.

It would be difficult to overstate the importance of scaling back the administrative structure, and of creditors' concessions on exemptions and involuntary bankruptcy, to the tenor of the 1898 act. Rather than a creditor collection device, as most previous bankruptcy laws had been, the first permanent U.S. law would be as sympathetic to debtors' interests as to those of creditors. By downsizing the administrative machinery, the 1898 act set up an adversarial, judicial process as the American model for bankruptcy. In contrast to England, where a governmental official plays a pervasive role, the referees under the 1898 act would have little incentive to get actively involved; and the process would be left largely to the parties themselves. This created an enormous demand for a bankruptcy bar, and, as we shall see, lawyers came out of the woodwork to fill the need. These characteristics—the generally debtor-friendly approach to bankruptcy, and the primacy of lawyers rather than an administrator—distinguish U.S. bankruptcy law from every other insolvency law in the world.

THE SHELTERING WING OF REPUBLICAN CONTROL

Neither the creditor organizations that lobbied so long for the 1898 act, nor the bar that the act inspired, explains why Congress finally passed the act in 1898, rather than 1890, 1895, or some other year. Crucial to the timing of the act, and to its early survival, was a simple shift in party politics. Each of the prior bankruptcy acts was enacted in years when the Republicans or their predecessors controlled both Congress and the presidency. The 1898 act was no different. In 1898, the Republican party controlled the presidency and both houses of Congress for the first time in years. The Republicans retained this control for more than a decade, as Theodore Roosevelt took over for President McKinley, and subsequently won a second term. Republican control helped put bankruptcy legislation on the front burner in 1898, and it helped keep the 1898 Bankruptcy Act in place long enough for the bankruptcy bar to develop and cement the coalition in favor of its retention.

Party control alone is not enough to assure the permanence of a law whose support is unstable, of course. Party dominance invariably comes to an end, as the Republicans found on losing the House in 1910. Even before this time, Republican support for the 1898 act was far from unanimous. The two Republican bills that were reconciled to create the 1898 act (the Henderson bill in the House, the Nelson bill in the Senate) differed dramatically in tone, as we have seen. Many creditors who had promoted the bankruptcy later chafed at the compromises that had been made to appease debtor-oriented lawmakers, and their disaffection was shared by at least a few Republican lawmakers.[55] Some observers believe that the act might have been repealed if Congress had not taken steps to tighten the discharge in 1903. (The act had also gotten an important boost the year earlier, when the Supreme Court held in 1902 that incorporating state law on exemptions did not violate the uniformity requirement.)[56] In 1905, the fate of the 1898 act was very much up for grabs as the Republican-controlled House Judiciary Committee advocated repeal. But the center held, and the continuing efforts for repeal had lost much of their force by the time the Republicans finally lost control of the levers of power in the second decade of the new century.

The most important effect of continued Republican control was that it enabled a federal bankruptcy bar to develop. Although bankruptcy lawyers immediately answered the call for their expertise, it takes time for a bar to mature. Republican control provided the necessary stability, and that turned out to make all the difference. In less than a decade, bankruptcy professionals supplied the final piece of the bankruptcy puzzle. Together with—and in time, even more than—the commercial interests that had inspired the act, the bankruptcy bar made sure that Complete Bankruptcy prevailed for good.

The Emergence of a Bankruptcy Bar After the 1898 Act

Spurred by the 1898 act, and by the need of both debtors and creditors for bankruptcy attorneys, the bankruptcy bar sprang almost immediately into existence. As we have seen, the ingredients for a bankruptcy bar had long been in place in the collection activities that dominated many lawyers' practice. Perhaps the best testimony on the rapid rise of a distinctive bankruptcy practice comes from the collective activities of lawyers' organizations and the emergence of bankruptcy "stars."

The earliest and most effective voices for the bankruptcy bar were lawyers' organizations such as the American Bar Association and the Commercial Law League. The first, and the first organization to give a nationwide voice to lawyers generally, was the ABA. Formed in 1878, the ABA predated the 1898 act by two full decades and was a somewhat unlikely spokesman for bankruptcy lawyers given the elitist orientation of its membership. In commercial law, the ABA was in the forefront of the movement to produce uniform commercial laws. In 1887, the committee voiced its support for the limited, "equity" bankruptcy bill that had been introduced several years earlier and would resurface in somewhat altered form in the next decade. Once the more expansive 1898 act had been enacted, however, the leading members of the newly emerging (and distinctly nonelitist) bankruptcy bar became a dominant influence on the Committee on Commercial Law—later called the Bankruptcy Committee. In the debates on repeal that began almost as soon as the act went into effect, the ABA consistently weighed in for retaining and expanding the 1898 act.

Unlike the ABA, which includes lawyers of all stripes, the Commercial Law League was, and is, much more directly tied to the bankruptcy bar. The Commercial Law League was first formed in 1895, shortly before Congress enacted the 1898 act. The league was designed as an analogue to general creditors organizations, but with a particular focus on legal issues. The fact that the league emerged during the final round of debates on the 1898 act is not accidental. Although it was (and is) concerned with a variety of commercial law issues, bankruptcy was an overriding concern of the league from its inception. Bankruptcy lawyers quickly became the principal members of the league. From the pages of the league's house organ, the *Bulletin* (later given the name *Commercial Law Journal*), bankruptcy lawyers reviewed bankruptcy developments and debated legislative strategies for promoting and protecting the 1898 act. During the buildup to the 1903 amendments, for instance, the editors of the *Bulletin* emphasized that "the League has uniformly and consistently advocated the principle of national bankruptcy legislation, while admitting the necessity for amendments to the present law in order to insure equity as between creditor and debtor."[57]

An even more vivid illustration was the early emergence and influence of bankruptcy "stars." One of the most prominent in the infancy of the 1898 act was Frank Remington. After practicing as a commercial lawyer in Cleveland prior to the act, Remington became one of the act's early referees. Although serving as a referee was not a particularly prestigious job, Remington quickly made a name for himself by, among other things, publishing one of the first comprehensive treatises on the 1898 act. From its inception in 1908, *Remington on Bankruptcy* quickly became a standard reference, and Remington figured prominently in the early bankruptcy debates.[58]

In some respects, the bankruptcy bar figured even more prominently than the creditors groups that served as its principal allies. The two groups spoke with equal fervor on the importance of an expansive federal bankruptcy law. But when lawmakers put overarching questions to one side in order to discuss the technical details of the act, creditors took less of an active interest. In hearings on issues such as the definition of insolvency and compensation for bankruptcy receivers, nearly all of the witnesses were lawyers and lawyers' groups. Frank Remington played a particularly visible role in these hearings. In addition to testifying, he cast himself, and was cast by the committee, as the expert on existing bankruptcy law. More than anyone else, it is Remington's voice that one hears in the deliberations that led to important amendments in 1903 and 1910.

Summary

The picture we have developed is a mosaic, with a variety of interrelated parts, but a small group of pieces tells much of the story. The backdrop of the 1898 act was decades of instability due to lawmakers' inconsistent views on federal bankruptcy legislation. Lawmakers' views divided loosely along geographical and party lines, with most northeastern and Republican lawmakers favoring bankruptcy, while southern and western lawmakers, and Democrats, were more hostile. Even within these groups, however, lawmakers held divergent views. Some wanted an expansive bankruptcy law, some did not want any bankruptcy law, and others preferred a limited, voluntary-only law. The single most important development at the end of the century was the formation of local chambers of commerce, boards of trade, and other merchant organizations across the country. These organizations provided a nationwide base of support for bankruptcy law and eventually persuaded Congress to enact the 1898 act.

Commercial organizations' support was not by itself enough to stabilize lawmakers' preferences, however. To soften opposition from states' rights, agrarian, populist, and other debtor-oriented lawmakers, the creditors were forced to cede authority over exemptions to the states and to minimize the act's administrative machinery. Creditors also bowed to prodebtor sentiment by offering discharge provisions that were much more lenient than in any previous act. The final hurdle was not cleared until the Republicans gained control of both houses of Congress and the presidency. Republican control assured passage in 1898, and continued Republican control kept the act in place long enough for the bankruptcy bar to develop. It was the emergence of the bankruptcy bar that reinforced the coalition for bankruptcy, a development that assured the permanence of the act.

The rise of the bankruptcy bar sets the stage for much of the rest of the bankruptcy story. Since 1898, bankruptcy professionals have been the single most important influence on the development of bankruptcy law. For readers who are familiar with the political science literature, this point may sound familiar. Political scientists have frequently noted that government agencies have a tendency to become self-perpetuating.[59] Once Congress establishes a new agency and creates jobs for a group of new government officials, these same officials will later serve as the primary bulwark against elimination of the agency. In a sense, the agency becomes its own political constituency. Although the bankruptcy bar is private rather than governmentally run, it has played a rather analogous role.

The influence of the bankruptcy bar was not, and has never been, unbounded, however. The same forces that were melded together to create the 1898 act—organized creditors and the prodebtor ideologies strengthened by American federalism—have continued to set the basic parameters of U.S. bankruptcy law. In chapter 3, we will examine the interest group and ideological dynamic in more detail, through the lens of public choice theory. First, however, we must consider the other half of U.S. bankruptcy law, the emergence of a judicial mechanism for reorganizing railroads and other large corporations.

Chapter Two

RAILROAD RECEIVERSHIP AND THE

ELITE REORGANIZATION BAR

A LTHOUGH CORPORATE REORGANIZATION has gone hand in glove with general bankruptcy law for many decades now, its origins are quite distinct. The bankruptcy debates that led to general legislation in 1800, 1841, 1867, and 1898 had little to do with the reorganization of large corporations. To be sure, both the 1867 act (after an amendment in 1874) and the 1898 act did include corporate bankruptcy. But lawmakers focused entirely on individuals and small corporations in their deliberations, and the Bankruptcy Act reflected this. The corporate bankruptcy provisions were useful only for small businesses; more substantial firms simply ignored them. To trace the real origins of corporate reorganization, we must look elsewhere.

The "elsewhere" that lies at the heart of early reorganization can be distilled to a single word: railroads. In a very real sense, the history of corporate reorganization is the history of nineteenth-century railroad failure. The periodic collapse of the railroads led to the first true reorganizations—which were called equity receiverships. When Congress finally added a meaningful corporate reorganization option to the Bankruptcy Act in the 1930s, it took all of its cues from the railroad receivership techniques that had long been used in the courts.

Although corporate reorganization traveled on a very different track than the rest of bankruptcy, we will see several familiar themes as we explore its origins. As with nineteenth-century bankruptcy legislation, American federalism, with its division of authority between Congress and the states, played a crucial role both in the emergence of the great railroad receiverships and in the shape the receiverships took. As with general bankruptcy, the process produced a powerful and distinctive bar. The bar, together with the Wall Street banks it represented, was the most obvious beneficiary, and a principal cause, of the reorganization technique. But that is the end of the story. Let us first go back to the colorful beginning.

THE GROWTH AND EFFECT OF THE RAILROADS

As scholars have often pointed out, the railroads were America's first great corporations.[1] The origins of the industry go back to the first half of the nineteenth century. In the early years, the construction of railroads, as with canals and bridges, was closely tied to state government. If state lawmakers concluded that they needed a railroad, the state would issue a corporate charter for this purpose, effectively granting a local monopoly to the lucky firm.

> Much of the work of [state] legislatures, in the first half of the 19th century, consisted of chartering transport companies, and amending these charters. Taking the Maryland laws of 1835–36 as a sample, we find in the first pages an amendment to "an act for building a bridge over the Little North-East, in Cecil County" . . . three more bridge laws, and an amendment to "the act incorporating the Annapolis and Potomac Canal Company" . . . all in January 1836.[2]

In a sense, the early firms were like an extension of state government. It is only a slight overstatement to call them our first state agencies.[3]

As with the other major innovations of this era, steamships and the telegraph, the first great boom of railroad construction began in the 1840s. To a total of 2,818 miles of track in 1840, nearly 5,000 miles were added in the 1840s, and even more—nearly 22,000 miles—in the decade that followed.[4] Although the states played a central role in these developments, the tight relationship between state government and the corporations they chartered had already begun to loosen by this time. State lawmakers faced strong political and economic pressures to grant corporate charters more freely. Not only was strict state control over charters assailed as undemocratic, but business was growing so rapidly that individualized review of each charter application made less and less sense. State legislators could increase their patronage opportunities, and overall support, by expanding access to corporate franchises. Legislators still had enormous influence over railroad development, but the railroads, like other state-chartered firms, acted more and more like private businesses, rather than simply arms of the state.

Closely related to this transition was the emergence of an investment-banking industry in the 1850s and 1860s.[5] The railroad construction boom created an enormous need for capital, and, because the construction was privately financed, somebody had to act as middleman between private investors and the expansion-oriented railroads. That somebody was the first investment banks. Pioneering firms such as Winslow, Lanier & Company sold railroad securities to both European and American investors. Many of these firms had cut their teeth selling the government bonds that were used to finance the Civil War. When the war ended, they turned their attention with renewed vigor to the largest and most capital intensive of the nation's private industries, the railroads.

The railroads had a transformative effect on nearly every aspect of American life. The largest dairy farming region of New York, Orange Country, lay only fifty miles from Manhattan, for instance, yet fresh milk was unavailable in the city before the railroads arrived. "Most New Yorkers," John Steele Gordon points out in his colorful history of the Erie Railway, "had to use milk from cows that were kept by brewers and distillers."[6] The cows that produced this "swill milk" were poorly fed and lived in deplorable conditions in the city. As a result, the milk they provided "was a major source of tuberculosis, cholera, and other potentially milk-borne diseases." With the arrival of the New York and Erie Rail Road in the early 1840s, all this changed. Fresh Orange County milk soon began to drive swill milk from New Yorkers' tables.

In a recent history of Chicago, William Cronon recounts the equally dramatic changes the railroads brought to the Midwest in the mid–nineteenth century. Rural merchants who once had to make annual buying trips to the East Coast for goods could now find many of the same goods in Chicago. For produce merchants, the "availability of rail transport, and the existence of a reliable cash market in Chicago, meant that merchants did not have to invest nearly so much money in the warehouse facilities they had formerly needed to hold the harvest until spring. Railroad cars could serve as warehouses of a sort, and the enormous grain elevators and packing plants in Chicago also removed some storage burdens from smaller towns."[7] For the rural shopkeepers who had previously monopolized their local markets, these developments were a disaster; but for consumers and the cash-starved entrepreneurs who could now afford to compete with existing merchants, they were a godsend.

Along with the magic came serious growing pains, however. The years of railroad expansion led, by the 1870s, to intense, and at times destructive, competition among the railroads. A recurrent problem was that the expansion often seemed to have little rhyme or reason; although thousands of miles of track had been laid, there was not always effective coordination among them. Added to this were the competitive pressures created by the railroads' high fixed costs. Because so much of a railroad's costs were incurred even if it had no business—"Ties rotted, bridges collapsed, and rails rusted no matter how few trains passed over them," as one historian puts it—even hopeless railroads had an incentive to set their rates low enough to attract business, even if this meant losing money.[8] Changes in technology introduced still other complexities. Many of the northern rails had used iron track, for instance, which had a narrower gauge than the steel track that came into vogue in the 1850s.

It was against this backdrop that the famous railroad magnates, men such as Daniel Drew, Cornelius Vanderbilt, and Jay Gould entered the scene. Each made fabulous fortunes in the railroad industry and other ventures through activities some saw as manipulation, others saw as savvy capitalism, and which often included a little of both. The fight over the Erie Railway in New York was the most famous clash involving all three and illustrates both the intensity and the stakes of their activities.[9] Prior to this struggle, Vanderbilt had put together a link from New York to the West by taking control of the New York Central and two smaller railroads, the Harlem and the Hudson River. The only other railroad that connected New York to the West was the Erie. In

1867 Vanderbilt launched an effort to acquire it, and thus to eliminate any competition for trans–New York traffic.

The principal obstacle in Vanderbilt's way was Daniel Drew, who for some years had been both a director and the treasurer of the Erie. After an agreement between the two fell through, Vanderbilt started buying Erie stock on Wall Street. When Drew responded by dumping millions of shares of new Erie stock into the market, Vanderbilt persuaded a friendly New York judge to enjoin Drew from issuing additional stock. Drew nevertheless continued to issue stock. Drew finally won the battle when the New York legislature, which had been heavily lobbied by both sides, passed a law that effectively legalized all of the securities Drew had issued in the course of the battle.[10]

The Erie battle was a particularly visible example of a pattern that repeated itself throughout the country. After the breathless expansion of the early years, competitive pressures led to mergers and other changes as railroad managers struggled to achieve profitability. Adding to the volatility was a widespread perception, particularly in the Midwest, that the railroads charged unnecessarily high rates in areas where the competition was less fierce. Lobbying by farmers and small merchants—the same agrarian forces that had resisted federal bankruptcy law, as we saw in chapter 1—prompted many states to adopt Granger laws that attempted to regulate railroad ratemaking. Enacted in Iowa, Illinois, Wisconsin, and Minnesota after the Civil War, these laws "delegated [authority] to regulatory commissions to enforce rate schedules designed to grant parity [to local and regional trade, as against longer rail routes]."[11] Although many of the laws were struck down on constitutional grounds, the pressure to harness the railroads remained strong and eventually led to the establishment of the Interstate Commerce Commission under the Interstate Commerce Act of 1885.

The continuous turmoil left many railroads in precarious financial condition. Only in the best of times could the railroads continue to meet their obligations under the mortgage bonds (that is, bonds that were secured by a mortgage on railroad track or other assets of the railroad) that had been used to finance their growth and operations. In bad times, many would come crashing down. Unfortunately, bad times came at distressingly regular intervals in the last half of nineteenth century, just as they had in the early decades. Last chapter we saw Emerson's reaction to an earlier depression, the Panic of 1837. The next great downturn, in 1857, was the first with a direct link in the public imagination to railroads. The Panic of 1857 would be followed by two more depressions of similar magnitude before the nineteenth century ended. First in 1873—with the downfall of Jay Cooke, who had pioneered the strategy of selling securities to the public and by this time controlled the Union Pacific— and then again in 1893, the railroads and the American economy as a whole were roiled by new panics. The period between the two panics was punctuated by an additional downturn in 1884. Between 1873 and the end of the nineteenth century, roughly one-third of all the railroads—some seven hundred in all—failed, and in some years nearly 20 percent of the nation's track was in receivership (table 2.1).[12]

Investment bankers and lawyers had played a prominent role in the rise of the railroad industry. Investment bankers underwrote the mortgage bonds that had financed expansion, and their lawyers wrestled with the legal issues that arose. But this was nothing compared to their role when the railroads failed.

OBSTACLES TO A LEGISLATIVE SOLUTION

The waves of railroad failures in the 1870s and thereafter, and to some extent even before, posed an enormous problem for the nation. Despite their private ownership, the railroads were widely viewed as public in character. Because the economy depended crucially on effective transportation, a crippled railroad system would be disastrous for everyone. There was a broad consensus, then, that troubled railroads had to be saved. What was far less obvious was how.

In a more centralized system, the government could intervene to protect the railroads. In England, Parliament exercised sweeping control over the railroads from cradle to grave. Parliament strictly defined their rights and responsibilities, and if a railroad ran into trouble, Parliament was well positioned to take action.[13] One would expect a similar response elsewhere.

Things were more complex in the United States. To a remarkable extent, neither federal nor state lawmakers could effectively intervene. It was these obstacles to intervention that assured that the judicial system would be the institution of choice for addressing railroad failure.

Consider Congress's authority under the Bankruptcy Clause. The power to make "uniform laws on the subject of bankruptcy" would seem to offer the perfect vehicle for setting up a framework for dealing with railroad insolvencies. Especially is this true given the extent of the public interest at stake. Yet the Bankruptcy Clause played almost no role whatsoever in addressing railroad failure. The crises that brought the railroads to their knees were precisely the downturns—1857, 1873, 1893—that stirred loud cries in Congress for federal bankruptcy legislation. But when lawmakers debated bankruptcy legislation, they made almost no connection between general bankruptcy and the distress of the nation's first large corporations. Why didn't lawmakers view the Bankruptcy Clause as a lifeline for the railroads, just as they (many of them, at least) did for individuals and small businesses?

The most obvious explanation is that Congress's Bankruptcy Clause authority was clouded by a serious constitutional issue that would have directly implicated the railroads. In the early and middle decades of the nineteenth century, there was heated debate whether the Bankruptcy Clause gave Congress the

TABLE 2.1
Railroads in Receivership, 1872–1898

Year	Railroads in Receivership	Total Mileage in Receivership	Percentage of Total U.S. Railroad Mileage
1872	6	941	1.56
1873	9	1,439	2.17
1874	17	2,329	3.31
1875	45	6,419	8.87
1876	75	12,267	16.56
1877	85	13,972	18.19
1878	94	12,988	16.42
1879	95	12,678	15.51
1880	73	10,099	11.67
1881	54	6,823	7.31
1882	29	3,773	3.66
1883	27	3,838	3.35
1884	23	3,430	2.82
1885	54	9,369	7.47
1886	76	15,926	12.41
1887	68	11,646	8.54
1888	51	8,585	5.76
1889	52	8,252	5.28
1890	50	8,325	5.16
1891	54	9,352	5.61
1892	60	7,049	4.13
1893	77	8,495	4.84
1894	191	34,496	19.41
1895	182	33,241	18.60
1896	171	30,961	17.10
1897	146	17,692	9.68
1898	132	14,101	7.64

Source: Henry H. Swain, *Economic Aspects of Railroad Receiverships*, Vol. 3, No. 2 of *Proceedings of the American Economic Association*, 70–71 (New York: McMillan Company, 1898).
   Note: Figures are as of January of each year.

power to regulate troubled corporations, rather than just individuals. The principal argument against congressional authority was quite simple: since corporations were chartered and regulated by the states, states should also be the ones to step in when firms defaulted on their obligations. "Corporations are artificial beings, created by the States," Senator Henry Clay thundered. "[The states] know when it is best to make or abolish them."[14] In the early decades of the nineteenth century, when corporations were closely tied to their domicile states, the argument was quite powerful. Relying on this reasoning, opponents of corporate bankruptcy managed to keep corporations out of the Bankruptcy Act of 1841. By the 1860s, as the link between corporations and state government loosened, the constitutional concern had lost much of its bite — and the argument would be especially weak with railroads, given that many already operated in more than one state. But constitutional uncertainty still would have complicated the inclusion of railroads in the 1867 bankruptcy law.

The bankruptcy laws that Congress did pass were not well designed to deal with the railroad problem. The Bankruptcy Act of 1867, the first bankruptcy law to include corporations, assumed that bankrupt corporations would simply be shut down and their assets liquidated. Such an approach did not make much sense for railroads, since everyone agreed that it was important to keep the railroads running. Congress did add a limited composition option for corporations in 1874. As an alternative to liquidation, this provision permitted a bankrupt firm to restructure its unsecured obligations. But the provision had small, mom-and-pop businesses in mind and would not have proven helpful for railroads, whose capital structure was dominated by mortgage (that is, secured) bonds. It is of course possible that lawmakers could have tailored any bankruptcy provisions they designed for railroads to the special circumstances of this industry. But the Bankruptcy Clause was not nearly so obvious a way to address railroad failure as it may seem to twenty-first-century eyes. At the end of the nineteenth century, one of the leading proponents of the 1898 act still questioned whether Congress could include railroads in the act even if it wanted to. "I do not understand," said Senator George Hoar of Massachusetts, "that the Supreme Court of the United States has ever held that a railroad corporation established by State authority is a fit subject for insolvency."[15] (In fact, Congress explicitly excluded railroads when it added corporations to the 1898 act.)

An additional problem was that, from the repeal of the 1867 act in 1878, to 1898, there was no federal bankruptcy law of any kind on the books. Any effort to use Congress's bankruptcy powers to address railroad failure would have gotten mired in the broader controversy whether to enact a federal bankruptcy law. In short, the prospects for including railroad insolvency in a federal bankruptcy law were not good. Behind the deceptively simple language of the Bankruptcy Clause lay serious obstacles to its use.

Congress's next most likely source of authority for regulating railroad distress was its power to regulate interstate commerce under the Commerce Clause.[16] As the nineteenth century wore on, calls for Commerce Clause–based regulation of some railroad issues did in fact become quite common. Much of clamor was prompted by the Granger laws that state legislatures enacted in the 1860s and 1870s to curb railroad rate increases. Like the Bankruptcy Clause, however, Commerce Clause–based regulation faced serious limitations as a solution to railroad failures. One problem was that Congress's Commerce Clause authority was much less sweeping than it later became. Not until 1886, in *Wabash, St. Louis and Pacific Railroad Company v. Illinois*, did the Supreme Court construe the Commerce Clause as giving Congress exclusive control over interstate commerce. And few observers would have been so bold as to suggest that Congress could invoke the Commerce Clause to regulate a railroad whose track lay entirely within a single state.

In addition to the question of Congress's authority, serious interest group obstacles would have impeded a congressional solution to railroad distress. The most natural constituencies for legislative relief, the managers of the largest railroads and the investment bankers who underwrote their securities, were deeply skeptical of congressional intervention. Given the pitched battles they waged from the 1860s onward to fend off federal rate regulation, which some condemned as a descent into socialism, it is hard to imagine the railroads welcoming a congressional solution to railroad failures. Moreover, the same southern and western lawmakers who opposed federal bankruptcy legislation could be expected to resist measures that seemed to bail out the managers who ran the large railroads and their Wall Street bankers.

If federal regulation was unlikely, what about looking to state legislatures instead? Early on, at least, the states were a more natural regulator of railroad insolvency than Congress. After all, states were the ones that chartered the railroads. The same argument lawmakers used to oppose federal regulation of corporate bankruptcy generally—that corporations were creatures of the states—could also be used to justify state intervention in railroad insolvency. As soon as railroads took on an interstate character, however—which did not take long, of course—state regulation faced a crippling limitation. Both state regulators and state laws lost all of their power once the railroad tracks crossed state lines. States' inability to regulate outside their own borders made a meaningful state response to railroad failure quite difficult, given that much of the track and thousands of the investors of many of the railroads lay beyond the boundaries of any single state.

I do not mean to suggest that state lawmakers simply stayed on the sidelines when major railroads failed. To an extent that has been forgotten by most commentators, state legislators did get involved when large railroads failed at the end of the nineteenth century. In his history of the Cravath, Swaine & Moore law firm, for instance, Robert Swaine recounts how, in 1890, the

Ohio & Mississippi railroad persuaded Ohio to pass (constitutionally suspect) legislation waving off the railroads' obligation under Ohio law to buy back the stock of shareholders who opposed its proposed reorganization. In 1896, Virginia lawmakers did their part in the Norfolk & Western reorganization by passing legislation that added special voting provisions to the reorganized railroad's charter.[17]

As crucial as these state interventions proved to be, they played a supportive, not a constitutive, role, and most came long after the basic template for railroad reorganization was in place. In years of the first railroad disasters, back in 1857 and 1873, there were serious obstacles to a legislative solution. Congress's power was uncertain, and state power was limited. Rather than federal or state legislators, the managers and investment bankers of troubled railroads looked to another governmental institution: the courts. The courts responded, and, in the history of American corporate bankruptcy law, that has made all the difference.

BIRTH OF THE EQUITY RECEIVERSHIP

During a summer vacation at the beach several years ago, my family and I watched as workers slowly disassembled a beach house over the course of several weeks. The work was painstakingly slow. When the workers started rebuilding the house, very little of the old house remained, except the foundation and a few structural support beams. Being a novice in construction matters, I asked a worker why they were dismantling the house piece by piece, rather than simply bulldozing it and starting over. His answer was simple. Getting zoning approval for the much different house that the new owners wished to build would have been nearly impossible. So long as the new owners technically left the old house in place, however, rather than completely tearing it down, the zoning regulations would not interfere with their plans. Although working with the existing structure was cumbersome and in many respects inefficient, this strategy gave the new owners enough flexibility to construct a beach house that fit their particular needs.

The beach house illustration is an apt metaphor for the process that led to corporate reorganization in this country. As with the old beach house, the standard reorganization device was derived from long-standing foundations in the common law, which courts then developed into a reorganization framework that looked almost nothing like the structure that had stood on the original foundation. Even the brief description that follows should give some flavor of the remarkable transformation that took place when railroads began to fail in the nineteenth century.

Because the railroads were the nation's first large corporations, the courts did not have any existing mechanism in place for dealing with a railroad failure. With a pervasive legislative response unlikely, and no adequate common-law precedents, reorganizers and courts cobbled together a new device from two powers that did have an established common-law pedigree: courts' equitable authority to appoint receivers to preserve the value of a debtor's property; and the right of a mortgage holder to foreclose on mortgaged property if the debtor defaults. In a remarkable display of common-law creativity, the reorganizers melded these powers into the so-called equity receivership, and, with judicial approval, railroad reorganization was born.

Receivership tradition has it that the oldest ancestor of the equity receivership was an 1848 Georgia case involving the Munroe Railroad and Banking Company.[18] When the Munroe, which owned a grand total of one hundred miles of track, became insolvent and foreclosure proceedings were commenced, the court ordered that the railroad's entire assets be sold at auction. This was seen as innovative because it had long been standard foreclosure practice to sell the mortgaged property piece by piece. The decision to sell the Munroe's property as an intact whole, which was affirmed by the Georgia Supreme Court, suggested that foreclosure need not be limited to piecemeal liquidation. The court also concluded that it made more sense to preserve a troubled railroad than to dismember it. "What disastrous consequences would have resulted," the court exclaimed, "if each judgement creditor had been allowed to seize and sell separate portions of the road, at different sales in the six different Counties through which it passed and to different purchasers? Would not this valuable property have been utterly sacrificed. . . ?"[19]

Only a visionary could have foreseen where this relatively mild deviation from ordinary foreclosure practice would lead. The Munroe and its peers belonged to an era when railroads were relatively small, their capital structures were quite simple, and the states still exercised significant control over railroad development. Once the railroads started tapping the private markets, their balance sheet profile became much more complicated. Throw in a wave of railroad mergers and the pattern of ownership, as well as the business itself, could become truly byzantine. The size of the railroads, and the chaos that ensued when they failed, was unprecedented. There was no rulebook explaining how railroads and their creditors—most prominently, the investment bankers who underwrote the railroads' mortgage bonds, and the lawyers who assisted them—should fit the railroads within the homely confines of traditional foreclosure law. So creditors and their lawyers developed their own rules.

What emerged was one of the most remarkable dances in the history of American common law. Railroad creditors continued to solemnly incant the magic words of foreclosure law, words like *foreclosure bill* and *judicial sale*. When the smoke had cleared, however, a body of law designed to liquidate the assets of an insolvent debtor had been reconfigured to effect the nation's first corporate reorganizations. (Referring to the elite Wall Street professionals who eventually dominated the process, New Dealer Jerome Frank later commented, with characteristically acerbic wit, that the words *prestige* and *prestidigitate* came from the same linguistic origins.)[20]

Here is how it worked.[21] The classic equity receiverships involved moderately large railroads—railroads whose tracks crossed several state lines, and which had issued common stock, preferred stock, and several different mortgage bonds to raise money over the years. If the railroad encountered financial distress and failed to make the requisite interest payments on its bonds, a creditor would first file a "creditor's bill" asking the court to appoint a receiver to oversee the defaulting railroad's property. The principal reason for appointing a receiver was that putting the receiver in place technically shifted control of the railroad's assets to the receiver and out of the reach of prying creditors. If a creditor tried to obtain a lien against railroad property, for instance, the receiver would simply ask the court for an injunction.

To analogize to current bankruptcy law, appointing a receiver pursuant to a creditor's bill served the same purpose, though in a more limited way, as the automatic stay does now. It forced most creditors to halt their collection efforts and provided a breathing space for the parties to try to work out plan of reorganization.[22]

The next step was to file a second "bill," the foreclosure bill. In form, the foreclosure bill asked the court to schedule a sale of the property (solemnly invoking the liquidation-oriented language of traditional foreclosure law, of course). In reality, the sale would be put off for months, often years, while the parties negotiated over the terms of a reorganization plan.

In the meantime, the investment banks that had underwritten the railroad's bonds would quickly form a bondholders' committee (referred to as a "protective" committee) to represent bondholders in the negotiations. If the firm had issued more than one class of bonds, several committees might form; and there might also be committees of common stockholders and preferred stockholders. The virtue of forming a committee was that it centralized the bargaining process and theoretically gave thousands of widely scattered bondholders a champion—which, in large receiverships at the turn of the century, usually meant J. P. Morgan and Company; Kuhn, Loeb; or one of a small group of others.

To ensure their authority, the committee representatives asked investors to "deposit" their bonds (or stock, for a stockholders committee) with the committee. By depositing their bonds, investors gave the committee complete control over the bonds for the duration of the negotiations, with one limitation: bondholders would have the right to withdraw their bond if they disapproved of the plan that the committee negotiated on their behalf.

The goal of the negotiations was to rework the railroad's capital structure, reducing its obligations so that it could get back on track financially after the receivership. Often this meant converting fixed obligations into variable ones, or reducing interest rates, or extending the payback period. A typical reorganization from the 1890s, for instance, proposed to give a class of junior bond-holders five hundred dollars of bonds with a 4 percent interest rate and five hundred dollars of preferred stock for each one thousand dollars of 5 percent bonds they exchanged. Senior bondholders would retain all of their existing rights, while common and preferred stockholders were offered fifty dollars of 4 percent bonds and different amounts of the reorganized firm's common stock if they turned in their old stock and paid a cash assessment.[23]

Once they had agreed to an overall plan, the committees were combined to form a single supercommittee called the reorganization committee. It was the reorganization committee that "purchased" the railroad's assets at the fore-closure "sale." Since the reorganization committee had all of the deposited securities at its disposal and could bid the face value of the securities as a substitute for cash, no one else bothered to bid at the auction. In the words of Paul Cravath, one of the leading receivership lawyers: "Counsel who have acted frequently for reorganization committees have spent a great many anx-ious hours preparing for the unexpected bidder, but in my own experience he has never appeared. . . . Manifestly in most sales where the security holders . . . have . . . placed their interest in the hands of a committee there is not likely to be serious competition at the sale."[24]

As soon as the reorganization committee purchased the assets, it transferred them to a shell corporation that had been set up for just this purpose. The stock and other securities of the new corporation were then distributed to the old investors on the terms laid out in the reorganization plan.

Each of steps I have described thus far can, at least in name, be attributed to traditional foreclosure law. Two problems remained, however, and each required an additional innovation.[25] The first was a problem that bedeviled a railroad's efforts to maintain business as usual for the months and sometimes years the receivership process took. The railroad could only keep running if its suppliers continued to supply coal for power and steel for track and the numerous other things the railroad needed. Unfortunately, suppliers had very good reasons to cut off the spigot. Because mortgage bondholders were enti-tled to first priority in the railroad's assets, any contributions a supplier made would be mostly for the bondholders' benefit. Suppliers would hold only a general, unsecured claim, and there would be little left for them once bond-holders were taken care of. (In the corporate finance literature, the suppliers' disincentive to contribute is referred to as an underinvestment, or *debt over-hang*, problem.)[26]

To remedy this problem, courts, at the behest of reorganization lawyers, created a device that became known as a *receivership certificate*. Receivership certificates gave special priority to the suppliers of essential goods and services. With a receivership certificate in hand, the receiver was authorized to pay suppliers on an ongoing basis—effectively moving suppliers to the front of the priority line. Since suppliers now were sure to get paid, they had every reason to keep making deliveries to the troubled railroad.

A second problem stemmed from the possibility of holdouts. Rather than agreeing to have the terms of their bonds reduced, bondholders might be better off if they refused to deposit their bonds, dissented from the proposed reorganization plan, and sought to be paid in full in connection with the judicial sale. Once again, courts came to the rescue. In the mid-1880s, courts started setting "upset prices" for the foreclosure sales in railroad reorganizations.[27] Much like the minimum bid requirement in an art or antique auction, the upset price was the lowest bid a court would accept at the sale. If the bid or bids came in under this amount, the court would simply prohibit the sale from going through. In theory, dissenting investors were the ones who benefited, since the upset price assured them that they would receive no less than their share of the specified amount. But the courts also were well aware that setting a high upset price would make reorganization more difficult. In practice, they set the upset prices extremely low, often at 10 to 80 percent less than the current market value of the bonds. "The upset price," noted a leading scholar of the time, "has ceased to be a protection for the minority, if it ever was one, and has become one of the most useful tools of the majority for forcing recalcitrants into line."[28] The effect of the upset price was to force nearly everyone to agree to the reorganization, since the upset price was an unattractive alternative.

As we will see when we explore the role of investment bankers and lawyers, the innovations did not stop with receivership certificates and upset prices. But these were the engines that made the process go. With the ability to pay ongoing expenses and with protection against holdouts, the reorganizers were poised to restructure thousands of miles of American railroads.

PUBLIC AND PRIVATE INTEREST IN REORGANIZING THE RAILROADS

The remarkable contortions required to convert the common law of foreclosure into equity receivership raise an obvious question: why were nineteenth-century judges so willing to distort common law to help bail the railroads out? In a fascinating if somewhat controversial book, Gerald Berk offers an ideological explanation, arguing that the federal judiciary was committed in the late nineteenth century to expanding interstate commerce. These judges, in Berk's mildly disdainful assessment, "had been appointed by the same national administrations that made huge land grants (the Union Pacific's was the size of New England)—that is, *continental development*—the pillars of economic development."[29] Since healthy railroads were an important part of this vision, it was not surprising that the federal courts were willing to stretch traditional foreclosure law to help the railroads reorganize.

Ideology in general, and the ideology of judges in particular, does offer a partial explanation for court's willingness to give their imprimatur to what, in retrospect, can only be seen as wild deviations from existing law. This assessment also fits nicely with important new work in the political science literature that has developed the "attitudinal model" of judicial decision making. Proponents of the attitudinal model contend that judicial ideology is the best predictor of how judges will rule in particular cases.[30]

While the federal judiciary does seem to have been ideologically predisposed to receivership (just as chapter 1 suggested that courts were inclined to interpret Congress's Bankruptcy Clause powers broadly), the federal judges were hardly alone in their desire to resuscitate the railroads. Many of the early receiverships, and some of the later ones, took place in state rather than federal court. By all accounts, state judges were as eager to save troubled railroads as their federal counterparts. Recall that the first great case, *Munroe*—whose author had exclaimed that if the proposed sale were rejected "this valuable property [would] have been utterly sacrificed" and "the rights and interests of the creditors as well as the objects and intentions of the Legislature . . . entirely defeated"[31]—was a state court decision. Jurisdictional limitations, rather than ideology, were the railroads' principal reason for favoring the federal courts. State legislatures, moreover, frequently helped out by eliminating corporate law obstacles to a reorganization plan, as noted earlier.

Rather than ideological lone rangers, the federal judges are best seen as reflecting the views of a remarkably broad consensus in favor of reorganizing the railroads. This consensus included not only the general perception that healthy railroads were crucial to the national interest, but also the self-interest of all of the participants in the railroad enterprise. The best way to appreciate this is to consider, by way of contrast, the conflicts one generally sees under current law when a troubled firm fails.

When a large corporation encounters financial distress, the firm's principal constituencies usually have sharply divergent interests. Managers, employees, and shareholders all would prefer that the firm restructure its debts and keep going. For managers and employees, this enthusiasm is directly tied to their jobs, which may be preserved if the firm is restructured rather than shut down. Although shareholders often have a less personal stake, they too see reorganization as a lifeline. When an insolvent firm is liquidated, shareholders get nothing, but they may get to keep an equity interest if it is reorganized.[32]

Creditors that have protected themselves by obtaining collateral tend to cast a much more skeptical eye on financial restructuring. If a troubled firm is simply closed up and its assets are sold off, priority creditors such as banks will often get paid in full from the proceeds. Keeping the firm going, by contrast, is a riskier proposition. Not only does this mean waiting longer to get paid, but, if the firm's fortunes continue to sink, even priority creditors might not get paid in full. These creditors often view reorganization as simply postponing the inevitable (and can trot out plenty of statistics showing how often reorgani-zations fail).

It is here, in the conflict between priority creditors and the other constituen-cies of a firm, that we begin to see how special the nineteenth-century railroads were. A key factor in the parties' convergence of interests was the unusual position of the railroads' priority creditors, the holders of mortgage bonds. Unlike the priority creditors of contemporary firms, who often hold security interests in all of a firm's assets, railroad bonds were secured by discrete sec-tions of track or other assets as collateral. In consequence, one class of bonds might be secured by a segment of track in one part of the state, another by track in a different part. As we saw earlier, this crazy quilt of security interests often was a historical artifact of the mergers through which the railroad had been pieced together from smaller roads. Unraveling the respective priorities of the bond issues in order to distribute the proceeds of a liquidation would have been a nightmare for a railroad of any size. Speaking of the famous Wabash reorganization, business historian Albro Martin concluded that "only a financial wizard . . . could have sorted out the property represented by the [railroad's] mortgages."[33] Perhaps more importantly, the collateral for any given bond issuance—say, one hundred miles of track in the middle of no-where—was essentially worthless unless the railroad remained intact.

(Interestingly, although the confused capital structure seems to have been accidental, these limited, overlapping mortgages may actually have had a beneficial effect on both the mortgage holders and the railroad. Because the segment of track included in a mortgage was worth little to the creditor but a great deal to the railroad, it may have given the railroad a powerful incentive to repay if possible, and at the same time discouraged the mortgage holder from prematurely foreclosing. Oliver Williamson has analogized ef-fects of this sort—provisions that encourage both parties to act cooperatively rather than opportunistically—to the exchange of hostages sometimes used in feudal times.)[34]

The upshot of this was that the bondholders, who under other circum-stances might have fiercely resisted managers' efforts to reorganize, had as much to gain from keeping the railroad intact as its managers and sharehold-ers did. Although bondholders did sometimes complain that courts were run-ning roughshod over their contractual right to priority, just about everyone interested in the railroads agreed that troubled railroads were worth more as going concerns than in liquidation.

Were it not for the idiosyncrasies of America's division of power between federal and state government, the widespread support for reorganization might have prompted a decisive legislative response. But the limitations that ham-strung both Congress and the states made a sweeping legislative solution un-likely. The judicial system was the only obvious institutional alternative. It was against this backdrop that the courts used their judicial magic to turn state foreclosure and receivership law into the equity receivership.

This is not to say that the courts were simply a fungible, alternative solution to the problem of railroad distress. For the parties most directly interested in a troubled railroad, the judicial system provided important institutional advantages over a legislative approach. A congressional debate about rescuing interstate railroads might have provoked agrarian or populist opposition, for instance, or a call for more direct governmental intervention in the industry. These potential critics of what could be seen as a railroad bailout did not, by contrast, have any obvious place in the courthouse. Judges saw only the parties who were directly affected by *this* railroad's failure—all of whom had a direct interest in seeing the railroad continue.

Thus, though there was no existing mechanism for reorganizing the railroads, ideological considerations and the interests of each of the relevant constituencies all lined up in support of judicial innovation. Courts were well aware that the equity receivership was a striking departure from existing law, but the pressure to reorganize was irresistible. In the most notorious receivership of all, the Wabash (whose notoriety we will consider in a moment), the presiding judge concluded that "an expenditure [must] be made for the benefit of all parties in interest . . . in order that [the railroad] shall be made a going concern. Otherwise, in the expressive language of a distinguished friend, you have nothing but a streak of iron-rust on the prairie."[35]

THE ROLE OF WALL STREET BANKS AND LAWYERS

The judiciary did not devise the receivership technique all by itself, of course. Help came from the investment bankers who had underwritten the railroads' bonds, and from the lawyers that represented them and the managers of the railroads. Almost from the beginning, these Wall Street bankers and lawyers were the guiding influences on the receivership process, and its most obvious beneficiaries.

Given that receiverships developed from mortgage foreclosure, there was a certain inevitability to Wall Street's role. Mortgage bonds were the principal source of railroad capital, and investment bankers were the ones who had underwritten the bonds, so it was only natural that they would figure prominently in any restructuring. Moreover, a large percentage of railroad bonds were held by foreign investors, and the Wall Street underwriters were the foreign investors' principal contact with the United States. Because the investment banks were centered in New York, they looked for legal support from the same Wall Street firms that represented the banks in their securities issuances. The Cravath firm, predecessor to today's Cravath, Swaine & Moore, represented Kuhn, Loeb in many of its bond offerings, so it made sense for

Cravath to come back on board if the railroad later defaulted on the bonds. Similarly, Francis Stetson's reputation as "Morgan's lawyer" stemmed from his involvement on Morgan's behalf both in securities underwriting and in Morgan's protective committee activities when firms defaulted.

The relationship between receivership law and the Wall Street banks and lawyers is so close that it is nearly impossible to determine how much the professionals molded the process to further their interests, and how much the process itself created a need for their expertise. The innovations we have seen, receivership certificates and upset prices, brought obvious benefits for bankers and lawyers. Because these Wall Street professionals spearheaded the process, any change that enhanced the efficacy of receivership meant additional influence and additional fees.

The grip of Wall Street bankers and lawyers on receivership only strengthened as the technique evolved in the 1880s, 1890s, and thereafter. The most famous development in receivership practice is often traced to the Wabash, St. Louis and Pacific Railway receivership in 1884.[36] On May 28 of that year, representatives of Jay Gould, who controlled the Wabash, made their way to the federal district court to start a receivership proceeding. The Wabash, a crucial piece in Gould's strategy to create a single dominant railroad from the Midwest to the West Coast, had been battered by cutthroat rate competition and the strain of overexpansion and was about to fail. The collapse of the Wabash boded ill for the 1880s railroad industry, to be sure, but the fact that the Wabash had landed in receivership was not so remarkable as the way it got there. Because receivership was a creditors' remedy, triggered by creditors' request for a receiver and a foreclosure by one or more classes of creditors, railroad creditors had been the ones who initiated a receivership proceeding. But Gould's men simply dispensed with this nicety of the traditional form. Rather than wait until the Wabash actually defaulted, and risk losing control of the process to the railroad's bondholders, Gould decided to make a preemptive strike. Before the first interest payment had been missed, his men marched into the district court and asked Judge Treat to appoint a receiver for their benefit. What they were asking for was a wholly voluntary corporate reorganization, a proceeding initiated not by creditors but by the railroad itself. To the astonishment of many, and the dismay of most commentators, Judge Treat signed the necessary orders.[37]

As remarkable as it seemed, the Wabash was simply the most vivid illustration of the fact that managers and their Wall Street professionals, not ordinary creditors, were the ones who controlled the reorganization process. Rather than filing themselves, managers who lacked Gould's audacity would select a "friendly" creditor and encourage that creditor to file the receivership papers. Since friendly creditors always asked the court to appoint an existing manager as receiver, the new strategy (which critics referred to as a "collusive" receivership) maximized the likelihood that the current managers would remain in control. In a study of 150 receiverships between 1870 and 1898, Henry Swaine found that insiders were appointed as receivers in 138 of the cases.[38] In addition to preserving their control, teaming up with a friendly creditor also proved to be managers' ticket into the federal courts. By choosing a creditor who was not just cooperative, but also lived in another state, the managers could create the diversity of citizenship they needed for federal court jurisdiction.

The principal practical difference between filing in the state courts, as was done in many earlier receiverships, and filing in the federal courts was jurisdictional. With state court receiverships, limitations on a state's authority over out-of-state property forced reorganizers to set up what, in effect, were separate receiverships in each state where the railroad had property.[39] Federal court receiverships enjoyed a much broader jurisdictional reach. This enabled the reorganizers to focus on a single, primary receivership in the district where the railroad had its principal assets. Although it still was necessary to set up ancillary receiverships in other districts, the process was centralized in the primary receivership.

Whatever the federal courts' reasons for giving their seal of approval— whether it be a desire for the prestige of overseeing prominent reorganizations,[40] ideological considerations, or other factors—friendly receiverships were a boon to the Wall Street banks and bar. The friendly receivership option gave managers an incentive to negotiate in advance with the bondholders who would determine the success or failure of the receivership process, in order to put in place as much of the reorganization as possible before the formal proceedings were commenced. This, of course, meant negotiating with J. P. Morgan, Kuhn, Loeb, and or one of a small handful of other banks that had underwritten the bonds and served as bond trustee.

By the 1890s, outside interests were, at most, an annoyance for the Wall Street professionals and railroad managers who negotiated the railroad's fate. Only when the bankers squabbled among themselves, as when different banks represented different bond committees in the most complicated reorganizations, was there likely to be any suspense as to who would be speaking on behalf of the railroad's investors.

It is tempting to see friendly receiverships as furthering the interests of Wall Street bankers and their lawyers at the expense of everyone else. Control of receivership reinforced the bankers' iron grip on large-scale capital, and the Wall Street professionals paid themselves handsomely. Yet to conclude that friendly receiverships were just a bonanza for bankers would seriously oversimplify the effects of this development. As pleasing as they were to bankers, friendly receiverships also could be seen as a desirable step forward for the process as a whole. By eliminating many of the jurisdictional snafus that could undermine a state court receivership, for instance, use of the federal courts significantly diminished the costs of receivership. Centralization of negotiations on a small group of bankers further streamlined the process, reducing the likelihood of a free-for-all that might stymie the reorganization effort.

This more sanguine view of friendly receiverships also draws support from the bankers' own interests. Since the bankers were the ones who underwrote the bonds, they had a vested interest in protecting bondholders as much as possible. Otherwise, investors would be less anxious to participate in the bank's next bond offering. This reputational stake was magnified by the fact that such a large percentage of U.S. railroad bonds were owned by investors in England and other European nations. If J. P. Morgan and its peers expected to continue selling bonds to foreign investors, it was essential that they show that the U.S. markets were safe and dependable. Indeed, a recent biography of the J. P. Morgan partnership argues that Pierpont Morgan's success in doing precisely this—in particular, protecting London investors in the 1880s—played a crucial role in the bank's rise to dominance on Wall Street.[41]

None of this undermines the point that Wall Street bankers and lawyers tended to push receivership practice in directions that benefited themselves, of course. Rather, it suggests a subtle, symbiotic relationship between the bankers and lawyers and railroad distress. Wall Street professionals responded to real needs but did so in a way that increased the importance of their own role and excluded potential rivals.

If we fast-forward several decades from the Wabash reorganization to the next major milestone in receivership practice, the Supreme Court's 1913 decision in *Northern Pacific v. Boyd*,[42] we will find a very similar pattern. Although *Boyd* was a major judicial setback for Wall Street professionals, it once again underscores their dominance in receivership practice. *Boyd* also is a convenient place to focus in a bit more detail on the emergence of the elite reorganization bar.

As receivership practice matured in the years after the Wabash receivership, reorganization lawyers tried to capture as much of its contours as possible in formal agreements.[43] The agreements governing committee powers, investors' deposit of their bonds, and the reorganization itself all became much more extensive. "There can be no doubt," wrote leading Wall Street lawyer Paul Cravath in the second decade of the new century, "that [receivership contracts] . . . have attained proportions, both in length and elaborateness of provision for all conceivable eventualities, of which the wildest imagination of the practitioner of fifty years ago could form no conception." When the Wabash returned to receivership in 1915, the reorganization agreement was, Cravath noted, "about three times as long" as the agreement in the Wabash's earlier reorganization.[44]

As with the friendly receivership technique, the increasing contractualization can be seen as evidence that Wall Street professionals were doing both good and well. The fact that reorganization had developed as a judicial proceeding assured that lawyers would always be needed, and the growing importance of receivership contracts significantly expanded the lawyers' role. It is therefore hardly surprising to read in the history of New York's powerful Cravath firm that, as early as 1885, the firm's principal emphasis had shifted from commercial litigation to corporate law and railroad receivership practice.[45] Yet the sprawling new documents, like friendly receiverships, can also be seen as more than simply assuring full employment for Wall Street. By consolidating existing practice, they reduced the uncertainty of the receivership process and thus increased the likelihood of a successful restructuring. Paul Cravath himself made a similar point in understandably self-congratulatory terms:

> The provisions of the modern reorganization agreement and the modern corporate mortgage are the result of the experience and prophetic vision of a great many able lawyers. Every new provision is suggested either by some decision of the courts or by an actual experience or by some lawyer's conception of a possible exigency.[46]

The *Boyd* case threw a monkey wrench into all of this. A standard practice in receiverships at this time was to give old bondholders a stake in the new company, to ask shareholders to contribute new cash in return for a continuing interest, but to exclude general unsecured creditors. Ten years after the reorganization of Northern Pacific Railway, Boyd, an unsecured creditor, cried foul. Because unsecured creditors have a higher priority interest in the firm than shareholders, Boyd argued, the reorganizers should not be permitted to give an ongoing interest to shareholders without giving anything to unsecured creditors. The Supreme Court agreed, announcing the "fixed principle" that William Douglas would eventually use to create bankruptcy's absolute priority rule.[47]

Boyd seriously complicated corporate reorganization. Forcing reorganizers to deal with unsecured creditors increased the number of constituencies they had to satisfy from two (mortgage bondholders and shareholders) to three.[48] Not only did more parties mean more risk of hitting an impasse, but it also made reorganization more costly, since unsecured creditors also had to be given a piece of the reorganization pie. In the wake of this thunderbolt from the Supreme Court, the leader of the Wall Street reorganization bar portrayed Boyd as "a veritable demon incarnate standing across the path of the reorganizer to-day."[49]

Yet the Wall Street reorganizers quickly adjusted. In the same year as *Boyd*, 1913, the St. Louis and San Francisco Railroad (the "Frisco") landed in receivership. Anxious to honor the letter and spirit of *Boyd*, the judge initially insisted that the reorganization provide a cash payment to unsecured creditors. According to Robert Swaine, however, a leading young Cravath lawyer of whom we will see more, "three days of friendly debate in [the judge's] chambers . . . persuaded the judge . . . [to approve] what became the standard practice for dealing with the Boyd Case problem in equity reorganizations."[50] The "Boyd Decree" stated that stockholders could participate only if unsecured creditors were given "a fair and timely offer of cash, or a fair and timely offer of participation in such corporation."[51] Rather than cash, the reorganizers offered general unsecured creditors a continuing interest in the reorganized firm so long as they, like the stockholders, paid a cash assessment.

The new strategy was a brilliant solution to the *Boyd* "problem." Although it did not avoid the need to negotiate with unsecured creditors, the decree took a potential cash drain—the obligation to give something to unsecured creditors—and turned it into a way to inject a little more cash into the reorganization. The technique caught on immediately as reorganization lawyers used it in case after case, adjusting the "scope, mechanics and draftsmanship" as they went along.[52]

As loudly as reorganization lawyers complained about *Boyd*, the case and their response reinforced the elite bar's hegemony over receivership practice.[53] Because the elite bar had participated in all the important receiverships and had developed contractual provisions for dealing with potential pitfalls, they had extremely useful documents to adapt to future cases. But form documents could of course be copied by other lawyers—upstarts outside of the inner circle. What could not be copied was the ability of Paul Cravath or Francis Stetson to bring his knowledge of what had and had not worked in the past into a judge's courtroom or chambers. These lawyers' ability to speak from personal experience about the importance of the Boyd Decree, and about other judges' willingness to approve it, was an enormous asset when it came time to persuade subsequent courts to approve a reorganization plan. Potential clients could be expected to be well aware of the virtues of selecting a lawyer who had "been there, done that."

The closest analogy to Paul Cravath and his peers in contemporary law is the Delaware corporate bar. With so many large firms incorporated in Delaware, the Delaware courts are our de facto national arbiter of corporate law. As with the old receivership bar, a small coterie of firms (a few in New York, and the rest in Wilmington, Delaware) appear in case after case.[54] The Delaware bar has the advantage of always appearing before the same judiciary—judges with whom they interact on both a social and a judicial basis. Receivership cases arose all across the country, so receivership lawyers did not appear before the same, limited group of judges. But everyone else was a repeat player, and most of them worked within a few blocks of one another on Wall Street.

Even apparently accidental aspects of the receivership practice tended to reinforce the dominance of the elite bar. A particularly good illustration is the standard practice with attorneys' fees. The fees could be enormous, and this was what captured everyone's attention at the time (often prompting howls of protest), but more interesting for our purposes was the timing of the check. Cravath speaks briefly to this in his famous 1917 speech. "When the Plan has been executed . . . and not until then, I am sorry to say, the time has come to pay your fee. . . . I know not why, but . . . from time immemorial it has been the custom for counsel not to receive or even ask for their fees until the reorganization has been consummated or abandoned."[55]

Cravath's words are full of regret, and no doubt heartfelt. But the apparent hardship of not being paid until months or years after a case began conferred a distinct advantage on the elite New York firms. Only a firm as well heeled and successful as Cravath could afford to wait so long to get paid. The fee arrangements were one more thing to emphasize that large railroad receivership practice belonged to the Wall Street bar, and not to the general run of lawyers.

No firm benefited more than Cravath. By the early part of the century, Cravath had five partners and a growing stable of associates. As the century advanced, the firm continued to expand, reaching thirteen partners and a total of forty-six associates and staff members by the early 1920s.[56] Along with several other New York firms, Cravath had left the days of solo and small partnership practice behind and was well on its way to becoming one of the nation's first major law firms. The receivership practice of the elite bar was a crucial piece in this development. Even more than corporate securities work, railroad receiverships were extraordinarily lawyer-intensive. The large number of railroad failures from the 1890s into the new century created a need for lawyers, and the elite bar was able to maintain enough of a monopoly to assure itself an ongoing supply of lucrative business.

Two Very Different Bankruptcy Bars

If we compare Cravath and its peers to their insolvency cousin, the general bankruptcy bar called into being by the 1898 Bankruptcy Act, the contrast could not be more stark. The general bankruptcy bar was fledgling in every respect at the turn of the century. The bar did not even exist until 1898, and the first bankruptcy lawyers were hardly the cream of the profession. The cases were small (almost all of the debtors were individuals and small businesses), the practice hardscrabble. Even as the bar matured, as it quickly did, there were repeated attacks on the credibility of bankruptcy lawyers.

The receivership bar, by contrast, was well established; and its members had always been drawn from the pinnacle of the New York bar. The Cravath firm's relationship with Kuhn, Loeb, like Francis Stetson's affiliation with J. P. Morgan, had been its ticket into railroad reorganization. Cravath drew its associates from the Harvard and Columbia law schools, and from families with impeccable pedigree. Looking back, the firm could count such eminent New York politicians as (Governor) Samuel Blatchford and (Senator and Secretary of State) William Seward in its ancestral line.[57]

As different as the receivership and bankruptcy bars were, their emergence did share one important theme. In both contexts, federalism played a defining role. Resistance by states' rights advocates and other opponents of federalization, together with creditors' own interest in controlling costs, forced the bankruptcy lobby to minimize the administrative structure of the 1898 Bankruptcy Act. The absence of significant administrative oversight then created the need for a bankruptcy bar. Like general bankruptcy law, receivership practice was shaped by the constraints of federalism. With legislative solutions to railroad distress all but precluded by the awkward division of authority between Congress and the states, judicial reorganization emerged as the obvious alternative. The judicial process was soon dominated by Wall Street bankers and their lawyers, and the receivership bar was born.

The general bankruptcy and elite bankruptcy bars would continue along their different, though somewhat parallel, paths for the first three decades of the twentieth century. Receivership lawyers had little to do with the bankruptcy bar, and vice versa. It was not until the New Deal, when corporate and railroad reorganization were added to the Bankruptcy Act, that the two bars finally came under the same roof. By then, general bankruptcy practice, like the large-scale receivership process, was well established. Ironically, it was the general bankruptcy bar that would survive the New Deal intact, whereas the receivership bar would, like its Wall Street banker clients, run headlong into the Wall Street–bashing New Deal reformers.

PART TWO

THE GREAT DEPRESSION AND NEW DEAL

Chapter Three

ESCAPING THE NEW DEAL: THE BANKRUPTCY
BAR IN THE 1930s

A S OF THE LATE 1920s, on the eve of the New Deal, general bankruptcy lawyers and the reorganization bar remained almost entirely distinct. Like the reorganization bar, general bankruptcy lawyers were notoriously clannish, even for lawyers, and they tended to congregate in urban areas—especially the urban Northeast. Distinguishing the two bars was, as we have seen, an enormous gulf in status and class. Unlike reorganization lawyers, the general bar was distinctly nonelite. From the earliest days of the 1898 act, general bankruptcy lawyers fought a continuous battle to rise above their mildly unsavory reputation.

A great irony of New Deal bankruptcy reform is that this somewhat unsavory bar, unlike its corporate reorganization counterpart, survived the New Deal unscathed—indeed, the bar emerged from the 1930s stronger in many respects than it had been at the outset of the decade. This chapter explores the how and the why of the general bankruptcy bar's success. Although the chapter places particular emphasis on the growing importance of the bankruptcy bar, the competing interests that were melded together in the 1898 act continued to set the parameters within which the influence of bankruptcy professionals played out. Ever since 1898, American bankruptcy law has been defined by creditors, the prodebtor forces unleashed by federalism, and the bankruptcy bar.

The relationship between these interests and the political parties was very much in flux. Democrats remained more sympathetic to prodebtor views, and creditors exerted much of their influence through the Republican party. By the end of the 1930s, however, Democrats rather than Republicans would be the principal advocates of expansive federal bankruptcy legislation, as the New Deal culture took hold. After the 1930s, creditors, prodebtor interests, and bankruptcy professionals would continue to dominate the bankruptcy debates, but party affiliation would fade further and further into the background.

The New Deal brought two very different sets of bankruptcy reforms, and these reforms will serve as the backdrop for this chapter and chapter 4. The first set of reforms had its roots in the pre–New Deal era. In 1929, at the outset of the Great Depression, simmering complaints about bankruptcy administration erupted into a full-scale scandal in the Southern District of New York. A district court investigation headed by William Donovan and a follow-up investigation launched by the Hoover administration produced a pair of highly critical reports—the Donovan report in 1931 and the Thacher report in 1932.[1] Based on the specific proposals outlined in the Thacher report, Senator Hastings of Delaware and Congressman Michener of Michigan introduced a bill (the Hastings-Michener bill) that called for sweeping reform of the administrative process of bankruptcy. At the heart of the bill was a proposal to appoint a staff of administrators to oversee bankruptcy. Although the House and Senate Judiciary Committees sprang into action and held lengthy hearings in 1932,[2] they did not send the bill to Congress. The following year, the legislation was reintroduced with many of its most controversial provisions deleted. Congress enacted part of the legislation at the end of the Hoover administration in 1933—including provisions for individual and farmer rehabilitation and the first codification of railroad reorganization—and lawmakers then added codified large-scale corporate reorganization for the first time in 1934.[3] By the time the 1933 and 1934 amendments were enacted, however, the principal Thacher report proposals were long gone.

The second stage of New Deal reforms commenced even before the first round was finished. After the 1932 hearings, a group of bankruptcy lawyers, academics, and judges banded together to form the National Bankruptcy Conference for the purpose of "perfecting" the bankruptcy laws. By 1935, the conference persuaded Representative Chandler to join the effort, and for the next several years they developed legislation that became known as the Chandler bill. At the end of 1936, as the process was perking along nicely, William Douglas and the Securities Exchange Commission suddenly crashed the party, urging Chandler and the National Bankruptcy Conference to replace the Chandler bill recommendations that dealt with large corporate reorganizations with a far more dramatic overhaul. Although many members of conference protested, and several criticized the SEC reforms in the legislative hearings that followed, the conference lent its formal support to the SEC's reorganization proposals in return for the SEC's support for the rest of the legislation. Out of this awkward alliance came the Chandler Act of 1938, the most extensive bankruptcy reform since the enactment of the 1898 act.[4] The changes to general bankruptcy practice were modest and incremental, the changes to large-scale reorganization revolutionary. The evolutionary changes will be our focus in this chapter, the revolutionary ones in chapter 4. Behind each, of course, lies a remarkable political story.

This chapter begins by describing the general bankruptcy bar of the 1920s and early 1930s—picking up, in a sense, where the discussion in chapter 1 left off. In addition to briefly profiling several of the leading members of the bar, the first section describes the Donovan and Thacher investigations that were prompted by complaints about bankruptcy practice. The next section then provides the theoretical apparatus for understanding the influence of bankruptcy lawyers and referees, as well as the limits of this influence. After a brief introduction to interest group theory, the section discusses a variety of interest groups other than lawyers, each of which has an important stake in the bankruptcy process—including debtors, borrowers who do *not* file for bankruptcy, unsecured creditors (that is, creditors whose loans are not collateralized), and secured lenders. Unlike each of these groups, whose influence is limited in one or more ways, bankruptcy professionals are well coordinated and have an enormous, ongoing stake in the shape of bankruptcy law. After discussing the nature of bankruptcy professionals' influence, the chapter chronicles the two most dramatic examples of the bar's success: the rapid demise of the proposed administrative reforms in 1932 and the expansion of general bankruptcy practice in 1938. Of particular interest is the role of the National Bankruptcy Conference, which was formed after the initial bankruptcy hearings and has become the single most prominent influence on bankruptcy legislation. The chapter concludes by briefly considering several issues—such as exemptions and individual rehabilitation plans—that underscore the continuing relevance of creditors and populist ideology.

The Donovan and Thacher Investigations

As was discussed in chapter 1, the bankruptcy bar benefited almost immediately from an effective lobbying base and from the efforts of several visible spokesmen. The Commercial Law League devoted much of its energy to bankruptcy issues; the American Bar Association could be counted on for support; and such prominent leaders as Frank Remington spoke and wrote widely and regularly testified before the House and Senate Judiciary Committees.

In the era after World War I, after the cries for bankruptcy repeal had largely subsided, a new group of bankruptcy leaders emerged. A particularly good example is Reuben Hunt, who would figure prominently prior to and throughout the New Deal. Located in California, Hunt, like many bankruptcy lawyers, represented a wide range of individuals and small businesses. From the 1920s on, he became increasingly prominent in the Commercial Law League, holding a variety of leadership posts and penning regular commentary for the *Bulletin* (which was later renamed as the *Commercial Law Journal*.[5] Hunt also served on the Commercial Law Section of the ABA, and in each of these capacities, he testified regularly before Congress.

On the East Coast, two of the most prominent bankruptcy professionals were Randolph Montgomery and Jacob Weinstein. Montgomery was located in New York and served for many years as counsel for the National Association of Credit Men, the principal lobbying group for unsecured creditors, and wrote regularly for the NACM publication *Credit Monthly*. Weinstein was located in Philadelphia and figured prominently in the same bankruptcy organizations as Hunt. Weinstein's prominence also reflects an important demographic characteristic of the early bankruptcy bar. In the Northeast especially, many bankruptcy lawyers were Jewish. Shut out of the most high-profile firms in New York, Philadelphia, and Boston, Jewish lawyers were forced to carve out niches outside of elite firm practice, in areas such as general bankruptcy practice.

With James McLaughlin, another early stalwart, came powerful evidence of the rapid maturation of the bankruptcy bar. McLaughlin was one of the first in a series of full-time law professors to champion bankruptcy law. Like several of his successors, McLaughlin taught at Harvard Law School, and he wrote more frequently in the pages of the *Harvard Law Review* than in practitioner periodicals such as the *Commercial Law Journal*. More even than Hunt, Montgomery, or Weinstein, it was McLaughlin who assumed Remington's mantle as the Judiciary Committee's de facto bankruptcy expert from the late 1930s through the 1950s. (In a revealing gesture, the conservative, sometimes prickly McLaughlin later changed his last name to *MacLachlan* after learning this was the original Scottish spelling.)

If Hunt, Montgomery, Weinstein, and McLaughlin personified the strength of the early bankruptcy bar, its festering sore was the perception that bankruptcy practice was grimy and, far worse, operated as a low-level racket. Bankruptcy lawyers handled the cases of individuals and small businesses, so the practice was not inherently lucrative. Debtors could not pay substantial fees; creditors often did not have enough at stake to justify hiring a lawyer. For many bankruptcy lawyers, serving as trustee was a more dependable source of income, though trustee fees were relatively small. Even better was serving as *counsel* for the trustee—particularly if one could obtain this appointment on a regular basis. Unlike the trustee, the trustee's counsel was not paid a set fee; he could charge an hourly wage for as many hours as it took to administer the estate. In theory, a debtor's creditors could select the trustee, and the trustee then hired the attorney of his choice. But in some areas bankruptcy lawyers quickly developed a device for commandeering the appointment process. Knowing that most creditors had little interest in getting actively involved, bankruptcy lawyers would obtain their proxies to vote for a trustee of the lawyer's choice. The trustee could then be expected to hire the lawyer or one of his friends as counsel. To make matters worse, bankruptcy lawyers sometimes short-circuited the process altogether by arranging to be appointed as receiver of the debtor's assets. Although the receiver's only job was to oversee the assets until a trustee could be appointed, bankruptcy professionals, acting as receiver, often delayed the appointment of a trustee until they had completed nearly all of the tasks of administering the bankruptcy estate. These were practices that outsiders bitterly attacked as the "bankruptcy ring."

In the late 1920s, the complaints about bankruptcy practice in New York City grew so loud that a federal grand jury issued a report concluding that bankruptcy practice had been "characterized by serious abuses and malpractices upon the part of attorneys, receivers, trustees, appraisers, custodians, auctioneers and other persons, associations or corporations within and subject to the jurisdiction of the United States District Court."[6] The Association of the Bar of the City of New York, which included most of the elite New York bar, then filed a formal petition with Judge Thomas Thacher asking to participate in an extensive investigation under the auspices of the district court. The judge agreed, and the association took charge. Heading up the investigation on behalf of the association was Colonel William Donovan. By Donovan's count, "Over 1,000 court files of cases, and some 4,000 witnesses were examined" during daily hearings that lasted from June to September 1929. Even as chronicled by a defender of existing practice, the findings of the Donovan investigation were dramatic and shocking and suggested a wide-ranging conspiracy to control bankruptcy administration:

> As a result of this investigation, twelve attorneys were indicted; one absconded and committed suicide; two pleaded guilty and received jail sentences; one was already serving sentence for subornation of perjury; four other attorneys resigned from the Bar of New York; four others were disbarred; another was censured, and disciplinary action was taken against other attorneys. The United States auctioneer and two custodians were indicted; a clerk of the Bankruptcy Record Room was dismissed and attempted to commit suicide, and during the progressive of investigation one Federal Judge resigned.[7]

In July 1930, in the wake of the Donovan report, President Hoover appointed Thomas Thacher, who had recently given up his district court judgeship to become solicitor general, "to undertake an exhaustive investigation into the whole question of bankruptcy law and practice."[8] Thacher's investigators then gathered extensive statistical data on every bankruptcy case closed during the fiscal year ending June 30, 1930, and visited the bankruptcy courts in twenty-one cities in a total of sixteen states. Although its details are not nearly as eye-popping as the Donovan report, the Thacher report reached essentially the same conclusions. The report worried that the process was shot through with conflicts of interest—the kinds of concerns that prompted allegations of a bankruptcy ring. "If there is a receiver," the report noted, "the attorney with the controlling claims [that is, the proxies of enough creditors to control the vote] will ordinarily vote for him as trustee with the assurance, in most cases, of being employed as his attorney. . . . It is impossible to escape the conclusion that in most cases the paramount motive is to obtain employment as attorney for the trustee rather than to select a trustee on merit alone."[9] Even apart from inappropriate behavior, the Thacher report concluded that payments to creditors were too small under the Bankruptcy Act of 1898, and debtors should not be given discharges so freely.

It is important not to simply take the findings of an investigative hearing at face value, of course. Would-be reformers often wish to make a name for themselves, and they may exaggerate the seriousness of the problems they discover. Held only a year or two after the Donovan and Thacher reports, the stock market hearings in Congress that inspired the securities law reforms of 1933 and 1934 have long been seen as having produced conclusive evidence of widespread stock manipulation, for instance, yet recent studies have raised doubts about nearly all of the evidence of fraudulent behavior.[10] The question, then, is this: were the hushed tones and somber indictments of the Donovan and Thacher reports legitimate?

With respect to New York, the principal focus of the reports, the evidence suggests that the complaints of corruption were well founded. One searches in vain the pages of *Credit Monthly*, the principal publication of the National Association of Credit Men, or the Commercial Law League's *Bulletin*, which spoke for the general bankruptcy bar, for any serious defense of bankruptcy practice in New York. When the district court responded to the New York problems by appointing a single bank, Irving Trust, as trustee for all New York cases, the New York bankruptcy bar bitterly complained about Irving Trust's monopoly on trusteeships. But no one argued that the indictments handed down in New York as a result of the Donovan report were mistaken or trumped up.

The real question was whether the corruption was limited to New York, or whether it could be found in bankruptcy practice throughout the country. Many bankruptcy lawyers insisted that New York was a blight on an otherwise clean practice, and the American Bar Association issued a report to this effect. Yet other observers were not so sure. Writing in *Credit Monthly*, Randolph Montgomery, who served as counsel to the National Association of Credit Men, pointed out that the Donovan investigators had examined several other cities in addition to New York. "It is difficult to reconcile the statements in the report of the American Bar Association to the effect that 'the only place where flagrant abuses and grossly illegal practices were found to exist . . . was in the Southern District of New York," Montgomery wrote, "with the same committee's conclusion that the primary reason for dissatisfaction with bankruptcy administration lies in the abuse and misuse of proxies. . . . [If the abuse of proxies] is prevalent 'in the larger communities,' . . . then the conclusion would seem to be inescapable that the conditions found by Colonel Donovan in the Southern District of New York are not unique, but are typical of those which exist in the larger communities everywhere."[11]

As Montgomery's comments suggest, although the level of corruption seems to have been extreme in New York, the system of selecting trustees through proxy voting reinforced the unsavory reputation of bankruptcy practice throughout the nation. In most cities, a small group of lawyers dominated the practice, a problem that had bedeviled general bankruptcy practice since the earliest years of the act.

To remedy the ills uncovered by the Donovan investigation, the Thacher report proposed a wide range of reforms to U.S. bankruptcy law. The most important of the reforms would have significantly altered bankruptcy's administrative structure, conforming it much more to the English approach. The Thacher report called for Congress to create "a staff of 10 full-time salaried administrators under the Attorney General."[12] The ten administrative overseers would hire, as civil service employees, a cadre of examiners to conduct a searching examination of each bankrupt who filed a bankruptcy petition. Another of the administrators' responsibilities was to police the appointment of trustees. Although creditors would retain their right to select a trustee (in larger cases, at least—no trustee would be appointed in small cases),[13] the administrators would help the court to assemble a list of authorized trustees and would report on the trustees' performance. The theme of the administrative changes was quite clear: lawmakers should shift a large dose of control from the parties and their lawyers to governmental administrators.

In addition to the administrative proposals, the Thacher report also recommended that the courts be authorized to suspend or delay a debtor's discharge, much as they do under English bankruptcy law. Courts must be "given power to discriminate between the different classes of bankrupts," the report concluded. Otherwise, "vast numbers of people for whom the law was never designed will continue to pervert its objects without the slightest hindrance, all to their own demoralization and the injury of the public interest."[14] Permitting courts to tailor the debtor's discharge to his or her specific circumstances would assure that debtors were discharged only from debts that they genuinely could not pay.

The Donovan and Thacher reports bore the unmistakable influence of Progressive thinking. Centered in the urban northeast, the Progressive movement of the early twentieth century sought to achieve wide-ranging social reform and often used empirical investigations to motivate the reform.[15] In contrast to their sometime allies, southern and western populists, the Progressives often came from the urban elite classes, and their reforms had a somewhat paternalistic flavor. Best known for the wage and working condition reforms they promoted early in the twentieth century, the Progressives included Presidents Theodore Roosevelt and Woodrow Wilson in their number. The Donovan and Thacher reform program was Progressive both in personnel and in its optimism about regulation. (Thacher's principal lieutenant, Lloyd Garrison, is a striking illustration. Garrison later became dean of the University of Wisconsin Law School, where he helped found the Progressive-influenced law-and-society movement.)

One of the principal contributors to the Donovan and Thacher reports was a man who would go on to become the single most important New Deal reformer on bankruptcy issues, and who will occupy much of our attention in chapter 4: William Douglas. Shortly before the Donovan and Thacher investigations began, Douglas had embarked on an extensive empirical study of New Jersey and Boston bankruptcy cases. Although Douglas has long been remembered as an advocate for the "little guy," he strongly believed, like the other members of the Donovan and Thacher investigations, that lawmakers and courts should distinguish between deserving and undeserving debtors. Debtors who had misbehaved or were capable of repaying their creditors should not, in Douglas's view, simply receive an immediate discharge.[16]

Propelled by the Donovan and Thacher findings, Senator Hastings and Representative Michener introduced the Thacher proposals as the Hastings-Michener bill in 1932. Given the shocking findings of the Donovan study and the support of Progressive reformers, the time seemed ripe for major reform of general bankruptcy practice. But the administrative reforms were not to be. Bankruptcy professionals derailed the administrative proposals for good in 1932. The Chandler Act reforms of 1938 would bring numerous amendments, but the bankruptcy bar—or at the least, its most prominent members—would be the source rather than the target of the changes. Despite the scandals and the enormous disruption brought by the Great Depression, the general bankruptcy bar survived.

An Interest Group Perspective on Bankruptcy Lawyers

How was it that this faintly disreputable segment of the bar proved so influential in the annals of bankruptcy law? The best way to answer this question is to start by taking a closer look at the nature of interest group influence.

Much as social choice theory helps to explain the instability of nineteenth-century bankruptcy law, another branch of public choice theory, interest group analysis, helps us to understand the prominence of the bankruptcy bar.[17] In some respects, the theory needs no explanation. The intuitions of interest group theory have so suffused the popular culture that we speak of interest group influence or the "tyranny" of special interests without thinking much about it. There is an analytical basis for these intuitions, and this section will briefly consider what it is.

The central insight of interest group theory is that concentrated interest groups often benefit at the expense of widely scattered groups, even if the diffuse group has more at stake overall. The reasoning is as follows. If voters act in their own self-interest when it comes time to select their congressional representatives, they have very little incentive to inform themselves and vote intelligently, due to the fact that their vote is unlikely to affect the outcome of any election. Even if the benefits of voting did exceed the costs, most voters still would decline to inform themselves in the hope they could free ride on the efforts of other, more diligent voters. Each voter is better off if other voters are the ones who go to the trouble to inform themselves and vote intelligently, since even ill-informed voters benefit from decisions made by an informed majority. These two problems—often referred to as rational apathy and the free rider problem—severely undermine the influence of general voters.

For a more concentrated group—that is, a group whose members have one or more shared interests and whose members have a significant amount at stake—the story is quite different. Smaller, concentrated groups are more likely to inform themselves, coordinate their activities, and participate actively in the political process.[18]

The distinction between ordinary voters and concentrated interest groups is not lost on legislators. A self-interested legislator will focus principally on getting reelected, since legislators who fail to do so quickly become ex-legislators. Because interest groups are better informed than ordinary voters and serve as an important source of political funding, legislators have a strong incentive to pay particular attention to the perspectives of interest groups.

Interest groups are not the whole story of legislative decision making, of course. If large numbers of voters hold similar moral or ethical views on an issue, their ideological concerns can play a transformative role, even if the voters do not formally organize. In an analysis of a 1977 law requiring the reclamation of strip-mined land, for instance, economists Joseph Kalt and Mark Zupan determined that ideology was an important factor in lawmakers' voting decisions.[19] As we have already seen, populist ideology figured prominently in the nineteenth-century bankruptcy debates. Similar ideological currents will resurface in this chapter and play a far more visible role in chapter 4.

Bankruptcy lawyers and other bankruptcy professionals have an enormous stake in the vitality of bankruptcy practice, but the bankruptcy bar is not the only group with a strong interest in bankruptcy law. Prospective debtors have an obvious stake, as do borrowers who never file for bankruptcy and the unsecured and secured creditors of bankruptcy debtors. Yet, of all these groups, bankruptcy professionals are the ones who have most strongly influenced the shape of U.S. bankruptcy law in the century since its enactment in 1898. The reasons will become clear if we briefly consider the roles of each of the other interest groups.

Perhaps the biggest surprise of the legislative process is how rarely individual debtors, prospective debtors, or, in the case of corporate debtors, their managers, participate. No one has as great an interest in the availability of bankruptcy, and the generosity of the discharge, as debtors. Yet even in the heart of the depression, few debtors ventured to Washington, or even wrote letters, to express their views on bankruptcy reform. One searches the legislative history in vain for any evidence of an individual debtor's speaking out on bankruptcy. The managers of corporate debtors did voice their views on occasion, as when Long Bell Lumber sent a telegram to its congressman urged passage of reform as beneficial to Long Bell Lumber's reorganization.[20] But missives of this sort were far more the exception than the norm. The obvious explanation for debtors' silence is a problem of timing. Future debtors often do not tend to think of themselves as debtors; even if they did, many would hesitate to lobby for debtors' interests, since active participation would signal to creditors that the debtor planned to seek a discharge from her debts. Once a debtor actually files for bankruptcy, she has an urgent interest in bankruptcy law. But even current debtors do not often take much interest in bankruptcy reform, since reforms generally apply only to subsequent cases.

For the same reasons, debtors and soon-to-be debtors cannot easily coordinate in order to act collectively. Most existing debtors do not expect to file additional bankruptcy petitions in the future, so they are not likely to show much interest in contributing to a lobbying organization for debtors. In times of economic disruption, potential debtors do, in a sense, influence the legislative debates. During the crushing depressions of the nineteenth century, and again in the Great Depression of the 1930s, the vast numbers of citizens facing financial ruin created great pressure for legislative action.[21] But these sentiments have not led to ongoing, prodebtor lobbying organizations, and these are best considered under the rubric of populism and related ideological concerns. (More recently, consumer advocacy groups have promoted debtors' interests. As is discussed in chapter 7, the principal consumer advocates in bankruptcy have been lawyers, and they have functioned as a subset of the bankruptcy bar.)

Like current and future debtors, consumers and businesses that will never file for bankruptcy also have a stake in the bankruptcy laws. We do not usually think of these individuals and firms—call them "repayers"—as a bankruptcy interest group, but of course they are. If bankruptcy gives debtors an easy, sweeping exit from their obligations, creditors will adjust their credit terms to reflect the increased risk that debtors will discharge their debts rather than repaying them. Lenders or suppliers may increase the interest rate they charge, for instance, or simply refuse to extend credit to financially precarious borrowers. Because creditors cannot perfectly predict which borrowers will default on their obligations, the group of borrowers who face more onerous credit terms will include many repayers—that is, many who will never file for bankruptcy—along with those who will in fact eventually make use of the bankruptcy laws.

Rather than bear these additional costs of credit, repayers should lobby for stricter bankruptcy laws. But the obstacles to repayers of acting collectively are even more daunting than those of debtors. For any given repayer, the costs of permissive bankruptcy laws are relatively small. Not only this, but the costs are often hidden, taking such forms as more intensive scrutiny by lenders. Given their limited stake in bankruptcy law, individual repayers cannot be expected to show much enthusiasm for an effort to coordinate their interests. If repayers had already organized for other reasons, they might steer the organization's lobbying efforts to bankruptcy from time to time, but rarely have there been organizations that served this function. In the second decade of the twentieth century, the Antibankruptcy Law Association briefly played something like this role. In the debates whether to repeal the 1898 act, the association excoriated federal bankruptcy law as an abomination. Whether the association truly acted on behalf of repayers is questionable, however. Its members seem mostly to have been creditors disgusted with the current law. The president of the association, for instance, was head of the Wholesale Grocers Association. As will become clear in a moment, grocers were an important source of credit for consumers and felt particularly vulnerable at the outset of the Great Depression.

Like debtors and repayers, unsecured creditors—that is, suppliers and other creditors who do not take collateral—are widely scattered and often have a relatively small stake when a debtor encounters financial distress. The unsecured creditors of a individual or small business that files for bankruptcy might include vendors such as the local stationery store or cleaning service—or in the 1930s, the local grocery. Some unsecured creditors do have a significant stake, however, and even those who do not tend to be repeat players. They deal not just with one borrower, but with many borrowers. In consequence, unsecured creditors have much more incentive to organize, and to coordinate their lobbying activities. This, of course, is precisely what unsecured creditors have done. As we saw in chapter 1, the emergence on a national basis of business organizations such as chambers of commerce and boards of trade had a transformative effect on the nineteenth-century bankruptcy debates. Creditors viewed bankruptcy as essential to the creation of a national economy, and their sustained lobbying activities finally came to fruition in 1898.

Unsecured creditors have continued to participate in the bankruptcy debates, most prominently through the activities of the National Association of Credit Men. ("Men" was eventually changed to "Managers" to remove the implicit sexism without altering the NACM acronym.) From time to time, other organizations of unsecured creditors have entered the fray. In the 1930s, for instance, many of the trade groups that had sprung up in every sector of the economy weighed in on the proposed bankruptcy reforms, as did a few individual creditors. A representative of the American Paint and Varnish Manufacturers Association applauded the proposal to establish a bankruptcy agency and the proposed restrictions on debtors' right to an immediate discharge. "[T]he members of our association," he testified during the 1932 hearings, "believe that the specific amendments suggested by this bill . . . provide a system which is more just than the present one to creditors while not unduly harsh upon debtors." The president of Crompton Company, a cotton goods manufacturer, echoed this sentiment. He found the administrative proposals especially welcome. "[W]e cannot personally be present at every bankruptcy that occurs, that may be 3,000 miles away," he noted, "and we would feel very much better if there were an official that we knew had to look into [each bankruptcy] . . . in order to ascertain the exact facts of the situation."[22] After this brief flurry of activity in the early 1930s, however, trade groups largely receded from the picture, and in subsequent years unsecured creditors have exerted less influence than their early prominence might suggest. One reason for this is that, while firms large enough to have a credit manager are represented by organizations such as the NACM, small unsecured creditors do not have an effective mouthpiece. For them, collective action problems do pose a real obstacle to participation. Second, and at least as important for many unsecured creditors, is the simple fact that their interest in bankruptcy law is quite limited. What unsecured creditors most wanted in the nineteenth century was a uniform bankruptcy law that prohibited debtors from making preferential prebankruptcy transfers to family members and local creditors. Although the 1898 act seemed too generous to debtors, it gave creditors the basic protections they felt they needed.

As much as unsecured creditors would have preferred a stricter bankruptcy law—and many grumbled loudly after the 1898 act was passed—the effect of bankruptcy reform on most unsecured creditors is sharply reduced in one straightforward way: except in extreme competitive matches, consensual creditors pass on the costs to their borrowers. As noted above, if changes in the bankruptcy laws cause more debtors to discharge their debts, for instance, creditors will scrutinize their borrowers more carefully and either ration credit or charge higher interest rates. This solution has downsides for creditors, of course. Rationing credit means making fewer loans. And raising interest rates creates an adverse selection problem: the higher interest rates may drive low-risk borrowers out of the credit market, leaving a disproportionate percentage of high-risk borrowers. In either case, however, much of the cost will be passed on to borrowers.

There are two factors that can make creditors much more vulnerable. The first is transition costs. Although creditors can pass on the cost of debtor-friendly bankruptcy changes to subsequent borrowers, they do not have the same flexibility with existing borrowers. Loans to existing borrowers have already been made, so debtor-friendly changes retroactively alter the terms of the existing loan. The effect is to subject creditors to new risks that the creditor did not bargain for initially. With existing loans, bankruptcy reform can thus impose real costs. Particularly is this so in a time of widespread economic collapse. During the Great Depression, for instance, the National Retail Grocers Association lobbied repeatedly for stricter bankruptcy laws. Thousands of local grocers had permitted their customers to run a tab—that is, the grocers had extended small amounts of credit—and the spike in bankruptcy filings triggered by the depression put much of this credit at risk. Grocers complained that numerous consumers who had no other significant obligations were filing for bankruptcy to discharge their grocery bills. At the least, they insisted (unsuccessfully, as it turned out), Congress should prohibit debtors who owed less than one thousand dollars to creditors from filing for bankruptcy, or make obligations incurred for "necessities" nondischargeable.

For many creditors, however, under many circumstances, the vulnerability of existing loans does not set off wild alarms. Creditors who extend credit on a continual and short-term basis and are just as continually repaid—that is, who do not run tabs for significant periods of time—may have relatively small amounts tied up in prior loans at any one time. Moreover, the likelihood that any given borrower will file for bankruptcy may be remote, especially in an era when economic conditions are good and overall filings low.

A second concern that can stir placid creditors into action is changes that directly affect their market share vis-à-vis a competing kind of credit. A good illustration, though one that involves secured rather than unsecured creditors, is the relationship between banks and finance companies. Banks lend to comparatively "safe" credit risks, whereas finance companies often make higher-risk, higher-interest rate loans secured by items such as consumer goods.[23] A decision to expand (or contract) either the range of consumer goods a debtor can exempt, or debtors' ability to avoid security interests in otherwise exempt goods, has important implications for the relationship between banks and finance companies. Such an expansion would make finance companies' strategy of taking security interests in consumer goods less effective. If finance companies responded by charging higher rates, this adjustment would make it harder for finance companies to compete with a bank loan. Financial companies therefore have a powerful incentive to resist such changes, and banks have good reason to support them.

In recent years, the most visible creditor activists in consumer bankruptcy have been credit card companies (the battle between credit card companies and bankruptcy professionals will in fact be a central theme in chapter 7). Credit card companies are motivated by both of the factors that inspire unsecured creditor lobbying. The enormous amount of outstanding consumer debt gives credit card firms a huge stake in the transition effects of a change to more stringent bankruptcy laws. Similarly, more restrictive bankruptcy laws would diminish credit card companies' expected losses and expand their attractiveness as a source of consumer loans.

Although the credit card firms are a high-profile exception, the vast majority of unsecured creditors do not participate in bankruptcy politics, either because they are scattered and unrepresented or because they can pass on their expected costs.

The final relevant group is secured creditors such as banks, savings and loans, and finance companies, who do some or all of their lending on a collateralized basis. An obvious difference between secured and unsecured creditors is that secured creditors face far fewer collective action problems than do unsecured creditors. Each bank tends to have large stake, and secured creditors are well represented overall by nationwide industry groups. The American Bankers Association, which hits the pavement on behalf of commercial banks, is notoriously effective in promoting bankers' interests. Local banks, savings and loans, and finance companies enjoy similarly effective representation in Congress.

Banks and other secured creditors do make their presence known when Congress takes up bankruptcy issues, but less vociferously than with other issues. In the 1930s, as in the nineteenth-century bankruptcy debates, secured lenders had comparatively little to say. One reason is precisely the same explanation (with the same exceptions) as just discussed with unsecured creditors. To the extent bankruptcy law increases secured creditors' costs, they often can pass these costs on. It is future borrowers, not the secured creditor, who bear the brunt of any increase in the costs of failure. At least as important is the factor that distinguishes secured from unsecured creditors: their priority. Because collateralized creditors are paid first, they have less at risk in the bankruptcy process. As a result, their interests in bankruptcy reform are relatively narrow. Banks and other secured creditors are concerned that the bankruptcy laws protect their collateral, and they also throw their weight behind proposals that would streamline the bankruptcy process and thus reduce its costs. As long as these objectives are met, secured lenders tend to remain quiet, and this was precisely what happened on bankruptcy issues in the 1930s. (On related issues such as moratoria on mortgage obligations, by contrast, banks found themselves in pitched battles that ultimately turned on the Supreme Court's Fifth Amendment jurisprudence.) As we will see in chapter 5, secured lenders figured more prominently in the debates that led to the 1978 Bankruptcy Code. Yet even in 1978, secured creditors could be pacified so long as the bankruptcy laws generally protected their property rights in the collateral securing their loans.

BANKRUPTCY LAWYERS IN ACTION

Against this backdrop, the influence of bankruptcy professionals is less puzzling than it seemed at first glance. Despite the poor reputation of its rank and file, the general bankruptcy bar had enormous advantages as an interest group. Bankruptcy lawyers, together with bankruptcy referees, were spread throughout the country. Yet, in any given locality, particularly in cities, bankruptcy practice was quite concentrated. (This, of course, is simply another side of the qualities, such as insularity, that reinforced outsiders' distrust of the bar.) The combination of local concentration and a nationwide presence made it much easier for bankruptcy lawyers than for many other groups to coordinate. And coordinate they did. As we have seen, bankruptcy lawyers exerted national influence through organizations such as the Commercial Law League and the Commercial Law Section of the ABA. Bankruptcy referees also were well coordinated, through the National Association of

Referees in Bankruptcy, which they formed in 1929, and enjoyed a similar national presence.

This broad-based influence immediately distinguishes the bankruptcy bar from debtors, repayers, and most unsecured creditors. Although it does not differentiate bankruptcy lawyers from banks, which could call on equally widespread sources of influence, banks' interests have generally been narrow, as just noted. Then, as now, they and other financiers took a passionate interest in a few issues but could often be pacified so long as their property interests were protected.

Another crucial factor in the influence of bankruptcy professionals is the perceived complexity of bankruptcy law. Despite my protestations to the contrary at the beginning of the book, many observers view bankruptcy as hopelessly arcane and technical. In a complex area of the law, lawmakers may not be punished for acceding to interest group pressures because the overall effect is quite difficult for the public (and even for many lawmakers) to detect.[24] As a result, interest groups often prove most successful in complex areas of the law. The influence of bankruptcy lawyers on bankruptcy law is a good illustration of this phenomenon.

Bankruptcy hearings have never lacked for complexity. A central issue in one early set of hearings was whether the bankruptcy trustee should have the authority to take control of property that was beyond the debtor's reach at the time of bankruptcy; or whether the trustee could only exercise control over property in the debtor's possession. Make no mistake: a lot can turn on this distinction in an actual case. If the trustee cannot take title to a piece of equipment or land, selling it in order to raise cash to pay creditors becomes difficult or even impossible. But this simply is not the kind of discussion that captures the attention of lawmakers, and, needless to say, it took place well below the radar screen of public opinion. Because they were the only ones who understood or took an interest in technical details such as these, bankruptcy lawyers had enormous influence over the discussions. Moreover, it is easy to imagine how this influence would also extend to issues with a broader effect.

In their role as bankruptcy experts, then, bankruptcy lawyers have an ongoing opportunity to influence the legislative process. In hearing after hearing, one sees bankruptcy professionals testifying before the Judiciary Committee on bankruptcy-related issues. On technical issues especially, bankruptcy professionals often are the only ones who testify, and committee members' deference to their expertise is often quite explicit. At times, the Judiciary Committee has abandoned even the pretense of treating bankruptcy professionals as ordinary witnesses. In the House hearings on the Chandler bill in 1937, for instance, Representative Chandler asked various members of the National Bankruptcy Conference to introduce the provisions of the proposed legislation. Referee Watson Adair described the definitional provisions of the bill,

Randolph Montgomery and Jacob Weinstein each outlined a variety of technical changes, and James McLaughlin described the history of the legislation and the preference and setoff provisions.[25] The members of the conference functioned not merely as witnesses, but as de facto members of the Judiciary Committee for the purposes of the Chandler bill hearings.

In addition to their testimony at hearings, bankruptcy professionals leave their fingerprints on almost every other step of the process. When the committee itself drafts or alters proposed legislation, for instance, the staff members who actually draft the relevant language are often lawyers and frequently come from the bankruptcy bar. Given their participation in every phase of the legislative process, bankruptcy professionals have an enormous influence on the shape of any proposed legislation.

The discussion thus far has assumed that bankruptcy lawyers share a single, consistent set of interests. In reality, of course, their interests differ in important respects. Rather than having a single viewpoint, bankruptcy lawyers tend to take on the perspectives of their clients. The prominent bankruptcy lawyers mentioned earlier are a good illustration. Whereas Jacob Weinstein represented debtors and some creditors, Randolph Montgomery was a classic creditors' lawyer and served for many years as general counsel to the unsecured creditors' primary lobbying organization, the National Association of Credit Men.

In some respects, lawyers' status as representatives of other interests is grounds for optimism about the political economy of bankruptcy. Lawyers serve as the agents of a wide range of interests, and among these interests are several that might otherwise be underrepresented. Although one is hard-pressed to find many examples of current and future debtors testifying in the Judiciary Committee hearings, for instance, bankruptcy lawyers who usually represent debtors frequently make appeals on their behalf. Similarly, unsecured creditors are represented by the Commercial Law League (as well as by their own organization, the National Association of Credit Men), which consisted in the 1930s of collection lawyers and lawyers who served as receivers and trustees' counsel. To the extent every perspective has its claim on a portion of the bankruptcy bar, the lobbying of bankruptcy lawyers may assure that the full range of interests is represented. In effect, lawyers may help to complete the political marketplace and in doing so realize the pluralist's dream that politics translate the vigorous competition of opposing interest groups into legislation that benefits everyone.[26]

Bankruptcy lawyers do play something like this role in the legislative process, acting as agents for a variety of interests, but their representation is imperfect in two telling respects. First, as with all agents, lawyers' interests diverge to some extent from those of their principals—that is, the parties that lawyers represent. A lawyer that represents debtors, for instance, will argue vigorously for her clients' interests on most issues. Debtors' lawyers can be expected to support measures that give corporate debtors more room to reorganize, and oppose those that would diminish the scope of an individual debtor's discharge. In the 1930s, for instance, bankruptcy lawyers fiercely opposed the proposal to authorize courts to suspend or condition a debtor's discharge. (Jacob Weinstein lambasted the proposal as "un-American" and complained that it would hold debtors in bondage.)[27] On other issues, however, lawyers are likely to look out for their own interests. Limiting the fees that can be paid to lawyers might reduce the costs of bankruptcy for debtors, but one does not often see lawyers taking the lead on this kind of proposal. Nor does one often see creditors' lawyers lobbying for measures that would curtail debtors' right to file for bankruptcy, even if such a change would benefit creditors by reducing their losses in bankruptcy.

Similarly, although bankruptcy lawyers act as agents for some interests, others cannot easily find a place under the bankruptcy bar's umbrella. Probably the most important is the group we have referred to as repayers—borrowers who are not likely to ever invoke the bankruptcy laws. Because bankruptcy lawyers represent parties that find themselves inside the bankruptcy process, they do not often think from the perspective of repayers.

Given the influence of the bankruptcy bar, and the fact that bankruptcy professionals do not simply act as scribes for the interests of other parties, the question that arises is this: what shape does the influence of bankruptcy lawyers take? How has the bar influenced the evolution of American bankruptcy law? As we will see, bankruptcy lawyers have left their stamp on bankruptcy law in two important respects. The bar has thwarted efforts to establish a governmental overseer in bankruptcy, and it has spearheaded the relentless expansion of bankruptcy law over the course of the century. During the New Deal, the bar played the first role—acting as spoiler—with the reforms of the early 1930s and then promoted expansion in the 1938 Chandler Act. The next two sections will consider each of these developments in turn. To say that other interest groups have less pervasive an interest than lawyers in bankruptcy should not blind us to their important and sometimes pivotal role in the lobbying process, however. The final section of the chapter will place particular emphasis on this theme.

HEADING OFF THE PROPOSAL FOR ADMINISTRATIVE REFORM

In a well-known Sherlock Holmes detective story, the key to Holmes's success in solving the crime is his realization that a dog—which surely would have barked if an outside intruder had appeared—never barked. The most important clue was something that was missing—the dog's bark—rather than in anything that could be found at the crime site. If there is a "dog that didn't bark" in American bankruptcy law, surely it is the absence of governmental overseer serving as gatekeeper to the bankruptcy process. In other nations that permit debtors to discharge their debts, one or more governmental officials review each bankruptcy petition, examine the debtor, and have an important say in whether the debtor receives a discharge.

Most striking of all is the contrast between U.S. and English bankruptcy law. Given their numerous similarities, one might expect to see comparable bankruptcy regimes. Long after the Revolutionary War, U.S. lawmakers continued to mimic English regulation and the English market framework. Initially, at least, the borrowing also extended to bankruptcy. The Bankruptcy Act of 1800 was derived from English law, as were parts of the 1841 and 1867 acts; and the Lowell bill that inaugurated creditors' push for a permanent U.S. law took much of its inspiration from the English Bankruptcy Act of 1869. Yet, as was discussed in chapter 1, U.S. and English bankruptcy law went very separate ways during the course of the nineteenth century. English lawmakers adopted a heavily administrative system, which positions an official receiver between debtors and the possibility of a discharge. The Bankruptcy Act of 1898, by contrast, left much of the U.S. process to the parties themselves.

As we also saw in chapter 1, the original reason for the minimalist administrative structure of the 1898 act was U.S. politics. Cost was a central issue for both creditors and their prodebtor opponents—an issue that geography made much more problematic in the United States than in England. And bankruptcy opponents waged a bitter battle to minimize any increase in the size of the federal bureaucracy. For many southern and western lawmakers, a bankruptcy law that required numerous new officials was anathema.

Although the political factors that steered the bankruptcy debates away from an administrative, English-style system have never fully disappeared, serious movements to add a governmental overseer to bankruptcy emerged in both the 1930s and the 1970s. Of particular interest for present purposes is the earlier movement, which grew out of the Donovan and Thacher reports in the early 1930s. As we saw earlier, the Thacher report recommendations quickly found their way into Congress as the 1932 Hastings-Michener bill and were the subject of extensive hearings before the House and Senate Judiciary Committees. Although there was general agreement that bankruptcy practice in New York was corrupt, witnesses debated whether there were similar problems elsewhere and whether the administrative proposals were an appropriate solution.

Many of the complaints about the plan to appoint ten new administrators sound quite similar to objections made during the nineteenth-century bankruptcy debates. Critics bitterly complained that the proposal would create an unwieldy new federal bureaucracy and would dramatically increase the cost of bankruptcy. Rather than populists or advocates of states' rights, however, the loudest and most insistent critics were bankruptcy lawyers. As part of his attack on the proposed legislation, Jacob Weinstein submitted a letter on behalf of the National Association of Federal Practitioners, a group of bankruptcy lawyers formed to oppose the Hastings-Michener bill. "Should the measure pass," the letter warned,

> not only would the administration of bankrupt estates become distinctly political and under bureaucratic domination, and cost the taxpayers millions of dollars annually, but the rights of citizens, and indeed their liberty . . . would be seriously affected, while lawyers would practically cease to function in such cases.[28]

The Bankruptcy Committee of the American Bar Association concurred:

> We take the position that our bankruptcy law is sound in its conception, that it has made a tremendous contribution to the commercial and economic life of the country, and so we start with this premise—that this law must not be rejected for any projected substitute system, but that all that is good in the law . . . ought to be preserved, and, moreover, that the experience of the country of 33 years and more with this law ought not to be scrapped, and that the precedents and the judicial decisions through which rules of law and interpretation and application of law have been built up by the courts of this country ought to be preserved.[29]

The influence of the bankruptcy bar becomes clear if we consider the various parties' perspectives on adding administrators. In contrast to bankruptcy professionals, nearly all of the creditors and creditors' groups who testified spoke out in favor of the proposal. Small, relatively unorganized creditors were among the most enthusiastic supporters of all. Typical of their perspective was Harry Schwartz of Capital Paint and Varnish. Schwartz complained that creditors almost never received any payment under current practice. Adding a governmental administrator who conducted a thorough investigation when a debtor filed for bankruptcy surely would improve creditors' prospect for recovery.[30] At the other end of the spectrum, the American Bankers Association, the largest bank lobby in the nation, favored the same attributes of the reform. In endorsing the bill, the association singled out the use of an independent examiner for particular praise.[31]

Slightly less unified, but at least as revealing, was the view of the National Association of Credit Men. The Donovan and Thacher proposals sparked a vigorous debate among the membership of the NACM, with some members insisting on the need to clean up the bankruptcy process, and others contending that the process worked relatively well. Advocates of reform emphasized the sorry reputation of bankruptcy practice and the poor results for creditors in most bankruptcy cases. As we saw earlier, Randolph Montgomery believed that the proxy system for selecting bankruptcy trustees was irredeemably flawed. "Colonel Donovan's proposed system of licensed trustees and limited creditor control," he argued, "with the surrounding safeguards which he has suggested, would tend to eliminate the proxy evil."[32]

The principal argument in opposition was that the reforms would wrest control of bankruptcy from a debtor's creditors and give it to governmental officials. The "appointment of Trustees by the courts in the first instance in all cases," argued one opponent of the reforms, "will have the tendency . . . to spread through the United States . . . [a] system of court control . . . , and [lead to] the annulment of the primary and fundamental rights of creditors. There would be little satisfaction in the few rights left to creditors. . . . Credit men would doubtlessly feel that the only privilege left to them would be to lock the barn after the horse had been stolen."[33]

The tension within the National Association of Credit Men is intriguing for several reasons. It illustrates that many creditors, even the relatively sophisticated creditors represented by the NACM, were now willing to cede substantial authority to a governmental official. Moreover, the support of a substantial proportion of its membership for the Thacher reforms represented a significant break with the NACM's long-standing ally, the general bankruptcy bar. Although the NACM had repeatedly stood side by side with the Commercial Law League and ABA on bankruptcy issues, reforming the administrative process was an important issue on which many members parted ways with the bar. The National Association of Credit Men did not formally endorse the administrative reforms, but many local NACM representatives, like nearly all of the creditors who testified, were quite vocal in their support. A representative of the St. Louis Association of Credit Men, for instance, predicted that the bill would increase dividends to creditors and enhance the flexibility of the bankruptcy system. This group of "wholesalers, manufacturers, jobbers, and bankers in St. Louis" had given "a great deal of thought and study" to the proposals, and they endorsed the bill "in toto."[34]

When Congress first took up bankruptcy reform, then, the only organized groups that were dead set against a more administrative bankruptcy process were bankruptcy professionals. (It is also possible that populism reinforced the bankruptcy professionals' effectiveness in stymieing administrative reform. As often is the case with relatively unorganized groups, populists did not participate in any visible way in the legislative hearings, but their influence was quite audible when bankruptcy reform made its way to House and Senate floor in 1933 and 1934—by which point the administrative proposals had been abandoned. Perhaps the most dramatic evidence of populism was a filibuster by Senator Huey Long of Louisiana in support of farm debtors, which held up the hearings for several days.)

In short, the legislative evidence is too anecdotal to "prove" that bankruptcy lawyers deserve much of the credit (or blame) for thwarting the reforms, but the evidence surely is suggestive. And what it suggests is that lawyers were the principal obstacle to more sweeping, structural change. This view draws further support from lawmakers' references to the 1932 hearings during their deliberations in subsequent years. The sponsor of the 1938 Chandler Act,

Representative Chandler, stated on several occasions that the administrative reforms had been dropped because of concerns about cost and their effect on thirty years of bankruptcy practice.[35] Anyone familiar with the earlier hearings would, of course, have immediately linked these concerns with the group that had voiced them over and over—the bankruptcy bar.

The role of bankruptcy professionals in heading off administrative reform would be even clearer when the proposal resurfaced forty years later. As we will discuss in more detail in chapter 5, a National Bankruptcy Review Commission established in 1970 (with Professor Frank Kennedy as reporter) conducted an extensive study of existing bankruptcy practice and recommended sweeping reforms. Like the Donovan committee before it, the 1973 commission report advised Congress to set up a governmental overseer to act as gatekeeper to the bankruptcy process. Bankruptcy professionals (especially bankruptcy judges, whose influence increased significantly after the New Deal) immediately went on the attack, speaking out against the proposal early and often. Several lawyers were quite candid about the basis for their opposition. In addition to its cost and the effect on existing practice, these lawyers complained that administrative reform would destroy the consumer bankruptcy bar.

This, quite obviously, was the rub. If Congress appointed administrative overseers to investigate debtors and make formal recommendations as to whether each debtor should get a discharge, bankruptcy lawyers and judges would figure much less prominently in bankruptcy practice. This is precisely what has happened in England. England's move to an administrative system in 1883 left relatively little role for bankruptcy lawyers. The governmental overseers do depend on input from professionals, but accountants rather than lawyers are the ones who provide the necessary information. Since the 1898 act created a need for their services, U.S. bankruptcy lawyers have fought to preserve the original framework, and to thwart any move to shift to the English approach. So far, they have been entirely successful.

EXPANDING THE BANKRUPTCY PROCESS

Proposals to establish an administrative overseer have always brought out bankruptcy lawyers' passions faster than any other single issue. As traumatic as they have been for the bankruptcy bar, these proposals have surfaced only episodically. A second set of issues—the scope of the bankruptcy laws—has captured bankruptcy lawyers' interests on a more regular basis. Bankruptcy lawyers have repeatedly lobbied to expand the bankruptcy process, and they have opposed amendments that might diminish the use of bankruptcy. This trend predates the New Deal, and the extensive changes ushered in at the end of the 1930s reinforced rather than curbed the gradual extension of bankruptcy law.

The most important (if not the most vivid) illustration of lawyers' support for expansion has been the ongoing efforts to enlarge the jurisdiction of the bankruptcy court. In the years before the New Deal, these jurisdictional issues frequently focused on the relationship between the state courts and federal bankruptcy law. As we saw in chapter 1, the 1898 act imposed severe limitations on the jurisdiction of the bankruptcy court. If a debtor had fraudulently conveyed property prior to bankruptcy and the trustee wished to recover this property, the act required him to file the fraudulent conveyance action in state court. The requirement was neither accidental nor incidental, of course. Permitting state courts to retain jurisdiction over fraudulent conveyance actions had been an important concession to lawmakers who worried that bankruptcy legislation would cause a dramatic shift from state to federal decision makers.

Almost immediately, bankruptcy professionals started lobbying to undo this piece of the original compromise. Requiring bankruptcy trustees to move from one court to another, depending on the nature of the action, was costly and inefficient, they argued. Vesting jurisdiction both in the state courts and in the bankruptcy court, so that either one could resolve a fraudulent conveyance action, would promote judicial economy in many cases by permitting a bankruptcy court resolution. In cases where the defendant lived far away or would be prejudiced in some other way by bankruptcy court jurisdiction, the case could be tried in state court.[36]

Closely related to these jurisdictional issues were questions of the trustee's authority. Early in the century, courts repeatedly faced questions as to which prebankruptcy transfers the trustee could avoid. For example, it was not entirely clear whether involuntary transfers, such as a court judgment giving a creditor a lien on the debtor's property, could be treated as preferences, or whether the trustee could only attack transfers that the debtor had made voluntarily. Bankruptcy professionals vigorously and repeatedly supported expansion of the trustee's powers.[37]

Each of these issues is quite technical in nature, and bankruptcy professionals persuaded Congress to take action on both.[38] To be sure, bankruptcy lawyers did not simply get their way at the expense of everyone else. The bankruptcy bar advanced plausible public interest justifications for each of the changes. Expanding the bankruptcy court's jurisdiction would indeed enhance judicial economy, and increasing the trustee's power to invalidate transfers made and property interests obtained immediately before bankruptcy would reduce creditors' ability to grab assets to the detriment of other creditors. But these technical changes, and others like them, also offer obvious benefits to lawyers. Just as it streamlines the bankruptcy process, for instance, expanding the bankruptcy court's jurisdiction also diminishes the need for nonbankruptcy lawyers and increases the attractiveness of bankruptcy as a solution to financial distress.[39]

These changes reflect a pattern of expansion that continued throughout the century. Particularly on technical issues such as the two we have just considered, bankruptcy lawyers' prominence in the discussions suggests that the bar exerted a crucial influence. Bankruptcy lawyers' effectiveness in shaping U.S. bankruptcy law stemmed in part from their expertise. But expertise alone might not have counteracted the bar's unsavory reputation—especially in the wake of the scandals chronicled by the Donovan and Thacher reports. Another crucial variable is the fact that the most prominent bankruptcy professionals—the ones who frequently appeared at hearings on bankruptcy—were not involved in the practices of the "bankruptcy rings." These professionals— who now included Reuben Hunt, Jacob Weinstein, and James McLaughlin— lent credibility to the proposals to enlarge and perfect the bankruptcy process.

Bankruptcy professionals emerged from the first wave of Great Depression reforms unscathed, having helped to derail both the administrative and the substantive proposals of the Donovan committee, but many of leading members of the bar were dissatisfied. In their view, Congress, in its rush to pass broad bankruptcy relief measures of 1933 and 1934, had neglected a wide range of technical problems with the existing act. To remedy this problem, these eminences of the bankruptcy bar formed the National Bankruptcy Conference to draft specific proposals for perfecting the act. James McLaughlin would later recall the birth of the National Bankruptcy Conference in the most nostalgic of terms. As they shared their frustration on a train back to Boston after one of the 1932 hearings, McLaughlin and several prominent lawyers concluded that they should take a more active role and immediately began scrawling proposed amendments on napkins in the train's dining car:

> There were seven of us got together in Boston in 1932, and some of the gentlemen thought we were going to rewrite the Bankruptcy Act between Saturday night and Monday morning. But that was the germ of the national bankruptcy conference, which was gradually extended. We did not call ourselves that, at that time, but we asked ourselves, "Who knows something about bankruptcy, and who will be ready to put in some time and make some suggestions, and take the time of actually getting it into words?" We said, "You may think you have got something that is worthwhile, but until you actually get it in words, you are a long way from having any practical legislation."[40]

These first conversations soon led to the National Bankruptcy Conference. Initially comprised of the Commercial Law League, ABA, National Association of Credit Men, National Association of Referees in Bankruptcy, one full-time bankruptcy academic (McLaughlin), and individual bankruptcy lawyers, the National Bankruptcy Conference would enjoy remarkable influence throughout the 1930s and thereafter. More than sixty years later, the conference remains the single most important voice in bankruptcy reform.

Given the prominent role the National Bankruptcy Conference will play throughout the remainder of the book, we should pause to briefly consider the perspective the conference has taken since its formation. Perhaps the most striking attribute of the National Bankruptcy Conference has been the often public-spirited nature of its members' commitment to reform—a commitment that would bring them into conflict with the general bankruptcy bar in the 1970s. The basis for this orientation, and for the NBC's influence, becomes clear if we consider the origins of the conference. I alluded earlier to the fact that the membership of the NBC included the most respected members of the general bankruptcy bar—the same men (they were all men) who were generally called on to testify at Judiciary Committee hearings on bankruptcy issues. Not only did these lawyers tend to be the ones who already had a genuine interest in reform, but the NBC has always had a strong incentive to protect this reputation. So long as the NBC could be trusted to offer disinterested expertise on the technical problems with bankruptcy law, lawmakers would continue to defer to its recommendations. From the beginning, this is precisely what we have seen.

This does not mean that the NBC is a purely disinterested source of guidance on bankruptcy issues. The NBC has always consisted of bankruptcy professionals, and its reforms invariably assume that bankruptcy should play a more, rather than less, prominent role in issues involving financial distress. But within these parameters, the NBC has encouraged Congress to tackle many of the traditional problems with bankruptcy practice. This commitment has in fact increased as the NBC has matured as an organization, and as its links to Congress have solidified.

Within weeks of their original conversations, McLaughlin and the other members of the NBC had developed a full-blown set of proposals for reforming the Bankruptcy Act. Most had little resonance with the public but significant implications for the day-to-day practice of bankruptcy law. As always, the overall effect would be to "perfect" bankruptcy law in a way that made bankruptcy more useful, and thus more attractive as a response to financial distress. By giving bankruptcy referees nationwide jurisdiction over the property of the debtor, for instance, the Chandler Act resolved a longstanding debate as to whether a referee's jurisdiction was limited to the county in which the courthouse sat, and it sharply expanded the bankruptcy court's jurisdiction.[41] The Chandler Act made other changes of similar import as well.[42] The overall pattern is familiar and clear: the Chandler Act sought to perfect bankruptcy by extending its reach and attempting to make bankruptcy a one-stop solution to financial distress. Almost all that remained of the sweeping Hastings-Michener bill proposals were a few provisions designed to ensure a slightly more rigorous examination of debtors, together with a halfhearted

effort to address concerns about collusive solicitation of proxies for the election of trustees. Rather than curbing or ending proxy voting, the Chandler
Act required only that a list of creditors be made available at the beginning of
the case, so that insiders would not be the only ones with access to the list.[43]

By 1935, the NBC had persuaded Congressman Chandler of Tennessee to
sponsor its proposed legislation. Introduced in early 1936 and further adjusted
in the next two years, the Chandler bill proposals had almost nothing to
do with the flurry of New Deal legislation swirling through Congress in the
mid-1930s. There would be no bankruptcy agency or other governmental
intervention into general bankruptcy practice. But the National Bankruptcy
Conference would have a major New Deal encounter before the Chandler
Act finally passed. In 1934, as part of the Securities Exchange Act of 1934,
Congress had instructed the newly formed Securities and Exchange Commission to investigate and report on the protective committees used in equity
receiverships. As we will discuss in detail in chapter 4, William Douglas, the
SEC's chair, turned the investigation into a wide-ranging referendum on
large-scale corporate reorganization practice. In late 1936, after Congressman
Chandler and the National Bankruptcy Conference had been developing the
Chandler bill for several years, the SEC dramatically intervened. In place of
the limited changes the Chandler bill had in mind for corporate reorganization, the SEC proposed an entirely new chapter for the reorganization of
publicly held firms.

In effect, the SEC, which spoke for the interests of the New Deal, and the
general bankruptcy bar struck a deal. The reformers would cede control over
all of bankruptcy law other than large reorganizations to the bar, so long as
the bar agreed to the sweeping revisions the SEC sought for publicly held
firms. It was a marriage of convenience for both sides. Douglas had little
interest in the general bankruptcy bar, and his work with Thacher ivestigation
cannot have left a particularly favorable impression. The membership of the
National Bankruptcy Conference was similarly, and more overtly, conflicted.
The NBC agreed to include the SEC's provisions for regulating publicly held
corporations by a closely divided vote, at a meeting from which many of its
members were absent. In the congressional hearings that followed, several
NBC members openly criticized the SEC's handiwork. Like nearly every
bankruptcy lawyer who spoke, Edwin Sunderland questioned the SEC's proposal to install a trustee in every case. "I want to say to you this," he complained, "from experience it has been demonstrated that there is a great number of cases where it is not necessary to have a trustee." John Gerdes
complained that the overall framework was simply too inflexible.[44]

Chapter 4 will explore in detail how the SEC's reforms transformed large-
scale reorganization. For present purposes, however, the uneasy alliance between the SEC and the bankruptcy bar is most remarkable for what it suggests
about the influence of the bankruptcy bar. Even at the height of the New

Deal, the reformers concluded that working with the NBC and the general bankruptcy bar was the best way to reform large-firm reorganization practice. The rest of bankruptcy practice they left to the bankruptcy bar—the same bar that had drawn so much criticism in the Donovan and Thacher reports that had set the reform process in motion only a few years earlier.

THE CONTINUING INFLUENCE OF CREDITORS AND PRODEBTOR IDEOLOGY

Our discussion thus far might, by itself, seem to suggest that bankruptcy lawyers dominated bankruptcy discourse in the 1930s, and that no other interest group got a word in edgewise. That, of course, is not the case. At various points, other interest groups lobbied vigorously for or against particular provisions. Railroad lessees, who sold or leased railroad cars to the railroads on credit, persuaded Congress to carve out an exception for them from the automatic stay. (Recall that the automatic stay forbids creditors from foreclosing once a debtor files for bankruptcy.) An issue that banks cared deeply about was their common-law right of setoff—in particular, their right to use a debtor's deposit account at the bank to offset, or pay down, the amount that a debtor owed to the bank. James McLaughlin wanted to treat setoffs effected prior to bankruptcy as preferential transfers, and he persuaded the National Bankruptcy Conference to include such a proposal in an early draft of the Chandler bill. Banks fiercely resisted this assault on their traditional setoff rights (which functioned very much like a security interest), however, and McLaughlin was forced to back down. "I am not going to revisit [the setoff proposal] all over again," he said in the 1937 Chandler Act hearings. "I think that would constitute breach of faith with my banker friends."[45]

Just as creditors continued to play a role, populism also exerted an obvious influence. In many respects, populism reinforced the interests of the bankruptcy bar, since by the mid-1930s both favored expansive use of bankruptcy. The inclusion of general rehabilitation provisions for individuals and small firms in 1933 and the enactment in 1938 of a new chapter authorizing wage earner plans illustrates the convergence of the general bankruptcy bar and prodebtor ideology. In its original, 1932 conception, rehabilitation was designed to include both a carrot and a stick. As an enticement, the reforms proposed that debtors who opted for rehabilitation rather than an immediate discharge would be called *debtors*, rather than the more pejorative *bankrupts*. (The distinction would disappear in 1978, when Congress abandoned the term *bankrupt* altogether in an effort to reduce the stigma of bankruptcy.) The stick was the suspended or conditional discharge, which would have given courts the authority to force debtors to continue paying their creditors. Well aware that suspended discharge would discourage some debtors from filing for bankruptcy, the bankruptcy bar subjected the proposals to sustained attack. As noted earlier, Jacob Weinstein complained that the proposed changes would hold debtors in bondage until they finally received their discharge.[46]

A variation of the rehabilitation provision resurfaced in 1933, but the new incarnation differed in telling respects. Gone was any suggestion that debtors should be forced to accept a delayed discharge. The new provision, which permitted debtors to renegotiate and scale down their obligations, would be entirely optional, an additional choice for debtors who committed some of their future earnings to the current creditors. So different was the 1933 version of composition from the original proposals, that the Progressive senator Robert La Follette insisted on including an analogous provision to help out farm debtors. The trend was reinforced in 1938, when the Chandler Act introduced the first full-blown individual rehabilitation chapter, Chapter XIII—the precursor to current Chapter 13—and made this alternative entirely optional.

The original 1933 provisions were seldom used, with one major exception. In Birmingham, Alabama, a large percentage of the debtors in Referee Valentine Nesbit's court proposed repayment plans. Nesbit appears to have achieved this result both through creative interpretation of the 1933 provision, and by prodding his debtors away from immediate discharge. In the 1937 hearings, Nesbit described his procedures in some detail. "Those debtors who have no intention of paying their debts and who are trying to use the court to avoid payment," he testified, "are soon found out and are not tolerated. Their petitions are forthwith dismissed."[47] Nesbit insisted that debtors genuinely wished to pay, however, and supporters of Chapter XIII in 1938 believed that debtors who could pay would feel obligated to do so and would voluntarily opt for Chapter XIII. As we will see in chapters 5 and 7, the rehabilitation provisions have never worked out as their advocates hoped. In Alabama, a large percentage of debtors continued to choose Chapter XIII over Chapter VII, but almost everywhere else the opposite was true.

Another striking illustration of the continuing influence of ideology—and of the significance of American federalism—involved the long-standing issue whether Congress or the states should determine what property a debtor can exempt from creditors. The evidence for the continued relevance of the deal struck in 1898 did not come in a vigorous New Deal debate. Quite to the contrary, in this era of massive federalization, there was almost no discussion of the exemptions issue in any of the hearings. The one reference to exemptions in the Chandler hearings speaks volumes about lawmakers' commitment to state control of this issue. The National Bankruptcy Conference considered proposing uniform federal exemptions, according to Jacob Weinstein, but quickly abandoned the notion. "It . . . occurred to us," he told the Judiciary Committee, "that any limitation on the present exemption allowances under the bankruptcy law would be met with vigorous political opposition, particularly from the representatives of farmer States. Therefore we abandoned for the present the drafting of a uniform exemption provision."[47]

For all the excitement and disruption that the Great Depression and New Deal brought to general bankruptcy practice, then, the political determinants that came together with the Bankruptcy Act of 1898 remained firmly in place. Bankruptcy law reflected an ongoing compromise between creditors and pro-debtor interests, with bankruptcy professionals pushing to expand and "perfect" its scope.

Given that lawyers are everywhere in U.S. society, the influence of bankruptcy lawyers over bankruptcy law seems almost inevitable. Perhaps the shape and the evolution of bankruptcy law are also inevitable. After all, the tempering of creditors' interests with sympathy for "honest but unfortunate" debtors, for the possibility of a second chance, resonates deeply in the American imagination. Perhaps the developments I have described were more or less preordained.

But perhaps not. The best way to appreciate how U.S. bankruptcy law could have taken on a very different look is to consider a simple counterfactual. Suppose the nation had continued without a federal bankruptcy law into the twentieth century. If federal bankruptcy had remained precarious into the New Deal, Congress might have dealt with insolvency issues quite differently. Nearly all of the welfare state, from welfare to social security, was put into place in this era. Bankruptcy can be seen as a natural part of this overall project. Like the other components of the welfare state, bankruptcy is central to the safety net created during the New Deal. Each of the other strands of the net is administrative rather than judicial in nature. It does not take too great a leap of imagination to speculate that New Deal lawmakers, if they had been writing on a clean slate, might well have crafted an administrative bankruptcy system. In form, at least, and probably in result as well, an administrative system would have developed quite differently than the judicial approach with which we are familiar. By the time the Great Depression hit and the New Deal ascended, however, the pattern of U.S. bankruptcy law was already set. At the heart of U.S. bankruptcy was the bankruptcy bar, and, for better or worse, bankruptcy lawyers were not about to permit this to change.

Chapter Four

WILLIAM DOUGLAS AND THE RISE OF THE
SECURITIES AND EXCHANGE COMMISSION

I N AN ODD WAY, the general bankruptcy bar could look back on the
Great Depression and New Deal as an era of triumph. Bankruptcy practice was hardly prestigious, and bankruptcy lawyers remained rather low
in the hierarchy of the legal profession, but the New Deal left existing bankruptcy practice almost entirely intact.

The trajectory of the elite reorganization bar over this period could not
have been more different. From the late nineteenth century into the 1930s,
the same Wall Street lawyers and firms had dominated the practice. By the
end of the 1930s, however, the Chandler Act—with a small assist from the
Trust Indenture Act of 1939, another important New Deal reform—had decimated existing reorganization practice. Within a few years, Wall Street professionals would all but abandon the area. Interestingly, the demise was not immediate. To the contrary, the New Deal got off to a promising start for the
elite reorganization bar. The reorganizers enthusiastically supported the early
New Deal reforms, and the first set of reforms (in 1933 and 1934) largely
codified existing practice. Only at the second stage was the framework that
the Wall Street bar had pioneered dismantled.

This chapter will attempt to make sense of each of these developments. The
chapter begins with the first puzzle posed by the reforms: why did the elite
reorganization bar begin by supporting rather than attacking the codification
of reorganization practice in 1933 and 1934? We then will consider the monu-
mental study of reorganization practice that William Douglas conducted for
the SEC from 1934 to 1939, and the strategic decisions Douglas made as he and
the New Deal reformers converted the study into epoch-making bankruptcy
legislation. By inserting their reforms into the Chandler legislation drafted by
the National Bankruptcy Conference, the reformers altered the course of large-
scale reorganization for the next forty years. Unlike the general bankruptcy bar,
which managed to partially co-opt populism, the Wall Street banks and bar
were the primary target of this sentiment. In the end, the elite bar was gone.

Codifying Corporate Reorganization with the
Blessing of the Wall Street Bar

By the early 1930s, a few of the names had changed, but Wall Street reorganization practice looked much the same as where we left it at the end of chapter

2. The firm Francis Stetson had formed, which later become Davis, Polk & Wardwell, together with the Cravath firm, Sullivan & Cromwell, and one or two other Wall Street lawyers figured prominently in nearly every reorganization case.[1]

At Cravath, Paul Cravath had recently died (in part, due to the stress of years of overwork). Several of his partners, including Edward Henderson, ranked among the leaders of the reorganization bar. The most renowned of these, and the one who would step into Cravath's shoes, was Robert Swaine. Swaine had survived the "Cravath system," which foreshadowed the hiring and promotion practices that are now commonplace in the nation's largest law firms. Starting in the early years of the twentieth century, Cravath hired a group of bright law school graduates as associates each year. Rather than grooming most or all of them for partnership, Cravath assumed that many would depart after a few years. "Cravath used to say," Swaine recalled in his biography of the Cravath firm, "that, except for a few research scholars and specialists, no one should be permitted to stay in the office more than six years unless the partners had determined to admit him into the partnership."[2] In words that are as true now as they were then, Swaine noted that it "is often difficult to keep the best men [and women, we would now say] long enough to determine whether they shall be made partners, for Cravath-trained men are always in demand. . . . Because among the many called to the staff only a few can be chosen as partners, even good men are likely to feel that the odds against them are so great that they should accept flattering offers from others."

Swaine would prove to be one of the few who made it. Swaine joined the firm in 1910, shortly after graduating from Harvard Law School. Swaine, too, nearly left. In 1915, he prepared to open his own practice, in part due to the stress of working with Cravath himself. Yet the Cravath partners insisted that Swaine talk things over with Cravath. "In less than an hour, succumbing to the dominating personality he had sought to escape and to the promise of a partnership," Swaine recalled, "[I] agreed to remain."[3] It was Swaine whose name would later join Cravath's on the Cravath firm letterhead, and who would joust with William Douglas and the New Deal reformers when they set out to tame, and in effect to destroy, the traditional Wall Street reorganization practice.

One of the small ironies of William Douglas's quest to dismantle the cliquish Wall Street bar with the Chandler Act of 1938, and of Swaine's spirited defense of the reorganizers, was that Douglas himself had once cast his lot with the Cravath system. Douglas spent only two of his many years in the law in private practice, and the firm he spent these two years with was Cravath. After graduating from Columbia Law School in 1925, Douglas toiled for parts of the next several years researching technical reorganization issues, and drafting memos for Henderson, Chester McLain, and other Cravath partners. Adding to the irony was the fact that Douglas worked quite extensively on the

Chicago, Milwaukee, St. Paul & Pacific Railway Company receivership. The St. Paul receivership became a bête noire of the New Deal reformers during the late 1920s and 1930s—due in part to a book by Max Lowenthal that portrayed the case, and the role played by the Wall Street banks and bar, in bitterly critical terms.[4]

Douglas's correspondence with Chester McLain after his departure offers a fascinating window into both Douglas and the Cravath firm. In early 1929, McLain worried that "there seems to be a tendency among men from the Yale Law School to avoid this office, chiefly, I think, because of our reputation for hard work. I hope that you," McLain requested, "who have had some opportunity to become acquainted with the real character of the office and the opportunities which it offers, will be able to do something to counteract this tendency in the future."[5] In both this year and the previous one, Douglas had dutifully sent lists of the most promising law school graduates for the Cravath partners to consider. Among the names he forwarded were two men who had worked for Douglas on his extensive study of general bankruptcy practice (the study that had led to Douglas's involvement in the Donovan and Thacher reports). Douglas recommended his two student assistants as "highly thought of" and "rather anxious to practice in New York."[6]

Douglas himself did not see any particular irony in his association with Wall Street. For him, at least in retrospect, his Cravath years functioned as a recognizance mission, a chance to gather information behind enemy lines. "I saw just enough of the horrors of Wall Street," he told Felix Frankfurter in late 1933, "to know that an adequate control of [Wall Street] practices must be uncompromising."[7] Only later, however, would this antagonism fully emerge.

When Congress took up bankruptcy reform in 1932 in response to the Donovan and Thacher investigations, lawmakers' most pressing concern had been bankruptcy administration and the general bankruptcy issues we considered in the last chapter. Almost as an afterthought, the Thacher report also proposed codification of equity receivership practice, which even at this late date was still a creature of the common law. At first glance, one might expect to find reorganizers like Swaine and his Cravath partners fiercely resisting congressional intervention in receivership practice. Aside from occasional hiccups, such as the question of how to deal with the *Boyd* case, the traditional technique worked just fine. The common law had proven remarkably flexible, and the federal courts were generally sympathetic with the reorganizers' efforts. Moreover, Swaine and his peers had a near monopoly on the practice. If Congress entered the picture after staying on the sidelines for more than half a century, the reorganizers ran the risk that lawmakers would foul up the system.

Surprisingly enough, Swaine and the reorganization bar enthusiastically supported the early reforms—especially the codification of corporate reorganization in 1934. Swaine gave speeches throughout the country and published a symposium article in the *Virginia Law Review,* all vigorously promoting federal legislation. "[T]he judicial machinery provided for . . . reorganization," he complained,

> is that adapted to the era of the localized factory, the butcher shop, . . . and the railroad venturing into but one or two states. . . . That the inefficiency and waste involved in the present judicial machinery for corporate reorganizations should have continued through three decades of the twentieth century is well nigh unbelievable. That it should continue further . . . would be a scandal both upon the Bar and upon Congress.[8]

Why was he so anxious to shift equity receivership practice from the common law to the statute books?

Much of the explanation lies in the frictions, or inefficiencies, of the equity receivership procedure. Perhaps most troublesome was the cost of dealing with investors who refused to sign on to the reorganization plan. Dissenters had the right to insist on payment in cash. Although dissenters' payout was set by the court, and courts often fixed relatively low "upset prices," paying the dissenters was a drain on the reorganized firm's cash just when the firm needed it most.

The second problem was ancillary receiverships. If a large interstate railroad failed, its receivership actually consisted of several different receiverships. Even a federal court enjoyed only limited jurisdiction over property in other states, which required the reorganizers to set up separate, "ancillary" receiverships in each state where the firm owned property. If a railroad was headquartered in Illinois, for instance, but its track extended into Indiana and Ohio, the court would need to set up ancillary receiverships in Indiana and Ohio to administer the property in those states. Ancillary receiverships were a tempting source of patronage for out-of-state judges. Serving as an ancillary receiver (or the receiver's attorney) was often lucrative, and the courts (in Indiana and Ohio in our illustration) could use their authority to choose the receiver to generate substantial goodwill. But it was also quite costly to run a series of connected receiverships rather than a single centralized one.

Neither of these costs was new, of course; as we saw in chapter 2, both had long been necessary evils of the receivership process. What made these costs more problematic by the 1930s was the economic crisis unleashed by the Great Depression. Raising new cash to fund a reorganization became more and more difficult as the depression dried up the nation's money supply. "In present times," Robert Swaine warned, "this is a burden which should not be imposed upon a reorganization."[9]

In addition to costs, another concern also had begun to trouble the reorganizers' sleep. Nearly all of the early receiverships had involved troubled railroads, and railroads still were central, but other kinds of firms had become an increasingly large part of the reorganizers' practice as the century wore on.

"Despite national prosperity," Robert Swaine wrote about the period before the depression, "the [Cravath] firm is never without an industrial reorganization."[10] Swaine and the other reorganizers naturally used the same strategy with these firms as with railroads. A friendly creditor would be found to assure diversity jurisdiction, the reorganizers would set up the primary and ancillary receiverships, and the corporation would be reorganized through the fiction of a foreclosure "sale."

Although the receivership technique easily could be adapted to nonrailroad corporations, the standard justification for railroad receivership—that railroads were public in nature and could not be allowed to fail—often did not apply to nonrailroad firms. As a result, the ideological consensus in favor of reorganizing troubled railroads lost some of its force outside of the railroad context. Starting in the 1920s, the Supreme Court began hinting darkly that the railroads were in fact a special case, and that the Court had serious doubts about giving other firms the same flexibility to use the receivership process. In *Harkin v. Brundage*, the Court suggested that, in nonrailroad cases, it would take a more skeptical look at the collusive techniques that the reorganizers employed in railroad receiverships to establish jurisdiction. The Court was still more explicit in *Shapiro v. Wilgus*, where it indicated that these techniques passed muster in railroad cases only because a railroad was a "public service corporation" that provided a "service in furtherance of the public good."[11]

By the 1930s, then, Swaine and his colleagues had several good reasons to join in the movement to codify equity receivership practice. If nothing else, federal legislation would stabilize the jurisdictional basis of the reorganization process. A federal statute would give troubled firms direct access to the federal courts; no longer would they need to arrange for a friendly creditor to perform the awkward fiction of diversity jurisdiction. The reorganizers also held out hope that Congress would solve their practical problems with dissenters and ancillary receiverships. To address the first issue, the cost of paying dissenters, the reorganizers advocated a simple majority or supermajority voting rule. If the vote were binding, dissenters would lose their claim on the troubled firm's precious cash. Every creditor in a class, including those who dissented, would receive the treatment proposed by the reorganization plan so long as the appropriate majority voted in favor of the plan.

As for the cost and inconvenience of ancillary receiverships, Congress could eliminate this complication by authorizing nationwide jurisdiction. The bankruptcy court where the firm filed for bankruptcy would administer all of the firm's property, regardless of where the property was located.

First at the end of the Hoover administration in early 1933, and then under Roosevelt in 1934, Congress enacted much of what the reorganizers had asked for. As we discussed in chapter 3, the reforms were preceded by lengthy hearings on the Thacher recommendations (as embodied in the Hastings-Miche-

ner bill) in 1932. Although the 1932 hearings focused on bankruptcy administration, the proposed legislation also called for the codification of corporate
reorganization. Several corporate reorganization lawyers enthusiastically supported the proposed codification. Harold Gallagher, a member of the prominent reorganization firm Hornblower, Miller, Miller & Boston, praised the
proposal for eliminating the need for federal diversity jurisdiction and ancillary
receiverships.[12] (Harold Remington, by contrast, a prominent member of the
general bankruptcy bar, was unenthusiastic both about the reforms in general
and about adding large-scale reorganization to the Bankruptcy Act: "The fact
is," he complained, "the minuteness with which [the reorganization provi-
sion] is done at once spots the amendment as coming from New York, because
it is New York that has always tangled itself up with countless red tape.")[13]

In addition to adding (largely ineffectual) rehabilitation provisions for individuals and small firms and for farmers, the 1933 reform sought, in its initial
incarnation, to codify both railroad reorganization and the reorganization of
other corporations. As he rushed the bill through the Senate, Senator Daniel
Hastings of Delaware dropped the railroad and corporate reorganization sections for fear they would bog down the bill in controversy. Given the large
number of insolvent railroads, he subsequently reversed course with the railroad provision and reintroduced it as part of the bill that Congress forwarded
for President Hoover's signature a few weeks later.[14]

The reorganization bar was generally pleased with the new railroad provisions (called *Section 77*, after the section they added to the Bankruptcy Act).
The new provisions provided for a binding two-thirds vote by classes of creditors, and for nationwide jurisdiction, thus solving the principal problems
with the existing approach. The 1933 amendments also assured a prominent
role for the Interstate Commerce Commission in railroad reorganizations.
Since its inception in 1887, the ICC had extended its tentacles into all aspects
of the railroad industry, from rate regulation (its best-known function) to approval of railroad mergers. The 1933 amendments gave the ICC similarly
broad authority in railroad reorganization. Under the new provisions, the ICC
would propose trustees, set limits on the compensation of lawyers and other
professionals, and, most importantly, pass judgment on any proposed reorganization plan.

To the extent the reorganizers grumbled, they grumbled about the ICC's
new prominence in railroad reorganization. Although the ICC's powers were
not nearly so sweeping as some lawmakers wanted, they promised to increase
the role of governmental oversight to the detriment of private negotiations
among the parties themselves. On the other hand, the reorganizers still fore-
saw a prominent role for themselves, and ICC regulation in other areas had
sometimes created more rather than less need for lawyers.[15]

With railroad reorganization taken care of, Congress turned its attention to
corporate reorganization the following year. Congress's consideration of these

amendments, which became Section 77B of the Bankruptcy Act, was just as rushed as its efforts the previous term. Roosevelt had replaced Hoover in the White House, but the process played out much as it had the year before. At the end of lengthy hearings on the hot button issue of municipal bankruptcy, the House Judiciary Committee added a cursory hearing on the corporate reorganization proposal. The hearing included little more than an introduction by Representative McKeown and a telegram suggesting that the bill would help the Long Bell Lumber Company reorganization in Missouri. In support of the provision, Representative McKeown emphasized that the provision had been "materially improved . . . because it has been submitted to . . . lawyers in the country who are interested . . . in corporate reorganizations [and] . . . those who represent the indebtedness of corporations."[16] The provision was then rushed to the Senate floor for consideration. After a colorful filibuster on the floor of the Senate by Huey Long, who wanted farm relief, Congress enacted it.

From the reorganizers' perspective, section 77B was an even greater success than the railroad provisions had been. In addition to binding dissenters and ending the need for ancillary receiverships, Section 77B provided a firm jurisdictional basis for reorganizing firms other than railroads. The unsettling statements in recent Supreme Court opinions would soon be a thing of the past. Best of all, in some respects, was that Congress left the process entirely to the parties themselves. Unlike the railroad provisions, the new corporate reorganization amendment did not provide for any additional governmental oversight.

Given the depth of the economic crisis, the fact that Congress passed a set of bankruptcy reforms designed to smooth the reorganization process for distressed railroads and corporations seems understandable. The populist impulse to protect troubled debtors—especially individuals, but often corporate debtors, too—is strongest when the economy is at its worst. Echoing the populist defense of free silver in the hearings on the 1898 act, some commentators went so far as to suggest that lawmakers' only real choices for restoring the economy during the Great Depression were to inflate the currency, pass bankruptcy reform, or to do both. "The enactment of [a] new bankruptcy law," according to the title of one article, "will check the tendency toward currency inflation."[17]

From another perspective, however, Congress's homage to existing practice could not have been more surprising. The bête noire of the New Deal reformers, from the very first days of the New Deal, was Wall Street bankers and lawyers. By the end of 1934, the reformers had already embarked on an ambitious program to destroy the Wall Street banks' apparent monopoly on American finance. The Securities Act of 1933 and Securities Exchange Act of 1934 gave the SEC broad powers to police the markets and sought to demystify the issuance and trading of securities by imposing stringent new disclosure requirements. Even more sweeping were the New Deal banking reforms. Of these, the Glass-Steagall Act, which prohibited banks from engaging in both commercial and investment banking, was already in place by mid-1933. The 1933 and 1934 bankruptcy reforms offer a striking contrast to this overall project. At the same time that an activist Congress sought to ensure that the Wall Street bankers would be—in William Douglas's barbed word—"superceded," Congress also passed a set of bankruptcy reforms that put the Wall Street–dominated receivership practice on much firmer ground.

This irony was not lost on everyone. In a 1934 letter to William Douglas, E. Merrick Dodd, a prominent Columbia law professor and enthusiastic advocate of the New Deal, complained that the corporate reorganization reform Congress was about to enact did almost nothing to address the abuses of the current receivership process. Dodd had drafted a lengthy memo criticizing the proposed amendments, and he invited Douglas both to comment on the memo and to join Dodd's opposition to the reform. In response to this call to arms, Douglas demurred. It is never advisable to fight something with nothing, Douglas advised. Rather than wage a rearguard action against the current proposals, the reformers should wait until they had developed concrete proposals of their own. "[A]ny opposition," he concluded, "would be more effective if it envisaged a rather definite alternative."[18]

As of early 1934, then, the reformers simply were not ready to inject the New Deal vision into bankruptcy. But the time for bankruptcy was on the horizon. Shortly after the exchange between Dodd and Douglas, the reformers planted the seed that would give rise to the SEC's contribution to the Chandler Act of 1938. Buried in the Securities Exchange Act of 1934, which created the SEC and gave it rather than the FTC jurisdiction over the securities laws, was a provision instructing the SEC to investigate and report on the protective committees used in corporate and railroad receiverships.[19] (Because the protective committees set up by Wall Street professionals lay at the heart of equity receivership practice, the charge to investigate protective committees was, in effect, an instruction to scrutinize every aspect of large-scale reorganization.) Although the reorganization study would tie the reformers' hands for several years, it also offered several crucial benefits. Most obviously, the findings of the study could be used to buttress the case for subsequent reform. Rather than political arguments alone, the reformers could point to the study's findings to demonstrate the need for reform. Separating bankruptcy from the other reforms also reduced the risk that the interest groups harmed by different New Deal proposals would join together to form a single, concerted opposition.[20] If the reforms were introduced as a unified package, the reformers would face the collective wrath of the Wall Street bankers affected by the financial reforms, the stock market professionals targeted by the market reforms, and the Wall Street reorganization lawyers who would be stung by the

New Deal vision for bankruptcy. The strategy was to divide and conquer, and in the short run at least, it proved marvelously effective.

William Douglas and the SEC Report

Headed by Joseph Kennedy, the father of the future president, the SEC itself was brand new in 1934. One of the first tasks of the new agency was to select the person who would oversee its protective committee study. As the SEC and its staff considered possible appointees, they quickly gravitated toward a single name: William Douglas. Prior to the Donovan and Thacher investigations, Douglas had undertaken an extensive study of bankruptcy cases in Massachusetts and New Jersey during his years as a law professor at Yale. Working with Judge Samuel Clark of New Jersey, Douglas had sent questionnaires to hundreds of bankruptcy debtors in order to determine, among other things, why they had failed and whether they received a discharge. In a press release issued in 1930, classically Progressive in its tone, Douglas expressed the hope that the information developed by the study "respecting causes of failures" would lead to "more scientific legislation in the bankruptcy field."[21] Douglas's study fit neatly within the efforts of the Donovan and Thacher reports, and he was both a participant in, and enthusiastic supporter of, the Thacher proposals.

In addition to his study of individual and small-business bankruptcy, Douglas conducted a study of medium-sized equity receiverships, and he had written extensively on the new securities laws.[22] Although Douglas's initial securities law scholarship was viewed by some observers as quite sympathetic to the Wall Street banks that dominated large-scale finance, he had already begun to adopt a more critical stance by 1934. (We will consider the question *why* Douglas's views shifted so dramatically at the end of the chapter—as we shall see, two important factors seem to have been Douglas's ambition for political advancement and the influence of several prominent New Dealer friends.)

Douglas's extensive study of bankruptcy filings, together with his work on corporate law and railroad reorganization, made him an obvious choice to oversee the protective committee study.[23] He also had impeccable New Deal credentials. As a law professor at Columbia and now Yale, Douglas knew and worked with several key members of Roosevelt's "Brain Trust," and he had been deeply involved in the reformers' discussions on corporate law reform from the very beginning. In an exchange with Brain Truster Adolph Berle, a Columbia University law professor, Douglas told Berle, "You can count on me to pull an oar" in the effort to establish federal control over corporate law, which had long been regulated by the states.[24] It did not hurt that Douglas had been described as "the outstanding professor of law in the nation."[25] In early 1934, Commissioner James Landis contacted Douglas on behalf of Kennedy and offered him the post. From the moment Douglas accepted, he became the administration's point person on bankruptcy. By 1937, when he became SEC chairman, he spoke for the administration on corporate and financial issues generally.

Douglas wasted no time assembling a staff, and the work of the committee took on a frenetic pace. Douglas wanted Abe Fortas, who was working for prominent New Dealer Jerome Frank at the Agricultural Adjustment Administration, to serve as his second-in-command. "What soon transpired," as recounted by Douglas's biographer, "was an extraordinary exchange of letters between Douglas and Frank, in which Douglas, with an impressive combination of audacity, good humor and persistence, wrenched Fortas away from his protesting employer."[26] Fortas, who like Douglas would later become a Supreme Court justice, began by developing an extensive questionnaire, which the SEC's investigators sent to the lawyers and banks in nearly every large reorganization case in the country. The investigators supplemented these questionnaires by interviewing many of the same professionals in person. Although Fortas and Douglas were often in different places, Fortas reported regularly to Douglas on developments in the study, and the two exchanged frequent notes on sensitive issues such as the question whether the committee had the power to subpoena reluctant witnesses.

Before they completed the investigation, Douglas and his investigators questioned many of the leading lawyers and bankers in the country. Both John Foster Dulles, the future secretary of state, and Samuel Untermyer, who was well known for his role as counsel to an earlier congressional investigation, were subjected to withering scrutiny in connection with the collapse of the Kreuger and Toll business empire. Douglas claimed in his often apocryphal autobiography that Robert Swaine, the prominent reorganization lawyer and Douglas's former boss, felt as though he had been held upside down and shaken "until all of his fillings fell out" after Douglas finishing his questioning.[27]

To paraphrase from the movie *Casablanca*, Douglas, Fortas, and the staff were shocked, simply shocked at what their investigation revealed. Like everyone else, the reorganizers already knew that receivership proceedings were dominated by the Wall Street investment bankers who set up and ran the protective committees used to effect a reorganization, together with their Wall Street lawyers. Douglas, as we have seen, had personally participated in the practice. It was not so much their dominance that drew the reformers' ire, though this surely was a contributing factor, as the extent to which the bankers and lawyers seemed to further their own interests rather than those of their clients. The bankers paid themselves generous fees for running the reorganization, including a substantial underwriting fee when the firm issued new securities to its old investors. The lawyers, too, received their fees before anyone else was paid, and, because the cases sometimes lasted several years, the lawyers' fees might run to millions of dollars. The bankers and lawyers were further compromised by their relationship, which usually predated bankruptcy, with the managers of the troubled firm. Rather than vigorously pursuing litigation against managers who had mismanaged the firm—litigation that could put a few more dollars back in investors' pockets—the bankers and lawyers simply looked the other way.[28]

Much of the SEC's report consisted of case studies that explored these problems in vivid detail. The first case study, the reorganization of Paramount Pictures, recounts the efforts of a minority group, led by Harold A. Fortington, who represented a group of insurance companies, to challenge the hegemony of Paramount's investment bankers over the reorganization process.[29] The report suggests that Fortington sought to minimize the expenses of the receivership and to pursue litigation alleging that Paramount's board of directors had caused Paramount to improperly repurchase stock prior to bankruptcy. But Paramount's directors cut a deal with the dissidents, the challenge petered out, and Paramount's bankers and their lawyers enjoyed all of the benefits to which they were accustomed. "The history of this group," the SEC report concluded, "illustrates how those who enter the reorganization in the independent advocacy of the interests of the real owners can readily take unto themselves the spoils of victory." The general pattern—and the scathing conclusions—are repeated in one case study after another.

The SEC report attacked the Wall Street banks and bar at every turn and sounded a call for sweeping reform. "Managements and bankers seek perpetuation of [their] control for the business patronage it commands," the report complained, "which they take for themselves or allot to others, as they will. They seek also to perpetuate that control in order to stifle careful scrutiny of the past history of the corporation. Thereby, claims based on fraud or mismanagement are stilled."[30] The report was equally critical of the elite bankruptcy bar. "[C]ounsel fees frequently constitute the largest single item on the list of reorganization fees," the report noted. "The vice is that the bar has been charging all that the traffic will bear. It has forsaken the tradition that its members are officers of the court, and should request and expect only modest fees."

The Wall Street bar was suitably outraged. Abe Fortas's account to Douglas of a visit by Cravath's Robert Swaine, the nation's most prominent reorganization lawyer, to Fortas's reorganization class at Yale Law School illustrates the depth of the hostility that the SEC report aroused. "Approximately an hour and a half was taken up with a defense of himself and an attack of Part I of our report," Fortas reported. "[Swaine] assured the boys that Part I designated him as a liar and a perjurer; he pointed out the many sections in which, according to his interpretation, he was accused of avarice. He entered a most vigorous denial of all the charges."[31]

Were Swaine and his peers, and the investment bankers they served, as ruthless and unprincipled as the SEC report suggested? Perhaps, but the report's most sweeping claims of abuse almost certainly were overstated. (Douglas himself acknowledged in a congressional hearing that the report was "in the nature of briefs.")[32] Consider how an investment bank such as J. P. Morgan that wished to protect its own interests would look at receivership. As a firm's principal investment banker, Morgan could usually count on controlling, or at least influencing, the protective committee process. Morgan and its peers might plausibly have used their influence to fleece the widely scattered investors of a troubled firm. But the bankers had a strong reputational interest in treating investors fairly. If J. P. Morgan routinely profited at the expense of the bondholders who bought the bonds it had underwritten, investors would remember this the next time J. P. Morgan tried to sell bonds. Investors would demand higher interest rates to offset the risk that J. P. Morgan would serve itself rather than them if the firm later failed. Because they knew they would be underwriting countless future bond issuances, bankers like J. P. Morgan had a strong incentive to establish and protect a reputation for fair dealing. Recent empirical evidence on J. P. Morgan's influence in other contexts seems to confirm these intuitions: firms with a J. P. Morgan partner on their board of directors performed appreciably better than their counterparts without Morgan directors.[33]

The experience of bondholders—the investors that Douglas and the SEC feared were especially vulnerable—offers additional evidence that conditions may not have been so bleak as the SEC findings suggest. Not only did bondholders as a whole fare quite well during this period, but distressed bonds were often undervalued at the time of default—that is, they performed better than expected after default. According to a classic study of bonds issued from 1900 to 1943, "some of the best buys in the bond market during the period covered by the study were low-grade bonds near the date of default,"[34] which suggests that the effects of default were not as devastating as the SEC report might suggest.

Although these observations suggest that the SEC's conclusions should not simply be taken at face value, there may also have been an element of truth to the findings. Even if J. P. Morgan generally protected investors' interests, the bank and its lawyers might still have parlayed their influence into lucrative fees. So long as the fees were a relatively small percentage of the reorganized firm's assets, Wall Street professionals could treat themselves well without risking serious punishment by the market.[35]

Whatever the precise mix of accuracy and imagination, the SEC's attack resonated deeply at a time when much of the public viewed Wall Street with suspicion. The New Deal reformers already had tapped into this populist hostility to pass the Glass-Steagall Act and other banking reforms, as well as the securities acts of 1933 and 1934. The SEC report led the New Deal charge into bankruptcy. Nothing less, the report insisted, than ousting managers in favor of an independent trustee and curbing the role of Wall Street professionals would suffice to loosen Wall Street's stranglehold on large-scale corporate reorganization. These recommendations would eventually become Chapter X of the Chandler Act of 1938.

The Sabath, Chandler, and Lea Bills

The SEC reforms were so dramatic, and so important, that we will want to consider the key provisions as enacted in Chapter X at greater length. But before we do this, we first should take a closer look at the legislative history and the strategic choices William Douglas made once the findings of the SEC report were in place. It turns out that the Chandler bill was only one of three different bills that proposed to add extensive governmental oversight to bankruptcy. The SEC's decision to cast its lot with the Chandler bill would have a great deal to do with the SEC's initial success in transforming corporate reorganization practice; it also would contribute (as we will see in chapter 6) to the eventual demise of the SEC's vision for bankruptcy.

The first of the three bills was the Sabath bill, named for its sponsor, Representative Adolf Sabath of Illinois. The Sabath bill grew out of a lengthy investigation of real estate reorganization practice that documented abuses in Chicago and several other cities. The committee uncovered evidence that several Chicago judges routinely gave lucrative trustee appointments to relatives and friends. The investigation had been rocky at times, and Sabath was slow to translate his findings into specific reforms. "After two days," the *New York World-Telegram* gasped in late 1934, "the committee suspends hearings and goes into a huddle, with little or nothing accomplished! So far Chairman Sabath and his fellow committeemen have shown themselves singularly vague and unprepared in tackling their job here."[36] Although his perspective should perhaps be discounted, for reasons that will become apparent below, Abe Fortas claimed to William Douglas that the Sabath investigation was even more troubled than the newspaper accounts suggested. "I understand," he wrote, "that these write-ups are an understatement of the actual condition existing."[37]

Nevertheless, by 1936 Sabath and his committee had developed and held hearings on a set of proposed reforms. The centerpiece of the Sabath bill was a proposal to establish a new bankruptcy "conservator" who would perform many of the functions that the Donovan and Thacher reports had envisioned in their unsuccessful efforts to create a bankruptcy administrator earlier in the decade.[38] Located in the Department of Justice, the conservator would have wide-ranging powers to police the bankruptcy process. The conservator and his staff would examine the debtors in personal bankruptcy cases, for instance, and also would review any reorganization plan proposed for a corporate debtor. The goal of the Sabath approach was to interpose a governmental overseer in place of the existing approach to bankruptcy administration, which, in permitting the parties themselves to select trustees and other officials, had led to cronyism, patronage appointments, and other evils.

Because it proposed to overhaul the existing Bankruptcy Act, the Sabath bill was assigned to the Judiciary Committee, which had had jurisdiction over bankruptcy legislation since early in the nineteenth century. (The choice of committees is a factor that will figure prominently in our postmortem on the Chandler Act era in chapter 6.)

The second of the three bills was the one that would eventually pass, the Chandler bill. As we have seen, the Chandler bill developed as a collaboration between Senator Chandler of Tennessee and the National Bankruptcy Conference. The antecedents of the bill dated back to the formation of the conference in 1932, and Representative Chandler had begun holding hearings on an early version of the bill in 1935. The Chandler bill, like the Sabath bill, was assigned to the Judiciary Committee, and Representative Chandler was himself a member of that committee.

A final bill, the Lea bill (named for its sponsor, Representative Clarence Lea), emerged slightly later than the other serious proposals for insolvency reform.[39] Introduced in early 1937, the Lea bill differed from the Sabath and Chandler bills in subtle but crucial respects. Unlike the two bankruptcy bills, the Lea bill came directly from the SEC and reflected the SEC vision in undiluted form. Rather than targeting all of bankruptcy, the Lea bill focused only on firms that had issued securities to the public—that is, large, publicly held corporations. (These, of course, were precisely the firms that the Wall Street bankers and lawyers had used equity receiverships to reorganize, and which were not added to the Bankruptcy Act until 1933 and 1934.) The Lea bill called for sweeping regulation of the protective committee process. In order to undermine Wall Street bankers' advantages in organizing the committees, the Lea bill gave the SEC wide-ranging authority over the deposit agreements pursuant to which investors ceded control over their securities to a committee. Bankers were prohibited from seeking deposits until the SEC had approved the agreement; lists of the names and addresses of depositors would be publicly available; and, most dramatic of all, any investment bank that had unwritten securities for the debtor prior to bankruptcy was disqualified from serving on a protective committee in bankruptcy.

The Lea bill was framed as amendments to the Securities Act of 1933. Although the Lea bill treated issues central to the reorganization process, it viewed everything through the lens of publicly issued securities and the concern to protect small investors. Unlike the Sabath and Chandler bills, the Lea bill was therefore assigned to the Senate Banking and House Interstate Commerce Committees, which had jurisdiction over the securities laws. (The pattern of assigning securities law issues to a different committee in the Senate—the Banking Committee—than in the House—Interstate Commerce—

dates to a jurisdictional squabble from 1933, when Congress held the hearings that led to the Securities Act of 1933.)[40]

These, then, were the principal bankruptcy bills that would work their way through Congress in the mid-1930s. The Sabath bill proved in some respects to be a throwback to the initial Donovan and Thacher efforts to reengineer bankruptcy; and the Chandler Act represented the bankruptcy bar's proposals (through the National Bankruptcy Conference) for "perfecting" the existing regime. The Lea bill differed both in its exclusive focus on large corporations that had issued publicly held securities, and in its assignment to the Senate Banking and House Commerce Committees, rather than the Judiciary Committee.

In late 1936, the SEC neared completion of the first volume of its protective committee study. In addition to case studies, the initial volume would summarize the SEC's findings and recommendations. With the basic findings of the report in place, Douglas decided it was time to strike.

The two bills making their way through Congress as the SEC prepared to dive in were the first two we considered, the Sabath bill and the Chandler bill. At first glance, one might have expected the SEC to join forces with the drafters of the Sabath bill. Unlike the Chandler bill, which consisted of a large number of mostly technical changes drafted by lawyers with little obvious connection to the New Deal vision, the Sabath bill called for the kind of governmental intervention that characterized many New Deal efforts. The conservator would police everyone, from the attorneys and trustees to the debtors, and would focus on investor protection in the larger cases. In reality, the SEC viewed the Sabath bill quite differently. The SEC's public response to the Sabath bill was tepid, at best; and the private correspondence among William Douglas, Abe Fortas, and others reveals active hostility to the bill.

The explanation for the SEC's hostility was quite simple. The SEC and Sabath investigations covered very similar ground (both covered the activities of protective committees in real estate insolvencies, for instance), and the SEC saw the Sabath committee, which was already under way when the SEC study got started, as a threat to its project from the beginning. The committees had gone through the motions of coordinating their efforts. Shortly after his appointment to run the SEC study, Douglas sent a letter to Representative Sabath proposing that they compare notes, and Joseph Kennedy, the chairman of the SEC, sent a very similar letter two weeks later.[41] There is little evidence of real collaboration between the two committees, however, and substantial evidence to the contrary. By January 1935, a member of the SEC staff had learned that at least one member of the Sabath committee had "suggested introducing a bill in the House of Representatives, called a preemptive bill, which in effect would nullify the authority which the [SEC] study now has to investigate the reorganization of real estate bonds."[42] The competition between the two investigations destroyed any real chance of cooperation, and by late 1935, Abe Fortas expressed the concern that the friction between the two committees might provoke each to sabotage any bill proposed by the other. "I think we are confronted with a very serious situation," he suggested darkly to Douglas. "I . . . believe that it is vital to pursue some course of action which will assure us that our legislation will receive adequate consideration and that the fruits of our study will not be lost."[43]

The bill that Sabath proposed did little to ease the tensions. The conservator, rather than the SEC, would serve as the primary overseer in bankruptcy. There were plausible reasons for limiting the SEC's role. Sabath's conservator would oversee every bankruptcy debtor, for instance, both individuals and corporations, whereas the SEC's mandate extended only to large corporations whose securities were held by widely scattered investors. However logical this reasoning might be, the SEC could not be expected to generate much enthusiasm for a bill that largely sidestepped the expertise of the SEC. The SEC's hostility was fully shared by the bankruptcy bar. Like previous efforts to establish a bankruptcy administrator, the Sabath bill embodied a frontal assault on existing practice. The bankruptcy bar trotted out its usual defenders, and each of them dutifully lambasted the conservator proposal as exorbitantly expensive and unnecessary.

The Sabath bill was, as a result, a sinking ship that had nothing to offer the SEC when the SEC entered the fray. Rather than joining the Sabath effort, the SEC drafted the Lea bill and, shortly thereafter, suddenly intervened in the Chandler bill deliberations, asking Chandler and the National Bankruptcy Conference to include the SEC's proposed reforms to large-scale reorganization as part of the Chandler bill. Although the National Bankruptcy Conference formally agreed to include the SEC proposals, the members were sharply divided. As recounted by John Gerdes:

> At a meeting of the conference, held [in December 1936], a subcommittee, consisting of Professor [James] McLaughlin, [Jacob] Weinstein, and [Referee Watson] Adair, was appointed to confer with the Securities and Exchange Commission to find out what changes it intended to recommend in corporate reorganization and to try to agree on a statute upon which both groups could unite. . . . The recommendations of this subcommittee [to agree to include the provisions that became Chapter X] were considered at a meeting of the National Bankruptcy Conference held in March [1937]. Copies of the proposed changes were not sent to the members of the conference with the notice of the meeting. There are 44 members of the conference. . . . Only 14 out of 44 members of the conference attended the meeting. These new provisions—highly controversial, as they were—were adopted in practically every instance by a majority of one, or two at the most.[44]

Like Gerdes, several other members of the National Bankruptcy Conference joined the corporate bankruptcy bar in attacking the SEC proposals—particularly the proposal to replace a firm's managers with an independent trustee in every case—during the hearings on the Chandler bill. In his overview of the hearings, Reuben Hunt, a leading member of the general bankruptcy bar, characterized "these new and radical changes" as having been "vigorously defended by Messrs. Douglas and Riger of the SEC," and "as vigorously opposed by Attorneys John Gerdes, Edwin S. S. Sunderland, David Teitelbaum and Irving Ernst, prominent attorneys of New York." In contrast to the attorneys, "all of whom . . . had considerable practical experience in corporate reorganization matters," the article noted rather pointedly about the SEC reformers that "none of them have had a great deal of practical experience in corporate reorganization matters."[45]

At roughly the same time, the House Commerce Committee held hearings on the Lea bill. Everyone involved treated the two bills as part of an overall package, with the Chandler bill focusing on bankruptcy-specific issues such as the appointment of an independent trustee, and the Lea bill regulating bankers' use of protective committees and deposit agreements to restructure the terms of publicly issued securities. (The package also included a third bill, which proposed to regulate the indenture agreements that governed publicly issued bonds, and which eventually became the Trust Indenture Act of 1939. We will briefly consider this legislation later in the chapter, but for now we can put it to one side.) Much as lawyers spoke out against the SEC in the Chandler bill hearings, investment bankers criticized the SEC's Lea bill proposals as far too draconian. After voicing his support for stronger disclosure requirements, for instance, a representative of the Investment Bankers Association of America complained that the Lea proposals went far beyond this; in effect, they instructed the SEC to pass judgment on the fairness of deposit agreements and invited it to second-guess the parties' contractual agreements.[16]

In response to the opposition from Wall Street bankers and the elite reorganization bar, the SEC had a series of strategic decisions to make. The most obvious question was whether to tone down the SEC proposals in order to achieve a compromise; the SEC also faced a choice whether to continue to push both the Lea and Chandler bills, or focus principally on one or the other. It is important to underscore that each of these decisions was strategic in nature and might have been made differently. The political science literature on public choice sometimes seems to assume that congressional legislation simply replicates the relative strengths of the interest groups that have a stake in the issues involved: what goes into the process is precisely what comes out, once it is suitably mixed in the legislative blender. In reality, the decisions of particular individuals often play a crucial role, and the 1930s bankruptcy reforms are a prime example.

To see this, consider the road not taken, a theme we will revisit in more detail when we explore the SEC's eventual decline in bankruptcy in chapter 6. William Douglas, who at this time was SEC chair and the Roosevelt administration's leading strategist on bankruptcy issues, could have scaled back some of the most dramatic reforms and, since the SEC study grew out of the new securities law, made a special effort to ensure that the Lea bill, the only bill truly rooted in the securities laws, was enacted. As just noted, reorganization lawyers and investment bankers pleaded throughout the Lea bill hearings for the SEC to soften some of its reforms in favor of a disclosure-based approach like that of the securities laws. Both in the Chandler Act hearings and in the hearings on the Lea bill, Wall Street professionals acknowledged that SEC oversight might improve the reorganization process, but they insisted that the most dramatic reforms, such as displacement of the firm's managers in favor of an independent trustee, would prove counterproductive. Douglas, of course, had no interest in (or incentive for) placating Wall Street, but one could easily imagine him and the SEC softening the mandatory trustee requirement (perhaps the trustee might investigate the debtor's business, but leave the debtor's managers in place to run it) in the Chandler Act and tinkering with the Lea bill enough to ensure its passage. The Lea bill might naturally have provided the basis for the SEC's involvement in large reorganizations.[47]

Douglas had little sympathy for serious conciliation, however. Douglas wanted to hit a home run—to devastate existing reorganization practice, not just to clean it up—and he believed the best way to do this was to keep bankruptcy reform outside of the securities laws. In an exchange with Adolph Berle several years earlier, Douglas had complained that the Securities Act of 1933 was "a rather laborious and untimely effort to turn back the clock and quite antithetical to many of the other significant current developments."[48] Douglas's distaste for disclosure-based regulation, and his commitment to more aggressive governmental intervention, grew even stronger as the New Deal wore on. Isolating bankruptcy from the securities acts helped to assure that the less draconian approach of the securities laws would not influence the philosophy of the bankruptcy reforms. Probably more importantly, working within the Chandler Act enabled him to create a temporary alliance with the National Bankruptcy Conference and the bankruptcy bar.

Partially neutralizing an important interest group was a strategy Douglas would also employ with the Trust Indenture Act of 1939. There he struck a shaky but effective deal with the commercial bankers' lobbying organization, the American Bankers Association, just as he did with bankruptcy lawyers and the National Bankruptcy Conference in the Chandler Act. In each case, he seems to have made a few small concessions to mollify the group in question. With the bankruptcy bar, Douglas apparently agreed to limit the SEC to an advisory role, rather than insisting on sweeping authority of the sort the Interstate Commerce Commission enjoyed in railroad reorganizations.[49] On the most dramatic provision, however, the mandatory trustee requirement, however, Douglas refused to budge.

Underwriting the effort was the widespread New Deal aversion to Wall Street and large Democratic majorities in the House and Senate. In the brief congressional debates on the Chandler Act, Senator King of Utah denounced Chapter X at length, complaining that it "contained provisions which would prevent reorganization[, . . .] novel, extreme, and wholly unjust and unfair provisions which would destroy many corporations that were entitled to reorganization and prove injurious not only to stockholders and creditors, but to employees and the public generally."[50] But no one bothered to respond to his complaints, and the legislation was quickly passed.

Although Douglas's Chandler Act strategy would eventually prove costly for the SEC, it was a smashing success in the short run. The SEC's reforms were incorporated in the Chandler Act with very little modification. The world of large-scale corporate reorganization would soon become a very different place, and the SEC's bankruptcy project had a great deal to do with this.

THE CHANDLER ACT APPROACH TO CORPORATE REORGANIZATION

Having recounted in overview how Douglas and the SEC transformed the nature of corporate reorganization, injecting pervasive governmental oversight into a practice that previously had consisted largely of private arrangements, this section gets down to the gritty detail of just how the SEC proposals altered corporate reorganization. Readers who are interested more in the general narrative than in the technical details should feel free to skip over this section. But the detail is well worth understanding, and I will try to keep the description clear.

Recall that, in describing the emergence of corporate reorganization, chapter 2 analogized the reorganizers' heady, early days to homeowners who leave only the foundation in place as they rebuild their house. To overextend the metaphor a bit, Chapter X of the Chandler Act agreed, in effect, that the family could rebuild its house. But the moment it committed to start rebuilding, a government official would step in and would make all of the decisions as to what would be done. To rebuild was to put the house in someone else's hands.

The defining provision was the one we have seen, the principle on which Douglas had adamantly refused to give ground: mandatory trustees. Whenever a firm with at least $250,000 in liabilities filed for bankruptcy, the Chandler Act called for an independent trustee. Unlike the world the reorganizers had known, where firms' existing managers had continued to run the business while their bankers ran the reorganization, the Chandler Act turned both of these responsibilities over to the trustee. The act gave the trustee explicit authority to take over the business activities of the bankrupt firm; and the new law took the power to formulate a reorganization plan out of the hands of the creditors and vested it in the trustee. Creditors and other parties could, in theory, make suggestions to the trustee; but the trustee, and the trustee alone, was the one who would develop the terms of any reorganization.[51]

The SEC reforms made clear that the firms' bankers and their attorneys were precluded from either serving as the trustee or advising the trustee. The key provision was a requirement that the trustee be "disinterested." The definition of disinterestedness explicitly excluded anyone who had served as "an underwriter of any of the outstanding securities of the debtor." Lest Robert Swaine and his peers in the reorganization bar slip through the cracks, Chapter X also required that the trustee's attorney satisfy a closely analogous disinterestedness requirement.[52] In short, Chapter X insisted that the trustee and its advisors be outsiders, with no significant prebankruptcy connection to the bankrupt firm. (Swaine denounced this requirement as assuring that the process would be managed and the business run by someone who knew nothing about the operations of the firm.)[53]

In addition to the power it vested in the mandatory trustee, the new law included a variety of other measures aimed at the Wall Street banks. One source of the bankers' influence had been their informational advantage. As the underwriter of a debtor's securities, the firm's bank knew who all of its security holders were and, as a result, had an enormous head start when it came time to organize a protective committee on their behalf. J. P. Morgan had a list (or could easily compile one) of all the investors who held a class of bonds it had underwritten. If the corporation ran into trouble, Morgan knew whom to contact and how to contact them as it tried to round up investors to form a protective committee. Lacking this access, outside groups faced a substantial disadvantage if they wished to set up a competing committee. By refusing to share the list, banks made it very difficult for their competition. The new law (as reinforced by comparable provisions in the Trust Indenture Act of 1939) cut through this cozy arrangement by authorizing the court to insist that the bankers divulge the list.[54]

Even more dramatic were the new requirements for soliciting votes on a reorganization plan. Chapter X prohibited anyone from soliciting either the acceptance of a plan, or the right to accept a plan, until *after* the court entered an order approving the plan in question.[55] To appreciate how dramatically this altered the traditional process, recall that the whole point of the protective committee process had been to "solicit . . . the right to accept a plan" by lining up "deposits" before the bargaining began. Under long-standing practice, J. P. Morgan or Kuhn, Loeb would contact the troubled firm's outstanding bondholders and ask them to deposit their securities with a protective committee. If she deposited her bond, the bondholder was giving the protective committee the right to accept a reorganization plan on her behalf. In effect, Chapter X completely reversed the timing of the process. Whereas the protective committee approach assumed that security holders would commit to the process first and that the parties *then* would negotiate the terms of the reorganization, the new law required that the plan be proposed and approved by the court before anyone could commit to it. As a result, nothing the Wall Street banks might do before bankruptcy could have any effect.

The obvious cost of these changes—as implied in Swaine's complaint that the principal qualification of the mandatory trustee was ignorance—was that the new regime sacrificed the bank underwriters' familiarity with the debtor and reputational incentive to protect the security holders of bonds it had underwritten. The reformers questioned whether banks really protected the investors, however, as we have seen. Moreover, court oversight alone would not solve the problem, because the court did not become involved until too late in the process—after the parties had completed their negotiations and sought approval of the plan.[56] Prohibiting prebankruptcy solicitations, the reformers believed, would give the court a much more meaningful role by forcing the parties to obtain the court's blessing *before* they started soliciting votes.

Where there is regulation, of course, there will be efforts to circumvent it. The SEC anticipated this and used the companion bill that became the Trust Indenture Act of 1939 to address a potential limitation of the Chandler Act. The limitation was this: even if the Chandler Act shut down the traditional reorganization process once a firm filed for bankruptcy, the bankers and reorganization bar could still play a role in any restructuring that took place entirely outside of bankruptcy. By persuading a firm's public bondholders to accept less than full payment, and perhaps to postpone the repayment schedule, reorganizers might help the firm adjust its capital structure without actually filing for bankruptcy. Coordinating thousands and sometimes millions of bondholders without the procedural advantages of bankruptcy would be difficult, especially given that each bondholder had the right to insist on being paid in full, but the investment banks had already devised a way to simplify the process somewhat. During the 1930s, issuers and their underwriters had begun to include voting provisions in the contracts (*trust indentures*) that governed a publicly issued class of bonds. Under the voting provision, if a majority agreed to scale down the debt, the entire class of bonds was bound, just as in bankruptcy.

The SEC would have nothing of this. At the SEC's urging, Congress passed the Trust Indenture Act a year after the Chandler Act became law. In addition to imposing extensive new obligations on the trustees who acted on bondholders' behalf, the Trust Indenture Act also included a provision, the so-called voting prohibition, that guaranteed each bondholder the individual right to decide whether to restructure the principal payment terms of her bond. Although William Douglas persuaded the American Bankers Association, the leading organization of commercial bankers, not to oppose the Trust Indenture Act, both they and the investment bankers chafed at the voting prohibition. In a speech sent to Douglas for comments, and which generally defended the proposed regulations, the chairman of the mortgage trustee committee of the American Bankers Association warned that the voting provision was "of real importance from the standpoint of the business structure of the country. We have argued [it] fully and regret that we have failed to convince the [SEC]."[57] The bankers' complaints were to no avail. The legislation passed, and the voting prohibition has been in place ever since.[58] Only in bankruptcy could public bondholders be bound by a majority vote; and there, the independent trustee, not J. P. Morgan or Kuhn, Loeb, would be calling the shots.

The SEC also wrote itself into the Chandler Act script, giving itself a prominent role as policeman on investors' behalf of all large-scale corporate reorganizations. The SEC's most important role was to scrutinize every proposed reorganization involving a publicly held corporation. Before the court could approve a reorganization plan for any debtor that had more than $3 million in outstanding obligations, it was required to forward the plan to the SEC "for investigation, examination, or report." The SEC would take the proposed plan under advisement and address issues such as the fairness of the plan, and whether it adequately addressed the firm's underlying problems. In addition to the SEC's explicit role in evaluating proposed plans, Chapter X gave the SEC general authority to weigh in on any issue that arose in the course of the bankruptcy by explicitly defining the SEC as a party in interest.[59]

Under the new system, then, a trustee would take over when a large corporation filed for bankruptcy, and the current managers would be sent packing. The firm's Wall Street underwriters and lawyers could neither serve as trustee, nor attempt to organize its bondholders while everyone waited for the trustee to propose a reorganization plan. Looking over everyone's shoulders to make sure there were no surprises was the SEC. Out were private negotiation and the wiles of Wall Street, in was pervasive governmental oversight.

It is important to emphasize how dramatically this vision of corporate bankruptcy departed from William Douglas's views of only a few years earlier. In a famous exchange with Max Lowenthal in the pages of the *Harvard Law Review* in 1934, Douglas had insisted that the linchpin of effective reorganization was vigorous committees who would negotiate over the terms of the debtor's reorganization plan.[60] The government, he argued, should actively oversee the process, but its role was to police for manipulation or misbehavior, not to involve itself in the details of the negotiations. Chapter X reflected a very different vision. The independent trustee, not the parties, would develop the reorganization plan; and the same reformer who had extolled the virtues of active committees left little role for them in Chapter X.

What lay between Douglas's initial views and his subsequent ones were, of course, the discoveries of the SEC's protective committee investigation. But several other factors also seem to have come into play. One factor was Douglas's friendship with other prominent New Dealers such as Thurmond Arnold and Jerome Frank. Commenting on a draft of Douglas's 1934 *Harvard Law*

Review article, Frank chided Douglas for not having more faith in the virtues of governmental intervention—particularly the role that an agency might play in reorganization. "I am not thoroughly convinced that the technique you advocate is the best one," Frank wrote. "If the [Interstate Commerce] Commission has too many duties to permit it to undertake, on its own, the formation of a Plan, then it seems to me some agency or agencies should be set up with all the powers you advocate."[61] It is quite possible that the apparent shift in Douglas's views owed a great deal to the persuasive powers of advocates of governmental intervention such as Frank.

The second factor was Douglas's ambition. Douglas had his eye on the Supreme Court, and in the New Deal, such aspirations required an unquestioned commitment to governmental control of business and finance. A reputation for being soft on Wall Street could undermine his prospects for advancement (and Douglas was in fact criticized for precisely this when President Roosevelt nominated him for the Supreme Court in 1939).

Whether through the persuasion of Frank and others, or for other reasons, Douglas became an increasingly enthusiastic supporter of New Deal–style intervention. Responding to a suggestion by Professor Felix Frankfurter, a New Dealer who would soon be appointed to the Supreme Court, that Douglas's work "champion[ed] the cause of the Street" and "houses like J. P. Morgan and Kuhn, Loeb," Douglas insisted that Frankfurter was mistaken:

> I still hear Wall St. comment on my article in the December [1933] issue of the Yale Law Journal. It is not what you apparently imagine. . . . They deplore the fact that I have gone 'administrative.' . . . So malign and libel me as you will. I only ask that you give me at least the benefit of a small doubt. And just because I have a deep understanding of corporate finance do not infer that I am [a lackey] for Wall St. The Securities Act will be fully justified if it drives the government into the investment banking business. I wonder how the clients you are trying to thrust upon me would like to hear that?[62]

Three years later, Douglas's efforts to defend Chapter X were a testimony to how far his thinking had evolved. Whatever they thought of his early work, no one could accuse Douglas of coddling Wall Street with the SEC's bankruptcy reforms.

USHERING WALL STREET OUT OF CORPORATE BANKRUPTCY

The best way to appreciate how the Chandler Act affected corporate bankruptcy law in the United States is to put the reforms in larger perspective. The Chandler Act came at the end of a remarkable string of New Deal business reforms, most of which we have already alluded to. The securities acts of 1933 and 1934 injected the SEC into the securities markets. The Glass-Steagall

Act severed commercial banking from investment banking, and other sections of the same legislation set up the deposit insurance system, which now guarantees up to one hundred thousand dollars in any single bank account.

As the SEC's Chandler Act reforms neared enactment, Douglas assured President Roosevelt that Chapter X would further advance this project. "[T]he reorganization study and investigation," he promised, "is now culminating in a comprehensive legislative program which should go far towards carrying into the reorganization field the high standards for finance which you have sponsored."[63] In retrospect, it is clear that the Chandler Act played a crucial role in the overall New Deal project. Drawing in no small part on the populist hostility to Wall Street that had been stoked by the depression, the New Deal banking reforms were designed to diminish the influence J. P. Morgan and other Wall Street banks had over large-scale finance in the United States, and to prevent them from controlling the governance of nonfinancial firms. In addition to their role as underwriters and at times board members for nonfinancial firms, J. P. Morgan and its peers also dominated the receivership process. If the New Deal reformers had left bankruptcy alone, this piece of the Wall Street influence might have remained at least partially intact. But Chapter X made sure that the banks' role in reorganization was destroyed.

In a sense, even the enactment of the Chandler Act in 1938 did not complete the SEC's Chapter X reforms. In 1939, Douglas was appointed to the Supreme Court to fill the vacancy created by Justice Brandeis's retirement. Douglas almost immediately had several opportunities to further the reformers' project through decisions he wrote for the Court. Two of most important of the decisions interpreted a provision, included in both Chapter X and prior law, that required that any proposed reorganization plan be "fair and equitable."[64] In *Case v. Los Angeles Lumber Products* and again in *Consolidated Rock Products v. DuBois*, Justice Douglas construed "fair and equitable" as a shorthand reference to the absolute priority rule, which requires that higher-priority creditors be paid in full before lower-priority creditors or shareholders can receive any payment from or stake in the reorganized firm. Given the reformers' commitment to absolute priority as a means of preventing senior creditors and shareholders from colluding to squeeze out junior creditors, as discussed in chapter 2, and the fact that nothing else in Chapter X specially required absolute priority, Douglas's somewhat imaginative interpretation of "fair and equitable" added a crucial piece to the Chapter X framework. (The chapter for small firms, Chapter XI, also included the "fair and equitable" requirement, which quickly led to problems because absolute priority did not accord with the rest of the Chapter XI framework, as we will see in chapter 6.)

Justice Douglas was quite proud of the contribution *Los Angeles Lumber Products* made to the SEC's Chandler Act reforms. Shortly before the opinion was published, Douglas described his handiwork in a diary he kept in his early years on the Court:

Nov. 4, 1939. The opinion in Case v. Los Angeles Lumber Products Co. was cleared today. [Chief Justice Hughes] tried to get [Justice] Reed to write a dissent. Reed was tempted but finally declined. So he and the [chief justice] and [Justice] McReynolds acquiesced. The opinion should have a healthy effect and curb the reorganization racketeers—the holding companies and the investment bankers who want to keep their preserves inviolate and under their control.[65]

In his insistence on absolute priority treatment in Chapter X, Douglas hammered one more nail into the coffin of the Wall Street practice that had characterized large-scale reorganization for so many years.

By any plausible yardstick, the Chandler Act reforms had a remarkable and immediate impact. The independent trustee requirement discouraged the managers of large firms from filing for bankruptcy if there was any way to avoid it. Due both to the Chandler Act and the winnowing out that had already occurred as a result of the depression, fewer and fewer large firms filed for bankruptcy. Whereas more than five hundred corporations filed for Chapter X in 1938, the number dropped to sixty-eight in 1944 and fluctuated around one hundred per year for much of the 1950s and 1960s (table 4.1).

For the few cases that remained, the Chandler Act requirements of a "disinterested" trustee and trustee's counsel, together with the prohibition on prebankruptcy solicitations, simply left no room for the Wall Street bankers to participate. Within a few years, the starring role that the Wall Street bankers had played for more than fifty years was a thing of the past. Because the fortunes of the Wall Street reorganization bar had always been tied to those of their clients, the Wall Street law firms disappeared along with the Wall Street banks.

The Chandler Act limited its focus to nonrailroad corporations and left the earlier New Deal reforms in place for railroad reorganization. Although these earlier reforms had dramatically altered railroad reorganization, they did not require the displacement of the railroad's managers and did not prohibit its underwriters and lawyers from participating in the reorganization process. Robert Swaine and his peers would therefore remain on the scene for a few more years.[66] As the number of railroad reorganizations dwindled after World War II, the elite reorganization lawyers slowly faded away.

Ironically, the hard line that Douglas and the reformers took on bankruptcy reform, and that came to such spectacular fruition in the Chandler Act, would eventually undermine the SEC's role in bankruptcy. As we shall see, the Chandler Act left the SEC with little interest group support, and firms started evading Chapter X by filing under Chapter XI, the provisions designed for small firms. In contrast to Chapter X, Chapter XI allowed managers to stay in

TABLE 4.1.
Chapter X Filings, 1945–1970

Year	Cases Filed	Assets ($ millions)	Liabilities ($ millions)
1939	577	550	440
1940	291	1,580	860
1941	291	135	98
1942	165	128	92
1943	109	94	71
1944	95	131	74
1945	70	281	257
1946	60	10	12
1947	94	15	13
1948	105	28	33
1949	113	108	99
1950	102	25	29
1951	75	3	3
1952	64	9	6
1953	61	8	4
1954	90	9	17
1955	80	113	113
1956	61	16	17
1957	71	n/a	n/a
1958	75	n/a	n/a
1959	99	62	39
1960	112	26	28
1961	119	32	28
1962	104	108	86
1963	133	152	143
1964	103	72	70
1965	88	168	150
1966	93	105	109
1967	138	200	131
1968	128	140	120
1969	87	181	154
1970	115	227	156

Source: Hearings on S. 235 and S. 236 before the Subcommittee on Improvements in Judicial Machinery of the Senate Committee on the Judiciary, 94th Cong., 1st sess., 778 (1975).

control, let the firms shareholders retain their stock, and did not provide for SEC oversight. In time, even the largest firms often managed to reorganize under the more hospitable provisions of Chapter XI. But that was much later. For now, the protective committee project seemed an unequivocal success.

It is worth emphasizing one more time the contrasting fortunes of the elite reorganization lawyers and the general bankruptcy bar during the course of the New Deal. The very virtues of the elite bar—its geographical concentration, its elite status—made it particularly vulnerable to the New Deal reformers' ideology-fueled crusade. The general bankruptcy bar, by contrast, had a nationwide presence and made a somewhat more complicated target for populist ire. When the New Deal reformers had completed their work, only the general bankruptcy bar was still standing.

PART THREE

THE REVITALIZATION OF BANKRUPTCY

Chapter Five

RAISING THE BAR WITH THE 1978

BANKRUPTCY CODE

W E COME NOW TO THE LAST of the three eras of American bankruptcy law. As we have seen, the first age, comprising nearly all of the nineteenth century, was an era of tumult. Bankruptcy laws came and went as lawmakers struggled to find a sustainable common ground. Only with the rise of creditor organizations at the end of the century did permanent federal bankruptcy become a reality. The second era arrived in the midst of the Great Depression. In corporate bankruptcy the New Deal injected sweeping governmental controls into a regime that had previously relied on contract and private negotiations, and the reformers ushered the Wall Street banks and bar out of large-scale reorganization. Although concerns about the general bankruptcy bar had inspired the sweeping investigations that first put bankruptcy on the legislative agenda in the 1930s, the general bar emerged from the era largely unscathed. If anything, the Chandler Act of 1938 reinforced and enhanced existing practice.

The touchstone of the current era of American bankruptcy was the 1978 Bankruptcy Code, which has brought the full flowering of bankruptcy law in the United States. In this chapter, we will explore the structural and consumer changes proposed and enacted in the 1978 legislation. We then will turn to the 1978 Code's equally dramatic reforms for large-scale corporate bankruptcy in chapter 6. It is no overstatement to say that the 1978 Code has had a transformative effect on bankruptcy as we know it, so we will want to explore the origins of the Code with some care.

In contrast to its effect on the Wall Street reorganization bar, which was destroyed, the Chandler Act had a relatively modest influence on general bankruptcy practice. It introduced consumer repayment plans—Chapter XIII—and expanded the scope of bankruptcy practice in some respects. The amendments did little, however, to counteract bankruptcy's faintly unsavory reputation—a reputation reinforced by the dominance in most cities of a small cluster of bankruptcy lawyers. Nevertheless, for several decades after the Chandler Act's enactment in 1938, there was no serious push for a more extensive overhaul.

All of this changed in the 1960s. A sharp increase in bankruptcy filings—which pundits attributed to the rise of consumer credit, the diminished stigma of bankruptcy, or some combination of the two—focused increasing attention on the limitations of the existing bankruptcy process. In 1970, Congress appointed a Bankruptcy Commission to conduct a thoroughgoing study of bankruptcy, and the commission's 1973 report served as the starting point for the reforms that Congress finally enacted five years later.

To an almost uncanny extent, the path to the 1978 legislation followed the same course as the bankruptcy reforms of the 1930s. The 1973 commission report served much the same function as Donovan and Thacher reports of the early 1930s, and it, like its predecessors, called for Congress to establish a bankruptcy agency to shoulder much of the oversight responsibility long located in the judicial system. As in the 1930s, bankruptcy professionals—this time, bankruptcy judges in particular—quickly derailed the proposal. The commission also proposed to expand the reach of bankruptcy law and to enhance consumer debtors' access to a discharge. Here, the commission report proved much more influential.

These, in brief compass, are the events we will explore in the discussion that follows. The chapter begins with a brief description of general bankruptcy practice in the years after the Chandler Act was enacted. In addition to the lawyers who handled consumer and small-firm bankruptcies—and who thus had the most at stake in the 1978 Code's structural and consumer provisions— we also will focus on the corporate bankruptcy bar (whose leaders played a surprisingly central role even in the reforms we consider in this chapter), bankruptcy academics, and the consumer interest movement. The second section summarizes the legislative history of the 1978 reforms, and the third considers the political economy of the general and consumer reforms in some detail. Of particular interest is the role of the National Bankruptcy Conference, which did both good and well in the bankruptcy reform process. By keeping the temperature of the debates low, the NBC and the other reform proponents achieved sweeping reform with remarkably little controversy. Although the Democrats controlled both Congress and the presidency, the legislation had widespread support on both sides of the aisle. Only on the question whether bankruptcy judges should be given Article III status—an issue of great concern to other federal judges—did tempers frequently flare.

General Bankruptcy Practice After the 1930s

As we saw in chapter 4, the Chandler Act of 1938 devastated the Wall Street reorganization bar. Within a few years, firms like Cravath, Swaine & Moore and the predecessor of today's Davis, Polk & Wardwell had disappeared from the bankruptcy courts.

For the general bankruptcy bar—that is, bankruptcy lawyers who handled personal and small-firm bankruptcies—the Chandler Act era was, by contrast, more of the same. A bankruptcy lawyer of the 1920s would not have felt significantly out of place if he were suddenly transported to the bankruptcy courts of the 1950s and 1960s.

As we saw in chapter 3, the Chandler Act expanded bankruptcy jurisdiction in a variety of ways, and it also enhanced the decision-making authority of bankruptcy referees by giving them the power to grant discharges. But none of the changes was on anything like the scale of William Douglas's handiwork for large-scale corporate reorganization. Probably the most lasting change to personal bankruptcy was the introduction of consumer repayment plans under Chapter XIII. When Chapter XIII was enacted, lawmakers believed that many debtors would choose this option in order to minimize the stigma of their bankruptcy filing. In reality, most did not, and the percentage of Chapter XIII plans, as compared to immediate discharges, varied dramatically from district to district. Debtors "use Chapter XIII," according to an influential 1971 Brookings Institution study, "only if it is favored by local usage or if it is the preference of their lawyers."[1] In Alabama, whose referees had pioneered the approach, a substantial majority of debtors used Chapter XIII. Elsewhere, the reverse was true, as most debtors sought an immediate discharge.

The dark side of the continuity in general bankruptcy practice was, not surprisingly, continued complaints that urban bankruptcy practice was controlled by "bankruptcy rings." In the 1940s and thereafter, the Bankruptcy Act still authorized creditors to select the trustee for each case, and the Chandler Act had done nothing to prevent bankruptcy lawyers from soliciting proxies for the election.

The *Commercial Law Journal*, the principal journal of the general bankruptcy bar, offers powerful (and somewhat embarrassed) testimony to the seriousness of the perceived problem. Writing in 1950, Charles Nadler, a longtime bankruptcy lawyer who had recently become an academic, apologized at length to his readers before raising the "hush-hush subject of Solicitation in Bankruptcy Matters."[2] An enthusiast for allegorical stories, Nadler opened his remarks by suggesting that, unless he first made clear his love for bankruptcy and bankruptcy practice, he would find himself "very much in the same position as those talkative women who buttonholed a fisherman who was minding his own business and said 'Aren't you ashamed of yourself?' "

> "A great fellow like you might be better occupied than in cruelly catching little fish like these." "Maybe you're right, lady," the fisherman replied tartly, "but if these fish had kept their mouths shut they wouldn't be here."

Having thus introduced "the ticklish and controversial question of the propriety of solicitation," Nadler went on to suggest that perhaps the bankruptcy bar should take at least modest steps to clean up its act. Perhaps a middle ground would be possible. Although prohibiting all "solicitation in bankruptcy matters definitely defeats the fundamental function and operation of this 'creditors' court,' " Nadler contended, "[i]t must be conceded that unrestrained and unrestricted solicitation in bankruptcy matters is, to say the very least, undignified and dishonorable."[3] Nadler concluded by urging the Commercial Law League to "courageously and formally adopt[]" a rule that had been developed by the Northern District of Ohio, and that permitted bankruptcy lawyers to solicit creditors' proxies only if they had already represented one of the debtor's creditors prior to the bankruptcy case. Under such a rule, bankruptcy lawyers would be restrained from coming out of the woodwork after a bankruptcy filing, finding a creditor to represent, and then lining up votes for a favored trustee.

Nadler's proposal seems to have stirred up a hornet's nest of debate within the general bankruptcy bar, but in the end it led nowhere. After considering Nadler's suggested rule, the Bankruptcy Committee of the Commercial Law League (whose membership included a familiar elder statesman, Jacob Weinstein) reported back in 1951 that "it was the unanimous opinion of the [committee] that the League should not go on record as in favor of or against any particular local rule or propose any alternative rule or plan any campaign to bring about the adoption of any rule or canon on this particular subject."[4]

As of the late 1960s, when Stanley and Girth conducted the study that led to their important Brookings Institution report in 1971, very little had changed. With obvious distaste, they described a familiar pattern in general bankruptcy practice:

> [I]t is not difficult for creditors' attorneys to arrange elections among themselves. In one district, we observed attorneys who regularly appeared in bankruptcy proceedings comparing claims before the court session was called to order. Whoever represented the creditor with the largest claim voted for himself, and no one else voted.[5]

The demographics of the bankruptcy bar continued to reflect its faintly undesirable status. Bankruptcy was widely viewed as a "Jewish" practice. Many of the bar's leading figures, including Harvey Miller and Ronald Trost, were in fact Jewish—bright young lawyers who were excluded from the nation's elite firms because of their religion. Trost recalls that when he graduated from the University of Texas School of Law at the top of his class—he was an editor of the law review and one of a small handful of recipients of the law school's prestigious Chancellor Awards—none of the major Dallas law firms would even interview him. The firms compiled a list of the students they would talk to, and the law school's two leading Jewish law students were excluded from every single list. Both the Jewishness and the second-class status of the bar was, of course, an old story in bankruptcy. What was new was that these traits now defined all of bankruptcy, including corporate reorganization, not just the general bankruptcy bar.

The leading organizational voices for the bankruptcy bar remained much the same as in earlier decades. The National Bankruptcy Conference included many of the most prominent members of the bar (most of whom were corporate bankruptcy lawyers), together with a group of academics and bankruptcy judges. The conference frequently consulted with the Judiciary Committee when bankruptcy issues arose in Congress. In the oral history he gave when he retired from the University of Michigan in 1985, Professor Frank Kennedy, a longtime member of the NBC, described the conference's ongoing influence in the legislative process. Whenever a bankruptcy issue made its way to the Judiciary Committee, Kennedy recalled, the committee "always informed us, and paid considerable respect to the views that were expressed by the NBC members."[6]

The Commercial Law League spoke more directly for the general bankruptcy bar. Its ranks continued to be filled with the lawyers who handled small and medium-sized bankruptcies, and who comprised the heart of the general bankruptcy bar.

Alongside the bar, a new generation of bankruptcy academics had taken the reigns from predecessors such as James McLaughlin. Of these, the two most prominent were Frank Kennedy and Vern Countryman. Kennedy (along with Professor Lawrence King of New York University) was perhaps the closest successor to McLaughlin. A professor at the University of Iowa before he moved to the University of Michigan for the last two decades of his career, Kennedy focused on the technical details of the Bankruptcy Act and how its overall structure might be improved. When asked in his oral history to describe his most important contributions to the academic literature, Kennedy emphasized an early article of his that had pointed out a doctrinal problem involving the treatment of tax liabilities in bankruptcy.

Countryman also wrote extensively on doctrinal issues, but his work had a more overtly theoretical and ideological component—a strand that connects him to the New Deal reformers. As we will see in chapter 8, this connection was more than simply academic. Countryman had close ties to William Douglas throughout his career, first as a law clerk for Douglas on the Supreme Court and then as Douglas's most vigorous intellectual advocate. Throughout the 1960s and 1970s, Countryman tirelessly promoted the interests of consumer debtors.

As an advocate for consumer debtors, Countryman also served as the most visible representative of yet another perspective—that of the consumer protection movement. In 1965, Ralph Nader's populist manifesto against the auto industry, *Unsafe at Any Speed*, propelled the consumer protection movement into mainstream political discourse.[7] Although the consumer protection movement is generally traced back to hearings on the drug industry held by Senator Estes Kefauver in the late 1950s, Nader's campaign highlighted in a more immediate way the risks to consumers of a wide range of ordinary products, from kitchen appliances to automobiles. (Nader's career got perhaps its biggest boost when it became known that General Motors had hired private investigators to scrutinize Nader's private life.) For much of the 1960s, consumer advocates focused their attention on issues such as product warranties and lender disclosure rules, rather than bankruptcy. Since that time, however, bankruptcy has become an increasingly important issue for consumer advocates, and one of the few areas where the consumer protection movement continues to thrive. Not only did Vern Countryman serve as a founding member of the National Consumer Law Center, a leading consumer advocacy center, but his congressional testimony in the 1960s can be seen as the earliest evidence of consumer advocacy in bankruptcy reform.

The various groups of bankruptcy professionals—practicing lawyers, their lobbying and reform organizations, consumer advocates, and bankruptcy academics—did not see eye to eye on everything. But in one crucial respect nearly everyone agreed: one goal (and perhaps *the* goal) of any legislative reform should be to improve the reputation and status of bankruptcy law. Everyone suffered from the poor reputation of bankruptcy—the perception that bankruptcy courts, in George Triester's phrase, "dispensed an inferior brand of justice."[8] For judges and academics it meant lower status than that of other judges and academics; and for bankruptcy lawyers it meant both lower status and, for some, less business. For bankruptcy professionals, one of the great triumphs of the 1978 Code was that it addressed precisely this problem. As we shall see, the Code expanded and improved bankruptcy practice and enhanced its image, to an extent that had previously seemed unimaginable.

THE HEARINGS THAT LED TO THE 1978 CODE

With the 1960s came increasingly vocal calls for Congress to undertake its first global reconsideration of the bankruptcy laws since the Chandler Act. The reason for the sudden interest in bankruptcy was simple: bankruptcy filings had risen to previously unheard-of levels, and each year seemed to bring a new record. After hovering around 10,000 per year in the mid-1940s, the number of personal bankruptcies had begun a steady climb thereafter. In 1960, the filings reached 97,750; and they surged over 100,000 the following year, to 131,402—more than a tenfold increase in a period of just fifteen years (table 5.1). These numbers seem almost quaint now, in an era that has seen over a million filings in each of the past several years. But at the time, most observers saw the numbers as real cause for alarm.

Nearly everyone suspected the record number of bankruptcy filings was somehow related to the rise of consumer credit. This was the dawn of credit cards, and an era when consumers incurred more installment credit than ever before. As Vern Countryman would later point out in the legislative hearings, consumer debt expanded from $30 billion in 1945 to $569 billion in 1974.[9] Then, as now, there was a rough consensus that bankruptcy and consumer credit went hand in hand. But then, as now, observers sharply disputed

TABLE 5-1
Personal Bankruptcy Filings, 1945–1970

Year	Personal Bankruptcy Filings	Personal Bankruptcy Rate[a]
1945	11,051	12.0
1946	8,566	9.1
1947	10,234	10.8
1948	13,537	14.1
1949	19,144	19.6
1950	25,040	25.3
1951	27,806	27.6
1952	28,331	27.8
1953	33,315	32.4
1954	44,248	42.6
1955	50,219	47.9
1956	52,608	49.7
1957	63,617	59.5
1958	80,265	74.3
1959	88,943	81.6
1960	97,750	88.8
1961	131,402	118.3
1962	132,125	117.7
1963	139,190	122.7
1964	155,209	135.0
1965	163,413	140.5
1966	175,924	149.5
1967	191,729	161.1
1968	181,266	149.4
1969	169,500	137.4
1970	178,202	142.2

Source: David T. Stanley and Marjorie Girth, Bankruptcy: Problem, Process, Reform, 25 (Washington, D.C.: Brookings Institution, 1971).
[a] Filings per 100,000 in population of age 20 or older.

whether debtors and a decline in the stigma associated with bankruptcy, or creditors and too-easy credit, were to blame.

As the debate heated up, it naturally focused attention on the existing bankruptcy laws. In the glare of this renewed scrutiny, the bankruptcy process was widely seen as inadequate, a throwback to an earlier era. In addition to concerns about a "bankruptcy ring," George Triester and other leaders of the bankruptcy bar worried about referees' involvement in both administrative and judicial tasks. Because they presided over the initial creditors meeting, for instance, which provides for an examination of the debtor, the referees were privy to information that might prejudice their view of subsequent legal disputes. For Triester, eliminating this perceived conflict of interest was perhaps the single most important goal of bankruptcy reform.

It bears repeating that Triester, like nearly all of the bankruptcy lawyers who figured prominently in the reform process, was a corporate bankruptcy lawyer—one who focused on bankruptcies involving medium-sized and large firms, rather than consumers or small businesses. These lawyers' role in the corporate bankruptcy reforms we will consider in the next chapter is easy to understand, since the changes in this context directly improved their practice. Their passion for structural reform is not so easily pigeonholed, however. Destroying the unsavory practices that sustained the "bankruptcy ring" and minimizing bankruptcy judges' involvement in administrative tasks improved the overall reputation of bankruptcy practice and thus provided indirect benefits to Triester and his peers. But these indirect benefits cannot fully explain their passion for reform. Purely public-spirited motives also seem to have been at work.

Starting in the late 1960s, Congress began the process that culminated a decade later with the 1978 Code.[10] The path of the legislation was unusually complex, so I will begin by providing a very brief overview of the highlights. We then will consider the major proposals for structural and consumer bankruptcy reform, and how they fit into the now-familiar political pattern for reform of the bankruptcy laws.[11] The chapter concludes with a brief reprise of the conflict between the bankruptcy and district court judges that colored much of the debate.

Congress got the ball rolling in 1968 and 1969, when the Judiciary Committee held relatively brief hearings on a proposal to establish a commission to conduct a sweeping study of bankruptcy law.[12] There was little dispute about the need to set up a commission, and nearly all of the witnesses enthusiastically supported the project. They stridently disagreed, however, about how the members of the commission should be selected. The original resolution proposed that the president, chief justice, president of the Senate, and Speaker of the House select the members and required that the commission include at least two bankruptcy lawyers and two bankruptcy judges (or referees, as they were called until 1973). Several district court judges and their allies on the Judicial

Conference, which served as the mouthpiece for federal district and circuit court judges, objected bitterly to the requirement that two of the commission members be bankruptcy judges. The chief justice and other selectors should have free reign to choose whoever they want, the district judges insisted. The district judges also wondered aloud whether bankruptcy judges were too close to the bankruptcy process to provide an objective assessment. The bankruptcy judges had an obvious rejoinder to this, of course: it was essential that the commission include bankruptcy judges, they argued, since bankruptcy judges understood the complexities of bankruptcy law better than anyone else.

In the end, the district court judges won, and the bankruptcy judges' worst fears were confirmed by the events that followed. Congress authorized a National Bankruptcy Review Commission in 1970 and put no restrictions on whom the selectors could choose. President Nixon chose Harold Marsh, a prominent Los Angeles corporate bankruptcy lawyer and member of the National Bankruptcy Conference, to chair the commission. The other members of the commission included two district court judges, Edward Weinfeld and Hubert Will, but nary a bankruptcy judge. (The reporter for the commission was Frank Kennedy, also a member of the National Bankruptcy Conference.) To make matters worse, Judge Weinfeld proved to be a relentless critic of any effort to enhance the bankruptcy judges' status.

For the next two years, the commission conducted an extensive review of existing bankruptcy law. In July 1973, the commission forwarded its report, which included a wide range of proposed changes, together with a proposed new statute and section-by-section commentary on the reasons for each suggested change.[13] The centerpiece of the 1973 commission report was a proposal to establish a new bankruptcy agency, the United States Bankruptcy Administration, in the executive branch of the government. The Bankruptcy Administration would assume all of the administrative functions previously performed by bankruptcy judges and would provide counseling services for would-be debtors. The commission also proposed that Congress adopt uniform federal exemptions, called for an expansion of the jurisdictional reach of the bankruptcy laws, and proposed additional protections for consumer debtors.

Furious at their exclusion from the commission, the bankruptcy judges responded with the bankruptcy equivalent of the Salon des Réfusés from art history lore. When Monet, Manet, and the early impressionists were rejected by the fashionable Paris Salon, they set up their own exhibition, which they called the Salon des Réfusés. It stood as a direct challenge to its more established predecessor and has long been seen as a defining moment in the early history of impressionism.

Although bankruptcy judges such as Conrad Cyr and Joe Lee are not quite so famous as the impressionists, they adopted a very similar strategy. Working through their lobbying organization, the National Association of Bankruptcy Judges, the judges developed their own bill at the same time as the commis-

sion was completing its report. Under the judges' bill, bankruptcy would retain its judicial orientation. A few of the judges' administrative tasks would be
shifted to trustees, but the bankruptcy judges would remain at the heart of the
bankruptcy process. Like the commission report, the judges' bill also proposed
to expand the reach of bankruptcy in various ways.

In 1975, subcommittees of the House and Senate Judiciary Committees
held extensive hearings on the commission's and judges' bills, which by this
time were invariably considered in tandem.[14] The two bills were eventually
consolidated into a single bill in the House, which became House Bill 8200
through a rather remarkable reconciliation process. As Ron Trost recalls it,
Representative Edwards, a member of the 1970 commission and the leading
congressional advocate for reform, told the bankruptcy judges and National
Bankruptcy Conference that there would be no reform unless they resolved
their differences. The two groups then met in Atlanta and hammered out a
series of compromises that gave rise to the House bill. Congress then held
additional hearings to consider the bill in 1977.[15] Under the House bill, bankruptcy judges would be elevated to Article III status (this meant lifetime tenure, just like the district judges). For consumers, the House bill provided
minimum federal exemption standards (but also gave debtors the option to
rely on state exemptions instead).

After holding hearings on roughly the same schedule as the House—first in
1975 and then in 1977, the Senate passed a radically different version of the
bankruptcy bill in early 1978. The Senate bill had less glamorous aspirations
for bankruptcy judges than the House: rather than enjoying lifetime tenure
under Article III, the judges would be appointed for twelve-year terms. Like
existing law, the Senate bill would simply incorporate state law on exemptions.

On one issue, the House and Senate saw eye to eye: neither bill included
the bankruptcy agency that had figured so prominently in the early discussions.

Rather than setting up a formal conference committee, the floor managers
of the House and Senate bills negotiated among themselves for several weeks
in the fall of 1978, in an effort to reconcile the two bills. By October, they
had reached agreement and obtained the blessings of both the House and the
Senate. Under the final compromise, which reached the president's desk in
November, bankruptcy judges were given new powers (as proposed by the
House) but would not enjoy Article III status. Debtors would permitted to
choose between state and federal exemptions under a complicated arrangement that authorized each state to eliminate the federal options if state lawmakers preferred that its debtors use the state exemptions.

In the final stages of the legislative debates especially, the chief justice of
the Supreme Court, Warren Burger, became something of an evil angel in the
deliberations. The chief justice actively opposed efforts to elevate bankruptcy
judges to Article III status, and his involvement in the legislative process struck

many observers as unseemly. Ironically, the Supreme Court would later strike down as unconstitutional the very compromise Burger helped to negotiate as to the status of bankruptcy judges vis-à-vis the district courts. We will return to this battle at the end of the chapter. To begin, however, the chapter will focus first on the 1973 commission proposals for structural and consumer bankruptcy reform and consider in each case how the proposals fared in the buildup to 1978.

THE 1973 COMMISSION REPORT PROPOSALS

Throughout the debates that would lead to the 1978 reforms, the 1973 commission report provided both the intellectual underpinning and much of the framework for the reforms that Congress eventually adopted. Not all of the commission's proposals survived, of course; in fact, the proposal most central to the commission's vision for consumer bankruptcy was long gone when President Carter finally signed the Code into law. The question we will consider throughout this section is, what distinguished the successful commission proposals from those that failed? As we will see, the same political factors that loomed large in previous bankruptcy legislation also left their fingerprints on this most recent of reforms. What we will not see is much evidence of a partisan divide between Democrats and Republicans. By the 1970s, bankruptcy had long since lost its partisan edge. In the absence of visible ideological debate, interest group activity becomes especially important in a technical area such as bankruptcy, and it is interest group activity we will see.

The commission's general and consumer-oriented reforms fall into four general categories. The first category can be described as structural and includes the commission's single most sweeping recommendation: its proposal to set up a bankruptcy agency, which would handle a wide range of administrative functions, in the executive branch of the government. (The proposals to enhance bankruptcy judges' status also were structural in nature, but they will be considered at the end of the chapter.) I will refer to a second category of proposals as *scope expanding*. A scope-expanding proposal is one that would extend the reach of the bankruptcy process. The commission's proposals to expand the jurisdiction of the bankruptcy courts (to give bankruptcy courts the power to decide issues that previously went to other courts) and to resolve unmatured as well as matured claims qualify as scope expanding. Third was the question whether Congress or the states should regulate exemptions, and the final category includes a variety of recommendations that would alter the balance of power between creditors and debtors in personal bankruptcy cases.

Structural Reform: The Bankruptcy Agency

The commission's proposal to establish an executive branch bankruptcy administrator had a distinguished pedigree in U.S. bankruptcy history. As we saw in chapter 3, the Donovan and Thacher investigations had reached precisely the same conclusion. The unseemly practices of the bankruptcy bar, especially in New York, persuaded the drafters of the Donovan and Thacher reports that Congress should shift much of the bankruptcy process to an administrative agency. As evidence of the virtues of an administrative approach the drafters pointed to England, whose administrative process seemed much more effective than the judicially oriented American approach.

Following its quick demise in the legislative debates of the New Deal, the proposal disappeared, more or less, for the next several decades. Its return can be traced quite directly to the influential Brookings Institution study conducted in the 1960s and published in 1971.[16] In order to make sense of the explosive increase in bankruptcy filings, two Brookings Institution scholars, Margaret Girth and David Stanley, undertook an extensive survey of the bankruptcy system based on cases filed in 1965. Girth and Stanley were appalled by what they found. (As should be evident by now, investigators almost always find themselves "appalled" by what they see in bankruptcy.) The bankruptcy judges had far too cozy a relationship with the trustees they appointed, and, in many metropolitan areas, a small group of bankruptcy lawyers seemed to dominate the appointment process—the dreaded "bankruptcy ring." Girth and Stanley also criticized the wide variations from one region to the next on issues such as the percentage of debtors who proposed rehabilitation plans rather than seeking an immediate discharge.

The Brookings report called for Congress to completely rethink the bankruptcy process. Much of bankruptcy seemed administrative, not judicial, in nature. In a substantial majority of personal bankruptcy cases, the debtor had no nonexempt assets, and there was no hope of any payment to creditors. These proceedings were (and still are, one might add) entirely pro forma; the debtor filed the appropriate forms, the court issued a discharge canceling the debtor's obligations as a matter of course, and that was that.

Rather than using judicial resources in these no-asset cases, the report argued, Congress should simply establish a bankruptcy agency to handle them. "We have seen," Stanley and Girth concluded, "that bankruptcy problems are in most cases problems of guidance and management. The major need is for speedy, discriminating, understanding processing of [several hundred thousand small cases] each year. This is an administrative function rather than a judicial function."[17] An administrator could gather facts and issue the discharge. In corporate bankruptcy, the administrator could select the trustee and set up the creditors committee. Courts would not fade away altogether. Courts would still resolve issues such as litigation by a trustee to recover preferential transfers or fraudulent conveyances. But bankruptcy would take on a much more administrative tone.

The National Bankruptcy Review Commission, which started its work just as the Brookings report appeared, relied heavily on the report's empirical work and adopted many of its recommendations. Most dramatically, the commission agreed that much of the bankruptcy process could, and should, be handled by an administrative agency. In the commission's framework, an executive branch agency called the U.S. Bankruptcy Administration would assume all of the administrative tasks currently performed by bankruptcy judges. For most consumers, bankruptcy would become an administrative process like social security or Veterans Administration benefits. (In corporate bankruptcy, the bankruptcy administrator would take over most of the SEC's responsibilities.) The commission also believed that the administrator could address consumers' general ignorance about bankruptcy. "The Commission's investigations have convinced it that the average consumer bankrupt today has no understanding of the options available to him under the Bankruptcy Act," the commissioners wrote, and "probably no ability to calculate unassisted which option [as between immediate discharge or an individual rehabilitation plan] may be feasible or desirable for him." The commission's solution was to authorize the bankruptcy administrator to provide counseling on these issues.[18]

The commission's proposal to establish a bankruptcy agency obviously would mean big changes for the practice of bankruptcy in the United States. The most likely losers would be the people with the largest stake in the existing framework: bankruptcy judges and some bankruptcy lawyers, especially consumer bankruptcy lawyers. Not surprisingly, bankruptcy professionals launched an immediate assault on the proposed agency.

Most vociferous in their criticism were the bankruptcy judges. The judges were already angry at having been excluded from membership on the commission, and the proposal to turn bankruptcy into an administrative process showed just how much their exclusion had mattered. As soon as the commission's recommendations came out, Conrad Cyr and several other leaders of the National Association of Bankruptcy Judges took up their arms. Judge Cyr (who, in a mildly ironic twist, subsequently became a federal circuit court judge) argued that the bankruptcy administrator would suffer from precisely the same conflicts of interest that observers had criticized in current practice. The agency would engage in both administrative and quasi-judicial tasks. If the same department of the agency investigated the debtor (an administrative task) and also ruled on the discharge (a judicial one), debtors could be prejudiced by the administrator's access to nonjudicial information. Judge Cyr also conjured up images of a sprawling, out-of-control governmental bureaucracy that would drive up costs and sharply diminish the quality of the bankruptcy. Cyr and his fellow judges frequently pointed out that the members of the commission were experts in business bankruptcy, and that not one of them had significant experience with consumer bankruptcy. This, the bankruptcy judges suggested, helped to explain the commission's support for such a wrongheaded proposal. "[T]he Commission report's use of beguiling adjectives in praise of its proposed administrative agency," Judge Cyr concluded, "amounts to little more than the narcissistic confusion of program goals for agency attributes."[19]

Behind the bankruptcy judges' substantive complaints lay a more immediate concern: the creation of a bankruptcy agency would cost many of them their jobs. The drafters of the 1973 commission report quite candidly predicted that their proposal would require roughly one-third less judges than were currently in place.[20] Although there was substantial discussion in the hearings on the commission bill about ways to ease the transition, the bottom line was that more than 70 of the 220 bankruptcy judges would no longer be needed. (Needless to say, the judges' bill did not propose that Congress establish an administrative agency; as noted earlier, the judges' bill would have ceded a few administrative responsibilities such as selecting trustees to another judicial branch official in order to address the concern about conflicting administrative and judicial functions; but the overall process would look much as it did under existing law.)

For bankruptcy judges, the commission proposals threatened their long, slow rise to respectability. The Chandler Act had given them important new powers, such as the right to grant discharges, and a set of amendments in 1946 finally shifted their compensation from a fee to a salary basis. In 1973, the very year that the commission forwarded its recommendation, the drafters (who included Professors Larry King and Frank Kennedy) of a sweeping set of new bankruptcy rules—rules that quite remarkably were deemed to trump any inconsistent statutory provision—promulgated a rule requiring that the bankruptcy judges be referred to as *judges* rather than *referees*. Unfortunately, the same developments that enhanced the status of bankruptcy judges also had made them increasingly similar to district court judges. Many district court judges saw this as a threat to their status, and the commission recommendations seemed to take the district court judges' perspective.

Many bankruptcy lawyers also opposed the agency, though with differing degrees of vigor. The most prominent members of the bar (several of whom had been involved in the commission) were the least hostile. For George Triester and other representatives of the National Bankruptcy Conference, the most important objective was to separate the judicial functions of bankruptcy from the administrative ones. So important was this reform that many of the leaders of the bar were willing to consider a modified agency approach. Thus, the National Bankruptcy Conference suggested that the administrator should be located in the judicial rather than the executive branch but was otherwise willing to go along with the proposal.[21] The NBC's sympathy for the reform can be seen in both public-spirited and interest group terms. Because the conference was dominated by corporate bankruptcy lawyers, most of its members had little to fear from the proposed agency and would at least indirectly benefit if the changes improved bankruptcy's reputation. Yet the leaders of the NBC also were motivated by an obvious commitment to reform, as evidenced by the thousands of hours they contributed to a cause that did not directly benefit them.

Other bankruptcy lawyers were far more antagonistic. Stoking concerns about the dangers of a faceless bureaucracy, a representative of the Dallas Bar Association predicted that the agency would "have all of the efficiency of the U.S. Postal Service, all the public interest orientation of the Bureau of Reclamation, all the heart of the Internal Revenue Service, and all the procedural due process of the Equal Employment Opportunities Commission."[22] A California lawyer who specialized in consumer bankruptcy complained that the agency would "destroy the private consumer bankruptcy bar" and replace it with a coterie of "lay counselors." No longer would consumer debtors receive the ongoing advice of a lawyer. Where would the administrator be, he wondered, if the debtor had trouble with a former creditor a year or two after bankruptcy?[23]

Although bankruptcy judges and bankruptcy lawyers took a more active interest than anyone else in the bankruptcy administrator proposal, other groups obviously had an interest, too. Interestingly, some members of the consumer credit industry also weighed in against the proposal to create a new agency. When the agency proposal had surfaced in the 1930s, many observers suspected that it would diminish the use of bankruptcy, and creditors were its most enthusiastic supporters. This is the effect the administrative bankruptcy process has long had in England. But forty years of experience with New Deal agencies and the welfare state had changed creditors' views on agencies. The agency's counselors might steer debtors into bankruptcy rather than away from it, and the commission's explicit goal of expanding the discharge did not give creditors any comfort on this score. "By encouraging a debtor to proceed in bankruptcy and without the assistance and guidance of a lawyer," worried Linn Twinen of Beneficial Finance, "a bankruptcy explosion could result." In a sense, these creditors preferred the devil they knew over the one they didn't.[24]

The response of consumer advocates suggests that they, too, believed that a bankruptcy agency might actually promote bankruptcy. Consumer advocates were generally open to the proposal, although they made clear that they were more concerned to expand bankruptcy's commitment to a fresh start than with the question whether bankruptcy should be administrative or judicial in nature.[25]

It is impossible to know how far the bankruptcy agency proposal might have gone if the commission had made a more conscious effort to appeal to creditors—or, for that matter, if it had arisen a few years earlier; by the mid-

1970s, the rising sentiment for deregulation had cast a damper on proposals to establish new agencies. Yet, to the extent history is a guide, it suggests that we probably would have ended up in precisely same place, even if the circumstances had otherwise been more auspicious. Twice in this century, proposals for a bankruptcy agency have been introduced in Congress with the backing of influential studies of the bankruptcy system. In each case, bankruptcy professionals have responded with immediate, vociferous opposition to the proposed agency. In each case, the study did lead to important legislation; but, by the time Congress gave its seal of approval, the bankruptcy agency was long gone.

Although the administrative agency proposal died an early death, several of the commission's proposals for structural change did ultimately come to pass. The most important and hotly contested were the proposals to upgrade the status of the bankruptcy judges themselves. These debates, which occupied much of the hearings, will be discussed briefly at the end of the chapter. Another facet of the commission proposals—the call for stricter controls on the election of trustees—illustrates once again that bankruptcy lawyers' interests were not homogenous in all respects. As we have seen, creditors' right to elect a bankruptcy trustee lay at the heart of long-standing complaints about a "bankruptcy ring." Taking advantage of creditors' generally passive role, bankruptcy lawyers solicited proxies for their favored candidate and doled out lucrative trustee and trustee's attorney assignments among themselves. The commission had proposed that the bankruptcy administrator serve as trustee unless at least 35 percent of the debtor's creditors asked for the right to elect a private, creditor-chosen trustee.[26] The minimum vote requirement was designed to make it harder for bankruptcy lawyers to use the proxies of a small number of creditors to control the trustee election.

The most prominent members of bankruptcy bar, who were well represented both in the National Bankruptcy Conference and on the Bankruptcy Commission, viewed the existing election process as a blight on bankruptcy practice. These lawyers had in fact been the driving force behind the proposed change. "[T]he election of trustees and the election of creditors committees," complained Harold Marsh, "is an election of lawyers, by lawyers, and for lawyers." The members of the Bankruptcy Commission, Marsh recalled, had concluded "that this was a most unseemly aspect of the entire bankruptcy picture."[27] The willingness of Marsh and other leaders of the bar to criticize existing practice once again demonstrates the depth of their genuine interest in bankruptcy reform. It is also important to keep in mind that reforming the "bankruptcy ring" would not undermine their own practice, since the leading members of the bar did not routinely serve as trustee or trustee's counsel. The lawyers who did participate in the proxy process were far less enthusiastic about the proposed changes. Speaking through the Commercial Law League, which reflected their interests much more than the elite National Bankruptcy

Conference, the general bankruptcy bar complained that a minimum vote requirement would interfere with creditors' right to select a trustee of their choice. "Even though we support the separation of administrative duties from the judicial duties of the court," the Commercial Law League's president explained, "we have to oppose anything that would take away from creditors the right to elect their trustee."[28] No other group stepped up to defend the current proxy process, however, and Commercial Law League's ostensible concern for creditors was not a particularly compelling argument for the status quo. Few observers believed, for instance, that the proxy system improved the payout to creditors. With the bar's reformers against them, and no other interest group visibly in their camp, the Commercial Law League could not derail the reform—though the 1978 Code did lower the percentage required for creditors to insist on their own choice of trustee to 20 percent.

Proposals to Expand the Scope of Bankruptcy Law

Bankruptcy professionals were far more united—this time in favor—of the second group of commission proposals—the proposals I have characterized as *scope expanding*. As a package, the scope-expanding proposals were nearly as sweeping in effect as establishing a bankruptcy agency would have been. But they generated surprisingly little opposition. These reforms would prove to be one of the most lasting legacies of the small band of bankruptcy lawyers who had set out to raise the level of bankruptcy practice and the bankruptcy bar.

A brief overview of three of the principal scope-expanding proposals will show the general contours of the reforms. The first and, in the view of many bankruptcy lawyers, most pressing, was jurisdiction. As we saw in chapter 1, the drafters of the Bankruptcy Act of 1898 had carefully limited the scope of the bankruptcy court's jurisdiction, in order to retain a substantial role for the states. Debtors and creditors had the right to insist on state court resolution of numerous issues, from a debtor's efforts to defend against an involuntary petition to the trustee's litigation to recover preferential and fraudulent transfers. Over the years, Congress steadily increased the bankruptcy court's jurisdiction, but irksome limitations remained. Most importantly, the bankruptcy court could only exercise jurisdiction over property that the debtor had in her possession at the beginning of the bankruptcy case. If the debtor had transferred property to a creditor, the bankruptcy court could assert jurisdiction over an action involving the property only if both parties consented.[29] Congress and the courts used the term *summary* to characterize the bankruptcy court's jurisdiction over property the debtor possessed, and *plenary* to denote the court's more limited authority over property the debtor did not.

The bankruptcy bar had long chafed at these restrictions. As a practical matter, the bankruptcy court's limited jurisdiction over plenary matters forced trustees to try many preference and fraudulent conveyance actions in state court, rather than in bankruptcy court. Bankruptcy professionals also saw the terms themselves as demeaning. Characterizing bankruptcy jurisdiction as summary seemed to suggest, in the words of George Triester referred to earlier, that the bankruptcy courts dispensed an inferior, less-thorough brand of justice. As a simple solution to these concerns, the commission report proposed much more expansive jurisdiction, and proposed to write the terms *summary* and *plenary* out of the bankruptcy laws altogether.

A second recommendation proposed to change the contours of the bankruptcy "estate." Under the 1898 act, the debtor's estate—that is, the property that would be available for distribution to creditors—consisted of all of the property that the debtor could have transferred to a third party outside of bankruptcy. If the debtor herself could not transfer the property, it also would not be available to creditors. Whether or not the debtor had a transferable interest gave rise to frequent, often esoteric disputes. The commission proposed to sweep these disputes away by adopting a much broader definition of "property of the estate." So long as the debtor had any legal or equitable interest, the property interest would be included.

The final expansion concerns the definition of *claim* and is, in a sense, the flip side of our second illustration. The second illustration focused on the bankruptcy "estate"—that is, what property is included in the pie that is available for distribution to the debtor's creditors. In asking who has a claim, we are asking which creditors will be given a piece of the bankruptcy pie.

As with jurisdiction and property of the estate, the Bankruptcy Act had developed a nuanced jurisprudence around the question of who did and did not have claims. To be included in the bankruptcy distribution, a claim had to qualify as both "provable" and "allowable." The most common sticking point was provability: creditors whose claims were specified by contract, or who had already sued and obtained a court judgment, had provable claims. If the claim was uncertain in amount and had not been reduced to judgment (it was *contingent*, or *unliquidated*, in bankruptcy lingo), however, it might not qualify as provable. Courts managed to stretch the definition of provable a bit over the years, but many claims still did not qualify. A tort claimant who had sued the debtor, but whose claim had not been resolved, often would not have a provable claim.

Interestingly, it may not always be in the creditor's best interest to have a provable claim, and thus to get a piece of the bankruptcy pie. To be sure, if the debtor were a corporation that was being liquidated, creditors with provable claims would get a share of the assets, whereas those who did not have provable claims would be excluded and get nothing. But being excluded did not look so bad when the debtor was an individual or a corporation that would be reorganized and keep going. In this case, creditors with provable claims would get their bankruptcy payout of, say, 10 percent, whereas the excluded creditor could insist on 100 percent payment after the bankruptcy was over, since her claim was not dealt with in the bankruptcy.

Whether this possible windfall was good or bad can be debated, but bankruptcy lawyers and the members of the 1970 commission wanted it fixed. If a substantial number of claims were excluded, bankruptcy would not provide as complete a resolution of financial distress as would otherwise be the case. To solve this problem, the commission once again proposed a sweeping solution. The concept of provability should be thrown out the window, the commission argued, and *claim* defined in the broadest of terms. Under the commission proposal, even claims that were contingent or unliquidated as of bankruptcy would be dealt with in the case.[30]

It is worth pausing for a moment to consider just why bankruptcy lawyers were so enthusiastic about the three changes. A common theme in the literature on lawyers and their interests is that lawyers benefit if laws are complex, rather than simple. (Having suffered through the welter of terms that have just been described, the reader will appreciate the complexity of the existing law.) There is an obvious reason for lawyers' taste for complexity: complicated laws create a greater demand for lawyers' services than straightforward laws do. This intuition is captured in the common complaint about mind-numbing regulation—often tax reform of one sort or another—that the legislation's real purpose is "full employment for lawyers."

From this perspective, bankruptcy lawyers' role in devising and promoting the scope-expanding reforms may seem at least mildly puzzling. All three of the scope-expanding reforms proposed to make bankruptcy *less* complex, by replacing the subtle distinctions of existing law with simple new rules. A moment's reflection on the reforms shows the benefits to the bankruptcy bar, however. If a law is *too* complex, it may discourage parties from using it— and thus prove counterproductive for lawyers.[31] Although streamlining the bankruptcy process would reduce the need (and thus the fees) for lawyers to litigate a variety of esoteric issues, the reforms would increase the flexibility and attractiveness of bankruptcy overall. If bankruptcy is more flexible, more firms will look to bankruptcy as a solution to their financial distress. Expanding the bankruptcy court's jurisdiction also would benefit bankruptcy lawyers in another way. Under existing law, the parties might well use nonbankruptcy lawyers to litigate issues such as fraudulent conveyance actions that had to be tried in state courts. If these actions could be litigated in the bankruptcy court, both sides would rely on bankruptcy lawyers for the bankruptcy court litigation—based on the "when in Rome" principle, if for no other reason.

In short, the leaders of the bankruptcy bar sought to transform bankruptcy from a mildly unsavory, often archaic practice to a more useful, attractive, and reputable response to financial distress. "Perfecting" the bankruptcy laws had been the National Bankruptcy Conference's main mission since the

1930s, and the 1970s reforms were very much in this spirit. It is easy to see why bankruptcy lawyers—both the reformers and the general bar—were so enthusiastic about these changes. But why was there so little opposition from anyone else?

The most important explanation is that each of the scope-expanding reforms enjoyed widespread support. Proponents of expanding the bankruptcy court's jurisdiction argued, for instance, that trying a preference action in state court was a waste of time and money; letting bankruptcy courts decide these issues would resolve them more quickly and cheaply and with less disruption. The cost argument was persuasive, and no one seriously argued that moving litigation of this sort to the state courts would improve the bankruptcy process. In 1898, prodebtor lawmakers would have vehemently voiced the need to try these issues in state court. The absence of such arguments is a testament to how much things had changed in the seven decades of the 1898 act. By the 1970s, state court jurisdiction was not seen as worth fighting about, although federal-state tensions continued to dominate a few issues such as exemptions policy, as we shall see.

The reforms did not benefit everyone. Expanding the definition of *claim* may not benefit a tort victim, for instance, if she might otherwise be able to obtain full payment from the debtor for her injury. Yet several factors (as we saw in chapter 3) ensured that the parties with the most to lose mounted little opposition to the scope-expanding reforms. First, these parties often were not well positioned to complain. Until tort victims actually suffer, or become aware of, an injury, they do not know who they are. Unless another group, such as trial lawyers, represents their interests, tort victims often do not have a place at the bargaining table. Small unsecured creditors also are not well organized, and they probably had the most to lose from an expansion of the bankruptcy process. (The National Association of Credit Managers represents the interests of larger unsecured creditors, but they did not speak out for small creditors or tort victims.) Added to this was another factor, complexity and expertise. Although the scope-expanding reforms were designed to simplify bankruptcy, it was nevertheless difficult for nonexperts to appreciate their likely effect. Each of the scope-expanding reforms looked like a characteristically mind-numbing technical adjustment, despite the potentially far-reaching effect of each.

Collectively, these factors explain the bankruptcy bar's remarkable success in expanding the scope of the U.S. bankruptcy laws. The changes were technical, so few observers other than the bar paid a great deal of attention to them. The participants who might be disadvantaged by the changes often were not well represented, and those with influence could be mollified by tinkering with the proposals. Underwriting all of this was the fact that the changes could be promoted as simplifying, modernizing, and in some respects undeniably improving bankruptcy law.

Federalism and Exemptions

Our analysis of the first two kinds of proposal—the commission's recommendations for structural and scope-expanding reforms—might seem to suggest that bankruptcy professionals dominated every aspect of the reform process. Bankruptcy judges were instrumental in thwarting the shift to a bankruptcy agency; and the leaders of the bankruptcy bar were the most active promoters of the commission's scope-expanding reforms. As influential as they were, bankruptcy professionals were only one set of voices, and their influence operated within substantial constraints. These larger constraints come to the fore as we turn to the third issue, the question whether Congress or the states should determine which property a debtor could exempt from her creditors. More than any other issue, the commission's proposal to enact federal standards for exemptions underscored the continuing importance of federalism to U.S. bankruptcy law.

Each of the bankruptcy reform proposals offered a different resolution of the exemptions issue. The Bankruptcy Commission put the issue on the table by proposing to displace state control of exemptions with a uniform federal framework. Under the commission proposal, all debtors would be entitled to exempt up to $5,000 of equity in a home and $1,000 in any personal property (plus $500 more for each dependent). These exemptions would displace any exemptions the debtor would otherwise have under state law. Rather than uniform federal standards, the judges' bill proposed a federal exemption scheme that would serve as a floor, while still permitting debtors to use their state exemptions. Under the judges' proposal, debtors could exempt $6,000 in a house and $3,000 in personal property. A debtor could also invoke any state exemptions, up to a maximum of $25,000. The House bill that reconciled the commission's and judges' proposals offered still more generous federal exemptions, protecting up to $10,000 in a home and $5,000 in personal property; the House bill also permitted debtors to forgo the federal exemptions in favor of their state's provisions. The Senate bill, by contrast, proposed to leave things where they were, with the states.

More remarkable even than the range of proposals, and the clever compromise that lawmakers finally agreed to, was the fact that this issue ever came up for consideration in the first place. In the debates leading up to the 1898 act, lawmakers had taken as a given that state lawmakers would be the ones to determine how much property debtors could exempt. The next major set of bankruptcy reforms came in the 1930s, an era that saw an unprecedented shift of authority to the federal government, and attempts at federal solutions for a wide range of social issues. Yet in a decade filled with bankruptcy hearings and bankruptcy reforms, there was almost no mention of exemptions.[32] The simple explanation for this was that, even in an era of federal ascendancy over the states, everyone assumed that proposing to federalize exemptions was politically untenable.

Given the long history of state control, why did the commission suddenly conclude that exemptions policy was once again up for grabs? The sudden prominence of the exemptions issue can be traced to several related factors. First, the meteoric rise in bankruptcy filings highlighted the remarkable differences in exemptions policy from state to state. It was one thing to know that some states (such as Texas) had astonishingly generous policies, while others (Maryland often came to mind) were just as astonishingly stingy. It was quite another to see Texas debtors filing for bankruptcy and using their state exemptions to protect a lavish home. As early as 1960, Vern Countryman criticized these divergences at length and called for a uniform federal solution.[33] Second and probably more important was the growing national success of the consumer protection movement. Consumer advocates had recently persuaded Congress to enact uniform national standards for debt collection issues such as garnishment.[34] If Congress was willing to intervene on these issues, which also had long been regulated by the states, it seemed plausible that the time might be right for a single, federal set of exemptions.

After more than seventy years of silent acceptance, the bankruptcy debates of the 1970s thus saw proposals taking every possible position on the issue whether Congress or the states should control exemptions policy: uniform federal standards (the commission proposal), minimum federal standards (the judges' bill), a choice between federal and state (House bill) and continued state control (Senate bill). The most plausible explanation for the positions staked out by each of the proposals comes from Eric Posner, and the interpretation that follows draws on his analysis.[35] The commission's enthusiasm for federal exemptions may reflect the nature of the commission's membership. Given that the commission included a senator, a congressman, and two federal district court judges, it is hardly surprising that the commission found the arguments for uniform federal exemptions compelling. Due in part to the persistent advocacy of Vern Countryman, the commission also placed a strong emphasis on consumer protection, and federal exemptions were seen as an important way to protect the interests of consumers, especially in states with stingy exemptions.

Although the bankruptcy judges also were federal judges, their orientation tends to be somewhat more local, given the large influence of state law on bankruptcy issues. This may begin to explain why the bankruptcy judges proposed minimum federal standards but declined to displace state control altogether. The judges also had a strong interest in defending the status quo, given the indignities to them of the commission process, and they were at pains to make their bill more politically palatable than the commission proposal wherever possible. An intermediate reform like minimum federal standards can be seen as attempting to juggle all of these concerns.

Despite the apparent support for federal exemptions, both the House and Senate bills proposed to retain a significant amount of state influence. Why did Congress once again abandon the quest for a uniform federal policy on exemptions? The best way to answer this question is to consider the nature of state lawmakers' interest in regulating an issue at the state rather than the federal level. If state lawmakers have developed a particular expertise in the area (as with corporate law), or if the states have a significant stake in tailoring legislation to their own citizens, they may be willing to "pay" Congress more for continued state control than federal lawmakers could expect from interest groups by enacting a federal law. (The "payment" comes in the form of benefits such as campaign contributions from interest groups interested in state regulation.) Exemptions policy seems to be precisely this kind of issue. State interest groups often care deeply about local exemption law, so both state lawmakers and federal lawmakers who are sensitive to state issues have a strong interest in state control. In stingy states like Maryland, for instance, state control enables lawmakers to keep creditor groups that favor limited exemptions happy, whereas Texas lawmakers can respond to the populist enthusiasm for generous protection.

Probably the strongest advocates for continued state control in the legislative hearings were insurance companies. Many states provide generous exemptions for insurance policies and related assets, giving consumers an additional reason to purchase insurance. Not surprisingly, insurance companies strongly favored continuation of this status.[36]

Bankruptcy professionals generally, but not unanimously, called for a significant federal role in exemptions policy. The National Bankruptcy Conference argued (as did the Consumer Law Center) that Congress should provide minimum exemption amounts to help out debtors in states with stingy exemptions, but that debtors should be entitled to use the state exemptions in generous states.[37] The Commercial Law League argued for an entirely federal approach. Texas lawyers, by contrast, stood by their state and its generous homestead exemption.[38]

The final version of the legislation included a last-minute compromise, which suggested that the constituency for federalization was larger than in the past, but that state lawmakers' interest in control is too great to permit true federalization. As enacted, the 1978 Code, like the House bill, gives debtors a choice between state exemptions and a set of federal options; but the Code also expressly authorized each state to remove the federal option and limit its debtors to the state provisions. Within a few years, a substantial majority of states took Congress up on its offer and enacted provisions limiting debtors to the state exemptions. Although the Bankruptcy Code now appears to include federal exemptions, for the debtors in most states this is merely a chimera: they continue to look to the state exemptions, just as they have since 1898.

Conflicts between Creditor Protection and Enhancing Debtors' Fresh Start

In addition to exemptions, the most important consumer bankruptcy issues involved the nature and scope of the bankruptcy discharge. Starting in the 1960s, the consumer credit industry had repeatedly urged lawmakers to adopt variations on what would now be called a "means test"—that is, a provision that forces debtors to use Chapter 13 rather than Chapter 7 if they are capable of repaying at least some of their debts. A crucial question for the 1970 commission was whether to develop a means-testing proposal.

In keeping with its generally prodebtor leanings on the substantive details of consumer bankruptcy, the commission rejected creditors calls for restrictions on Chapter 7. After noting that lawmakers had rejected means testing in the past and that groups such as the ABA continued to oppose this approach, the commission concluded that "forced participation in a [Chapter 13 plan] has so little prospect for success that it should not be adopted as a feature of the bankruptcy system."[39]

Although it rejected means testing, the commission did agree that not enough debtors invoked Chapter 13 and attempted to repay some of their obligations. Rather than mandating Chapter 13, the commission concluded that the best way to increase the percentage of Chapter 13 cases would be to make the repayment option more enticing—that is, to sweeten the Chapter 13 pot. The commission therefore proposed to give Chapter 13 debtors a variety of powers that would not be available if the debtor sought an immediate discharge—including the right to cure any defaults on the debtor's home mortgage and an injunction—referred to as a *co-debtor stay*—that required creditors to halt any collection efforts against anyone who was jointly responsible for any of the debtor's obligations. The co-debtor stay would significantly expand the protections that bankruptcy offered to a debtor, and creditors resisted the proposal throughout the hearings. "In effect," a representative of the National Consumer Finance Association complained, "the [commission's and judges' bills] invalidate the contractual rights between the creditor and the co-obligor or guarantor who is not before the court."[40] But prodebtor advocates insisted on retaining it, and the provision appeared in each of the major bills, as well as the legislation as finally enacted.

By the end of the hearings, the list of benefits that would be available in Chapter 13 but not Chapter 7 had grown still larger. A particularly important addition involved one the oldest limitations on a debtor's discharge—the denial of a discharge for any debt that was based on a fraudulent financial statement. Although the exception dated back to the 1898 act, consumer advocates claimed that creditors used this exception to undermine debtors' fresh start. Creditors looked the other way, they complained—and even encouraged debtors to understate their existing debt—so that they could later challenge the debtor's discharge if he filed for bankruptcy. (As creditors repeatedly pointed out during the hearings, these concerns had been partially addressed by a 1970 amendment—promoted by Vern Countryman—that required creditors to bring any objections to the discharge during the bankruptcy case, rather than thereafter.) The commission agreed with the consumer advocates' concerns, noting, "Substantial evidence of the abuses of this exception by creditors has come to the attention of the Commission," and the commission concluded that the exceptions should no longer apply to consumer debtors.[41] Creditors excoriated the commission's reasoning and repeatedly defended the exception. Once again, the stance of the National Consumer Finance Association was typical:

> We cannot believe that the Commission would be inclined to grant a dishonest debtor, consumer or otherwise, a discharge from all those debts incurred through his wrongdoing. . . . With the advent of restrictions on consumer credit reporting contained in the Fair Credit Reporting Act, . . . the representations of the prospective borrower become more important and are most frequently the only determination of the borrower's outstanding indebtedness and conversely his ability to pay.[42]

In the end, the creditors and prodebtor advocates reached a compromise. Although the fraud exception would be retained in Chapter 7, even fraudulently incurred obligations could be discharged as part of Chapter 13's so-called superdischarge.

It is easy to see why this kind of compromise proved attractive. In simple bargaining games, the parties often gravitate toward a solution that splits the difference between them. Adding a prodebtor provision to Chapter 13, but withholding it from debtors who seek an immediate discharge, has a very similar effect. Debtors gain an added protection, but only if they propose a repayment plan giving some of their future earnings to creditors. Both of the central interest groups thus had an incentive to agree to compromises that reinforced the commission's strategy of making Chapter 13 more enticing to debtors.

To most observers, this approach seems to make perfect sense. If not enough debtors choose repayment, why not offer a small carrot? The problem is that the new strategy—let's call it the "Chapter 13 bribe"—sharply conflicts with the ostensible purpose of Chapter 13, which is to give debtors who need temporary relief from creditors, but who feel a moral obligation to repay, the opportunity to do so. Now, no one has ever believed that Chapter 13 is only designed for debtors who feel morally compelled to, as the apostle Paul put it

(Rom. 13:8), "leave no debts outstanding." A debtor will often have mixed motives for repaying, including a desire to retain important property such as a house or to preserve her credit record so that she can continue to borrow money in the future. But Chapter 13, as restructured in 1978, goes well beyond this. It gives debtors (not to mention their attorneys) an overwhelming incentive to view the choice between Chapter 7 and Chapter 13 in crassly strategic terms. Debtors who wish to keep their house or car, or who wish to discharge items that are not dischargeable under Chapter 7, lean toward Chapter 13. Debtors who do not have significant nonexempt assets use Chapter 7. The Chapter 13 bribe is deeply inconsistent with the moral assumptions that underlie Chapter 13, and the parties' political interests reinforce the tension. (We will explore the current implications of this problem in chapter 7.)

Another issue that merits brief mention is the debate between creditors and prodebtor advocates over reaffirmations. A reaffirmation is an agreement by the debtor to honor an obligation that would otherwise be discharged in the debtor's bankruptcy. Debtor advocates believed that reaffirmations were inconsistent with the fresh start and should be prohibited. Based on this view, the 1973 commission report and the commission bill proposed to make any attempted reaffirmation invalid. As with the fraud exception, creditors aggressively resisted the commission's proposal throughout the hearings. "We believe this to be an unwarranted and perhaps unconstitutional interference with the freedom of contract between the debtor and creditor," the credit industry insisted, in a particularly stringent critique.[43] Once again, the final result was a compromise. Creditors successfully scuttled the proposed prohibition, though they made important concessions to prodebtor advocates along the way. As enacted, the 1978 Code requires explicit court approval of any proposed reaffirmation. (In a recent, much-noted case, Sears agreed to pay millions of dollars to a class of debtors for failing to obtain the required approval when the debtors agreed to reaffirm their debts.)

The mildly prodebtor effect of the 1978 reforms is best explained in terms of the factors we have seen throughout the book. By the 1970s, the principal proponents of enhancing bankruptcy's protections for debtors were bankruptcy professionals and consumer advocates, many of whom were themselves attorneys. Consumer advocacy groups such as the Consumer Law Center championed debtors' interests more vocally than anyone else. But their views, such as the Consumer Law Center's contention that most security interests in consumer goods should simply be invalidated, were well outside the mainstream of the deliberations.[44] Of greater practical significance was the sympathy of the National Bankruptcy Conference and leaders of the bankruptcy bar, most of whom did not practice in the consumer area. The staff attorneys who helped draft the House and Senate bills were similarly sympathetic — one, Ken Klee, was in fact a student of Vern Countryman and had been recommended by Countryman. Buttressing their efforts was the long-standing, widespread ideological commitment to helping troubled debtors. Aligned against this view were the creditors, who stood to lose if the bankruptcy laws were further loosened in debtors' favor.

The prodebtor interests had several political advantages in the discussions. In difficult economic times, prodebtor ideology tends to have particular resonance. Although the 1970s were a far cry from the depression, inflation and economic stagnation had produced the general anxiety that President Carter, borrowing from the sociologist Christopher Lasch, would famously refer to as "cultural malaise." Moreover, Democrats held the presidency and both houses of Congress as the bankruptcy reforms neared enactment. Nevertheless, a powerful lobbying effort by large creditors probably could have derailed the legislation. To prevent this, bankruptcy professionals sought to pacify large creditors by compromising on each of the troublesome issues—hence the modest gains for debtors—the reduced fraud exception, the tighter restrictions on reaffirmation. (Bankruptcy professionals also deliberately tried to lower the profile of the bankruptcy reforms, and to portray them as largely technical in nature.) The compromises generally satisfied creditors, yet offered additional protections to debtors and did so in a way that expanded the role of bankruptcy professionals, given that each compromise located the decisive decision-making authority squarely within the bankruptcy court.

Soon after the 1978 legislation was enacted, many large creditors concluded that they had given up too much in the compromises included in the Code. As we shall see in chapter 7, the reaction of some—most prominently, credit card lenders—has been a continuing theme in the legislative debates over consumer bankruptcy since 1978.

The Eleventh-Hour Maneuvers of Chief Justice Burger

Although the 1978 Code was prompted by escalating concerns about the number of consumer bankruptcy filings, and the Code completely reorganized bankruptcy practice, many of most animated debates did not concern either of these issues. Throughout the lengthy gestation of the Code, lawmakers wrestled with a single structural issue: the status of the bankruptcy judges. Much of the discussion was dominated by the question whether to give the judges lifetime appointment and all the trappings enjoyed by federal district court judges (that is, Article III status) or to define their position in some other way.

Along with nearly all of the principal interest groups—from bankruptcy lawyers to creditors—bankruptcy judges favored Article III status. Their chief opposition came from other federal judges, who quite candidly worried that elevating bankruptcy judges would diminish their prestige. The House bill took the bankruptcy judges' side—proposing full Article III status—whereas the Senate bill made only limited concessions to bankruptcy judge status. The compromise worked out between the House and Senate more or less split the differences between the two bills. Under the compromise, the bankruptcy judges would be appointed by the president, but they would not enjoy true Article III status. Bankruptcy judges would serve fourteen-year terms rather than receiving a lifetime appointment.

It was at this point that Chief Justice Warren Burger, in an unusual step for a sitting Supreme Court justice, actively intervened. Chief Justice Burger shared the district judges' concerns about diluting the federal bench and about the inferior quality of many bankruptcy judges. "Would *you* accept a bankruptcy judgeship?" he asked a legal academic privately during the legislative debates.[45] As the compromise gathered steam in 1978, Burger apparently telephoned Republican senators Strom Thurmond and Malcolm Wallop and persuaded them to stop the Senate from voting on it. In an effort to placate Burger, the managers of the legislation made several small adjustments.[46] The judicial council would be given authority to nominate bankruptcy judges, for instance, and the president instructed to "give due consideration" to the council's nominees. Still not satisfied, Chief Justice Burger tried to persuade President Carter not to sign the bill. But sign it the president did.

The constantly shifting compromise between bankruptcy judges and the current federal judiciary was far from resolved even when President Carter signed the bankruptcy bill into law in November 1978. In trying to strike a delicate balance that lifted bankruptcy judges up, but kept them beneath the district court, the final legislation created a ticklish constitutional difficulty. The Code authorized the bankruptcy judges to exercise federal jurisdiction of the sort vested in Article III courts, yet the bankruptcy judges did not have Article III status. Everyone knew there would be a constitutional challenge, and there was. In 1982, the Supreme Court struck down the 1978 Code as unconstitutional in *Northern Pipeline Construction Corporation v. Marathon Pipeline Co.*[47] Although the precise contours of the decision were obscured by a division within the Court as to the appropriate rationale, *Marathon Oil* made clear that the bankruptcy judges could not act like Article III judges unless they were given full Article III status. The saga continued after *Marathon Oil*, culminating in additional amendments in 1984 that attempted to strengthen the pretense that the district courts were the ones with bankruptcy jurisdiction, without interfering with bankruptcy judges' ability to run the show on a day-to-day basis. No one is quite sure whether the constitutional problems have been solved, but the bankruptcy courts have been open for business ever since.

The lengthy debates over the status of bankruptcy judges should not obscure the real effect of the 1978 Code. The technical changes to jurisdiction and consumer bankruptcy generated little attention in the media. Rare was the editorial that took any notice of the goings-on in Congress. The effect of the changes, however, has been to usher in a dramatically new bankruptcy regime. The political balance between debtors' and creditors' interests remains intact, but the "bankruptcy ring" has disappeared. For both better and worse, bankruptcy no longer is a mysterious process that takes place in dark rooms or behind closed doors.

Chapter Six

REPUDIATING THE NEW DEAL WITH CHAPTER 11 OF
THE BANKRUPTCY CODE

ALTHOUGH THE LEGISLATIVE activity that led to the Bankruptcy Code of 1978 had been prompted by the astonishing rise in consumer bankruptcies rather than business failures, many of the most prominent bankruptcy lawyers came from the corporate bankruptcy side. As we have seen, the principal officers of the National Bankruptcy Conference were such corporate bankruptcy experts as George Triester, Charles Seligson, and Larry King, and many of the members of the ABA Committee on Bankruptcy Law also had a corporate focus. (A crucial exception was Harvard's Vern Countryman, the persistent advocate of consumer debtors.) Even the membership of the National Bankruptcy Commission reflected this bias, as the bankruptcy judges pointed out with malicious glee in their assaults on the structural and consumer provisions in the commission bill.

The corporate bankruptcy lawyers were committed to and interested in structural and consumer bankruptcy reform, as we have seen. The leaders of the bar viewed reforming bankruptcy practice as a whole, and improving its image, as crucial to bankruptcy lawyers of every stripe. Moreover, many issues—such as the definition of *claim* and the preference rules—affect both personal and corporate bankruptcy. With so many corporate bankruptcy specialists involved, however, it was also inevitable that the reform process would devote significant attention to concerns about corporate bankruptcy practice. And it did. The commission bill proposed to soften the absolute priority rule, and to cede the SEC's responsibilities to the proposed bankruptcy administrator. The House bill proposed still more dramatic changes to the Chandler Act framework, while the Senate bill toed the line on existing law. As we will see, when the dust cleared, the House proposals prevailed, and Congress abandoned the New Deal vision that had defined corporate bankruptcy since 1938.

The big winners in the Code's reconfiguration of corporate reorganization were corporate bankruptcy lawyers and their clients. As we saw in chapter 4, the New Deal reformers' vision for bankruptcy had decimated the elite reorganization practice. As we shall see, the general bankruptcy bar filled the void, in large part through a remarkable manipulation of the chapter for small corporations, Chapter XI; but the process was fraught with uncertainty, and the bar yearned for a more flexible approach. In the words of one prominent bankruptcy lawyer, the SEC's authority to insist that cases be transferred to

Chapter X hung "like the sword of Damocles" over the proceedings.[1] The 1978 Code gave the bankruptcy bar more than they could have dared to hope.

Much more than with the structural and scope-expanding proposals, the new approach to corporate reorganization cannot be seen as a simple story about the influence of the bankruptcy bar, however. Although corporate bankruptcy lawyers do, of course, figure prominently, they were only one factor in the long series of developments that led to Chapter 11 of the 1978 Code. The great irony, as mentioned at the end of chapter 4, was that, by destroying elite reorganization practice so completely in the Chandler Act of 1938, the SEC and its New Deal allies sowed the seeds for their own demise. The story is important and has not previously been told, so we will start at the beginning, with the Chandler Act of 1938 itself. We will then consider a series of developments that took place between 1938 and 1978, most of which can be traced to the structure of Chapter X. Only in the context of these historical developments can we begin to make sense of Congress's dramatic repudiation of the SEC and the New Deal approach to large-scale corporate reorganization in 1978.

In brief, the story consists of five interconnected pieces. The narrative that follows will recount (1) how an accident of drafting left the door open for lawyers to manipulate Chapter XI; (2) how William Douglas himself as Supreme Court justice authored the very opinion that kept the strategy alive; (3) how the SEC's destruction of the elite reorganization bar created an interest group environment over which the SEC had far less control; (4) how the federal budget retrenchment of the Eisenhower years and persistent budget problems in the reorganization division thereafter compounded the SEC's difficulties; and (5) how the SEC's choice of bills in the 1930s, and thus of congressional oversight committees, later came back to haunt it. The theme running through all of these developments is that, by claiming so complete a victory in Chapter X of the Chandler Act, the SEC reformers unintentionally "wired" the 1938 legislation for demise. It was the confluence of these factors that ultimately doomed the New Deal vision for bankruptcy in 1978.

Although the passage of Chapter 11 was by far the most important corporate law reform, several other changes also have contributed to the flourishing of corporate reorganization since 1978. We will briefly consider the most important of the changes at the end of the chapter.

EVADING CHAPTER X AND THE SEC

As we have seen, the Chandler Act destroyed large-scale reorganization practice as it had previously existed. In addition to ushering Wall Street out of the practice, Chapter X also required that the managers of the firm be replaced by an independent trustee, which gave managers an incentive to avoid Chapter X at all costs. The draconian effect of Chapter X, together with the fact that so many large firms had already failed during the depression, caused a dramatic drop in Chapter X cases. As we saw in chapter 4, in the 1950s, there were frequently less than a hundred new cases in any given year.

Between the 1950s and the 1970s, a new group of corporate bankruptcy lawyers developed an increasingly vibrant practice outside of Chapter X. These lawyers included Benjamin Weintraub and Harris Levin in New York in the 1950s, and as well as subsequent leaders of the bar such as Charles Seligson and, on the West Coast, George Triester. It was the practice they carved out that would serve as the basis for Chapter 11, and for the complete repudiation of the New Deal vision for large-scale corporate reorganization.

The corporate reorganization practice was made possible, in part, by an important and accidental loophole in the framework of Chapter X. This gap quickly brought to the fore a series of problems, each tied to the structure of the Chandler Act reforms, that would bedevil the SEC for the next four decades. To appreciate the statutory goof and why it mattered, recall the differences between the two reorganization chapters of the Chandler Act. Chapter X called for an independent trustee, required strict compliance with the absolute priority rule, and gave the SEC a pervasive oversight role. In Chapter XI, the debtor's managers retained control, absolute priority was not required, and the SEC was nowhere to be seen.

It was clear to everyone that publicly held debtors were supposed to reorganize under Chapter X—and only that chapter—and that Chapter XI would be used for mom-and-pop firms and small corporate debtors. Moreover, since many large debtors had significant amounts of secured obligations, it no doubt seemed unlikely that publicly held firms could reorganize under Chapter XI, given that this chapter permitted debtors to restructure only their unsecured debt. This was why the SEC had focused all of its attention on Chapter X, for instance, and let the general bankruptcy bar have its way with Chapter XI and the rest of the Chandler Act amendments.

Obvious though it was that publicly held firms belonged in Chapter X, nothing in the Chandler Act explicitly *required* a publicly held firm to use that chapter. In fact, in what was as delicious an irony for the SEC's opponents as it was a nightmare for the SEC, the reformers got their threshold requirements exactly backward. By its terms, the Chandler Act limited access to Chapter X—only firms that could demonstrate a need for Chapter X were allowed in—but imposed no restrictions on access to Chapter XI.[2] Any firm that was so inclined, these requirements suggested, was welcome to file its petition in Chapter XI.

The irony here is that the managers of a troubled firm and their lawyers had powerful incentives to file for Chapter XI, and equally strong incentives to avoid the chapter designed for publicly held firms. Managers who could navigate their firm into the cozy waters of Chapter XI would remain in control of the firm, and the lawyers who assisted them could stay on as debtor's coun-sel. As Larry King explained to Congress during the hearings on the 1978 Code: "by filing a Chapter XI case not only does the debtor remain in posses-sion and in control, but the lawyer also remains in control." In Chapter X, after the lawyer files and the trustee is appointed, "there is literally nothing left for the attorney for the debtor to do, and he more or less drops out of the case."[3] By restricting access to Chapter X, but not Chapter XI, the SEC had accidentally posted a guard at the wrong door. (As it turns out, there is a simple explanation for the glitch. The entrance requirement dated back to former Section 77B, which firms *did* want to invoke, and the SEC neglected to delete the language when it imposed its harsher vision of corporate reorganization.)

Almost as soon as the Chandler Act was passed, the SEC realized that managers might point their firms toward Chapter XI in order to avoid Chapter X. The commission quickly sought to close the loophole both legislatively and judicially. In early 1940, the SEC introduced legislation that would have required any firm whose securities were held by one hundred or more investors to use Chapter X. While the legislation was pending, the SEC chal-lenged attempts by several corporations whose securities were held by public investors to file for bankruptcy under Chapter XI. In the same year, 1940, one of these challenges reached the Supreme Court. Superficially at least, the Supreme Court's decision in this case, *SEC v. United States Realty & Improve-ment Co.*,[4] seemed to solve the SEC's problem. After contrasting the investor protections of Chapter X with the relative absence of similar strictures in Chapter XI, the Supreme Court concluded that public policy dictated that the financial distress of firms like U.S. Realty be resolved in Chapter X. Of the two chapters, the Court concluded, only Chapter X could provide a thor-oughgoing restructuring and at the same time protect investors' interests. Based on the *U.S. Realty* case, the House Judiciary Committee issued a report concluding that there was no longer any pressing need to consider the SEC's proposal.[5]

In reality, the *U.S. Realty* case did not solve the SEC's dilemma at all. Because the Supreme Court framed the issue in public policy terms, rather than establishing a bright-line test for which chapter applied, the managers and lawyers of troubled firms could continue to try to navigate even publicly held firms into the hospitable waters of Chapter XI. To be sure, on the rare occasions when truly large firms filed for bankruptcy, courts could be expected to insist on Chapter X. In the much more common event that a middle-sized firm filed, however, it was a different story. With these firms—corporations that had issued at least one class of stock or debt to public investors, but were owned by one shareholder or a small group of them—the managers and their attorneys could plausibly argue that Chapter XI made sense. The SEC contin-ued to insist that all publicly held firms belonged in Chapter X, but the *U.S. Reality* case had left just enough room for at least some middle-sized firms to squeeze through. By the 1950s, two leading reorganization lawyers cautiously announced that Chapter XI was the chapter of choice for middle-sized firms.[6]

In 1956, the ongoing dance between the SEC and medium-sized firms and their lawyers once again reached the Supreme Court in *General Stores Corp. v. Shlensky.*[7] General Stores was a small chain of cigar shops that had a relatively small number of public shareholders and one issue of publicly held bonds. As in the earlier case and a third case the Supreme Court would decide in 1965, the SEC urged the Court to adopt a bright-line test for distinguishing the two chapters. If a corporate debtor had issued any securities to public investors, the SEC insisted, it belonged in Chapter X. In response, the attorneys for General Stores contended that the determination should be made on a case-by-case basis, and that there simply was no need for the elaborate apparatus of Chapter X with this debtor.

On the facts, the SEC won once again. But it was a victory that would offer the SEC little satisfaction in the ensuing years. In an opinion by Justice Douglas (the same William Douglas, of course, who had drafted Chapter X as chairman of the SEC), the Supreme Court agreed that General Stores belonged in Chapter X, not the more manager-friendly Chapter XI. To the SEC's chagrin, however, Douglas's majority opinion pointedly refused to require that all firms with public investors use Chapter X. In words that echoed through dozens of lower-court decisions in the years to follow, Douglas held that the choice of reorganization chapters required a case-by-case, factual inquiry focusing on the "needs to be met." If a debtor's attorneys could persuade a court that the firm's investors were generally capable of taking care of themselves, the friendly confines of Chapter XI would still be available. *Shlensky* put to rest any hope the SEC had of achieving a surgical solution to the jurisdictional issue. (The *Shlensky* case was not the last time General Stores would be heard from in the annals of bankruptcy history. After nine years in Chapter X, General Stores, which now had given up cigars to sell candy, emerged from bankruptcy while the Brookings Institution investigators were conducting their study, and earned the distinction of being the only successful Chapter X reorganization in the study.)

One of the more intriguing puzzles of the SEC saga is William Douglas's role. How could the same man who worked so hard to create Chapter X and secure its enactment later go on, as Supreme Court justice, to write the opinion that brought so much heartache to the SEC? We will explore this mystery in just a moment. For now, the important points are that the reformers' failure to define which firms belonged in each chapter of the Chandler Act had left the door open for debtors to sneak into Chapter XI; and that the *Shlensky* case, which affirmed the Supreme Court's initial decision in *U.S. Realty* and was itself reaffirmed by the Court nine years later, propped the door firmly open.

In the late 1950s and early 1960s, the number of firms that had publicly held securities but nonetheless filed for bankruptcy under Chapter XI grew substantially. This is not to say that the SEC was simply helpless against the onslaught. Both the SEC and the bankruptcy bar knew that, if the SEC dug in its heals, it could force many of the cases into Chapter XI. For bankruptcy lawyers, the prospect of an SEC challenge could cast a pall over the whole reorganization process. During the hearings that led to the 1978 Code, several offered horror stories of cases in which the SEC intervened in the waning moments of a reorganization, roiling the negotiations as they neared completion. (Most frequently mentioned was *SEC v. Canandaigua Enterprises*, where the SEC intervened after the parties had reached agreement on the terms of a reorganization. Although Judge Friendly concluded that he had no choice but to accede to the SEC's demand that the case be transferred to Chapter X, he did so with obvious reluctance. "We repeat," Judge Friendly said for the court, "our dislike at having to insist on a course which scarcely a creditor or stockholder has sought and which might lead to disaster. If we were holders of the debentures, we might well prefer [to remain in Chapter XI].")[8]

For its part, the SEC developed loose guidelines for deciding which Chapter XI filings to challenge—guidelines that reflected the SEC's charge to serve as champion for investors that hold publicly issued securities.[9] If a firm had issued bonds to public investors, the SEC pushed for Chapter X, since strict application of the absolute priority rule could protect the bondholders' interests. With firms that had issued stock but not bonds to public investors, on the other hand, the SEC generally took no action. In fact, the commission welcomed Chapter XI in these cases, since Chapter XI assured that shareholders' interests would be preserved, whereas the absolute priority rule might leave nothing for shareholders in Chapter X. Finally, with firms that had issued both stock and bonds to public investors, the SEC made an ad hoc determination whether to push for Chapter X. Rather than litigating the jurisdictional issue in every case where it decided to intervene, the SEC often struck a bargain with the debtor's attorneys. The SEC would insist on specified protections for the firm's public investors, and in return, the commission would agree to allow the case to remain in Chapter XI.

In short, the *Shlensky* decision did not prevent the SEC from playing a substantial role in corporate reorganization. The process continued to bear the SEC's fingerprints, not just in the SEC's formal challenges to Chapter XI filings but also in the many cases that remained in that chapter. But corporate reorganization looked less and less like the regime that Douglas, Fortas, and their peers had imagined. Rather than reigning unchallenged in Chapter X, the SEC was reduced to raising jurisdictional objections. And larger and larger firms began to make their way into Chapter XI. The list of firms that reorganized under the procedures originally designed for mom-and-pops included many of the nation's largest corporate bankruptcies—firms like Bohacks or Arlan's Department Stores.

THE CURVEBALL FROM JUSTICE DOUGLAS IN THE SHENSKY CASE

As noted above, perhaps the greatest puzzle of the *Shlensky* case is that Justice Douglas, the leading New Deal bankruptcy reformer, seemed to pass up a perfect opportunity to shut the door on Chapter XI for publicly held firms. The contrast to Douglas's other bankruptcy decisions as Supreme Court justice is quite striking. From the moment he was fitted for the black robe, Douglas had translated his views as scholar and SEC chairman into bankruptcy jurisprudence in cases such as *Case v. Los Angeles Lumber Products* and *Consolidated Rock v. DuBois*. In *Shlensky*, by contrast, Douglas seemed to go against his natural grain. Rather than solving the SEC's dilemma, Douglas left substantial room for debtors and their lawyers to maneuver.

Why did Douglas decline to provide a clear resolution? One possible explanation is that the Chandler Act had so transformed corporate reorganization by the 1950s that it no longer seemed necessary to steer every large debtor into Chapter X. The lawyers for debtors such as General Stores did not come from the old Wall Street bar, and the Wall Street banks were nowhere to be seen. On the other hand, there is no evidence that Douglas believed Chapter X had completed its work, and the SEC obviously was persuaded that its strictures were still necessary.

It is also possible that Douglas's views did not change at all, but that he was constrained by the exigencies of Supreme Court decision making. Even if Douglas believed that every firm with public investors belonged in Chapter X, he could not take that position for the Court unless at least four of the other eight justices agreed with him. Perhaps Douglas had to scale down his aspirations in order to assemble a five-justice majority. This, too, is faintly unsatisfying, however. Douglas was never known as a coalition builder on the Court. Quite to the contrary, he seemed to revel in taking an independent stance. His biographer, in fact, alluded to this in the title of his biography, *Independent Journey.*[10]

Although we may never know for sure, an internal memo that Douglas wrote for the *U.S. Realty* case in 1940 strongly suggests that neither of the obvious explanations has it quite right.[11] In the memo, Douglas set forth his views on *U.S. Realty*, the first of the Supreme Court's decisions on the jurisdiction issue. (Douglas did not actually participate in the decision; he recused himself at the strong urging of Chief Justice Hughes because he had been SEC chairman before joining the Court.) The striking similarities between the 1940 memo and Douglas's *Shlensky* opinion suggest both that *Shlensky* reflected Douglas's real views, and that his views did not change markedly in the decade and a half that followed. Of particular note, Douglas insisted in the memo, as in *Shlensky*, that the choice of reorganization chapter should be left to courts' discretion, and he expressly rejected his former SEC colleagues' contention that "all cases where a debtor has outstanding public offerings of securities automatically fall under [Chapter] X." Courts must look at the particular debtor, he concluded, before they can determine which chapter it belongs in. The memo also foreshadows Douglas's discussion in *Shlensky* of the technical factors that should guide a court's choice of reorganization chapter. In both places, Douglas suggests that courts should consider whether a debtor realistically could propose a Chapter XI reorganization plan that is "fair and equitable"—that is, that satisfies the absolute priority rule. If the debtor could not propose a plan that satisfied both the "fair and equitable" standard and the other requirements of Chapter XI, Douglas suggested, the firm must use Chapter X.

The technical parallel might not seem remarkable at first glance. Of course the reorganization belongs in Chapter X, the reader might mutter to herself, if the firm could not plausibly devise a plan that meets the requirements of the less formal chapter. But the bankruptcy laws had changed in a crucial and telling respect between 1940 and 1956. Prior to 1952, the requirement that plans be "fair and equitable" applied both to Chapter X and to Chapter XI. In 1952, however, Congress deleted the "fair and equitable" requirement from Chapter XI at the urging of the National Bankruptcy Conference, which argued that this stricture made it nearly impossible to meet the other requirements of Chapter XI. (This was because Chapter XI required that shareholders keep their stock, yet the absolute priority rule mandated by the "fair and equitable" requirement prohibited shareholders from retaining any interest unless every one of the firm's creditors was somehow paid in full—an impossibility if the firm was insolvent.) Thus, when Douglas refers to the fair-and-equitable requirement as bearing on the choice of chapters in *Shlensky*, he refers to a requirement that no longer exists in Chapter XI. Justice Frankfurter, his long-time colleague, pointed out the oddity, and arguable irrelevance of the requirement, in a sharply worded dissent. "Since the [*U.S. Realty*] decision to no small degree turned on the enforcement of the 'fair and equitable' rule," Frankfurter wrote, it is noteworthy that no consideration was given by the lower courts, and none is given by this Court, to the significance of this amendment by Congress."[12] Although we should not push the speculation too far, it is plausible that Douglas hewed to his original analysis even in the face of an intervening statutory change.

If, as the 1940 memo strongly suggests, Douglas's views did not change, where did the views come from in the first instance? Why not simply direct all publicly held debtors into Chapter X? The most obvious explanation is that *Shlensky* is a direct manifestation of Douglas's judicial philosophy— though one with unfortunate consequences for the SEC. Douglas was deeply committed to the legal realist view that lawmakers must look beyond the laws themselves—which often offer little insight into how things actually work—and take a more functional approach to legal decision making. Douglas's "needs to be served" standard is precisely this kind of approach. Although he believed that every debtor belonged in one of the two chapters, either Chapter X or Chapter XI, Douglas also believed that the choice should turn on the particular debtor rather than an artificial rule such as the presence or absence of publicly issued securities.

An additional, practical consideration may have been the SEC's limitations as an overseer. The SEC could not realistically intervene in every case involving publicly issued securities; nor would it want to. Even the most avid reformers believed that the SEC's resources were best spent focusing on cases where public investors' interests were genuinely at stake—cases with widely scattered security holders or complicated capital structures. SEC oversight of closely held debtors that happened to have a few publicly issued securities could distract the SEC from its mission of championing the interests of public investors.

THE SEC'S INTEREST GROUP WOES

As remarkable as the decision was, *Shlensky* did not by itself seal the SEC's fate. Only in combination with several other factors that, like the lack of a gatekeeping requirement, were set in motion in 1938 did the "needs to be served" test prove so disastrous.

The most devastating structural problem with the Chandler Act was that the New Deal reformers quite accidentally stacked the interest group deck against themselves. As we saw in chapter 4, the very prominence and geographical concentration of the elite Wall Street bankers and bar made them an easy target for the New Deal vision of finance. The good news for the SEC was that the Chandler Act reforms destroyed Wall Street's stranglehold on large scale reorganization. Unfortunately for the SEC, this may also have been the bad news. As the Wall Street firms disappeared, the general bankruptcy bar began to fill the void. As we have seen, bankruptcy practice was dominated by small, second- and third-tier firms—the bankruptcy "boutiques." Many of these bankruptcy firms specialized in business bankruptcy. The firms that handled the largest cases tended to be centered in large cities—Charles Seligson's New York firm dated back to 1920 and grew to a dozen or so lawyers by the 1960s. In Los Angeles, George Triester's firm, Stutman, Triester and Glatt, was similarly prominent. Because Chapter X required the displacement both of a firm's managers and of its attorneys, the interests of these firms obviously were directly opposed to those of the SEC. The SEC was the managers' and lawyers' principal obstacle to steering a bankrupt firm into Chapter XI, and the story of corporate reorganization under the Chandler Act is, as should already be clear, largely the story of the SEC's skirmishes with the new reorganization bar.

By most objective standards, the reorganization boutiques were not as prestigious as the Wall Street reorganizers had been. Yet they were a far more effective interest group in many respects. Unlike their predecessors, who were geographically concentrated, the new bar spanned the country. Acting through the National Bankruptcy Conference and the ABA, they could not easily be typecast as an insulated elite. The leading reorganization lawyers also were not closely connected to the "bankruptcy ring"—the lawyers who acted as trustee or the trustee's attorney in many cases in New York and other cities.

In addition to managers and the bankruptcy bar, the Chandler Act also aligned the SEC and the New Deal vision for bankruptcy against another interest group with antagonistic interests: the bankruptcy bench. The bankruptcy judges played a particularly important role—more subtle but more influential than their role in the congressional hearings of the 1970s—for the simple reason that the slow demise of the SEC in bankruptcy took place principally in the case law, and thus in the courtroom.

Each time the SEC challenged a debtor's attempt to steer a publicly held firm into Chapter XI, the challenge was resolved on the merits, of course. But the "needs to be served" standard gave the courts a great deal of discretion in determining which of the two reorganization chapters should apply in a given case. And the discretion clearly did not favor the SEC. To see why, we should start by noting that both bankruptcy and district court judges had a hand in the decision on chapter choice. Under settled practice for much of the life of the Chandler Act, bankruptcy judges oversaw Chapter XI cases, whereas the larger, more formal Chapter X cases were transferred to the district court. (This was one of many manifestations of the fact that bankruptcy judges were second-class adjuncts of the district court.) Given that large reorganizations were the most prestigious cases they saw, the bankruptcy judges had a powerful incentive to squeeze the case into Chapter XI, rather than shuffling the parties off to the district court. After a steady diet of personal and small-firm bankruptcies, a bankruptcy judge might be forgiven if he were reluctant to let go of, say, the Arlan's Department Store bankruptcy.[13]

Later on, when bankruptcy courts began hearing Chapter X cases themselves, they still had good reasons for preferring the small-firm alternative. Appointing a trustee was a distraction, and the trustee had to get up to speed on the firm. The SEC itself was a source of delay, since the parties had to wait for the SEC to review any proposed plan in large cases. Perhaps more importantly, although some courts welcomed its input, the SEC was in a sense a competing source of authority, since the SEC report inevitably carried great weight. The smoother waters of Chapter XI thus held a powerful allure for the bankruptcy judge, just as they did for the debtor's managers and lawyers.

The case law on chapter choice offers a striking confirmation of these general inclinations. The SEC's record in the lower courts was quite weak. A substantial majority of trial-level decisions refused to transfer the case to Chapter X. It was only at the appellate level that the SEC's record improved.[14] Unless the SEC was willing to litigate multiple appeals, it faced debtors and attorneys who were dead set against Chapter X, and judges likely to have similar inclinations. An obvious alternative, of course, would have been to ask Congress to remedy the SEC's problem, and the SEC attempted precisely this in the late 1950s. As we shall see when we consider congressional committee structure below, however, the SEC's prospects were nearly as bleak in the legislative sphere as in the courts.

The great irony of the SEC's interest group woes is that the SEC might actually have been better off in the long run—or at least lasted longer—if William Douglas and the reformers had weakened the Wall Street reorganization bar rather than destroying it. A comparison with the SEC's role under the 1933 and 1934 securities acts offers a revealing contrast in this regard. In order to pass the securities laws, New Deal lawmakers had to overcome resistance from the same investment banks that the SEC targeted with its bankruptcy reforms. As with the Chandler Act, the securities laws interposed the SEC as regulator in an area where investment bankers previously had enjoyed wide latitude. At the time, Wall Street responded with dire predictions that the reforms would destroy the hoped-for economic recovery and undermine corporate finance.[15] As broadly as the new securities laws swept, however, they, unlike the Chandler Act, preserved an important role for investment bankers (and Wall Street lawyers) in securities issuance. As a result, each of these interest groups now has a powerful incentive to ensure that the SEC retains its regulatory authority; and each has sided with the SEC in the SEC's jurisdictional battles with other agencies.[16] As the SEC wrestles with the Commodity Futures Trading Commission over the right to regulate derivative securities, for instance, investment banks and lawyers have strongly supported the SEC, the regulator they know, over the one they don't. By flatly prohibiting a debtor's current lawyers from serving in Chapter X, the Chandler Act left little room for this kind of symbiotic relationship to develop between the SEC and the reorganization bar. Instead, the SEC found itself aligned against every relevant interest group.

THE INEFFECTUALITY OF THE SEC ITSELF

As if the SEC's interest group opposition were not enough, its difficulties were compounded by the strict budget controls the Eisenhower administration implemented in the 1950s. Although Eisenhower did not have any particular animus against the SEC, the SEC was dealt the same sharp cuts as other agencies. In his already classic history of the SEC, Joel Seligman refers to the Eisenhower era commission as the "budget bureau's SEC."[17] Faced with a shrinking budget, the SEC was forced to reign in many of its enforcement activities. The SEC's reorganization division was particularly hard hit. In an odd way, the Chandler Act itself may have encouraged the SEC to respond to the cuts by retrenching in bankruptcy. As we have seen, the managers of troubled firms had an enormous disincentive to file for Chapter X under the Chandler Act, since the bankruptcy petition would also be a death sentence for their current jobs. Firms that could avoid Chapter X did precisely that, either by filing for Chapter XI or by struggling to stay out of bankruptcy. This, together with the fact that the depression had already winnowed out many firms, caused the number of Chapter X filings to plummet, as we saw in chapter 4. In 1939, there were 577 Chapter X cases; in the next five years, the number would drop to less than 100 per year and remain there in most years (see table 4.1). The dearth of Chapter X cases and the elimination the Wall Street reorganization bar made bankruptcy an obvious place to cut, and cut the SEC did—even after the SEC's budget began to increase again. The legislative history of the 1978 Code is filled with references to the pitiful state of the SEC's reorganization division. The complaints of Harold Marsh, chairman of the Bankruptcy Commission, were characteristic. "The reorganization branch has been starved by the commission for the past 20 years." By Marsh's reckoning, the reorganization budget amounted to only $500,000–600,000 out of a total SEC budget of $38–40 million each year. Even the SEC acknowledged its precarious status. "We do not have, and have not had for some time," an SEC commissioner told Congress, "enough money to do all of the varied things that the Commission has to do."[18]

The SEC's weakened state ratcheted up its interest group problems. Because the SEC was understaffed, it took longer for the SEC to complete its review of a proposed reorganization plan than might otherwise have been the case. As the SEC itself noted during the hearings that led to the 1978 Code, "it is all too often that it takes us longer than we would like to prepare the report." Responding to a bankruptcy judge's defense of the SEC, Congressman Edwards, who had been a member of the Bankruptcy Commission, echoed this concern, saying that "there was evidence [in the discussions of the commission] . . . that the SEC did drag its feet and put bankruptcy matters at the bottom of the pile."[19] The effect of SEC's tardiness was to exacerbate the delay that already characterized cases that were handled in Chapter X. This made Chapter XI look even better to bankruptcy lawyers and the bankruptcy court.

Although I have emphasized the importance of structural factors and the role of interest groups, an alternative theory might characterize the demise of the SEC in purely economic terms, as an illustration of the U.S. capital markets at work. The economic story goes as follows. By the late 1940s, the most troubled U.S. firms had been winnowed out by the depression—hence the steep decline in Chapter X cases. Starting in the 1950s, the U.S. capital markets were back on their feet, and the nature of U.S. business had changed in crucial respects. Railroads, whose complex capital structures had created the need for corporate reorganization in the first instance, were not nearly so important to the U.S. economy as in the past. Railroads had been replaced by a wide variety of industrial corporations—IBM and the auto manufacturers, for instance—that had less complex capital structures. Whereas the railroads had been financed by bonds and other debt securities, the new generation of U.S. firms relied more on the equity markets. The SEC stood ready to protect the small investors who had put their savings in bonds, and who needed a governmental champion. Unfortunately for the SEC, this paradigm no longer existed. In the new marketplace, small investors were more likely to invest in stock than in bonds, and the elaborate governmental apparatus provided by the Chandler Act no longer made sense. The economic story thus suggests that the decline and eventual fall of the SEC was the inevitable fate of a regulatory framework whose time had passed.

An obvious problem with this economic story, at least as I have related it, is that it puts too much weight on the changing business climate of the 1950s as a wholly external and independent explanation for the demise of the New Deal vision for large-scale reorganization. The return to strength of American business is one reason for the drop in large-scale corporate bankruptcies, for instance, but the Chandler Act itself was also part of the equation. By ushering Wall Street out of corporate reorganization, the Chandler Act severed the ties between bankruptcy and finance. Even in the best of times, at least some large firms still encountered financial distress and might have benefited from a thoroughgoing reorganization process. But troubled firms no longer viewed bankruptcy as part of the ordinary arsenal of weapons for solving corporate problems, and the managers of these firms had good reason to file for bankruptcy (and face immediate displacement in Chapter X) only as an absolute last resort.

The Chandler Act may also have influenced the financing decisions of healthy firms, and thus contributed to the precisely economic changes I described a moment ago.[20] To see this, consider how bondholders would have viewed the innovations put in place by William Douglas and his SEC allies. Whereas J. P. Morgan and the Wall Street banks had played a consistent, predictable role in the equity receivership era, bondholders, whose securities were the focus of the traditional restructuring process, now faced several crucial uncertainties. Probably the greatest wildcard was the role of the SEC. The SEC had no track record in bankruptcy, and bondholders had no way of knowing how aggressively the SEC would intervene in Chapter X, or what standards the SEC would use when it assessed proposed reorganizations. (As it turned out, the SEC's valuations did not solve this problem, as the commission's valuations seemed to many observers to be inconsistent and ad hoc.) Adding to the uncertainty was the fact that bondholders could not know for sure whether a future bankruptcy case would be resolved in Chapter X or under the very different procedures of Chapter XI.

In work that was published in the same decade as the changes we are considering, the 1950s, and that would eventually lead to a Nobel Prize, Merton Miller and Franco Modigliani argued (as one of the qualifications on their famous "Irrelevance Thesis") that firms will issue more stock and less debt as the cost of issuing bonds increases.[21] The Chandler Act may well have had precisely this effect on the securities markets. Bondholders' uncertainty translates to higher risk, which would cause rational bondholders to demand a higher return on their investment. The increased cost of issuing bonds may therefore have been one reason that managers of firms looked more to stock than to bonds for financing during the 1950s. By insisting that the traditional reorganization process be dramatically overhauled, William Douglas and the SEC therefore may have contributed to the very changes—such as the shift from debt to equity financing—that would make the SEC's role increasingly tenuous in the decades after the Chandler Act was enacted.

The relationship between the Chandler Act and the economic changes that took hold in the 1950s obviously is complex, and I do not want to overstate the impact of the 1938 legislation, but one thing is quite clear: the demise of the SEC was more than simply the accidental side effect of external market changes. The structure of the Chandler Act itself contributed to the SEC's woes in crucial respects. If the Chandler Act had been structured differently— most importantly, if William Douglas had heeded the widespread pleas to make the trustee requirement flexible rather than mandatory—the SEC could have preserved a meaningful role for itself in corporate reorganization. That is what we see in a variety of other New Deal financial reforms, such as the 1933 and 1934 securities acts, both of which are alive and well in the post– New Deal marketplace.

The Curse of an Unsympathetic Oversight Committee

The last factor we need to consider, and a daunting obstacle for the SEC when it turned to Congress for help, stemmed from a seemingly technical detail in the way the New Deal reforms had been framed: the identity of the congressional committee that would oversee any subsequent amendments. To appreciate the possibilities, recall from chapter 4 that when the SEC sprang into action in 1936, the reformers added their proposals to a pair of companion bills: the Chandler Act was designed to amend the Bankruptcy Act, whereas the closely related Lea bill was framed as amendments to the securities laws. When both bills encountered fierce opposition, the reformers refused to compromise on either bill and eventually let the Lea bill die. As we saw earlier, this was only one of several tacks the reformers could have taken. As an obvious alternative, Douglas could have tinkered enough with the Lea bill to ensure its passage. If the Lea bill had passed, the Interstate Commerce and Banking Committees would have had jurisdiction over any subsequent reforms, since these committees oversee the securities acts. By casting their lot with the Chandler bill, the reformers also assured that any future amendments would go to a different committee—the Judiciary Committee, which oversees bankruptcy legislation.

According to some scholars, it should not make any difference whether one congressional committee (here, the Judiciary Committee) has jurisdiction over a legislative proposal rather than another committee (here, Banking and Interstate Commerce). Committees are simply set up to make Congress's work a bit easier, and Congress (or, more precisely, the majority party in Congress) is the one that calls all the shots. By controlling the membership of committees, and the votes on any bill that comes out of a committee, the majority party determines what kinds of legislation get passed.[22]

Other scholars, by contrast, view committees as far more influential. Although committees act as "agents" for Congress, agents do not always blindly follow the wishes of the "principal" they represent. The nature of an oversight committee's role, these scholars argue, gives it an enormous influence over legislative outcomes. Committees are the ones who decide whether an issue is ever considered—and once enacted, whether legislation is revisited. When conference committees are set up to reconcile differences between the House and Senate versions of a bill, members of the relevant oversight committees almost always predominate, which gives the committee yet another opportunity to influence the shape of legislation.[23]

The reality almost certainly lies somewhere between the two views. Although committees are not omnipotent, they clearly can make a difference, at least at the margin. From the SEC's perspective, it is plain that the Judiciary Committee was a far less promising venue for launching or affecting future legislation than the Banking and Commerce Committees. Think first about the advantages the SEC would have enjoyed if the Banking and Commerce Committees were responsible for corporate bankruptcy reforms. Because Banking and Commerce have jurisdiction over the securities laws, and the SEC has a direct interest in nearly every proposed amendment to these acts, the SEC has long had frequent, direct, ongoing contact with these committees. This ongoing relationship has created both familiarity and a presumption of expertise when the SEC speaks on its activities under the securities laws. The SEC is, in fact, the Banking and Commerce Committees' principal expert on issues relating to the financial markets.

The SEC's relationship with the Judiciary Committee stands in marked contrast. The SEC does not appear before the Judiciary Committee with any regularity, since the Judiciary Committee does not oversee the other areas that the SEC regulates. Moreover, even in bankruptcy, the SEC's interest was always limited to issues involving large corporate debtors and public investors; it had no stake in consumer and small-business bankruptcies, which comprise the vast majority of all bankruptcies. In the late 1960s hearings that led to the National Bankruptcy Review Commission, Charles Seligson, the chair of the National Bankruptcy Conference, pointedly underscored this limitation. Responding to the question whether Congress should include an SEC representative on the Bankruptcy Commission, Seligson said, "I don't think they have the broad approach that is needed for representation."[24]

Rather than the SEC, it is the bankruptcy bar and organizations such as the National Bankruptcy Conference that appear before the Judiciary Committee year after year and enjoy a presumption of expertise. As we saw in chapter 5, in his oral history, Frank Kennedy, a longtime member of the NBC, recalled the relationship with great fondness: "Over the years, whenever any bankruptcy legislation was being considered . . . the House Judiciary Committee and the Senate Judiciary Committee always informed us, and asked us to comment on these proposals, and paid considerable respect to the views that were expressed by the NBC members.[25] Similarly, Congressman Edwards opened several House hearings in the 1970s by emphasizing that the proposed legislation had been developed in close cooperation with the National Bankruptcy Conference. Introducing Vern Countryman, a vice chairman of the NBC, Edwards described the conference as "a select group of bankruptcy practitioners, judges, and teachers that has often been of assistance to Congress in fashioning bankruptcy legislation.[26]

With the Judiciary Committee, then, came double trouble for the SEC: the SEC had much less clout there than with Banking and Commerce; and even worse, the one interest group that did have influence, bankruptcy professionals, had a great deal to gain if the SEC's reforms in Chapter X unraveled over time.

The SEC's intermittent efforts to pass legislation forcing publicly held debtors to use Chapter X illustrate the commission's trouble on the legislative front. In 1958, the SEC introduced (through Representative Celler) legislation that would have prohibited any corporation whose securities were held by one hundred or more persons from reorganizing under Chapter XI. In deference to the influence of the National Bankruptcy Conference both on bankruptcy issues in general, and with the Judiciary Committee in particular, the SEC met with the NBC in an effort to obtain the NBC's support.[27] When the conference made clear that it would oppose the SEC's proposal to limit access to Chapter XI, the SEC abandoned the new legislation. The SEC "does not feel that separate legislation need be offered," the SEC concluded in an internal memo, "with respect to [a proposal] on which there is fundamental disagreement with the National Bankruptcy Conference."[28]

The Chandler Act era was thus both the best and the worst of times for the New Deal vision of bankruptcy. The Chandler Act utterly destroyed Wall Street's traditional dominance of large-scale corporate reorganization and established the SEC as champion for the interests of small, public investors. But the structure of the Chandler Act subtly undermined the prospects for the New Deal vision and a permanent SEC role. The SEC's reforms went well beyond the goal of breaking Wall Street's grip on corporate reorganization and left the SEC with interest group enemies but no real allies. The interests of bankruptcy lawyers, bankruptcy judges, and—as will be discussed below—even large creditors conflicted with those of the SEC. The SEC's difficulties were exacerbated by the committee structure, which assured that any legislative efforts would go to a committee more sympathetic to bankruptcy lawyers than to the SEC, and by continual budget woes. Together these structural problems created ongoing hassles for the SEC and set the stage for the final indignity: the 1978 Code.

The Legislative History of the 1978 Reforms

The story of the 1978 Code's changes to corporate reorganization is, in a sense, a story of the reorganization bar achieving more than it could have dared to hope. For reorganization lawyers, Chapter X was the bankruptcy equivalent of the Berlin Wall, and the 1978 reforms brought it tumbling down. Bankruptcy lawyers were not the only ones who cheered; various other interest groups, most notably large creditors, also lobbied for more flexible reorganization provisions.

As in all things with the 1978 reforms, the commission bill made the opening bid on corporate reorganization and set the tone for all of the deliberations that followed. As noted at the beginning of the chapter, the commission bill proposed to retain the absolute priority rule, but in somewhat relaxed form, and to consolidate the two reorganization options into a single chapter. Although the commission proposed to remove the chief bugaboo of Chapter X, the mandatory trustee requirement, its bill included a presumption that the court would appoint a trustee in large cases. Each of these proposed changes was important, but the commission's most striking proposal, in some respects, involved the SEC. The commission proposed to relieve the SEC of all of its responsibilities, and to shift them to the proposed bankruptcy administrator.

The bankruptcy judges' alternative to the commission bill took a far more conservative stance on corporate reorganization. Under the judges' bill, the bankruptcy laws would continue to include two separate reorganization chapters, and the basic framework would remain the same. Trustees would be appointed as a matter of course for large corporations, and the SEC would continue to serve as the principal overseer for firms with publicly held securities.

Although the legislative history is replete with discussion of whether the bankruptcy laws should include two chapters for corporate reorganization, or just one, this was not the real issue. (And in fact, as Eric Posner has noted, speakers' views on this were misleading; a proponent of one chapter who believed that the chapter should include special provisions distinguishing between large corporations and small ones, for instance, was advocating essentially the same thing as proponents of two chapters.)[29] The real issues were whether Congress should continue to mandate trustees for large debtors, and whether the SEC should continue to oversee these cases.

Given bankruptcy lawyers' and judges' aversion to Chapter X, one might expect the congressional hearings to have been bristling with criticism of the SEC and the old framework for reorganizing large firms. The reality actually was more complex and interesting. Criticism by the bankruptcy bar and bench was muted at times, and the early hearings even included a few notes of support for the existing regime. Much of the complexity disappeared as the hearings went on, however, and the possibility of sweeping change became clear.

Perhaps the most striking note of support was the judges' bill itself. Although bankruptcy judges were not particularly sympathetic to the Chapter X framework and the role of the SEC, their bill proposed to keep nearly all of the existing framework in place, including both the SEC and the general apparatus of Chapter X. This apparent vote of confidence in the existing framework was misleading, however. Aside from a few kind words about the contributions of the SEC, the bankruptcy judges' support for the Chapter X framework was tepid at best. What the judges really cared about was defeating the proposal for a bankruptcy administrator, and protecting their role in the bankruptcy process. This meant defending the SEC — particularly given that the commission's bill proposed to transfer the SEC's responsibilities in corporate reorganization to the bankruptcy administrator — but the judges' commitment to the Chapter X was entirely strategic, and they made very little effort to defend the Chandler Act approach.

On the issue whether to replace the managers of a corporate debtor with a trustee, nearly everyone who testified argued for leaving the debtor's managers in place in small cases. Similarly, there was broad support for the Bankruptcy Commission's proposal to soften the requirement that trustees be appointed in large cases, by making the trustee presumptive, rather than mandatory. The National Bankruptcy Conference agreed with the use of a presumption, but argued that the reform should go still further — courts should be instructed to presume that a trustee would *not* be appointed. Almost the only countervailing view came, not surprisingly, from the SEC itself. SEC commissioner Loomis insisted that the trustee requirement should be mandatory in large cases, not simply presumptive, in order to assure adequate protection of small investors' interests.[30]

Interestingly, most of the creditors who testified were as firmly in favor of leaving the debtor's managers in control as bankruptcy lawyers were. Like the National Bankruptcy Conference, some thought that the commission proposal did not go far enough. John Creedon of the American Life Insurance Association, for instance, criticized the commission proposal, with its presumption in favor of appointing a trustee, as "leaning too far" toward Chapter X, rather than the more flexible Chapter XI approach. "If management is competent and honest and the debtor's financial plight is due to circumstances beyond management's control," he argued, "bringing in an outsider may not solve anything. Instead it may only slow the reorganization, add expense and restrict flexibility while the new trustee learns the business."[31]

Although the mandatory trustee requirement had enormous implications for the managers of troubled firms, managers played no visible role in the legislative hearings. The explanation for this remarkable anomaly—after all, managers are extremely well represented by groups such as the Business Roundtable—lies in the factors we considered in chapter 3. The managers of healthy firms do not tend to imagine their firm in bankruptcy, so they do not focus on insolvency-related issues. Corporate takeovers offer a revealing contrast in this regard. In the 1980s, many corporate managers worried that they would be taken over, and they actively lobbied state legislatures for protection from takeovers.[32] Bankruptcy, by contrast, does not seem so imminent. Once a firm does in fact fail, forcing its managers to think intensely about these issues, it is too late for the firm to benefit from future legislative changes. As a result, managers have always figured prominently in the judicial sphere, where they attempt to make the best of the existing rules, but they are represented only indirectly, by bankruptcy professionals, in the legislative debates.

In contrast to their unanimous support for eliminating the mandatory trustee requirement, bankruptcy lawyers' testimony on the SEC itself was more mixed. Their principal criticism concerned the uncertainty as to whether the SEC would challenge their attempt to use Chapter XI in any given case. A few were deeply skeptical of a continuing SEC role, but others seemed more ambivalent. Although prominent Los Angeles lawyer George Triester was "not wed" to retaining the SEC, for instance, and believed that a bankruptcy administrator could develop comparable expertise, he noted that the "SEC's attitude for moving cases from [Chapter XI to Chapter X] has toned down a lot."[33] The contrast in views seems to have reflected differing experiences in lawyers' interactions with the SEC. Some of the most prominent lawyers, such as Larry King, had developed workable relationships with the SEC and were willing to retain the SEC so long as the strictures of Chapter X were watered down. Those that had not, such as the chairman of the 1973 commission, Harold Marsh, were more hostile. (Ron Trost, who like Marsh practiced on the West Coast, was equally hostile; he recalls infuriating the SEC by suggesting that the best predictor of the SEC's staffing decisions was climate: the SEC staff devoted much more of their scarce resources to intervening in cases in California and Hawaii than in less pleasant locales.)[34] Early on, the more sympathetic view of the SEC seems to have commanded a majority within the National Bankruptcy Conference.[35] But bankruptcy lawyers' support for the SEC was not deep. Even lawyers who echoed Triester's view that the SEC had been less of an impediment in recent years were skeptical of the long-term prognosis. Several suggested that the SEC would keep a low profile only so long as its budget woes continued.

In short, bankruptcy lawyers as a group felt somewhat more sympathy for the SEC than they did for the elaborate reorganization apparatus of Chapter X. Both considerations were very much on the table when a new set of proposals replaced the commission's and judges' bills in 1977.

The differences between the commission's and judges' bills were striking in some respects, but they paled by comparison to the contrasts in the two bills that emerged in the second and final round of legislative deliberations. As we saw at the beginning of the chapter, the House bill took the tentative reforms of the commission bill and pushed them much further. This bill presumed that the debtor's managers would remain in place, waved off the absolute priority rule for classes of creditors that voted in favor of a reorganization plan, and eliminated the SEC. Under the House approach, the SEC would not even have standing to intervene. The only source of oversight, other than the court, would be a governmental official (eventually called the U.S. Trustee) located in the judicial branch of the government.

The Senate bill took precisely the opposite tack, hewing closely to the procedures of existing law. The Senate approach preserved the sharp distinctions between large- and small-firm reorganizations; required strict adherence to absolute priority; and continued to look to the SEC as protectors of investors' interests in cases involving publicly held firms. Far from retrenching on the Chandler Act, the Senate proposal actually strengthened the SEC's grip in several respects. Most importantly, all debtors with one hundred or more public investors would be subject to SEC oversight.

From the bankruptcy bar's perspective, the choice was quite stark and quite simple: the choice between a lawyers' bill (the House) and a bill that was, in some respects, worse than current law. Nor were they alone in their preference for the House approach to corporate reorganization. Banks, insurance companies, and other large creditors generally supported the more flexible approach of the House bill, which they defended as smoother, less costly, and more efficient than current Chapter X or the Senate bill. (In their recent book on the 1978 U.S. and 1986 British reforms, Carruthers and Halliday suggest that institutional creditors objected to the more relaxed approach that emerged in the hearings leading up to the 1978 Code and gave in only in the face of broad public support for a more rehabilitative regime.[36] This significantly overstates the pervasiveness of creditors' complaints. Although a few spokesmen for bankers did raise objections, bankers loudly and consistently argued for a flexible reorganization approach, one derived from Chapter XI rather than Chapter X.)

Particularly revealing was the view of the bankruptcy judges. As we saw a moment ago, the judges had initially proposed to keep much of the existing framework intact, including the oversight role of the SEC. By the second round, things had changed in one not-so-subtle respect: the bankruptcy agency proposal was now dead. With both bills assuming that judges rather than an administrator would rule the roost, the bankruptcy judges were more willing to call for reform. "[F]rom a time and cost savings standpoint," one judge testified, "as well as a practical problem caused by the SEC's picking and choosing its adherence to absolute priority, the SEC's role in reorganizations ought to be abolished or at least largely reduced."[37]

None of this is especially surprising, of course. We would expect bankruptcy judges, bankruptcy lawyers, and large creditors who could protect themselves to throw their support behind a proposal to expand the flexible Chapter XI approach, and to scale back Chapter X. What is more surprising is that the Senate would move so far in the opposite direction. Given the widespread support for a more relaxed approach, why did the Senate bill hold the line on the New Deal vision of bankruptcy?

The answer lies in the tireless advocacy of one lonely man, Aaron Levy of the SEC. His spirited but futile efforts to preserve the SEC's role were a faint echo of the SEC's influence on the Chandler Act of 1938 and underscore how much had changed. The structural time bomb that had been ticking for almost forty years was about to explode.

Levy had been the head of the SEC's reorganization staff for over a decade by the mid-1970s and had long kept a wary eye on efforts to chip away at the reach of Chapter X. (Levy appeared on the SEC's brief in the 1956 *Shlensky* case; spearheaded the failed effort for a legislative solution later that decade; and, when a wide-ranging set of proposed, nonlegislative bankruptcy rules (the same rules that would give bankruptcy referees the title of *bankruptcy judge* in 1973) was submitted to the Supreme Court for approval in the early 1970s, pleaded with Justice Douglas to intervene.) By the end of the first round of hearings, it was clear that the SEC had few allies in its battle to preserve the New Deal framework for large corporations. Despite the SEC's overall isolation, Levy managed to persuade one very useful advocate to the SEC's side: Robert Feidler. As research director for the Senate Judiciary Committee, Feidler was the staff member assigned to oversee the bankruptcy reform process. Along with Senator Burdick, Feidler was the only congressional representative who sat through and participated in all of the Senate bankruptcy hearings, and he was the primary drafter of the Senate bill.

As the staff of the Senate Judiciary Committee worked on the Senate bill, Levy kept in continuous contact with Feidler. "The basic approach of [the House bill]" he told Feidler, "is that a reorganization is based on a bargain among creditors of a distressed company. That is not a fitting approach for a public company. The mandatory appointment of a trustee and the [absolute priority rule] are the keystone to an effective reorganization."[38] To ensure that Feidler kept the faith, Levy sent him a steady stream of proposed amendments throughout 1977.[39] By mid-1978, Levy was able to look back with satisfaction on the shape of the Senate bill as he offered a few last suggestions. "Please accept my personal appreciation for the labors that went into [the Senate bill]," Levy told Feidler. "The spirit of this memorandum is best conveyed by the words of John Milton who over 300 years ago wrote that 'he who freely magnifies what hath been nobly done, and fears not to declare as freely what might be done better, gives ye the best covenant of his fidelity.' "[40]

At the Senate Judiciary Committee level, then, Levy and the SEC achieved notable success. In early 1978, the Senate passed the proposed legislation with the corporate reorganization provisions fully intact.

But the interest group opposition was simply too great, and the support for the Chapter X approach too thin even among the senators who voted for it. Prior to the Senate deliberations on the final bill, the House had passed its version of the legislation with the enthusiastic support of the bankruptcy bar, bankruptcy judges, banks, and insurance companies. When the House and Senate managers met to reconcile the two bills, they adopted the House provisions on corporate reorganization almost completely. As a sop to the SEC, the final version gave the commission the standing to intervene in corporate reorganization cases. But new Chapter 11 left the debtor's managers in control and significantly relaxed the absolute priority rule. In place of the SEC, the 1978 reforms and subsequent legislation established an entity known as the U.S. Trustee, whose duties are a pale echo of the SEC's former role. The U.S. Trustee oversees all cases, both individual and corporate, proposing trustees for Chapter 7 liquidations. In Chapter 11, its role is limited to appointing the creditors committee and occasionally intervening on matters such as approval of attorneys fees for the debtor's lawyers. With Chapter 11, the New Deal vision of bankruptcy was now dead.

BANKS AND THE 1978 CODE

Chapter 11 was by far the most important new development in corporate bankruptcy, but several other changes also contributed to the 1978 Code's emphasis on reorganizing rather than liquidating troubled firms. The best way to appreciate both the changes, and the limits on how far the changes could go, is to focus on the secured lenders who stood to lose if the new legislation conceded too much to the interests of debtors and rehabilitation. Throughout the hearings, banks expressed repeated concerns about three different commission proposals.[41] First, under the old Bankruptcy Act, the trustee could invalidate a prebankruptcy transfer as a "preference" only if he could show that the transferee—often the debtor's bank—"reasonably should have known" that the debtor was insolvent at the time of the transfer. The commission bill proposed to eliminate this requirement, and simply to presume that the debtor was insolvent at the time of the transfer. Second, the commission bill proposed to limit creditors' right to effect a setoff of any amounts the creditor owed to the debtor against the creditor's claim. Finally, the commission bill made it significantly easier than under prior law for the debtor to use collateral in which a lender held a security interest.

Each of these changes directly opposed lenders' concern to protect their interest against the interest of bankruptcy professionals in increasing the prospects for reorganization. Eliminating the "reasonably should have known" requirement made it easier for the trustee to recover prebankruptcy transfers. This would hurt lenders, who often benefited from the transfers, but help debtors and their lawyers, because it brought money into the bankruptcy process that could be used in the reorganization effort. The other two changes would have a very similar effect. The most important setoff right was a lender's right to use the debtor's deposit account to pay some or all of the amount that the debtor owed to the lender. Interfering with this right would undermine the lender's position and free up cash for the reorganization. Similarly, giving a debtor free use of its bank's collateral might help the reorganization effort, but it also would put the lender's collateral at risk.

The fate of the three proposals offers a revealing portrait of the dynamics of bankruptcy politics. Bankers argued repeatedly that these proposals would force banks to restrict access to credit and would end up hurting everyone. With the first proposal, the banks' complaints were unavailing. The "reasonable cause to believe" standard had led to repeated litigation, due to the difficulty of showing that a transferee (that is, the creditor who received a prebankruptcy payment) knew or should have known that the debtor was insolvent. The litigation was quite costly and made it difficult for the trustee to recover payments even when they clearly were preferential in nature. Lawmakers' unwillingness to concede on the preference issue suggests the limits even of a powerful interest group when the rule it defends is costly and lacks a persuasive public interest justification.

On the second and third proposals, the banks' interests were protected. The legislation that eventually passed preserved banks' long-standing right to setoff, with one caveat—if a creditor effected the setoff before bankruptcy, the trustee could avoid the setoff to the extent the creditor's position had improved in the period prior to the setoff. The 1978 Code protected banks' collateral by requiring court approval before the debtor could use cash that is subject to a security interest, and by requiring a hearing before the debtor can sell collateral outside of the ordinary course of business. At least as revealing as the banks' success on these issues, however, is the nature of the concessions made to them. As was discussed in chapter 5, bankruptcy professionals have often structured their compromises with other interest groups in such a way as to maximize the use of bankruptcy, and that is precisely what they did with both setoffs and the use of banks' collateral. Although banks have long refused to relinquish their setoff rights, by subjecting prebankruptcy setoffs to scrutiny, the drafters (who were, of course, bankruptcy lawyers themselves) gave banks a subtle incentive to forgo their setoff until after the debtor filed for bankruptcy. The effect was to give control over the timing of the setoff to the bankruptcy court and to keep the cash in the firm, thus enhancing the prospects for reorganization.[42] Similarly, the Code assured that banks' collateral would be protected, but the drafters did this by keeping the collateral firmly within the bankruptcy process. (The Code's cramdown provisions, which permit courts to confirm a reorganization plan over the objections of creditors, provide similar protections for creditors' property interests.) Debtors still cannot ignore the interests of their secured lenders, but the 1978 Code makes it more difficult than under prior law for a debtor's secured lenders to pull the plug on the reorganization effort.

As these brief comments indicate, two of the three principal factors in U.S. bankruptcy history—creditors and bankruptcy professionals—figured prominently in the enactment of Chapter 11. What about the third—prodebtor ideology? Does the fact that the one effort that sought to preserve the New Deal perspective, the Senate bill, was so decisively rejected mean that ideology no longer plays a role in the corporate bankruptcy context? Not at all. Despite both the failure of the Senate bill and the general absence of rhetorical fireworks, ideology nevertheless may have played at least an implicit role. Recall that populist hostility has traditionally been directed at elite Wall Street professionals—not at the fact of reorganization. Indeed, populists have generally supported reorganization, even when it involves large corporations. By 1978, the days when J. P. Morgan and other Wall Street banks ruled the bankruptcy roost were long gone, so there was much less reason for populists to oppose the new bankruptcy regime. To be sure, it is somewhat puzzling that the lack of governmental oversight in Chapter 11 did not raise more eyebrows, and we will return to the puzzle in chapter 8. For the moment, the important point is that the populist influence was muted in 1978, but we should never assume that it has disappeared.

PART FOUR

THE VIEW FROM THE TWENTY-FIRST CENTURY

Chapter Seven

CREDIT CARDS AND THE RETURN OF IDEOLOGY IN CONSUMER BANKRUPTCY

THE CONGRESSIONAL DEBATES on the 1978 Code seem almost Zen-like in their tranquility from our vantage point more than two decades later. Although the controversy over the status of bankruptcy judges flared up from time-to-time, especially in the final months, the vast majority of the debates and hearings drew little attention. The drafters of the Code made a deliberate choice to avoid controversy, and to a remarkable extent they succeeded. The debates over consumer bankruptcy at the dawn of the new century could not be more different. For the past decade, the consumer credit industry has been engaged with consumer advocates, bankruptcy academics, and the consumer bankruptcy bar in a fierce struggle over the future of consumer bankruptcy in the United States. Creditors point to the unprecedented number of bankruptcy filings and call for restrictions, while the bankruptcy bar points its finger at creditors as the source of the problem. Congress nearly enacted creditor-promoted legislation in fall 2000, and lawmakers are poised to complete the process in 2001.

The current struggles can be traced directly back to the 1978 Code itself. Almost as soon as the Code was enacted, the number of bankruptcy filings once again skyrocketed. From 1979, the year the new legislation became effective, to 1980, filings rose from 196,976 to 314,886 (table 7.1). Consumer creditors attributed that increase to the Bankruptcy Code and began lobbying for reform. Congress responded by tightening the bankruptcy laws in several respects in 1984, in connection with the reforms that attempted to fix the Code's jurisdictional problems. The 1984 amendments were merely a prologue to the most recent round of debates on consumer bankruptcy, however. The best and most contentious was yet to come.

The main story begins in 1994, when Congress authorized a new commission to conduct a sweeping study of bankruptcy law and to recommend changes. Unlike its predecessor, whose 1973 report provided the framework for the reforms that followed five years later, the most recent commission proved enormously controversial. In its consumer recommendations, the 1994 commission's report took a prodebtor cast, firmly rejecting calls to tighten the bankruptcy laws and vigorously defending consumer debtors' right to an immediate discharge. Consumer creditors were less than enthusiastic with the process. In an effort to preempt the commission's recommendations,

TABLE 7-1
Nonbusiness Filings, 1978–1998

Year	Nonbusiness Filings
1978	172,423
1979	196,976
1980	314,886
1981	315,833
1982	311,005
1983	289,859
1984	284,517
1985	341,189
1986	449,129
1987	492,850
1988	549,831
1989	616,753
1990	718,107
1991	872,438
1992	900,874
1993	812,898
1994	780,455
1995	874,642
1996	1,125,006
1997	1,350,118
1998	1,398,182

Source: *The 1999 Bankruptcy Yearbook and Almanac*, 10, 12 (Boston: New Generation Research, 1999)

Notes: 1978–80 filing numbers are for fiscal year ending June 30. All other filing numbers are calendar year. 1978 Bankruptcy Code became effective October 1, 1979.

consumer creditors introduced legislation that would tighten the bankruptcy discharge in a variety of ways. It is this legislation, rather than the commission report, that served as the starting point for the debates that followed.

Congress's embrace of the creditors' perspective on consumer bankruptcy forced the leaders of the 1994 commission, such as Chair Brady Williamson and Chief Advisor Elizabeth Warren, to shift from setting the agenda to a posture of loyal dissent, a role they assumed with relish. Unlike the bankruptcy technocrats of the 1970 commission, Williamson and Warren became vigorous partisan advocates, in keeping with the ideological tone of the overall debate. Professor Warren even found herself giving a private bankruptcy tutorial to then First Lady Hillary Clinton, who emerged as a leading critic of the proposed reform within the administration.

An obvious question, which we will consider in some detail, is this: what happened? Why did the 1994 commission prove so much more controversial than its 1970 predecessor, and why has consumer bankruptcy become such a partisan issue? To answer that question, we will begin by considering the interest groups on either side of the recent reforms. The chapter first recounts the rise of the consumer credit industry, and the enormous interest creditors have in tightening the screws on bankruptcy so that fewer debtors will discharge their obligations. We then will consider the most prominent debtor advocates, whose ranks include the consumer bankruptcy bar, prominent bankruptcy academics such as Elizabeth Warren, and consumer interest lawyers such as Henry Sommer.

After describing the principal players and the role each played in the 1984 amendments, we will turn to the main event: the 1994 commission and the legislative debates that have followed. Although consumer creditors and debtor advocates have continued to dominate the deliberations, we will need to take additional political factors into account to understand why bankruptcy suddenly became such an ideological battleground. The key political development came in 1994, when Newt Gingrich's "Contract with America" propelled the Republicans to control of Congress for the first time in decades. This transformation, together with several strategic decisions made by the commissioners, helps to explain why the commission proved so divisive. These factors also explain why the recent debates have taken on such an ideological tone.

Unfortunately, ideologically driven debates often make for bad reforms. To show just how confused the legislative process has been—with a high degree of disingenuousness on both sides—the chapter describes several of the key issues and proposals, which range from the "means testing" provision that would compel some debtors to use Chapter 13, to the latest incarnation of an old issue: the debate over several states' extravagant homestead exemptions. Not since the 1898 act have many of these issues been so hotly contested. Despite the shift from the consensus approach of the 1970s to a far more ideologically driven debate at the dawn of the new century, however, the political determinants of U.S. bankruptcy reform have not changed. For all the hoopla, U.S. bankruptcy law would retain its unique features even if Congress were to adopt all of the current proposals.

THE CREDIT CARD COMPANIES' COMPLAINTS

Each new generation marvels at the growth of consumer credit in the United States. In the heady days of the 1920s, outstanding consumer credit climbed to $7 billion, much of it in the form of small bank loans and installment sales.

Along with margin trading, critics blamed installment sales and Americans' "love of luxury" for the speculation frenzy that led to the stock market crash at the end of the decade.[1] A generation later, the $7 billion figure seemed quaint. By the late 1960s, the advent of credit cards and the relentless increase in installment credit had pushed consumer borrowing to several hundred billion dollars, and the numbers have continued to climb. Outstanding consumer credit now stands at more than 1.7 trillion dollars. As the 1997 commission report points out, "In 1978 . . . less than 40 percent of American families had a credit card. Today, four of every five families have at least one."[2]

As the amount of consumer credit has skyrocketed, the number of individuals seeking to discharge their obligations has increased at an even more startling clip. In 1946, 8,566 consumer debtors filed for bankruptcy. By 1967, the number had risen to 191,729, and it was 314,886 in 1980. In 1996, individual bankruptcy filings passed one million per year for the first time, and there have been more than a million filings in each succeeding year.

When individual debtors file for bankruptcy, much of what they discharge is consumer credit, since these obligations are generally unsecured and thus unprotected. This does not mean that credit card companies and other consumer creditors lose more and more money as the number of bankruptcy filings increases, of course. So long as consumer creditors can anticipate their losses, they can pass much of the cost on to future borrowers by raising interest rates or restricting access to credit. The cost of these adjustments falls on future debtors, not the consumer creditors. An increase or decrease in bankruptcy filings does affect *existing* credit, however. Once a loan has been made, the creditor benefits from changes that make repayment more likely and suffers if the likelihood of repayment falls.

For consumer creditors, the transition effects—that is, the effects on existing obligations—of shifts in repayment patterns are enormous, given the huge amount of outstanding consumer credit. Starting in the 1960s, consumer creditors sounded the alarm bells as bankruptcy filings increased at an exponential rate. Creditors' complaints played an important role in Congress's decision to establish the 1970 commission and can be seen as contributing to the 1978 legislation.[3] Creditors were quickly disillusioned by the results, however. The 1978 Code did nothing to stem the tide of personal bankruptcies. Rather than dropping, filings surged upward almost as soon as the Code was enacted, increasing a whopping 60 percent in the first year alone. Many creditors attributed the increase to changes such as the more generous federal exemptions added by the Code.

Consumer creditors took their complaints directly to Congress. Armed with a study conducted by Purdue University's Credit Research Center concluding that a large percentage of Chapter 7 debtors could have paid at least half of their debts in Chapter 13 (the so-called Purdue Study), the consumer credit industry insisted in 1981 that Congress should not permit these debtors to simply discharge all of their obligations. It is essential, a representative of the Credit Union National Association argued, "that future income be taken into account in determining the nature and scope of relief to be provided debtors in financial distress."[4] To curb the perceived abuse, creditors proposed that the discharge be withheld for any debt that qualified as "affordable"—that is, that the debtor was capable of repaying. With the doors of Chapter 7 shut, debtors with "affordable debt" would be forced to use Chapter 13. In effect, this approach would replace debtors' voluntary choice whether to use Chapter 13 with a command-and-control approach.

The creditors' brief for tighter bankruptcy laws was backed by a powerful moral argument, that debtors have a responsibility to make good on their obligations. This is not new, of course. It has appeared in one form or another in every bankruptcy debate. (And variations on the theme turn up in other areas as well: the 1996 welfare reform legislation was premised on the analogous argument that able-bodied citizens should be required to work for welfare benefits, rather than receiving a free handout.) In hearings on the 1978 Code, for instance, the National Consumer Finance Association had frequently referred to this obligation as "credit morality."

> [T]here remains a fundamental obligation to the people of this country to maintain and preserve a sense of public morality in connection with the extension of credit. We choose to call it "credit morality." . . . Society will continue to teach and demand that contractual obligations be honored lest we undermine or even destroy the principles upon which the credit industry was built.[5]

Although concerns about "credit morality" have a long-standing pedigree, the exponential rise in bankruptcy filings gave them a particular urgency for consumer creditors; and the Purdue study, together with other, more anecdotal evidence, seemed to lend credence to the creditors' concerns.

The consumer creditor proposals were stoutly resisted by the consumer bankruptcy bar, consumer advocacy groups, and bankruptcy academics. It is to this collection of debtor advocates that we now turn. Not surprisingly, these bankruptcy professionals and bankruptcy academics viewed the meteoric rise in bankruptcy filings in very different terms.

DEBTORS' DEFENDERS: CONSUMER INTEREST LAWYERS, LAW PROFESSORS, AND THE CONSUMER BANKRUPTCY BAR

Each of the groups that resisted efforts to tighten the bankruptcy discharge in the 1980s had taken a similar stance prior to the 1978 Code. In the years immediately before and after the 1978 legislation, the status of these groups was shifting—in no small part due to the 1978 Code itself. Their opposition helped to ensure that only a watered-down provision was enacted in 1984, and these groups have figured even more prominently in the most recent debates.

The consumer bankruptcy bar was a major beneficiary of precisely the trends that caused such deep distress for the credit industry. Even in the 1970s, relatively few lawyers devoted all or most of their time to consumer bankruptcy, and the practice had a rather ragtag quality. There was no national organization devoted solely to the consumer bankruptcy bar, and their presence during the hearings on the 1978 Code was sporadic. As the number of personal bankruptcies continued to soar in the 1970s and early 1980s, however, the practice expanded. The 1978 Code itself also enhanced consumer bankruptcy practice by lending bankruptcy much more respectability than it had in the past. Bankruptcy debtors were now called *debtors*, not bankrupts; the Code finally brought an end to the so-called bankruptcy ring; and the increasing visibility of corporate bankruptcy (which we will explore in detail in chapter 8) has had a positive ripple effect on the status of the consumer bankruptcy bar.

These developments took time, of course, and consumer bankruptcy lawyers still were relatively unorganized in the early 1980s. Not until 1992, with the formation of the National Association of Consumer Bankruptcy Attorneys, did the consumer bankruptcy bar begin to come of age. In the hearings that led to the 1984 amendments, the consumer bankruptcy bar played only a peripheral role.

Far more important to the earlier debates was the nonprofit face of consumer bankruptcy practice. As we saw in chapter 5, consumer protection organizations such as Community Legal Services and the National Consumer Law Center had testified on behalf of consumer debtors at various points in the hearings that led to the 1978 Code. By the early 1980s, more than a decade after Ralph Nader and "Nader's Raiders" had burst on the scene, the first wave of the consumer protection movement had clearly passed. A variety of factors, ranging from the death of prominent advocates such as Senator Paul Douglas to a general loss of enthusiasm for social engineering during the Reagan administration, had taken much of the wind out of the movement. (A 1982 book referred to these developments as the "rise and pause of the consumer movement.")[6] Yet the trajectory in bankruptcy was somewhat different. Financial distress was a crucial issue for many lower-middle-class families, and public interest attorneys found that bankruptcy was an increasingly important part of their mission. One prominent bankruptcy academic now calls consumer bankruptcy the last great stronghold of the consumer protection movement.[7]

The career of Henry Sommer, the dean of public interest bankruptcy lawyers, vividly illustrates the increasing emphasis on bankruptcy by consumer advocates. Indeed, Sommer himself can claim much of the credit for consumer interest lawyers' success both in using the bankruptcy laws and in protecting consumer debtors' interests in the legislative process. Although he attended Harvard Law School at the height of "Stern Vern" Countryman's career there, their paths did cross until much later. "I never took a course from him or even met him [at Harvard]," Sommer recalls, for he had no inkling that his "future would be in bankruptcy law."[8]

After graduating from Harvard in 1974, Sommer joined Community Legal Services in Philadelphia, where he would work for the next twenty-two years. (Sommer has since become of counsel to Miller, Frank & Miller, a Philadelphia law firm specializing in consumer and small-business bankruptcy.) The event that launched Sommer's bankruptcy career and would make bankruptcy a more important part of consumer interest law than ever before was the 1978 legislation itself. As he familiarized himself with the 1978 reforms, Sommer realized that the new bankruptcy law could become an important new resource for consumer interest lawyers. In article published in early 1979, Sommer made his case. "Especially in states where it will cause dramatic changes in property exemptions," he argued, "[the Code] will become a powerful tool available to consumer debtors and their representatives. In view of this fact, bankruptcy can no longer be ignored, as it has been in the past in many legal services offices."[9] To demonstrate his point, Sommer outlined a long list of changes (including the new federal exemptions and the ability to restructure secured debt in Chapter 13) that consumer advocates could use for the benefit of their clients.

Sommer's belief that the Code offered a "fresh start for legal services lawyers" proved to be prescient. Within a few years, bankruptcy overtook warranty and truth-in-lending litigation as the mainstay of consumer advocacy in commercial law, as organizations such as Community Legal Services in Philadelphia and the Consumer Law Center in Boston developed extensive bankruptcy practices for low-income debtors. Sommer himself would soon work almost entirely on bankruptcy matters. During the Reagan era, when consumer advocates worried that their congressional funding would be cut off, Sommer drafted a detailed treatise, *Consumer Bankruptcy Law and Practice*, as a means of preserving for future consumer advocates the insights he and his peers had developed about representing consumers in bankruptcy. In the 1980s and 1990s, Sommer and other consumer advocates were also a frequent presence in Washington, testifying on behalf of consumers each time bankruptcy legislation came before the Judiciary Committee. Throughout this time, consumer advocates repeatedly criticized creditors' proposals for means testing in consumer bankruptcy.

In the hearings that concern us at the moment, the debates that led to the 1984 amendments, Ellen Broadman of Consumers Union raised the concerns that consumer advocates voiced then and continue to voice now:

Consumers Union strongly opposes the proposed revision. The standards set forth are simply unworkable, arbitrary standards that will be applied differently from court to court, resulting in inequities and an enormous amount of litigation. . . . The proposal is totally at odds with the philosophy underlying the bankruptcy law of allowing individuals who are overwhelmed by crushing debt obligations to start a new, fresh life without debt burden.[10]

Bankruptcy judges were similarly hostile to the creditors' proposals throughout the 1981 hearings (and they have continued to resist proposals to implement mandatory means testing for debtors). The bankruptcy bench was particularly concerned about the administrative burden of means testing. "As to the future earnings test," the president of the National Conference of Bankruptcy Judges warned, "the first problem ... [would be] the deluge of cases that would be filed." He also worried that judges would be forced to conduct an inquisition into the finances of each individual debtor. Given that the proposal was based on "future income" and "future income obviously must relate to a [debtor's] future expenses," since only by deducting anticipated expenses could a court predict the debtor's likely net income, the proposal would place bankruptcy judges in the awkward position of attempting "to establish the reasonable norm of society in reference to expenses."[11]

The final ally for debtors' interests was bankruptcy academics. Vern Countryman once again served as the most vocal academic advocate for personal debtors. Countryman had no particular hostility to Chapter 13. For many years, in fact, he had argued that creditors should encourage debtors to propose repayment plans under Chapter 13 (and its predecessor, Chapter XIII) rather than seeking an immediate discharge. Writing in the midst of the previous "bankruptcy crisis" in the 1960s, Countryman chastised creditors for neglecting Chapter 13, a solution that was already available under the bankruptcy laws.[12] When it came to a *mandatory* Chapter 13 scheme, however, Countryman had no sympathy at all. Countryman noted that the creditors' proposal was similar in spirit to the unsuccessful 1932 effort (which had been inspired by the Thacher report) to give bankruptcy judges the power to limit debtors' access to an immediate discharge. That legislation, Countryman noted with disdain, was "to my knowledge, the only proposed bankruptcy legislation in this country to be characterized by witnesses as 'UnAmerican.' "

Countryman's antipathy for mandatory means testing had deep roots. An ardent civil libertarian, Countryman had actively and publicly supported several defendants who were accused of communist sympathies in the early 1950s. Many observers believed that Countryman's involvement in the loyalty cases rather than any scholarly shortcoming was the reason that Yale Law School passed him over for tenure. (Countryman ultimately got the last laugh when Harvard Law School gave him a tenured professorship in 1964.) An approach that encouraged debtors to file for Chapter 13 but left the choice firmly in their hands was fully consistent with Countryman's commitment to individual liberties. Taking this choice away and *forcing* debtors to use the Chapter 13 approach, by contrast, was anathema. Indeed, Countryman repeatedly took the position—a position rather foreign to the actual Supreme Court case law— that requiring debtors to attempt to repay their debtors, rather than permitting them to seek an immediate discharge, was a form of involuntary servitude and therefore violated the Thirteenth Amendment of the Constitution.

Countryman was by far the most prominent academic opponent of the creditors' means-testing proposal, but other academics — many of them similarly steeped in the values of the consumer protection movement — also took arms against the proposed reforms. Professor Phillip Shuchman joined Countryman in lambasting the creditors' proposal, and Shuchman presented an extensive empirical study that raised doubts as to how much debtors really could repay.[13]

In addition to Countryman and Shuchman, mention should also be made of Elizabeth Warren, who would soon become Countryman's successor as the leading academic advocate for consumer debtors. Prior to the 1984 amendments, Warren and her two coauthors, Teresa Sullivan and Jay Westbrook, had begun the first of three major empirical studies of the U.S. bankruptcy process. What their work added to the debates of the early 1980s was a scathing empirical critique of the Purdue study that creditors were using to buttress their case for reform. Sullivan, Warren, and Westbrook honed in on a series of assumptions that the study made and contended that each of the assumptions caused the study to overstate the ability of consumer debtors to repay some or all of their obligations. After an item-by-item assault on the study, the authors concluded,

> The Study lacks crucial expertise, is designed incorrectly, asks a series of inartful questions, gathers its data improperly, misanalyses the statistical data and draws erroneous and biased inferences from the data analysis. Moreover, error after error increases the count of the debtors who "could pay" and the amount of the debt that could be recovered.[14]

In the years since the 1984 amendments, Warren and her coauthors have weighed in with two book-length empirical studies of their own, *As We Forgive Our Debtors* in 1989 and *The Fragile Middle Class* in 2000, each of which develops a detailed defense of debtors' access to an immediate discharge.

The bankruptcy professionals, consumer advocates, and academics that I have just described have formed a tight, ongoing defense against creditors' efforts to amend the bankruptcy laws. It is important to recognize, however, that their interests are not simply interchangeable. Consumer bankruptcy lawyers who have a large Chapter 13 practice may be more enthusiastic about changes that encourage Chapter 13 than their peers who focus more on Chapter 7. Consumer advocates tend to be biased toward Chapter 7, since it offers a more sweeping discharge, and many in fact do not handle Chapter 13 cases. Interestingly, the most influential bankruptcy organization, the National Bankruptcy Conference, does not fit neatly within any of these camps. As we saw in chapter 5, the Conference has tended to draw most of its members from the corporate bankruptcy bar and has nurtured a reputation for technical expertise and evenhanded reform. (The only NBC member who focuses primarily on consumer bankruptcy issues is Henry Sommer, who joined the conference in the 1980s.) In the 1980s, the NBC advised Congress to reject calls for a mandatory repayment approach. The NBC concluded that debtors should be the ones to choose between Chapter 7 and Chapter 13. But the NBC suggested that Congress could increase the amount of repayment under Chapter 13 by requiring debtors who choose this alternative to pay their entire "disposable income" to creditors for at least three years.

The provision that Congress ultimately adopted in 1984 reflects something of a compromise between creditors and the bankruptcy professionals who opposed them, though one closer to the status quo than to the creditors' proposal. Rather than a true means test, the 1984 amendments authorize the bankruptcy court to dismiss a debtor's Chapter 7 petition if the petition constitutes a "substantial abuse."[15] If a court dismisses the debtor's petition, her only alternative if she wishes to obtain bankruptcy relief is to file under Chapter 13. In theory, bankruptcy judges could use their authority to force most debtors into Chapter 13. But the provision not only requires that the abuse be "substantial," it also instructs judges to presume that debtors are entitled to Chapter 7. Moreover, bankruptcy judges initially were the only ones who could invoke the "substantial abuse" provision. As we have already seen, bankruptcy judges were not exactly enthusiasts for the means-testing approach. Quite to the contrary, they never liked the idea in the first place.

In addition to the "substantial abuse" provision, the 1984 amendments also adopted the National Bankruptcy Conference's proposal to require that debtors commit all of their "disposable income" to repaying creditors for at least three years. The 1984 amendments thus tweaked the 1978 Code in response to creditors' concerns but did not seriously restrict debtor's access to an immediate discharge. Consumer bankruptcy lawyers and their allies viewed the outcome as a major success.

Why did the creditors' means-testing proposal lose so much of its bite? The most visible explanation was the efforts of Democratic senator Howard Metzenbaum on behalf of the prodebtor perspective. Metzenbaum had adamantly opposed the means-testing provision and persuaded Republican senator Strom Thurmond, the proponent of the legislation that eventually passed in the Senate, to retreat from the creditors' proposal.[16] At a more general level, the compromise fits a pattern we have seen again and again: when interest groups clash directly on an issue of real importance, lawmakers often resolve the conflict by devising a mushy, fact-driven compromise. "Substantial abuse" is malleable enough to permit courts to reach either result—to dismiss the debtor's petition or permit it—in almost any given case.

The other factor is simple party politics. The election of a conservative Republican president, Ronald Reagan, had encouraged consumer creditors to step up their lobbying efforts, but the Democrats still controlled both the House and the Senate. Democratic control made it unlikely that Congress would pass legislation that dramatically shifted the balance away from debtors and toward creditors. Thus, party politics may help to explain why Senator Metzenbaum's efforts were so successful, and why the final compromise left so little of the creditors' means-testing proposal in place.

Although the "substantial abuse" standard made major concessions to the prodebtor perspective, it is important to emphasize that creditors got something too. The "substantial abuse" provision validated creditors' contention that debtors should not have unfettered discretion to file for Chapter 7. As a result, it represented an important symbolic victory for creditors. Moreover, Congress strengthened the provision two years later by permitting the U.S. Trustee, rather than just the bankruptcy judge, to ask for dismissal; and the 1984 amendments can be seen as foreshadowing the far more dramatic efforts creditors have made to promote consumer bankruptcy reform in the past several years.

IDEOLOGICAL SPLITS ON THE 1994 COMMISSION

Rather than consumer bankruptcy reform, the driving force for the 1984 amendments was the need to calm the storm over bankruptcy court jurisdiction. The 1984 amendments seem to have done just this, although, interestingly enough, the Supreme Court has never ruled on the question whether the current system of Article I bankruptcy judges is in fact constitutional.

Although jurisdiction was the most pressing issue in 1984, it is the consumer bankruptcy amendments that most observers remember. None of the consumer changes was especially dramatic, yet they seemed to have stirred discontent on all sides. Debtor advocates criticized the new restrictions on the discharge, and creditors complained that the changes did little to stem the flow of new bankruptcy cases. The most significant effect of the "substantial abuse" provision seems to have been to reinforce the influence of "local legal culture"—that is, the norms of a particular district—on debtors' choice whether to file under Chapter 7 or Chapter 13. As we saw in chapter 5, the proportion of Chapter 13 cases varies dramatically from district to district, which suggests that bankruptcy judges and lawyers may steer debtors, either implicitly or explicitly, toward or away from Chapter 13. The "substantial abuse" standard strengthens judges' hand in this regard. Those bankruptcy judges who do believe that debtors should attempt to repay some of their obligations can use the threat of dismissal for "substantial abuse" as a means of subtly pushing debtors toward Chapter 13.

The next significant set of bankruptcy amendments came in 1994, when Congress made a large number of adjustments to the Code—many of them designed to overturn controversial court decisions. The most momentous decision of the 1994 amendments had no immediate effect on the Bankruptcy Code at all, however. Even more significant than the substantive adjustments was lawmakers' conclusion that the time had come to establish another bankruptcy commission to conduct an exhaustive review of the nation's bankruptcy laws.

To many observers, the timing was somewhat puzzling. In the past, governmental studies of bankruptcy and major reform have come at roughly forty-year intervals, and neither the passage of time nor any obvious signs of corruption seemed to call for a major review. The National Bankruptcy Conference, in fact, specifically argued that the time was not right for a new commission. Rather than shelve the idea, Congress did in fact authorize a commission, but explicitly stated that lawmakers were "generally satisfied with the basic framework established in the [1978 Code]," and instructed the commission "not [to] disturb the fundamental tenets of current law."[17]

Although its work was delayed by the illness and untimely death (from brain cancer) of its initial chairman, Congressman Michael Synar, the commission got off to an unremarkable start. In accordance with the authorizing legislation, President Clinton chose three members for the commission; William Rehnquist, the chief justice of the Supreme Court selected two; and the Senate and House majority and minority leaders picked one each. At its first formal meeting, in October 1995 the commission approved Synar's choice for chief reporter, Harvard Law professor Elizabeth Warren; and the commission began planning a series of public hearings on a variety of bankruptcy topics.[18]

After beginning in apparent consensus the commission dissolved into a state of sharp division, with a majority block of commissioners consisting of the chairman, Brady Williamson, and four other commissioners, frequently opposed by a dissenting block led by Judge Edith Jones, a judge on the United States Court of Appeals for the Fifth Circuit who had been appointed to the commission by Chief Justice Rehnquist. The tensions grew worse as the commission completed its work and culminated in a lengthy dissent by Judge Jones to the commission's recommendations. In consumer bankruptcy, the commission majority rejected calls for means testing and proposed to restrict reaffirmation, whereas Judge Jones took the opposite view on both issues. It is Judge Jones's perspective rather than the commission report, that has more in common with the legislation that Congress debated in 2000 and 2001.

There is an obvious puzzle here. How did so much dysfunction come from a commission whose innocuous-sounding charge was to look for ways to perfect a generally adequate framework? The answer cannot lie in the commission form itself, since the 1970 commission is viewed, at least in retrospect, as a model of reasoned debate and productive dialogue. The 1994 commission was selected in similar fashion—with commissioners chosen by the president, the leaders of the House and Senate, and the chief justice—but its deliberations became much more transparently ideological. It is the ideological turn that we need to locate. By showing where all of the bickering came from, we can begin to explain why the commission report served as a foil—not a basis— for the legislative debates that followed.

Much of the ideological tone of the commission's work can traced to two factors, a seismic shift in the political landscape at the time the commission was appointed and a sharp split in the academic literature on bankruptcy that made its way into the commission process. The saga begins with the first factor, party politics. The elections in 1994 gave the Republicans control of Congress for the first time in more than thirty years, and the Republicans retained control in the two elections that followed. As a result, the 1994 commission was established by a divided Congress in which Democrats held the House and Republicans the Senate, but it reported to an entirely Republican Congress. By the time the commission issued its report, its membership no longer reflected the balance of power in Washington.

At least as important as the fact that Republicans took control was the nature of the 1994 elections that brought them to power. After the collapse of the Clinton administration's efforts—led by Hillary Clinton and Ira Magaziner—to overhaul the U.S. health care system, the Republicans took advantage of the backlash with a highly ideological campaign that was masterminded by Representative Newt Gingrich and featured a "Contract with America" promising to diminish the role of government in American life. The 1994 elections were a dramatic manifestation of the increasing polarization of U.S. politics in the last two decades. Not only did the elections bring a cadre of notably ideological Republican candidates to office, but a disproportionate number of the Democratic representatives who survived were ideological Democrats from safely liberal districts. Against this backdrop, the commission can be seen as reflecting the larger, sharply ideological political landscape. It is not entirely surprising, from this perspective, that a commission report that was submitted by a Democrat committee chairman, and most fiercely opposed by several Republican appointees, would not be welcomed with open arms by a Republican-controlled Congress.[19]

The political background is an important part of the story, but it does not entirely explain why the commission itself was so sharply divided. For decades, bankruptcy had been seen as a relatively nonpartisan issue. In Berglof and Rosenthal's new study of roll call voting, for instance, they find little evidence of ideological division in the votes on the 1978 Code. Not only were there few role call votes, which tend to reflect congressional division, but both Democrats and Republicans voted for the 1978 reforms by large majorities.[20] If bankruptcy were still nonideological, one might have expected a relatively harmonious commission process, immune from the ideological battles taking place on other issues.

It is here that the second factor, the split within recent bankruptcy scholarship, helps to explain the emergence of a sharp ideological divide on the commission. By the time the 1978 Code was enacted, the "law-and-economics" movement had already begun to transform legal scholarship. Often associated with University of Chicago law professors such as Richard Posner (who now is chief judge of the U.S. Court of Appeals for the Seventh Circuit), law-and-economics scholars applied the tools of economics to legal issues. In place of traditional concepts such as fairness or equity, law-and-economics scholars introduced efficiency as the central goal of legal analysis. Based on the assumption that each individual tends to pursue her own best interest—which economists define as acting "rationally," a focus that has given rise to an endearing nickname for economics-influenced analysis, "Rat Choice"—law-and-economics advocates insisted that legal rules should be used instrumentally, as a means of promoting the efficient allocation of resources.

In bankruptcy, the early law-and-economics literature suggested that lawmakers could reverse the rise in bankruptcy filings by adjusting key bankruptcy provisions. Reducing the amount of property that debtors could exempt, for instance, might cause debtors to think twice before seeking an immediate discharge in bankruptcy. Starting with a seminal 1979 article, Thomas Jackson used the insights of law and economics to develop a more elaborate general theory of bankruptcy, which he and his frequent coauthor Douglas Baird called the "creditors' bargain." The creditors' bargain theory is more concerned with corporate than consumer bankruptcy, so we will wait until chapter 8 to revel in its intricacies. For now, we need only look to the title of Baird and Jackson's theory—and its emphasis on the *creditors*' bargain—to appreciate its significance for bankruptcy scholarship and the 1994 commission. Like nearly all of the law-and-economics analysis that has followed, Baird and Jackson concluded that an optimal bankruptcy regime would give creditors most or all of the same protections inside bankruptcy that they enjoy outside of bankruptcy.

The instrumental and creditor-oriented tendencies of law-and-economics scholarship have been anathema to traditional bankruptcy scholars, particularly those who would characterize themselves as progressives. Vern Countryman scoffed at Chicago School analysis decades before it entered the bankruptcy literature, and Elizabeth Warren has picked up the baton in recent years, waging an ongoing battle against law-and-economics scholarship. She has repeatedly criticized the assumption by law-and-economics scholars that debtors make a rational, calculated decision whether and when to file for bankruptcy. In one of her early articles, for instance, Warren lambasted the claim that reducing exemptions would encourage more debtors to use Chapter 13 rather than seeking an immediate discharge. "This premise," she complained, "calls to mind thousands of almost-bankrupt rational maximizers sitting anxiously on some hypothetical cost/benefit curve, waiting for the numbers to come down from Congress."[21] Warren also sharply criticized law-and-economics scholars for failing to emphasize the distributional consequences of bankruptcy—who wins and who loses.

Selecting Elizabeth Warren as chief reporter for the 1994 commission made great sense in many respects. Not only is Warren one of the nation's leading bankruptcy scholars, she also is a prominent member of the National Bankruptcy Conference and has excellent working relations with a wide range of bankruptcy professionals. Warren also is an eloquent defender of the existing framework, with which Congress had pronounced itself generally pleased. But Warren also is famously partisan, the standard bearer for one side in the academic debate between bankruptcy progressives and law-and-economics scholars. The contrast to Frank Kennedy, the reporter for the 1970 commission, could hardly be more stark. Whereas Kennedy was best known for his technical expertise and was described in one of the hearings on the 1978 Code as "saintly," Warren is more often characterized as a "street fighter." (Had the commission sought to appoint a less partisan reporter, an obvious choice would have been Larry King, a law professor at New York University and editor of the most widely used bankruptcy treatise until his death this year.)

Law-and-economics perspectives have dominated the bankruptcy literature since the early work of Baird and Jackson. Yet, as the commission went about its work, law-and-economics scholars were rarely seen—a fact that is widely attributed to Warren's influence. The commission relied extensively on reports prepared by bankruptcy experts, for instance, and none of the reports came from a law-and-economics scholar. Other than token appearances by law-and-economics scholars at several commission hearings, the law-and-economics perspective was excluded from serious consideration in the commission process.

Partisanship is nothing new in governmental studies, of course. We need only think back to the SEC report overseen by William Douglas to find evidence of full-fledged partisanship in the bankruptcy context. Douglas had no interest in evenhanded deliberation—he wanted to build a case—yet the SEC's policy recommendations made their way directly into the 1938 Chandler Act. For Douglas, there was no need to provide a more balanced report, since he could count on the support of President Roosevelt and an overwhelmingly Democratic Congress. Because congressional control had shifted, the 1994 commission did not have this luxury. If the commissioners wished to be heard in Congress, they would have to present a report that made sense to both sides, and which made concessions to creditors as well as debtors. The commission's hostility to law-and-economics scholarship made clear that this would not be the case. The law-and-economics perspective is not synonymous with creditors or Republicanism, and I am certain to hear from my law-and-economics colleagues if I neglect to make this clear. Yet, as I noted above, the prescriptions of law and economics have often seemed to come from a creditor-oriented perspective. The Republicans have tended to take a similar view, at least for consumer bankruptcy, echoing creditors' complaint that debtors have become too quick to discharge their obligations. By excluding the insights of law-and-economics, the commission majority signaled that they would stick to their guns in the bankruptcy wars, rather than attempting to tailor their report to the Congress that would be reading it.

Once again, we can see a combination of structural factors and strategic decisions affecting the course of legislative developments. The shift to Republican control after 1994 immediately complicated the prospects of a commission whose majority was appointed by the other side of the congressional aisle. If the commission had taken a resolutely technical and nonpartisan approach, its report might have been better received by Congress (though it would also have been less satisfying, no doubt, to the commission majority itself). The commissioners' decisions to appoint Elizabeth Warren as commissioner and then to exclude the law-and-economics perspective, together with the partisan divide that already existed within the commission, steered the process in a very different direction. "This Report . . . will be controversial," its drafters admitted. "It is meant to be controversial."[22] And it was.

MEANS TESTING AND OTHER PROPOSALS

If bankruptcy filings were relatively stable, the 1997 commission report might have been filed in Congress's cylindrical file and temporarily forgotten. But the explosion in consumer credit, and the equally dramatic increase in personal bankruptcy filings, made the stakes too high for creditors to ignore. Although both the players and the issues were the same as in the early 1980s, the potential benefits to creditors of altering what institutional economists call the "rules of the game" had sharply increased.[23] Even a small tightening of the discharge could have enormous benefits.

As the direction of the commission became clear, consumer creditors continued to pepper the commission with memos and testimony. But they also started laying the groundwork to blunt the effects of the commission's recommendations. In late 1996, before the commission had even completed its report, legislation drafted by the consumer credit industry was introduced in the House and Senate. Unlike the commission report, which rejected creditors' call for means testing, the new legislation would preclude debtors from using Chapter 7 if they were capable of making payments under Chapter 13. The creditors' proposals proved spectacularly successful at turning lawmakers' attention away from the 1994 commission. It is the creditors' proposed legislation, rather than the 172 recommendations of the 1997 commission report, that Congress debated and nearly passed.

According to one of the hoariest chestnuts of the law, "Hard cases make bad law." If hard cases make bad law, so too does the combination of complex issues and a highly polarized political environment. The tone of the recent bankruptcy legislation was set by the charges and countercharges of consumer creditors and bankruptcy professionals, each trying to attract the attention of a public (and as a result, to put pressure on legislators) that has long had little interest in the niceties of the U.S. bankruptcy system. Creditors' central claim has been that bankruptcy has lost so much of its stigma, that many debtors file for bankruptcy and seek an immediate discharge for obligations that the debtor could easily have repaid in part or full. The exponential increase in bankruptcy filings has given new credibility to the creditors' complaints, as have the ubiquitous lawyer advertisements encouraging debtors to "erase their debts fast.". (Creditors, on the other hand, are rather imperfect messengers for the message that debtors have a moral obligation to repay their debts, since creditors' interests are far more financial than moral.)

In 1998, creditors ratcheted up their media campaign by running newspaper ads with the headline, "What Do Bankruptcies Cost American Families?" The answer, according to a 1998 study, was that bankruptcy costs the U.S. economy $44 billion each year, an amount that translates to four hundred dollars (or a "month of groceries," in the more colorful imagery of the creditors' ad) for every American family.

For their part, the consumer advocates, bankruptcy academics, and the consumer bankruptcy bar sought to draw attention to the enormous amount of money (upwards of $80 million, by some accounts) that creditors have spent lobbying on the legislation. Debtor advocates also insisted that consumer creditors were the principal reason for the bankruptcy filing boom. If credit card companies exercised a little restraint in issuing card cards, debtor advocates argued, American consumers would be far less likely to incur debts that they had no hope of repaying. (Nearly everyone had their own favorite illustration of credit card companies' willingness to extend credit to any one. Babies, the deceased, and even cats and dogs have received "preapproved" credit card applications in the mail.)

In addition to criticizing the creditors who were promoting the legislation, debtor advocates also complained that the new legislation would hurt families—particularly families headed by women. Elizabeth Warren was an especially visible architect of this rhetorical strategy. In one of a series of op-eds criticizing the legislation, she pointed out that more than seven hundred thousand women file for bankruptcy each year and argued that the new legislation would "strip[] economic protection away from many of America's most vulnerable women."[24] A letter signed by eighty-two law professors echoed this theme, as did statements by numerous consumer bankruptcy lawyers and other opponents.

As if the ideological ante had not been raised enough, the committee that oversaw the bankruptcy legislation—the Judiciary Committee, which has handled bankruptcy since the early nineteenth century—is the same one that had just overseen the Clinton impeachment proceedings. During the impeachment hearings, commentators frequently speculated that the unusually partisan membership of the Judiciary Committee had exacerbated the tensions of the impeachment process. This partisanship also colored the bankruptcy hearings.

As we saw most recently with the "substantial abuse" provision adopted in 1984, when two interest groups clash directly on an issue, the impasse is often resolved by a compromise that vests significant discretion in the court. The proposed legislation followed something like this pattern. On several of the key issues, the legislation was modified to address the rhetorical claims made by its opponents. There is nothing especially surprising about this, of course. But the unusually ideological nature of the debate has led to provisions that solve largely imaginary problems by creating very real ones. To show this, I consider three key provisions below. I then describe the debate over a largely symbolic abortion provision and over generous state homestead exemptions, and the impact of these controversies on the final debates.

Steering Debtors toward Chapter 13 through Means Testing

The best-known provision in the proposed legislation requires means testing of consumer debtors. As we have seen, means testing has long been at the top of creditors' wish list for consumer bankruptcy. Congress took a serious look at means testing in the late 1960s and again in 1984, but creditors largely came up short in each case. In the most recent round of reforms, they have gone to the well one more time. Under the original proposal, a consumer debtor would have been prohibited from seeking an immediate discharge if it appeared that she had sufficient income to repay either five thousand dollars or 25 percent of her unsecured obligations.

A perennial problem with coercing debtors to propose a repayment plan rather than using Chapter 7 is the question of how to determine just how much a debtor could repay. How could a bankruptcy judge who has thousands of other cases on her docket sort through each debtor's finances to see if five thousand dollars or 25 percent is realistic? The creditors' solution was to piggyback on the expense guidelines that the Internal Revenue Service has set up for determining taxpayers' legitimate expenses. The original legislation instructed the court first to determine the debtor's expenses, as conformed to the IRS guidelines, and any payments due on secured obligations such as her house or car, and then to subtract this amount from the debtor's current income. If the debtor's income exceeded her expenses, the surplus should be available for paying her unsecured debts.

Consumer interests and the consumer bankruptcy bar assailed the means-testing proposal, calling it an unconscionable burden on the poor, and the National Bankruptcy Conference also weighed in against the proposed legislation. The IRS standards were notoriously stingy—a "bread and water" approach. The standards would make the means-testing provision overinclusive, critics argued, seriously exaggerating the number of debtors who could repay some of their obligations. Critics also contended, as Vern Countryman had so often done in the past, that this approach should be seen as a modern-day form of involuntary servitude.

In response to these criticisms, the legislation was amended so that it would only apply to debtors whose income exceeded the state median (The repayment minimum was also raised from five thousand to ten thousand dollars). Middle- and upper-income debtors would be forced through the means-testing grinder, but the new framework would have no effect on lower-income debtors. Although the revised provision continued to look to the IRS for guidance on expenses, it cleverly neutralized the contention that means testing has a disproportionate impact on the poor. It is hard to argue with the notion that middle- and upper-income debtors should repay some of their debts if they are capable of doing so.

Yet the revised means-testing proposal poses an intriguing puzzle. Even apart from the possibility that debtors would manipulate their finances to evade the test—a much-noted concern—limiting means testing to middle- and upper-income debtors has a curious effect. Because the vast majority of bankruptcy debtors earn less than the median income when they file for bankruptcy, the means-testing net is not likely to catch many debtors. Why were creditors so anxious to enact a provision with so little real bite? One possibility is that the new provision was simply the most recent salvo in a long-term plan to promote ever stricter standards. Although the new provision would not have had an enormous effect, it promised to move creditors one step closer to a more rigorous bankruptcy system like the one we see in England. From a historical perspective, moreover, the trajectory looks rather promising: failure in 1967, followed by a weak compromise provision in 1984 and now a more serious provision to start the new millennium.

A second, and related, possibility is creditors concluded that a means test that catches only a few debtors is better than no means-testing provision at all. The third and last explanation may be the most inportant. Although the means test would not reach a large number of debtors, it would appreciably raise the cost of the bankruptcy process. Every Chapter 7 bankruptcy case would require a determination whether the provision applies, and for debtors at or above the median income, this determination would entail a detailed calculation of the debtor's financial prospects. The benefit to creditors is that the increased cost of bankruptcy could discourage some debtors who would otherwise be eligible to file for bankruptcy from doing so. There is a case for tightening access to bankruptcy, of course, but raising the cost by complicating the process is a particularly unattractive mechanism for achieving this.

Nondischargeable Credit Card Debts, Alimony, and the American Family

Almost as high on creditors' wish list was a second provision that is equally technical and equally controversial. In addition to complaining that many debtors could repay some of their debts but do not, creditors also insist that debtors who plan to file for bankruptcy often deliberately run up their credit cards first—knowing that it is the credit card company who will be stuck with the bill. In one particularly vivid case, a debtor used his credit card to obtain large cash advances, gambled the money away in Los Vegas, and then filed for bankruptcy.[25] To curb the abuse, creditors proposed that debtors should be prohibited from discharging credit card debts that were incurred shortly before bankruptcy. Such a debtor could obtain an immediate discharge under Chapter 7, but the discharge simply would not apply to the credit card debt. The credit card issuer could continue to insist on payment. (As it turns out, bankruptcy judges already have the authority to make "fraudulently" incurred debts nondischargeable—this was a provision creditors fought to preserve in 1978. But courts often conclude that a debtor's prebankruptcy use of her credit cards is not fraudulent if she intended to repay her obligations from hoped-for gambling winnings. The new provision is designed to make nondischargeability mandatory.)

It was this proposal that reform opponents lambasted as antiwomen and antifamily. What in the world does withholding the discharge under these circumstances have to do with the American family? Why is this a "women's issue?" Here's how it works. Divorce and other family problems are a factor in a large number of bankruptcy cases. A long-standing concern in these cases is that the husband will file for bankruptcy and use bankruptcy to discharge the alimony or child support obligations he promised to pay. Almost no one thinks this should be permitted. To prevent husbands from evading their responsibilities to ex-wives and children, the Bankruptcy Code makes alimony and child support payments nondischargeable. This is where the new credit card provision comes in. Under current law, the list of nondischargeable obligations is relatively small, so alimony and support payments occupy a special status. Reform opponents insisted that adding credit card debts to this list would be devastating for divorced women. Rather than having first dibs on her ex-husband's assets after bankruptcy, women, in Elizabeth Warren's words, "would have to compete against big lenders and their collection departments." "At a time when most divorced mothers cannot collect more than 40 percent of the child support they are owed," she insisted, "this provision is shameful."[26]

The ratio of rhetoric to reality in this complaint is quite high. The new credit card provision simply expands an existing provision. Even as expanded, it would apply to a small portion of all credit card debt—credit card obligations incurred immediately before bankruptcy. Not only are all other credit card obligations fully dischargeable, but the inability to discharge last-minute obligations may well cause many debtors to limit their credit card spending at the eve of bankruptcy. The ability of many and probably most spouses to collect alimony and child support would not be undermined in any serious way by the new provision. Despite the exaggeration, however, the complaints made an effective sound bite. Most lawmakers do not follow bankruptcy very closely, but they know enough to shy away from a reform that will be viewed as hostile to women and families.

Rather than trying to defend the legislation as it stood, proponents sought to recapture the rhetorical high ground by proposing a special new priority for alimony and child support payments. Alimony and child support payments already enjoyed higher priority than most obligations, including all general unsecured debts. The new adjustments moved alimony and child support still higher, to the very top of the list, ahead of even—gasp!—attorneys' fees, and second in line only to debts that are secured.

Notice that this response by advocates of reform takes a different tack than the "antifamily" complaint it is designed to address. The objection to making some credit card obligations nondischargeable focuses on claims against the debtor's assets *after* bankruptcy—by making exceptions to the general rule that bankruptcy wipes the debtor's slate clean. By contrast, the response—increasing the priority of alimony and child support—comes into play *during* bankruptcy, when the trustee divvies up the debtor's assets among the debtor's creditors. The ex-spouse can continue to collect any unpaid amounts after bankruptcy, since alimony and child support are also nondischargeable. But the special priority makes this less crucial, because it is now more likely (at least in theory) that the debtor's existing alimony and child support obligations will be paid in bankruptcy.

For rhetorical purposes, the special priority was a clever response, one that seemed to signal that reform proponents care about women and children too. The practical effect is more dubious, however. The special priority would indeed assure somewhat larger payments to ex-wives in bankruptcy. Because nearly all of the assets of most debtors are either exempt or encumbered by security interests, however, alimony and child support still would not be paid in full in most cases. Much worse is the fact, as noted above, that the special priority puts these obligations ahead of attorneys fees. Most of us will not feel especially sorry for the bankruptcy bar, of course, but the simple truth is that bankruptcy attorneys will not take these cases unless they can collect their fees. Bankruptcy attorneys no doubt would devise a way to get paid—most likely, they will insist on payment in full in advance. The effect would be to ratchet up the initial costs of bankruptcy for divorced debtors.

The Proposed Consumer Counseling Requirements

Unlike the means-testing and credit card nondischargeability provisions, which have inspired endless debate, the third set of changes attracted remarkably little attention. From the earliest days of the debate, the bankruptcy legislation included provisions requiring every debtor to submit to credit counseling before filing for bankruptcy, and again after the conclusion of the bankruptcy case. The theory is that educating debtors about their financial needs could keep them from falling back into financial trouble after their bankruptcy and may even avoid some bankruptcy filings in the first instance.

The counseling provisions fit perfectly into consumer creditors' campaign to promote "credit morality." Counseling could help teach debtors how to manage their obligations and reinforce the importance of repaying. So long as the message of consumer counseling is fiscal responsibility, it is likely to encourage more repayment and fewer bankruptcies on the margin.

Given the obvious benefits to consumer creditors, one might expect debtor advocates uniformly to resist the new requirements. The reality is quite different, however. Consumer education has a long pedigree in progressive thought and, as we saw in chapter 5, the 1970 commission made counseling a centerpiece of its proposed reforms. In a memo to the 1994 commission, progressive scholar Karen Gross revisited this theme. "Who can be against creditor counseling," she asked before making an enthusiastic case for implementing a system of debtor education. Indeed, Gross has recently set up a pilot program (Henry Sommer is also involved) to provide bankruptcy counseling for debtors. There are several crucial differences between this program and the proposals in the new legislation, however. Whereas Gross's program is entirely voluntary and made available after a debtor files for bankruptcy, the legislation proposes to make counseling a prerequisite to invoking the bankruptcy laws. As with means testing and the alimony priority, the most obvious effect would be to discourage debtors' bankruptcy filings in a rather indirect and inefficient way: by making bankruptcy more costly and cumbersome.

Homestead Exemptions and Wealthy Deadbeats

By early 2000, creditors and the lawmakers supporting their call for restricting bankruptcy law had largely won the rhetorical debate (no doubt with the help of the substantial campaign contributions made by consumer creditors). Critics continued to attack the proposed reform as "antifamily," but versions of the bill passed by large, bipartisan majorities of the House and Senate in early 2000. As the House and Senate met to work out their differences, however, the bill suddenly became even more controversial. The lightening rod for the renewed criticism was a lengthy *Time* magazine article by investigative reporters Donald Barlett and James Steele. Entitled "Soaked by Congress," the article contrasted the credit industry's costly lobbying efforts with vignettes about families that had been forced to file for bankruptcy by circumstances beyond their control. "Lavished with campaign cash," the article proclaimed in its tagline, "law makers are 'reforming' bankruptcy—punishing the downtrodden to catch a few cheats."[27]

Although the article's complaints and tone were not new, the length and visibility of the critique gave a number of the reform's Democratic supporters serious second thoughts. An even more important effect of the article was to highlight an additional, populist critique of the bill: its failure to curb the unlimited homestead exemptions that debtors in states like Florida and Texas can use to protect their houses. "[L]et's consider the story of two homeowners in bankruptcy," the article proposed: "One is James Villa, a 42-year-old one-time stockbroker who lives in a $1.4 million home in Boca Raton, Fla. The other is Allen Smith, a 73-year-old retired autoworker with throat cancer who lives in a deteriorating $80,000 home in Wilmington, Del." Unlike the auto-worker, who was forced to give up his house, the stockbroker fled to Florida after Massachusetts securities regulators concluded that his firm had bilked investors through various fraudulent practices. Because of Florida's generous homestead exemption, none of these investors can touch Villa's extravagant new home. The *Time* article's complaint quickly made its way into other accounts of the reform effort. The *New York Times*, to take one prominent example, which previously had expressed cautious support for the reform, complained that "the overwhelming impact [of bankruptcy reform] would be to hurt unsophisticated debtors and go easy on the well-healed. The proposal fails to override state laws that allow debtors to lock away millions in trust, a huge benefit to the wealthy."[28]

Focusing on lavish state exemptions was a brilliant rhetorical move. The number of debtors who take advantage of the Florida and Texas homestead exemptions is quite small. The exemption is only useful to a debtor who can buy his million-dollar house with cash, since it only protects value above and beyond any mortgage on the property. Yet there are a few James Villas out there, and their existence has enormous symbolic value. Even better for critics of reform, the exemptions issue created serious political complications for advocates of reform. Most reform advocates would be happy to clamp down on unlimited homestead exemptions—after all, restrictions would make more assets available for creditors. Yet, as we have seen throughout the book, any effort to federalize exemptions prompts immediate resistance on states' rights grounds.[29]

A second, even more symbolic sticking point was a proposed abortion amendment. Under the amendment, which was suggested by Senator Schumer of New York, debtors would not be permitted to discharge any obliga-tions arising from damage to an abortion clinic. It was clear to everyone that the actual effect of the amendment was minuscule. Debtors already are prohib-ited from discharging obligations arising from "willful or malicious" injury to property in Chapter 7, and the number of debtors who would be affected is obviously not large. Nevertheless, many Republican lawmakers did not want to sign on to legislation that seemed to favor abortion, and many Democrats insisted that the amendment remain in order to send the opposite signal.

Both of these issues, as well as the general attack on the legislation as antifamily, emboldened President Clinton to refuse to sign the bill in fall 2000. The homestead exemption has continued to complicate passage of the bill in 2001.

THE MORAL CONFUSION IN U.S. CONSUMER BANKRUPTCY

Things have changed a great deal since the first permanent U.S. bankruptcy law in 1898. In 1898, carriages rather than cars were the principal form of transport, television did not exist, and consumer credit was still rather exotic. The number of filings was much closer to ten thousand per year than to 1 million. Neither the consumer credit industry nor debtor advocates such as consumer interest organizations existed in anything like their current form.

Yet for all the differences, the basic political contours of consumer bankruptcy have stayed remarkably consistent. The bankruptcy laws still reflect a rough balance between the interests of creditor groups, and of debtor advocates whose influence is both magnified and channeled by the nation's federalist structure. Federal bankruptcy law is now seen less as a creditor remedy than as a debtor protection, but the battle lines have remained the same. Debtors are most closely allied with Democrats and the Senate, creditors with Republicans and the House. Bankruptcy professionals play a prominent role in shaping the laws—especially with reforms that can be portrayed as technical in nature.

As an institutional matter, creditors' campaign for means testing is an attempt to take the decision whether to repay out of debtors' hands. The original, 1930s proposal for restricting the discharge had been to vest discretion in a judge, and the "substantial abuse" provision enacted in 1984 can be seen as a watered-down version of this strategy. But most bankruptcy judges have little interest in forcing debtors into Chapter 13. As an alternative to judicial discretion, the new means-testing proposal (like the nondischargeability provision for credit card debts) has therefore shifted to a command-and-control approach setting forth a precise test for determining which debtors do not belong in Chapter 7. Although means testing can be defended in principle— surely, debtors should repay some of their obligations if they can realistically do so—mechanical guidelines are both an artificial and manipulable strategy for inducing debtors to pay. (Nor does it help that the expense provisions of the proposed legislation look to the IRS—not the most sympathetic regulator—as a role model.)

As we saw in chapter 5, the 1978 Code offered a different approach to repayment by consumer debtors. Rather than forcing debtors to use Chapter 13, lawmakers added a variety of provisions designed to entice debtors to opt for Chapter 13. The problem with these provisions—which include the "superdischarge," the co-debtor stay, and the right to reduce secured claims to the value of the collateral—is that they conflict with Chapter 13's original purpose of giving debtors who genuinely wish to repay an opportunity to do so. Now that lawmakers have scattered carrots throughout Chapter 13, debtors and their lawyers have even more of an incentive than might otherwise be the case to decide on crassly strategic grounds whether to seek an immediate discharge or to propose a reorganization plan. Ideally, bankruptcy reform would seek to diminish these strategic incentives, and to move toward a more morally coherent approach to consumer bankruptcy. The first step in this direction would be to eliminate the superdischarge, so that the same debts are dischargeable in both of the consumer bankruptcy chapters.

In another context, progressive scholar Bill Whitford has contended that Chapter 13 should be eliminated altogether.[30] Whitford bases this rather dramatic proposal on the facts that a large majority of Chapter 13 rehabilitation plans are never completed, and that "local legal culture" rather than debtors themselves seems to determine whether personal debtors file for Chapter 7 or Chapter 13. An intriguing effect of Whitford's proposal would be to eliminate the moral confusion I have identified. But eliminating Chapter 13 might also increase bankruptcy filings by making bankruptcy more alluring, a possibility that suggests that the consumer credit lobby would fiercely resist such a proposal. (Interestingly, even progressive scholars are somewhat reluctant to endorse Whitford's proposal, in part because it might threaten some of the special protections available in current Chapter 13.)

None of the principal parties has much incentive to focus on the moral coherence of the bankruptcy framework unless this translates directly to more repayment (for creditors) or a broader discharge (for debtor advocates), and there was little discussion of the confusion of the current approach in the recent legislative debates. The debates continue to focus on means testing, and creditors' efforts to force debtors to repay more of their consumer debt.

What can we look for in the future? So long as consumer debt remains at its current, astronomical levels (or even increases), the benefits to consumer creditors of continuing to lobby for bankruptcy reform will remain extremely high. Their prospects for success are likely to be inversely related to the nation's economic health. In a recession, lawmakers will quickly lose their taste for "credit morality." Either way, the most remarkable lesson of the recent bankruptcy debates is how resilient the compromise reached in 1898 has been. Even if the creditors' proposed reforms are enacted, as seems likely, American bankruptcy law will still have the most generous discharge in the world, but one that also takes creditors' interests into account.

Chapter Eight

BANKRUPTCY AS A BUSINESS ADDRESS: THE

GROWTH OF CHAPTER 11 IN PRACTICE AND THEORY

I
F ASKED TO POINT to a single case that marked the transition from the low-profile bankruptcy practice of the Chandler Act decades to bankruptcy's current prominence in the American legal imagination, many bankruptcy lawyers point to the massive Penn Central railroad bankruptcy in the 1970s. Although it actually predates the 1978 Code by several years (and unfolded under the railroad provisions of the old Bankruptcy Act, rather than either of the corporate reorganization chapters), the Penn Central bankruptcy foreshadows several of the central themes of this chapter. When the railroad and numerous of its corporate subsidiaries filed their bankruptcy petitions at the federal courthouse in Philadelphia in 1970, they initiated one of the largest reorganization cases the nation had ever seen. Penn Central had billions of dollars in assets (and even more liabilities), and its track covered much of the northeastern United States. So consuming was the task of shepherding Penn Central through bankruptcy that one of District Judge Fullman's law clerks, Walter Taggart, continued to work part-time on the case from 1970, when he joined the Villanova University law faculty, until the consummation of Penn Central's reorganization in 1978.

Penn Central presaged current bankruptcy practice in several important respects, each of which can be traced to the enormity of the case. First, the size of the debtor and many of its creditors brought unprecedented numbers of attorneys into the proceedings. For the first time in decades, the corridors of the courthouse were filled with lawyers from the nation's most prominent firms. Nearly every major firm in Philadelphia had an interest in the case, as did many of the white shoe New York firms. In addition, during the course of the case, an active market developed for the buying and selling of claims against Penn Central. Like the involvement of prominent firms, claims trading was another practice that both harked back to the glory days of the old Wall Street reorganization bar and looked forward to the great Chapter 11 cases of the 1980s and 1990s.

Although Penn Central was a unique case, an increasing number of large firms had begun making their way into bankruptcy in the 1960s and 1970s. After the enactment of the 1978 Code, the trickle grew to what seemed at times a flood. In their study of the largest Chapter 11 cases filed during the

1980s, Lynn LoPucki and Bill Whitford found forty-three cases that involved more than $100 million in assets.[1] The enactment of Chapter 11 was not the only reason for the surge in large-scale corporate bankruptcy filings—which, after all, predated 1978 to some extent—but the new reorganization provisions clearly have played a crucial role. Because they continue to run the firm in bankruptcy, managers no longer try to avoid bankruptcy at all costs. Moreover, managers' assurance that they will retain control (at least initially—many are replaced during the case, as we shall see) has increased their willingness to take risks while the firm is financially healthy. Some of these firms will find themselves in bankruptcy as a result. The net effect is that more substantial firms now file for bankruptcy, and they do not wait so long to do so.

This chapter explores the most important changes in corporate reorganization practice since the enactment of the 1978 Code. The chapter begins by considering two of the most high-profile developments of the Code's first two decades, the increasing number of large firms that landed in bankruptcy after failed leveraged buyouts, and the upsurge in mass tort cases such as Johns Manville and A. H. Robins. Of particular interest is the extent to which Chapter 11 has encouraged these cases. The chapter then describes the transformation of the corporate bankruptcy bar that has resulted. After decades in the shadows, current reorganization practice now looks remarkably like the Wall Street reorganization practice of the 1920s and 1930s, although with the important distinction that the bar is much less centralized on Wall Street than in the earlier era. As we have seen throughout the book, bankruptcy scholars have figured prominently in judicial and legislative developments since the early twentieth century. After considering the transformation of bankruptcy practice in the wake of the 1978 Code, we will focus on an issue that came up in the last chapter: the recent division of the scholarly literature into two antagonistic strands, progressive scholarship and the law-and-economics movement. The scholarly debate is filled with apparent anomalies. Although Chapter 11 has almost completely repudiated the New Deal vision of corporate bankruptcy, for instance, progressive scholars—William Douglas's heirs in the bankruptcy literature—have tended to defend rather than criticize the new order. The most radical proposals for change have come not from progressives but from law-and-economics scholars. Law-and-economics scholars and their insights had remarkably little influence on the 1994 commission, as we have seen, but actual bankruptcy practice has taken on many of the market-oriented characteristics that these scholars have advocated.

The final section of the chapter considers the implications of these developments and takes us to the heart of current practice, by exploring four of the most hotly contested corporate reorganization issues: "prepackaged" bankruptcy and firms' efforts to opt out of bankruptcy; a raging debate over Delaware's success in attracting a large percentage of the nation's biggest corporate bankruptcy cases; the uncertain status of the new value exception to the absolute priority rule; and the growing concern about international insolvency cases.

BANKRUPTCY AND THE 1980s TAKEOVER BOOM

The initial rise of corporate reorganization can be traced in part to a development that took place outside of bankruptcy: the corporate takeover boom of the 1980s. Corporate takeovers underscore the intimate relationship between corporate reorganization and general corporate law.[2] Although the Chandler Act obscured the connection for four decades, Chapter 11 has reestablished the former link between corporate reorganization and general corporate and securities law.

Corporate takeovers frequently take the form of a leveraged buyout. In a leveraged buyout, the acquirer or "bidder"—either the managers of the target corporation or an outside bidder—makes a tender offer or merger proposal offering to buy the target corporation's stock or assets at a price significantly higher than the current market price. The buyout is referred to as "leveraged" because the bidder causes the target firm to incur enormous amounts of new debt (the "leverage") to help pay for the acquisition. For the purchase price, the bidder uses the proceeds of the new debt, plus a small amount of cash— somewhat as a home buyer does when she buys a new house. If all goes well, the bidder then uses revenues generated by the target corporation to repay the debt incurred to finance the takeover.

If all does not go well, however, the firm can quickly end up in bankruptcy. Because they often take on a great deal of debt in a takeover, and the price of the takeover is so high, bidders must immediately generate value by breaking up the firm (if parts of the firm can be sold for more than the firm is worth as a whole) or by improving its operations. If the bidder overpays, or if some unexpected change—anything from an increase in the cost of oil to a downturn in sales—cuts into the firm's revenues, the firm will default on its debt obligations. After a takeover, there often is very little margin for error. With the dramatic increase in takeovers in the 1980s came a large number of takeover-related bankruptcies.

The Federated Department Stores bankruptcy illustrates many of these factors.[3] In 1988, the Canadian investor Robert Campeau and his firm, Campeau Corporation, acquired Federated, which owned a group of ten department stores, after a takeover contest with Macy's. Campeau paid $8.17 billion to acquire Federated and financed this price largely with new debt. The transition proved rocky. Campeau's existing stores did not fit neatly with the stores acquired in the takeover, and Campeau made several strategic missteps in the months after the takeover. Less than two years later, Federated could no longer meet the payments due on its takeover debt, and it filed for bankruptcy. (The story would eventually have a happy ending, at least for Campeau; Federated restructured its obligations in Chapter 11; emerged with a much more sensible capital structure; and more recently acquired Macy's during the Macy's bankruptcy.)

As our discussion suggests, and as was apparent to just about everyone during the 1980s and early 1990s, an increase in takeovers can quickly lead to an increase in large Chapter 11 cases. What is less obvious is that the changes ushered in by the 1978 Code can also be seen as having contributed to the takeover trend in intriguing respects.

Perhaps the simplest way to see this is to focus first on the managers of takeover *bidders*. If the managers of a bidder firm knew they would be displaced if the takeover misfired and led to bankruptcy, they might think twice about engaging in takeover activity. With Federated, for instance, Campeau might not have been quite so anxious to launch an expensive takeover bid if he stood to lose control of the firm in bankruptcy. Thus, the manager-friendly rules of Chapter 11 tend to encourage takeover activity, whereas a harsher regime might discourage the market for corporate control, at least on the margin.

Now consider the managers of possible takeover *targets*. For target managers, takeovers pose a serious threat, since target managers are often ousted when the firm is taken over. One popular defense (in addition to "poison pills" and the like) is for managers to incur substantial amounts of debt. Taking on debt acts as a preemptive strike, since the target firm's debt-laden capital structure makes it hard for an aspiring bidder to assume still more debt in order to finance a takeover. This strategy also has a downside, of course: taking on more debt increases the risk of bankruptcy. If bankruptcy meant immediate removal, just as takeovers do, target managers might therefore try to protect themselves from takeovers in some other way.

In other developed nations, such as Germany and Japan, where bankruptcy does mean immediate removal, corporate managers have protected themselves by forging alliances with banks and other institutional investors.[4] In both nations, institutional shareholders hold large percentages of the stock of many widely held corporations. In return for the influence they enjoy due to their large stake in the firm, institutional shareholders traditionally have insulated the firm's managers from the risk of a takeover by implicitly committing not to sell their shares to any outside bidder. In the United States, by contrast, this strategy was foreclosed by the (recently repealed) Glass-Steagall Act and other New Deal reforms that undermined institutional investors' ability to actively participate in the governance of U.S. firms. Rather than relying on relational investors, managers and their lawyers pushed throughout the 1950s and 1960s, as we have seen, to evade the harsh, manager-displacing provisions of Chapter

X by filing under Chapter XI if the firm ran into financial distress. The enactment of Chapter 11 was the climax of this triumphant story.

By adopting an explicitly manager-friendly approach to corporate reorganization, Chapter 11 thus fit hand in glove with the expanding corporate takeover market. When takeovers took off in the 1980s, Chapter 11 provided a smooth landing both for the managers of takeover bidders whose takeovers misfired, as with Federated, and for the managers of potential target firms that took on too much debt in an effort to protect themselves.

The connections between Chapter 11 and corporate law are evident in other recent developments as well. Just as firms' stock and bonds are bought and sold prior to bankruptcy, active markets for claims have developed in many large bankruptcy cases. Often, buyers purchase claims in an effort to assert control of the reorganization process, much as bidders buy stock in order to effect a change in control outside of bankruptcy. In the Macy's bankruptcy, Federated Department Stores bought large amounts of senior debt and used its position to force Macy's to sell the business to Federated. In the bankruptcy of Allegheny International, Japonica Partners had taken this strategy even further. In order to assemble a large block of claims to vote in the reorganization, Japonica made a tender offer to Allegheny bondholders for their bonds. Like Federated, Japonica eventually used its bankruptcy voting rights to buttress a successful campaign to buy the debtor's assets.[5]

The location of many large bankruptcies offers still more evidence that Chapter 11 has become a business address. Nearly half of the nation's largest corporations are incorporated in Delaware. Just as the most important corporate law disputes are resolved by Delaware state court judges, a high percentage of large corporate debtors now file for bankruptcy in Delaware. A recent study found that 82.5 percent of all large corporate debtors that filed somewhere other than the location of their headquarters filed in Delaware.[6] (As discussed in more detail later in the chapter, non-Delaware bankruptcy judges and bankruptcy lawyers have loudly criticized this trend, and the 1997 commission report proposed that firms be prohibited from filing in Delaware.)

The corporatization of Chapter 11 illustrates just how much corporate bankruptcy has changed. Rather than a last resort for firms with no little hope of survival, Chapter 11 is now closely tied to developments in general corporate law, much as it was in the pre–New Deal era of J. P. Morgan and Kuhn, Loeb.

Interestingly, one can see evidence of analogous developments outside of the United States. Both in Europe and in Japan, traditional patterns of relational shareholding in corporate law are now under great stress, as a more shareholder-centered, U.S.-style perspective has begun to take hold. At the same time, there has been an increasing interest in adopting corporate reorganization provisions that look much more like Chapter 11 than does existing law. Germany, for instance, has enacted a new corporate bankruptcy framework that was quite explicitly modeled on the U.S. approach. Although important differences remain, in both countries we see corporate bankruptcy playing an increasingly important role in corporate law.

BANKRUPTCY AS A SOLUTION TO MASS TORT LIABILITY

In addition to the manager-friendly reorganization provisions that smoothed the skids for numerous failed leveraged buyouts, other aspects of the 1978 Code also have contributed to the dramatic increase in large reorganization cases. Especially important have been the reforms I referred to earlier as scope expanding. One of these changes, the expanded definition of *claim* (together with the Code's elimination of any requirement that a debtor be insolvent when it files for bankruptcy) has played a crucial role in some of the most visible bankruptcy cases of the past two decades, the "mass tort" cases—bankruptcies filed by Johns Manville, A. H. Robins, Dow Corning, and other firms after they were sued by thousands of actual and potential tort victims. Although these cases represent only a tiny percentage of all Chapter 11 cases, they have proven disproportionately important to the perception—deeply held by bankruptcy professionals and now shared by many others—that bankruptcy offers a solution to any economic disaster.

The touchstone for all of the major mass tort cases was Johns Manville.[7] As many readers will recall, Johns Manville had pioneered the manufacture of asbestos, which was first used to insulate houses and ships, and eventually for a wide range of other purposes as well. In 1964, an extensive study demonstrated a link between asbestos exposure and lung cancer. Prompted by the medical evidence, a steadily growing number of victims began to sue. One commentator calculated that the "pace of litigation against Manville had increased by 1982 to an average filing rate of 3 cases per hour[, with] over 16,500 lawsuits pending." Because asbestos-related disease often does not appear until many years after exposure, Manville could expect to face a continuing stream of lawsuits even if it were to stop selling asbestos immediately. On August 26, 1982, at a time when the firm was still fully solvent, Johns Manville filed for bankruptcy in an effort to deal with its litigation crisis. Manville's managers spent the next four years negotiating with its creditors over the terms of a reorganization. In the end, they set aside slightly over $2 billion to set up a trust fund to pay current and future victims.

Since Manville, Chapter 11 has been used not just by many of Manville's competitors in the asbestos industry, but also by other corporations faced with catastrophic tort liability. The next prominent mass tort bankruptcy involved A. H. Robins, whose enormously profitable business selling the Dalkon

Shield, an intrauterine contraceptive device, turned into a liability quagmire when thousands of women began experiencing serious complications. More recently, Dow Corning filed for bankruptcy after women who had received breast implants made by Dow Corning sued the firm in large numbers. The pattern in each of these cases has been the same. The firm's managers have filed for bankruptcy preemptively, before the firm was overwhelmed by liability, and have attempted to use Chapter 11 to reach a global solution for its liability problems. In each case, the centerpiece of the reorganization has been a trust fund set up to compensate current and future victims of the debtor's products.

It is possible, of course, that these cases would have landed in bankruptcy, in more or less the same fashion, even under the old Bankruptcy Act regime. But the process would have been fraught with uncertainty for the managers of firms like Johns Manville. Under the old act, Johns Manville theoretically could discharge only "provable" claims. The "provability" requirement would have raised even more questions than current law as to the bankruptcy court's authority to discharge the tort victim's claims. Not just future claims, but also many claimants whose symptoms had already arisen could have argued that they had no claim in bankruptcy and thus were entitled to ask payment in full after the case. Perhaps a bankruptcy court would have bent the rules a bit to address the avalanche of claims faced by Manville. The court might have stretched the definition of *provable* to its breaking point, for instance, and issued an injunction requiring future claimants to comply with the terms of the reorganization (and thus to accept partial rather than full payment), much as the court did in the actual case. But the only way to find out would have been for the managers of Manville to file for bankruptcy and face almost certain displacement if the case ended up in Chapter X. With the enactment of Chapter 11, by contrast, Manville's managers were assured that they could continue in control. And by expanding the definition of *claim* to include "any legal or equitable right," even those that are "contingent" or "unliquidated," the Bankruptcy Code sends a clear signal that bankruptcy judges should pull as many creditors as possible into the bankruptcy case. Together, these changes made the current Code far more hospitable to firms like Johns Manville than the old Bankruptcy Act; and these firms have responded by using bankruptcy to achieve a global solution to their litigation woes.

The expansion of bankruptcy to resolve mass tort liability has generated enormous controversy in some quarters. In his book on the A. H. Robins bankruptcy, *Bending the Law*, Richard Sobol voices many of the most prominent criticisms.[8] As in Manville and other cases, the trust set up in A. H. Robins purports to bind victims who did not even know they had been injured. These future claimants therefore had no opportunity to challenge the terms of the trust arrangement. Another pressing concern is the difficulty of predicting how large the firm's total liability will be, how much money to put into the trust for the benefit of the victims, and how to handle each new claim that arises. In A. H. Robins, the court set up a payout framework that imposed strict dollar limits on how much each victim would be paid based on the nature of her injury. The strict limits have assured that the fund does not run out before future victims are paid, but they have been attacked by Sobol and others as too stingy. In Manville, by contrast, the trust offered generous payout terms, but the money was almost immediately used up, and the bankruptcy court was forced to restructure it.

In the academic literature, commentators have offered intriguing solutions to the valuation issues that have bedeviled the mass tort cases. One possible solution is to issue a new security —referred to as "tort debentures"—to the victims of firms like Johns Manville.[9] The face amount of the debenture would correspond to the full amount of harm suffered by the victim, and a debenture would be issued to each victim after her injury arose. The bankruptcy court would then sell some or all of the assets of the firm, pay priority creditors, and use the rest of the sale proceeds to establish a trust fund for the tort victims. The payment date for the trust fund would be set far in the future—well after the last future victim would have received her debenture. In the meantime, the debentures could be bought and sold (with each debenture representing the right to share in the trust fund at the payout date). The virtues of the approach are that each victim would get a full opportunity to demonstrate the extent of her injury once it had actually arisen, and the market rather than a bankruptcy judge would be the one to predict (through the prices buyers are willing to pay for a victim's tort debenture in the secondary market) what percentage of each victim's damages should be paid. An important question with tort debentures is whether a dependable market would in fact develop— otherwise, tort victims who desperately needed cash might sell their claims too cheaply.

Although the tort debenture proposal strikes many readers as far-fetched, and bankruptcy judges have not yet shown any inclination to adopt such a strategy, the continuing expansion of bankruptcy to accommodate the mass tort cases is in some respects equally remarkable.[10] Even under the broadest possible reading, the Code's expanded definition of *claim* does not seem to encompass many victims whose injuries have not yet arisen at the time of bankruptcy. As noted a moment ago, the court in Johns Manville swept future victims into the Manville reorganization by issuing an injunction requiring them to abide by the terms of the trust. From the debtor's perspective, this approach is a clever strategy for solving the litigation problem once and for all. Future claimants are not likely to find the solution quite so appealing, however, because it subjects them to the terms of a reorganization they had no real voice in. Even after Manville, it remains to be seen whether these claimants can in fact be bound, consistent with their constitutional right to due process.

Like the managers of these firms, bankruptcy professionals also have an obvious interest in seeing the Manville strategy succeed. For bankruptcy judges, there are substantial reputational benefits if bankruptcy becomes the forum of choice for resolving prickly social problems such as mass tort liability. These benefits are most pronounced for the judge who guides a case like Manville or Dow Corning to reorganization, of course, but they also enhance the prestige of bankruptcy judges generally. Corporate bankruptcy lawyers receive a similar boost in prestige, as well as the more tangible benefit of an additional source of lucrative, high-profile cases. In 1994, bankruptcy professionals and the managers of Manville itself persuaded Congress to give its explicit imprimatur on the Manville solution to the question of how to bind future claimants. (Notice that this is a rare exception to managers' tendency not to participate in debates on bankruptcy legislation.) A new provision attempts to validate trust funds that sweep in future as well as current victims of asbestos-related injuries, so long as 75 percent of the existing victims approve the plan and future victims are represented in absentia by an appointed representative.[11] In keeping with its general enthusiasm for existing practice, the 1997 Bankruptcy Commission report proposed to expand the reach of bankruptcy still further, by applying a similar approach to all firms, including those outside the asbestos industry.[12]

An interesting puzzle has been trial lawyers' role in the mass tort bankruptcies. Trial lawyers have an extremely effective lobbying organization, the American Trial Lawyers Association. Because bankruptcy imposes an automatic stay on tort plaintiffs' efforts to pursue litigation against the debtor and has often imposed additional constraints such as halting litigation against co-defendants and other third parties, one might expect trial lawyers and ATLA to resist the use of bankruptcy to resolve mass tort issues. So far, however, trial lawyers have been more supportive than critical of bankruptcy's role in mass tort. Early on, trial lawyers' acquiescence may have reflected the novelty of the bankruptcy strategy. Their recent support, however, appears to reflect the comparative attractions of bankruptcy as opposed to bringing class action litigation outside of bankruptcy. Recent Supreme Court cases such as *Amchem Products, Inc. v. Windsor*[13] have made it much more difficult to certify a class action outside of bankruptcy, and attorneys have fared quite well under the trust fund arrangements employed in many of the mass tort bankruptcies. As a result, bankruptcy offers significant benefits to trial lawyers, despite the limits it imposes on the ability to litigate individual cases. Although future victims might prefer not to be included in the case, they are represented only indirectly, by trial lawyers (and by an appointed representative in individual cases) whose interests do not fully reflect their own.

If the 1978 Code had never been passed, and corporate reorganization had retained its uninviting New Deal parameters, the mass tort crises of recent years would no doubt have been dealt with in some other way, even in the wake of Supreme Court limitations on the availability of private class action treatment. One obvious possibility would be for Congress to use multidistrict litigation panels to deal with the avalanche of litigation. Another is simply to permit the individual trials or limited class actions to go forward. Through the reforms they achieved in 1978, and the expansion of bankruptcy's domain, bankruptcy professionals established bankruptcy as a more plausible alternative. The new, more flexible Bankruptcy Code, together with the Supreme Court's retrenchment on class action certification, has made bankruptcy the forum of choice for resolving the modern dilemma of mass tort liability.

The Return of White Shoe Law Firms to Bankruptcy

The leveraged buyout and mass tort cases are specific instances of the broader transformation that has affected all of bankruptcy practice. Because managers are assured they will remain in control, and both bankruptcy lawyers and bankruptcy judges are biased toward reorganization, large debtors have used Chapter 11 to address a wide variety of economic problems. For every megabankruptcy, hundreds of smaller corporations file for Chapter 11. In a substantial majority of the smaller cases, the reorganization effort fails. But the guiding impulse is the same. Current bankruptcy law gives the managers of troubled firms one last chance to reverse their firms' decline.

The most obvious beneficiaries of the newfound prominence of corporate bankruptcy have been bankruptcy lawyers. Once reviled, corporate bankruptcy attained an undeniable cachet. By the late 1980s, the *American Lawyer* and other national legal publications regularly included bankruptcy on their lists of the hottest practice areas for new law school graduates. "Insolvency lawyers," the *National Law Journal* proclaimed,

> are expecting the excesses of the 1980s to lead to business failures that will keep them busy for at least the next five years. Ten years ago, before large corporate clients began to use the 1978 Bankruptcy Code as a way out of short-term financial problems, most large firms ignored the field altogether. Now they are scrambling to bolster and promote their insolvency practices.[14]

In the same 1992 article, the *National Law Journal* published a list of the top bankruptcy lawyers in the nation. Included on the list were many of the lawyers who had worked so tirelessly to reform bankruptcy practice in the years before the 1978 Code. Harvey Miller made the role of honor, as did Leonard Rosen, Ron Trost, and Ken Klee.[15] But the list reflects a remarkable change in the nature of the reorganization bar. In stark contrast to the bankruptcy bar under the old Bankruptcy Act, most of the honorees now worked for the nation's most prestigious law firms. A recent history of bankruptcy practice in the New York area tells a similar story: forty-nine of the fifty largest New York law firms now claim to have a bankruptcy practice.[16]

The simplest way for prominent law firms to develop an effective bankruptcy practice was to hire lawyers away from the bankruptcy boutiques, or to simply acquire the boutique in toto, and this is precisely what large firms did. One of the first was New York's Weil, Gotshal, whose bankruptcy practice is now widely viewed as preeminent in the nation. Starting in the 1960s, Weil, Gotshal sought to lure both Harvey Miller and Charles Seligson from Seligson's firm Seligson, Morris & Newburger. In the early 1970s, both made the shift. Numerous other bankruptcy lawyers made similar moves thereafter, and precisely the same shift occurred in other major cities as well. As in New York, bankruptcy practice in Philadelphia had long been dominated by a small cluster of specialty firms. In the 1970s, leaders of the corporate bankruptcy bar such as Leon Forman and Ray Shapiro began moving to the city's elite law firms, with Forman moving to Wolf, Block & Schorr and Shapiro setting up shop at Blank, Rome, Comisky & McCauley. Small and midsized law firms continued to play an active role in bankruptcy practice. But the lawyers at the top of the bar—the ones who handled the largest and most prominent cases—now came disproportionately from the largest law firms.

The exodus of leading bankruptcy lawyers to major law firms has given bankruptcy practice a striking back-to-the-future quality. Much as in the era before the Chandler Act severed the ties between Wall Street and corporate bankruptcy, corporate bankruptcy has increasingly become the domain of the megafirms—the "haves" of the U.S. legal profession. Although the number of large bankruptcy cases declined during the economic boom of the mid and late 1990s, corporate reorganization has retained its connections with large-firm practice. And many firms are gearing up for a wave of large bankruptcies at the outset of the twenty-first century.[17]

The newfound prominence of corporate bankruptcy practice has also been reflected in the academic literature. In the law schools, bankruptcy had for many years been as much a backwater as bankruptcy practice. With a few exceptions, such as a pioneering casebook by Vern Countryman in 1951, there was little activity or interest in bankruptcy in the 1950s and 1960s. All of this changed in the wake of the 1978 Code. Bright young academic stars such as Stanford Law School's Tom Jackson used the new visibility of Chapter 11 to rekindle academic and student interest in bankruptcy. Jackson emerged as the most prominent advocate in the bankruptcy literature of the law-and-economics perspective, and his work has inspired a talented new generation of bankruptcy scholars. Jackson's insights sharply conflicted with the stance of the progressive scholars who follow in the tradition of William Douglas. The most important progressive, Vern Countryman—an elder statesman when Jackson arrived on the scene—was instinctively hostile to law-and-economics analysis, and his successors have shared Countryman's disdain. The next two sections will take a closer look at the debates between these two perspectives and the extent to which each has influenced bankruptcy politics. We begin with the current progressives.

DEFENDING CHAPTER 11: THE PROGRESSIVES

Each of the developments we have seen—the increasing resort by large corporations to bankruptcy, and the return of the elite law firms—has been encouraged by the 1978 Code's repudiation of the New Deal vision of corporate bankruptcy. Forty years after William Douglas and the SEC ended the elite Wall Street reorganization practice, Congress opened the door for its return. One can easily imagine the angry words William Douglas might have had for the recent strategic bankruptcy filings and the fancy lawyers at the top of the bankruptcy bar. One might also imagine that Douglas's intellectual heirs— the current generation of progressive scholars—would take up the banner right where Douglas left it, decrying the return of an elite corporate bankruptcy practice. The remarkable thing is that they have not. Rather than attacking the changes ushered in by the 1978 Code, recent progressive scholars have been the Code's most vigorous *defenders*.

This section explains the unlikely stance of recent progressive scholars— their defense of a bankruptcy regime that looks suspiciously like the world that William Douglas, the most famous bankruptcy progressive of the last century, so fiercely attacked. As we shall see, the explanation for this thinking is mixed: recent progressives have responded to a world that has changed in important respects since the Wall Street–dominated era that Douglas knew, but their stance has also been shaped by close ties to the corporate bankruptcy bar and by their resistance to the rise of law-and-economics scholarship.

The crowning achievement of William Douglas and the early bankruptcy progressives was the SEC report that Douglas and his staff issued in stages from 1936 to 1940. As we saw in chapter 4, the SEC report took direct aim at the corporate managers and Wall Street professionals who had long dominated corporate bankruptcy. The report excoriated managers and their Wall Street bankers for furthering their own interests rather than the interests of the scattered investors of the troubled corporation. Because the firm's managers stayed in control, and its bankers focused principally on their own fees, no one investigated the possibility that the firm's investors had been victimized by fraud or mismanagement prior to bankruptcy. As we also saw in chapter 4, the report and Douglas's other writings repeatedly criticized the elite reorganization bar.

Despite the similarities between current bankruptcy law and corporate reorganization prior to the New Deal, current progressives have enthusiastically defended current Chapter 11. The most prominent current progressive, Professor Elizabeth Warren of Harvard Law School, defends precisely those aspects of current law that have repudiated the New Deal vision: managers' right to remain in control, the relaxed treatment of absolute priority, and the overall flexibility of the reorganization provisions. "In some cases," she notes, with implicit approval, "a creditor's nonbankruptcy rights can be impaired, forcing it to share in the losses of bankruptcy, in order to give the failing business a chance to survive."[18] Warren and other current progressives extoll Chapter 11 as a success, not a failure.

Why does current progressive thinking look so different from William Douglas and the first generation of progressive scholars? In other work I have highlighted the importance of Vern Countryman, who was one of William Douglas's early law clerks on the Supreme Court and a longtime ally, as the crucial link between Douglas and the very different insights of Elizabeth Warren and other leading current progressives.[19] For our purposes, three aspects of that story loom especially large. The first is the dramatic change in corporate bankruptcy practice in the years after the Chandler Act of 1938. As we saw in chapter 4, the principal target of the New Dealers' ire was Wall Street, and the Wall Street banks and bar simply disappeared from reorganization practice after the Chandler Act reforms. For Countryman, the bankruptcy bar (particularly in its reformist mode, with the National Bankruptcy Conference) was an ally rather than a nemesis, and the ties of Elizabeth Warren and current progressives to bankruptcy professionals are, if anything, even closer. The second factor follows from the first. Flexible, manager-friendly reorganization rules seemed most pernicious when the process was dominated by Wall Street elites. But populists and their allies have always been sympathetic to reorganization, even if it involves large corporations. Although Countryman himself protested the repudiation in 1978 of the New Deal vision for corporate reorganization, the absence of Wall Street domination has made it much easier for current progressives to embrace the new Chapter 11 reorganization framework.

The final factor is progressive scholars' instinctive hostility to the rise of economics-influenced scholarship in the law schools over the past two decades. Law-and-economics scholars have tended to call for strict enforcement of creditors' priority rights, even when this diminishes the likelihood of reorganization, based on the assumption that clear priorities increase the certainty (and ultimately, the efficiency) of securities markets. The most influential work in this vein was done by Douglas Baird and Thomas Jackson in the 1980s. Baird and Jackson developed a "creditors' bargain" model for bankruptcy that advocated strict compliance with state law priority rules. As we will discuss in the next section, more recent work has taken this impulse still further and suggested that Congress should replace current Chapter 11 with market-driven, liquidation-based alternatives. In response to this literature, which they view as creditor-oriented and conservative, progressive scholars have dug in their heels. They, along with the practicing bar, have fiercely defended the existing framework.

Together, these developments in bankruptcy practice and in the more rarefied world of academic theory have made current progressives much more sympathetic to existing practice than William Douglas and other reformers were with the reorganization procedures of their day. Gone are the calls for governmental intervention and sweeping reform.

THE BRAVE NEW WORLD OF LAW-AND-ECONOMICS THEORY

In contrast to the 1930s, the most sweeping calls for reform in recent years have come not from progressive scholars, but from the very different scholars of the law-and-economics movement. The origins of law-and-economics scholarship in the corporate bankruptcy literature can be traced to the work of two scholars I mentioned a moment ago, Thomas Jackson and his frequent coauthor, Douglas Baird.[20] As a young faculty member at Stanford Law School in the late 1970s, Jackson described bankruptcy as the solution to a collective action, or common pool, problem.[21] Thomas Jackson contended that if creditors could bargain as a group, they would agree to halt their collection efforts and wait until the group decided whether to liquidate or preserve the firm. Because the creditors of a troubled firm are too widely scattered to reach such an agreement, however, each creditor has an incentive to sue the debtor and levy on its assets in an attempt to be one of the fortunate few who get repaid before the firm is dismembered. Bankruptcy's automatic stay solves this problem by forcing creditors to stop trying to collect until creditors as a group can agree whether the firm should be liquidated or preserved.

More startling than his characterization of bankruptcy as solving a collective action problem was the conclusion that Jackson derived from this. Jackson insisted that addressing creditors' collective action problem was not simply one of bankruptcy's goals; it is the *only* proper goal for bankruptcy. With his coauthor, Douglas Baird, Jackson argued that bankruptcy should not create any new substantive rights for any of the parties. In support of their creditors' bargain model, Baird and Jackson contended that unless it respected the parties' nonbankruptcy property rights, bankruptcy would inspire costly forum-shopping fights. Parties favored by bankruptcy would have an incentive to invoke the bankruptcy laws, whereas disfavored parties would fight bankruptcy, for reasons having nothing to do with whether or not the firm belonged in bankruptcy. If bankruptcy fails to fully honor a creditor's security interest, for instance, the parties will take costly steps to invoke (the debtor) or resist (the creditor) bankruptcy.

Subsequent law-and-economics scholars have pushed the insights of Baird and Jackson even further. Although Baird and Jackson called for a sharply restricted bankruptcy framework that interfered as little as possible with market transactions and nonbankruptcy law, their creditors' bargain model assumed that the existing reorganization rules were necessary, due to the collective action problems. A second generation of law-and-economics scholars insists that the parties themselves could solve any collective action problems by contract. The key to this new analysis is the debtor itself. Although the debtor's creditors cannot easily bargain with one another, the new scholars argue, the debtor deals with each of the creditors. The debtor could therefore serve as an intermediary.[22] At the same time (and often in the same work) law-and-economics scholars began to devise alternative schemes that, in their view, would work better than the costly, time-consuming Chapter 11 reorganization rules.

The most prominent of the new proposals was an argument by Michael Bradley and Michael Rosenzweig, and at roughly the same time by Barry Adler, stock cancellation scheme.[23] Bradley and Rosenzweig argued that when a firm defaulted, the stock of its current stockholders should simply be canceled, and the interests of its lowest-priority creditors converted from debt into stock. Bradley and Rosenzweig's stock cancellation scheme sparked a spirited debate with progressive scholars, who sharply criticized both their proposal and the empirical evidence they had marshaled to illustrate the deficiencies of existing reorganization law. In a characteristically tart critique, one progressive scholar dismissed their analysis as "strange visions in a strange world."[24]

In addition to Bradley and Rosenzweig's, and Adler's, stock cancellation scheme, other law-and-economics scholars have advocated that corporate reorganization should be replaced by an auction regime in which bankrupt firms would be sold to the highest bidder, either through a straight sale or through a complicated system of options.[25] Still another proposal suggested that Congress should simply provide a menu of different bankruptcy regimes, ranging from current Chapter 11 to the stock cancellation and auction approaches. In its original certificate of incorporation, the debtor would select the approach that made the most sense for that firm.

Despite their striking differences, the proposed alternatives to Chapter 11 (I put the menu proposal to one side, as it does not propose a specific approach) share several key characteristics. In contrast to Chapter 11, each uses strict adherence to absolute priority as its starting point. (The parties can vary this by contract if they wish). The proposals also undermine the status of the debtor's managers. Unlike Chapter 11, where the managers remain in control at the outset of the case, most of the proposed schemes trigger adjustments that would immediately shift authority out of the managers' hands. Each also is much more market-oriented than current law and therefore depends on smoothly functioning markets—stock cancellation that does not cause systemic disruption, auctions where plenty of bidders show up.

The most recent work by law-and-economics scholars has focused on the question whether debtors could devise their own bankruptcy rules by contract. Alan Schwartz has demonstrated that, given the appropriate assumptions, the parties could devise a contract that gives the managers of a firm an incentive to choose liquidation rather than reorganization when this alternative is best, rather than invariably pushing for reorganization in order to retain control.[26]

As we saw in chapter 7, the insights of law-and-economics scholars have played curiously little role in the legislative debates. One obvious explanation for the lack of legislative influence is that the proposals seem inconsistent with the traditional American balance between creditor- and debtor-oriented perspectives. (In more creditor-oriented England, by contrast, one of the new proposals received serious attention when Britain revisited its insolvency laws in the mid-1990s.) Law-and-economics scholars also have made little effort to translate their theoretical proposals into realistic reforms.

Although the law-and-economics proposals have had little legislative influence, market forces play an increasingly prominent role in the Chapter 11 process, as law- and economics scholars have long advocated. Managers are often replaced during the reorganization process; many cases are resolved through auctions, rather than negotiated reorganizations; there are increasingly liquid markets for the claims of many large corporate debtors; and the deviation from absolute priority in many cases turns out to be quite small.

The Rise of Delaware and Other Bankruptcy Controversies

One does not need a crystal ball, or any special prescience, to predict the general trajectory of corporate bankruptcy in the coming years. Absent catastrophic change in the U.S. markets, bankruptcy will retain its current characteristics: control by managers and the debtor's attorneys, and a flexible approach to absolute priority. Bankruptcy lawyers have an enormous stake in this framework (and the support of progressive scholars), and there is no obvious, cohesive constituency for harsher reorganization rules. Although the elite law firms have returned to corporate bankruptcy practice, the bar is not confined to Wall Street as it was in the 1930s. Even populists are often sympathetic to the current approach, with its emphasis on rescuing troubled firms.

Despite the general stability of Chapter 11, several crucial issues are very much up for grabs, and their resolution will have a significant effect on corporate reorganization practice in the coming years. To conclude our analysis, this section will briefly consider four: (1) efforts to opt out of bankruptcy; (2) Delaware's recent and much-debated dominance as the filing location of choice for large corporate debtors; (3) the new value exception to absolute priority; and (4) international insolvency cases. Each of the first three issues harkens back in interesting respects to the elite Wall Street reorganization practice of the 1930s. Together with the recent fascination with international insolvency, they also tell a great deal about the future of U.S. corporate bankruptcy law.

Opting Out of Bankruptcy

Debtors can opt out of the bankruptcy laws in a variety of ways. In recent years, the lenders of many individuals and small firms have required debtors to agree to provisions waiving the automatic stay if the debtor later files for bankruptcy. By agreeing to a stay waiver, the debtor partially opts out of bankruptcy, since the waiver amounts to a promise that the lender will not be bound by the automatic stay that would otherwise preclude the lender from retrieving its collateral in bankruptcy. Like a stay waiver, prepackaged bankruptcies also can be seen as partially opting out of bankruptcy. In a prepackaged bankruptcy, the debtor negotiates the general terms of its reorganization plan with creditors before filing for bankruptcy, then files its bankruptcy petition and proposed plan at the same time. Although the court must still confirm the reorganization plan, prepackaged bankruptcy short-circuits the lengthy negotiations that characterize other Chapter 11 cases. Prepackaged bankruptcies generally last several months, rather than several years.[27]

In addition to stay waivers and prepackaged bankruptcy, one can also imagine more complete efforts to opt out of bankruptcy. As we have seen, this impulse has motivated a great deal of the recent law-and-economics literature. Law-and-economics scholars have argued that a firm could sidestep bankruptcy altogether by devising a set of bankruptcy rules to include in its certificate of incorporation or contracts with creditors.

Bankruptcy professionals have long viewed prepackaged bankruptcy quite differently than efforts to more fully opt out of bankruptcy. For decades, received wisdom has held that efforts to completely opt out of bankruptcy are unenforceable, and bankruptcy lawyers have loudly condemned any suggestion that an individual or firm should be permitted to waive bankruptcy. (This is why stay waiver provisions purport to waive only the automatic stay, rather than precluding bankruptcy altogether, although the effect is essentially the same if the creditor in question is the debtor's principal lender.) In contrast to their relentless hostility to bankruptcy waiver, bankruptcy professionals have long defended prepackaged bankruptcy. In the hearings on the 1978 Code, bankruptcy lawyers frequently praised prebankruptcy workouts and argued that the Bankruptcy Code should honor these agreements.[28]

It is not difficult to imagine why bankruptcy lawyers find true waiver pernicious, and prepackaged bankruptcy just the opposite. Widespread waiver of bankruptcy would diminish the demand for bankruptcy, and thus the demand for bankruptcy lawyers. Bankruptcy lawyers have a powerful interest in preserving the Bankruptcy Code's role as the principal mechanism for resolving financial distress, so they can be expected to take issue with any suggestion that debtors could devise an alternative approach. (Indeed, this is an area where the National Bankruptcy Conference has little interest in substantial reform; the conference has repeatedly criticized proposals for permitting significant opting out of bankruptcy.) Prepackaged bankruptcies are another story. Although prepackaged bankruptcies truncate the bankruptcy process, too, they make use of the bankruptcy framework; even the prebankruptcy negotiations take place in the shadow of bankruptcy; and, as a result, they invariably require the services of bankruptcy lawyers. To be sure, prepackaged bankruptcies are less lawyer-intensive than a full-blown bankruptcy case. But the prepackaged option also makes bankruptcy more attractive for firms that might otherwise resist filing. Along with the rise of Delaware, the increasing use of prepackaged bankruptcy is the single most important development in corporate bankruptcy practice. Rare before 1990, prepacks have become almost routine, particularly for firms with publicly held debt.

The Rise of Delaware as Venue of Choice

During the same period as bankruptcy professionals have perfected the prepackaged bankruptcy, Delaware has surged to prominence as the nation's leading bankruptcy court.(Indeed there is an important link between the two developments: a large majority of prepacks are filed in Delaware, as we shall see.) The story of Delaware's rise to dominance and the controversy it has caused are both quite remarkable, so I will briefly describe each in turn.

Bankruptcy's venue provision is quite flexible, permitting a troubled corporation to file for bankruptcy in any district where it has its principal place of business, principal assets or domicile, or where an affiliated firm has already filed for bankruptcy.[29] For much of the 1980s, debtors used this flexibility to file important cases in New York. Starting in the early 1990s, however, all this changed. As Continental Airlines prepared to file for Chapter 11 for the second time, its managers had three filing options. As Robert Rasmussen and Randall Thomas have described, Houston, the location of Continental's headquarters, "was unattractive because Continental had previously filed for bankruptcy there and the case had not gone smoothly." New York, where Continental affiliate Eastern Airlines was already in bankruptcy, was a second option, but it, too, was "a poor candidate because the Eastern Airline's bankruptcy had turned into a contentious affair."[30] The one remaining choice was Delaware, Continental's state of incorporation. Continental's managers decided to take their chances on the devil they did not know, rather than the two they knew. Although the parties had little idea what to expect from the Delaware bankruptcy judge, Helen Balick, she handled the Continental reorganization quickly and effectively, and her efforts put Delaware on the bankruptcy map. By the mid-1980s, as noted earlier, well over 80 percent of the large firms that filed for bankruptcy somewhere other than the location of their headquarters were taking their cases to Delaware.

Delaware's growing dominance has generated loud complaints.[31] Critics first complained that Delaware was an inconvenient location, especially for small creditors. A second objection was that Delaware's bankruptcy judges had too cozy a relationship with the bankruptcy bar and engaged in inappropriate ex parte communications. (This complaint was directed at Judge Balick in particular, but she has since retired, so it has lost some of its steam.) The latest salvo is an empirical study suggesting that firms that reorganize in Delaware are more likely to wind up back in bankruptcy a second time than corporations that file for bankruptcy elsewhere.

By 1997, Delaware's critics had achieved several small successes. Early in the year, the chief judge of Delaware's federal district court, Joseph J. Farnan, started assigning some of Delaware's cases to the district court judges, rather than letting all of the cases go directly to the two bankruptcy judges. (The ostensible reason for the change was to reduce the bankruptcy judges' caseload, but most observers believe that Judge Farnan was responding to the complaints about their oversight.) Delaware skeptics also persuaded the National Bankruptcy Review Commission to propose in its 1997 report that state of incorporation be removed as a filing option, and an anti-Delaware provision was inserted into proposed bankruptcy legislation in 1998. Congress has not done anything yet, but the crusade against Delaware continues.

The criticisms of Delaware's regulatory influence over corporations that are incorporated in Delaware but have few assets there have a long populist pedigree. Although the complaints usually are aimed at Delaware's regulation of state corporate law, there is similar precedent in the insolvency context. In the early New Deal bankruptcy debates, Senator (and later Supreme Court justice) Hugo Black complained that permitting debtors to file for bankruptcy in a state far from their principal operations "would encourage a continuation of the conditions with reference to the freedom and laxness of corporate laws in certain states."[32] Although Black did not mention any state by name, everyone knew his remarks were aimed at Delaware.

On the merits, the current criticism of corporate debtors' penchant for filing in Delaware is questionable. Outside of bankruptcy, commentators have long debated whether Delaware's status as the nation's leading state of incorporation is desirable or pernicious. I will not rehash the debate here, other than to say that many commentators, myself included, are persuaded that Delaware's success depends on the effectiveness of its lawmakers and judges as overseers in corporate law. Given the large revenues Delaware receives from the firms that call it home—nearly 20 percent of Delaware's yearly income comes from franchise taxes and other chartering-related income—its lawmakers have an enormous stake in maintaining Delaware's success.[33] Many of the same forces that pressure Delaware to enact desirable corporate law will also influence the decision making of Delaware's bankruptcy judges. Indeed, the best approach to corporate bankruptcy would be to cede control over bankruptcy to the states altogether. As a political matter, the likelihood that Congress will turn over the reins to the states is, of course, close to nil. When I advocated this step in an op-ed in the *New York Times* several years ago, a bankruptcy lawyer wrote a letter to the *Times* characterizing my view as "educational malpractice."

To be sure, permitting Delaware corporations to file for bankruptcy in Delaware's federal bankruptcy court is not quite as effective as shifting authority to the states would be. Because bankruptcy law is federal, Delaware has no control over the Bankruptcy Code or the selection of bankruptcy judges. In addition, the facts that the managers of a troubled firm often have several venue choices at the time of the bankruptcy, and that they make the choice without any shareholder or creditor input, create the risk that managers will take only their own interests into account—and that bankruptcy judges who wish to attract cases will be forced to cater to managers' interests. Yet there are silver linings with each of these concerns. Although the Bankruptcy Code is federal, it leaves considerable room for discretion, and Delaware's bankruptcy judges have used this discretion to develop a quick, administratively efficient bankruptcy process. Similarly, it is unlikely that Delaware's bankruptcy judges will simply cater to managers. Delaware's bankruptcy judges operate within the same corporate culture that shapes Delaware's role in corporate law. If Delaware's bankruptcy judges focused on managers' interests at the expense of the insolvent firm, they would face enormous social pressure in Delaware to mend their ways. Most judges care deeply about their reputation, and the way to enhance one's reputation in Delaware is to demonstrate the kind of sophistication and responsiveness that we see in the Delaware state courts' handling of general corporate law issues.

Much as critics fail to appreciate the benefits of Delaware venue, they also overstate the significance of Delaware's inconvenience. Large creditors will of course have no trouble participating in a bankruptcy case in Delaware. Although traveling to Delaware might not be cost effective for small creditors, the firms that seek out Delaware's bankruptcy court are large and publicly held; most large firms have assets and creditors in many different states, so any filing location would be inconvenient to large numbers of creditors. Moreover, small creditors rarely participate even in convenient cases.

The real impulse behind the push to prevent Delaware firms from filing for bankruptcy is political and centers on two influences we have seen throughout the book: bankruptcy professionals and the forces of federalism. The loudest critics of Delaware venue have been bankruptcy lawyers and bankruptcy judges. Their criticism is quite understandable. For judges and lawyers, large corporate bankruptcies are the most exciting and prestigious cases they see. Each high-profile Delaware filing, from Continental Airlines to Marvel Comics, is a case that would otherwise have gone to another court-house because few of the firms have any meaningful business operations in Delaware. Ending Delaware venue would be a gain for the rest of the bank-ruptcy bench and bar, just as Delaware's gain has been their loss.

A recent pronouncement by the bankruptcy judges of the Southern District of Texas is a striking illustration of their perceived stake in the venue issue. To discourage Texas firms from filing their bankruptcy petitions in Delaware, the judges announced in open court that "the war on fees is over"—that is, that they intended to award generous attorneys fees to the debtor's attorneys in cases filed in the Southern District of Texas from now on.[34]

In addition to bankruptcy professionals, the same populist winds that stirred Senator Black's sails in the 1930s can still be expected to favor the challenge to Delaware. Although the hostility to Delaware's preeminence in corporate law has been muted in recent years, it has never disappeared, and the same will be true with bankruptcy.

In corporate law, Delaware has an enormous, long-standing commitment to continued state control, as noted earlier, and other states also can be expected to support the current division of authority. In bankruptcy, by contrast, only Delaware benefits, and its interest is quite recent.

From a political perspective, then, Delaware venue is somewhat precarious. In the most recent bankruptcy debates, the proposal to reform the venue provision failed for a very simple reason: a well-placed federal lawmaker. Delaware's Joseph Biden is an influential senator and a long-standing member of the Judiciary Committee, and he has made clear that he will resist any effort eliminate domicile-based venue. Should Biden retire or his influence wane, the dynamics could change. The longer Delaware retains its venue, however, the greater its stake will be and the more aggressively Delaware lawmakers will fight to retain the current rule.

For now, at least, Delaware has transformed the nature of corporate bank-ruptcy practice. As a leading bankruptcy lawyer noted to me, Delaware decides cases quickly, and its judges are viewed as having a realistic perspective on what must be done to get a firm in and out of bankruptcy.[35] Delaware also has perfected the prepackaged bankruptcy process. When a firm files in Delaware, it can be confident that Delaware's judges will not provide unexpected sur-prises. Each of these factors are characteristics that have long been associated with Delaware's handling of corporations that have not encountered financial distress. At the outset of the twenty-first century, prepackaged bankruptcy has become the strategy of choice for even major corporations with complicated financial structures, and troubled firms go to the same place that healthy ones do: Delaware.

Absolute Priority and the New Value Exception

Absolute priority first surfaced as an issue in the early years of corporate reorganization, and it never quite seems to go away. As we saw in chapter 5, the 1978 Code dramatically relaxed the contours of absolute priority, waving it off altogether for classes of claims that voted in favor of the reorganization plan. This relaxed approach to absolute priority, and the changes that went with it, are unlikely to disappear anytime soon. Bankruptcy lawyers have a powerful interest in the Chapter 11 approach, and large creditors such as banks also prefer Chapter 11 over the elaborate administrative apparatus of old Chapter X.

While the Code's modified absolute priority rule itself is comfortably established, one of its contours—the so-called new value exception—has roiled the bankruptcy waters ever since the 1978 Code was enacted. Under the new value exception, a debtor's old shareholders are permitted to retain an interest in the firm even though higher priority creditors are not paid in full (thus, absolute priority is not met) and at least one class of the creditors objects to the proposed reorganization (thus, absolute priority is not waved off), so long as the shareholders contribute "money or money's worth" to the reorganization effort.[36]

The significance of the new value exception has changed in remarkable ways in the years since its origins during the equity receivership era.[37] In the beginning, new value took the form of cash assessments paid by the old shareholders to help finance a large-scale reorganization. Because Chapter X of the Chandler Act required that managers be replaced by a trustee, and managers and their Wall Street professionals had been the ones who coordinated the new value strategy, the exception disappeared from Chapter X. Nor was the new value exception used in Chapter XI, given that Chapter XI already required that shareholders retain their equity interest. As a result, there was little need for the new value exception, and for forty years it disappeared into the ash heap of bankruptcy history.

Congress's repudiation of the Chandler Act with the 1978 Code created the conditions for the new value exception to reemerge, though in a very different context. Unlike the Chandler Act, Chapter 11 subjects small firms to the same reorganization rules as large firms. Since 1978, small firms have thus faced the same absolute priority requirements as large firms, rather than the special rules of Chapter XI. (Recall that Congress made clear in 1952 that the absolute priority rule did not apply in Chapter XI.) Chapter 11's absolute priority rule is waved off if the firm's creditors agree to a reorganization plan. But if a small firm's creditors dig in their heels, then its owners—mom and pop—have a problem. Strict application of the absolute priority rule suggests that the owners cannot retain their interest unless they pay all of their higher-priority creditors in full. After 1978, dozens of troubled mom-and-pops were stymied by recalcitrant creditors (usually their bank, whose enormous deficiency claim gave it control over the class of unsecured creditors) and would lose their stake in the business unless they could somehow get around the absolute priority rule. The solution devised by the lawyers of small-firm debtors was to dust off the new value exception. If mom and pop could contribute value to the reorganization, perhaps the court would confirm a reorganization plan even over the objections of creditors under the Chapter 11 cramdown provision. Thus, the new value exception was reborn. No longer a device for raising cash in large-scale reorganizations, it now was a strategy for helping mom and pop reorganize their small business.

Creditors objected to this strategy on two grounds. In cases where the old shareholders offered something other than cash, creditors argued that the proposed contribution failed to meet the "money or money's worth" requirement. More radically, they insisted that the new value exception was superseded by the 1978 Code. Nowhere in the Code is the new value exception mentioned, and the Code's elaborate reorganization scheme leaves no room for the new value approach. The Supreme Court has attempted on two occasions to resolve the confusion over the new value exception. In 1988, the Court held that the debtors' promise to contribute their labor and expertise to their family farm did not qualify as "money or money's worth."[38] Since the new value exception was not satisfied, the Court saw no need to address the larger question of whether the exception still exists. In its most recent case, *203 N. LaSalle Street*, the Court confronted the new value issue more directly, holding that old shareholders cannot retain an interest if they are the only ones who are given the right to contribute.[39] This solution offers a defensible middle ground between eliminating the exception, on the one hand, and unbridled acceptance, on the other, but it almost certainly will not resolve the new value issue. The whole point of the new value strategy is to assure that existing shareholders retain control, rather than outsiders. As a result, we can expect continued fights over whether new value arrangements have been structured to exclude outside interests.

For bankruptcy lawyers who handle mostly large cases, the controversy over the new value exception has limited significance, since it concerns mostly small debtors. But bankruptcy lawyers who do handle smaller cases care deeply about the exception, as do most progressive bankruptcy scholars. The principal opposing view comes from large creditors such as banks and insurance companies who have the most to lose if courts help small firms confirm hopeless reorganization plans. Despite the influence financial institutions have in Congress, advocates of the exception have several important advantages. First, the exception has significant ideological resonance. Because it gives small, failing businesses one more chance, the new value exception appeals to the populist dimension in U.S. bankruptcy politics. Second, new value is an area where large creditors' opposition can be neutralized by addressing banks' greatest concerns. Congress did precisely this in 1994 by making it easier for lenders to obtain relief from the automatic stay in "single asset real estate" cases—a category that includes a large percentage of the new value cases. (Moreover, the new provision is structured in a way that assures that most of the cases will remain in bankruptcy—the stay is lifted only if, among other things, the debtor fails to propose a reorganization plan within ninety days.) The likely future of the new value exception, then, is this: courts will probably require some accommodation of hypothetical outside investors but continue to confirm new value plans.[40]

International Insolvency Cases

In 1993, the Maxwell Communications empire collapsed. Liquidating so large and prominent a business organization in bankruptcy would have been an intricate project under any circumstances. For Maxwell, bankruptcy was further complicated by the international scope of the corporate group: Maxwell had its headquarters in Great Britain, but most of its assets were located in the United States. The question whether U.S. bankruptcy law should apply to the U.S. assets and British law to the assets in Great Britain, or whether one nation's laws should apply throughout, was a central theme in the liquidation. Due in large part to good relations between the United States and Britain, and the relative compatibility of the two nation's bankruptcy laws, the Maxwell bankruptcy proceeded smoothly. But many commentators fear that the coming years will bring a wave of international insolvencies that make Maxwell seem simple by comparison—and that this will be the new frontier in corporate bankruptcy law.

There is an obvious analogy between the plethora of national bankruptcy laws in the international insolvency context, on the one hand, and the state-specific insolvency frameworks in the United States in the nineteenth century. The divergences among different states' approaches, and the jurisdictional difficulties posed by debtors who had assets in different states, were a central theme in the calls for a single, uniform bankruptcy regime—the regime that was finally established with the 1898 act. Although commentators have not called for a single, transnational bankruptcy regime, most have argued that every multinational bankruptcy case should be governed by the laws of a single nation. (There is much less agreement, however, as to how to determine which nation's laws should apply—some commentators argue for the firm's domicile, others for its headquarters or the location of its principal assets.) This approach, usually referred to as *universalism*, would eliminate many of the problems created by *territorialism*, which assumes that the bankruptcy laws of each nation where assets are located will apply to any assets within its boundaries.[41]

The politics of international insolvency are ambiguous in the United States, and the ambiguity is magnified by the fact that international insolvencies are still quite uncommon. Consider the perspective of the corporate bankruptcy bar. On balance, corporate bankruptcy lawyers might favor the universalist approach, since it would simplify international cases where U.S. law applies, and universalism resonates with bankruptcy lawyers' sympathy for using a single, overarching bankruptcy law in U.S. cases. Yet the universalist approach also might mean losing control of cases involving firms that had significant assets in the United States. For large creditors, universalism could increase the predictability of transactions by making it easier to determine in advance what bankruptcy rules would apply in the event of insolvency. Yet large U.S. creditors might well prefer to know that U.S. law would ordinarily apply to transactions on U.S. soil, even if the debtor has headquarters or most of its assets elsewhere.

As a practical matter, the differences among the bankruptcy laws and cultures of different nations are too great for a true universalist approach to succeed. More likely are limited treaties among nations whose approach to bankruptcy is generally similar, and that is the approach that lawmakers have taken thus far. The most ambitious project to date, for instance, is an American Law Institute project that would encourage lawmakers to use limited treaties to coordinate international insolvencies involving the signatory nations. Whatever the result, it remains unclear how important an issue international insolvency will be, and it is safe to assume that U.S. bankruptcy law will continue to govern the U.S. assets of multinational firms that fail.

THE ROAD FROM HERE

Two decades after the most dramatic bankruptcy reform in forty years, the contours of corporate bankruptcy remain dynamic. Prepackaged bankruptcy and the prospect of bankruptcy contract have sharply reinforced the market component of the bankruptcy process, and Delaware now occupies the same status in large-scale reorganization that it enjoys in corporate law generally. In the minds of some theorists, at least, the traditional bankruptcy laws could become obsolete for many firms. As the continuing battles over the new value exception suggest, however, the core of U.S. corporate reorganization remains solid. For the vast majority of firms, Chapter 11 continues to assure that the managers of troubled firms can remain in control, and that reorganization will be a negotiated process limited only by a flexible version of absolute priority. Bankruptcy lawyers favor this approach because it gives them a central role. Even creditors, who might seem to suffer from Chapter 11's bias toward rehabilitation, prefer this approach over a more intrusive system such as Chapter X of the former Bankruptcy Act. With a more widespread elite corporate bar replacing the insular Wall Street bar of the equity receivership era, it is difficult to imagine a set of circumstances that would lead to serious alteration of the current reorganization framework.

In the nineteenth century, corporate reorganization emerged as a response to the perceived public interest in protecting insolvent railroads. In the course of the twentieth century, the reorganization framework extended far beyond the context of firms such as the railroads that the public has an obvious interest in protecting. In recent years, the corporate reorganization provisions have been used to address a new kind of public interest—the public interest in devising a collective solution to the recent mass tort disasters. The expansion of U.S. corporate reorganization is likely to continue as new crises arise, and there is no obvious end in sight.

Epilogue

GLOBALIZATION AND U.S. BANKRUPTCY LAW

COMMENTATORS HAVE OFTEN marveled (or grimaced, as the case may be) at the unique attributes of American bankruptcy law. In many other nations, consumer debtors have no right to discharge their debts—or at best, the discharge is subject to strict limitations such as a requirement that the debtor continue paying her debts for an extended period of time. The newly *liberalized* Norwegian bankruptcy law, for instance, instructs the court to determine whether discharge would be morally offensive and ordinarily requires that debtors continue to pay for at least five, and sometimes as long as ten, years.[1] The differences are no less striking with corporate bankruptcy. Nearly every other nation in the world takes—in the words of one commentator—a "salvage" approach to corporate bankruptcy. If a corporation fails, its managers are immediately displaced, an outside official takes over, and the firm's assets are sold to whoever will have them, often at scrap prices. U.S. bankruptcy law, by contrast, is designed to "rescue" firms that fail. As if to suggest that bankruptcy is business as usual, Chapter 11 permits the firm's managers to continue to run the firm while the parties negotiate the terms of a reorganization plan. The clear goal of the process is to preserve the firm as a going concern rather than to liquidate it.

The differences between U.S. bankruptcy law and the insolvency regulation of other nations are fundamental and are a matter of continual discussion among economic commentators. Yet they are routinely taken as a given; almost no one has attempted to explain *why* the U.S. approach looks so different. The classic history of U.S. bankruptcy law, Charles Warren's *Bankruptcy in United States History*, predates a vast, recent literature on the nature of lawmaking and offers only a loose, breezy interpretation of the birth of U.S. bankruptcy regulation. Subsequent efforts have been partial and often superficial. There is both room, and a real need, for an account that is both complete and up-to-date. This book has tried to address that need.

In the eight chapters of the book, we have viewed the evolution of American bankruptcy regulation through the perspectives of contemporary political science, history, and economics. Let me briefly recap what we have seen—American bankruptcy past and present—before I conclude by speculating on American bankruptcy future.

The heart of our journey began in the nineteenth century, with the passionate struggle between Federalists and Jeffersonian Democrats over personal and small-business bankruptcy. From the beginning, the debate divided along political and sectional lines, with conservatives—especially those in the Northeast—insisting on bankruptcy as essential to a commercial economy, and more liberal lawmakers—particularly in the South and West—worrying that bankruptcy would undermine agrarian life. Rather than simply falling into one or the other of these two camps, lawmakers held a variety of views, which contributed to the remarkable instability of bankruptcy law throughout the nineteenth century. In 1800, 1841, and again in 1867, Congress enacted federal legislation in response to financial panics, but then quickly repealed the legislation in each instance. By the end of the century, the proliferation of creditors groups such as local boards of trade and chambers of commerce led to an organized campaign for permanent bankruptcy legislation. It was these creditors who inspired and promoted the 1898 act, and who fought for nearly two decades to keep bankruptcy on the legislative agenda.

The task of these creditors and their champion—the indefatigable, future Rough Rider Jay Torrey—was complicated by the continued opposition of populist lawmakers whose influence was magnified by attributes of the nation's federalist political structure, such as the fact that even the least populated, agrarian state was entitled to the same number of senators as urban New York or Massachusetts. To assure enough votes for passage, creditors and their Republican allies adopted a minimalist administrative structure and agreed to the generous, prodebtor discharge policies—a veritable "jubilee," in the words of an early critic—that make U.S. bankruptcy law so different from that of other nations. Although even creditors had second thoughts about the legislation after its enactment, continued Republican control kept the 1898 act in place long enough for a bankruptcy bar to develop. And the rest is history. The three forces that determined the early shape of U.S. bankruptcy law—organized creditors, agrarian and populist lawmakers, and bankruptcy professionals—have continued to play this role ever since.

The origins of large-scale corporate reorganization were both very different and very much the same. Once again, America's federalist structure played a starring role. When the railroads, the nation's first large corporations, failed, the division of power between Congress and the states seriously limited the options for a legislative solution. As a result, the parties took to the courts instead, and American-style corporate reorganization was born. In time, the same three influences we saw in personal and small-business bankruptcy would prove equally central to large-scale reorganization. Both creditors and bankruptcy professionals were there in the beginning. The third factor, populism, was important more for its absence from the early judicial reorganizations than for any affirmative influence (indeed, avoiding the populist outcry that legislative efforts to bail out the railroads might have prompted was one of the benefits of the judicial context for railroad managers), but populism and related ideologies would figure much more prominently by the time large-scale corporate reorganization was added to the Bankruptcy Act in the twentieth century.

I have referred to the nineteenth century throughout the book as the first "era" of U.S. bankruptcy law. The twentieth century brought the second and third eras, and each of these eras was characterized by a dramatic economic shift. The second major era came in the 1930s with the Great Depression. Although this era brought only limited changes in personal and small-business bankruptcy—a tribute to the tenacity of the general bankruptcy bar—it produced a remarkable transformation of large-scale corporate reorganization. Masterminded by William Douglas, Chapter X reflected a dramatic, populist revolt against the traditional methods of large-scale corporate reorganization. For the Wall Street reorganization bar, the Chandler Act of 1938 brought forty years in the wilderness. The most startling developments of the third and most recent era have been the repudiation of Chapter X by the 1978 Code and, in consumer bankruptcy, the remarkable growth of the consumer credit industry. In corporate bankruptcy, we have seen a return to many of the reorganization techniques that were used in the early years of the twentieth century. In consumer bankruptcy, we have seen an escalating, ideological battle between consumer creditors, who wish to tighten the bankruptcy discharge, and a group of bankruptcy professionals and consumer advocates who have sought to align themselves with the spirit of prodebtor populism.

In the work for which he was awarded the Nobel Prize, Douglass North argues that institutional change takes place when there are significant benefits to one or more parties to promoting such change. "To the degree that there are large payoffs to influencing the rules and their enforcement," he contends, "it will pay to create intermediary organizations (trade associations, lobbying groups, political action committees) between economic organizations and political bodies to realize the potential gains of political change." In this context, "political or economic entrepreneurs may devote their talents or tacit knowledge to ferreting out profitable margins, estimating the likelihood of success, and risking the organization's resources to capture the potential gains."[2]

Each of the three eras of American bankruptcy law can be seen as evidence of this pattern. In each era, one or more groups sought to renegotiate the regulatory rules to take advantage of potential gains: creditors wanted a permanent bankruptcy law, William Douglas and the New Deal reformers sought to neutralize Wall Street, consumer creditors now wish to tighten the bankruptcy discharge to curb the enormous number of consumer bankruptcy filings. Despite all of the changes we have seen, however, American bankruptcy regulation retains many of the same contours it had at the end of the nineteenth century. The same three forces that explained the 1898 act are still a handy and reliable guide to the wilds of U.S. bankruptcy law.

What about the future? The most obvious pressure on commercial interaction in recent years has come from the vast, ill-defined trend we call "globalization." It may not be clear just what "globalization" means, but its effects are everywhere. As I write these words, I need only pull out today's newspaper for striking illustrations. In Germany, as reported in the *Wall Street Journal*, Chancellor Gerhard Schroeder just "rammed through Parliament" a tax reform that slices the capital gains tax that firms must pay if they sell the stock of other corporations. The reform will give firms that hold large blocks of shares much more flexibility to buy and sell shares, thus injecting additional market forces into German corporate governance. Because firms will no longer be forced to hold stock indefinitely, "the change is expected to unleash a wave of divestitures, spinoffs and acquisitions," and to "boost[] momentum for further restructuring of Germany and the rest of continental Europe."[3] Flipping to the editorial page, the focus shifts to Japan. The lead editorial, "The Big Bankruptcy," marvels that Japan's ruling party has decided to let a major department store chain, Sogo, fail, rather than following through on a contemplated bailout.[4] "The dramatic decision to let Sogo go bankrupt," and the popular pressure that prompted it, the writers conclude, mean that the "deconstruction of Japan's curious form of free market socialism just passed the point of no return."

Each of these developments can be traced, at least in part, to the pressure of international market forces—globalization—and each has profound implications for the nation's insolvency framework. Does this mean that globalization will also force lawmakers to alter U.S. bankruptcy law? The rather remarkable answer is no. Although the new, worldwide economy will have important effects, the basic parameters of American bankruptcy law are unlikely to change. We will continue to see the same three forces—creditors, prodebtor ideology, and bankruptcy professionals—and the shape of the bankruptcy process will remain roughly the same.

The best way to show why I can be so confident in this prediction is simply to take another look at the international changes I have just described. In each case, the effect of the change is to make the nation's corporate law and/ or insolvency framework *more* like the American approach. The German tax reform focuses most directly on Germany's relational approach to corporate governance, which, as we saw in chapter 8, stands in sharp contrast to the market-oriented U.S. approach. Relational governance, with its "cobweb of cross-holdings," the article on Germany's new tax law concludes, "is now regarded as a hindrance to competitiveness and to the growing focus on shareholder value." If shareholder value and market-oriented governance become the norm, as seems to be the trend, the shift will also create pressure for a reorganization-based insolvency framework like Chapter 11 of the U.S. system to deal with the inevitable failures.

In fact, Germany has already taken the first tentative steps in this direction. In 1994, Germany enacted a new corporate bankruptcy framework (which went into effect in 1999) that drew quite explicitly from Chapter 11. The new approach stops far short of wholesale adoption of Chapter 11. Managers are quickly replaced when a firm files for bankruptcy, for instance, and each case starts out as a liquidation rather than a reorganization.[5] Nevertheless, the reforms are a clear shift away from the traditional liquidation procedure, and the seismic changes in Germany's corporate culture could well lead to further change on the insolvency front.

The relational framework in Japan has been roiled to a similar extent in recent years, as alternative forms of finance have begun to challenge the role of the relational banks, and the first serious hostile takeover attempts have begun. The decision to let Sogo fail is additional evidence of these trends. If the government permits more troubled firms to fail, this shift almost certainly will create pressure to use the bankruptcy laws to reorganize firms that default, rather than invariably liquidating them as under current law.

Although we have been talking exclusively about corporations, the same trends have similar implications for consumer bankruptcy. A key issue in the decision to let Sogo fail was the inevitable job loss that would result. Japanese firms have traditionally offered lifetime employment to all of their employees, thus assuring employees that they need not fear the disruption of job loss. The Asian economic crisis of the 1990s made this cultural tradition increasingly difficult to sustain, since the cost of keeping unproductive employees hurts Japanese businesses when they compete with firms that do not have this commitment. The decision to let Sogo fail was one more indication that lifetime employment, like firms that never fail, may soon be a thing of the past.

Like Japan, the European democracies have a tradition of extensive social protection, and here, too, the internationalization of markets has begun to force sweeping change. An obvious illustration is the European Union, which is designed to help European nations compete globally. The strict economic requirements imposed by the European Union have made it difficult for member states to maintain social benefits such as health care and unemployment protection at current levels, and many will be forced to scale back their governmental expenditures in these areas.[6]

As we look into the future, the obvious question is this: what will happen to the Japanese worker who loses her job, or the French consumer who is overwhelmed by medical costs that are not fully covered by his health insurance? In the United States, bankruptcy has long served as a partial substitute for the more generous social protections provided by other nations. Unlike many nations, the U.S. does not provide national health insurance, and our unemployment compensation system is quite limited. The only recourse for many families who lose their source of income or face unexpected medical costs may be bankruptcy. This, in fact, is a major theme of the recent study of U.S. consumer bankruptcy by Teresa Sullivan, Elizabeth Warren, and Jay Westbrook. In *The Fragile Middle Class*, Sullivan et al. found that job stress figured in two-thirds of all bankruptcy filings; and almost twenty percent of the debtors in their study listed medical complications as a reason for their bankruptcy filing.[7]

Because the existing consumer bankruptcy laws of most nations offer little relief to troubled debtors, one does not have to be a visionary to see that any decline in social protections will create new pressure to liberalize bankruptcy regulation. Bankruptcy does not necessarily solve these problems, but for many it can offer "a chance—often a last chance—to retain their middle class status."[8] As social protections decline, bankruptcy regulation suddenly increases in importance. Once again, there already are obvious hints of this. The Norwegian bankruptcy law I mentioned in the opening paragraph is just one illustration of a much larger trend. Prior to the 1990s, few other nations offered a meaningful discharge for individual debtors. Since then, one European nation after another has either put a new bankruptcy law on the books or liberalized an existing one.[9]

It is important not to get carried overboard, and to conclude from these changes that we will soon see a global convergence on insolvency issues. As Douglass North has emphasized in the work on institutional change noted above, even when formal rules change, widely held cultural norms may limit the effect of an apparent transformation. In Europe and Japan, these norms could discourage firms from using insolvency law as a business tool and may continue to stigmatize consumer bankruptcy filings. Moreover, even the formal changes we have seen have thus far been only partial. The liberalized insolvency laws adopted thus far fall well short of the U.S. approach, with its generous discharge and manager-friendly corporate reorganization provisions.

The important point, however, is that all of the pressure unleashed by globalization is pushing in this direction. All around the world, other nations are beginning to adopt some of the features of U.S. bankruptcy law. There is little evidence of a trend in any other direction, in the United States or elsewhere. Perhaps this will change with some unexpected jolt to worldwide commerce. Yet at least in the United States, even a jolt seems unlikely to alter the political infrastructure of the American approach to financial distress. The basic contours of our consumer and small-business bankruptcy laws date back to the days of the horse and buggy, and we owe our rules for large-scale corporate reorganization to the railroads, but the overall approach should be good for another century.

NOTES

INTRODUCTION

1. The emergence of England's bankruptcy laws in the nineteenth century is chronicled at length in V. Markam Lester, *Victorian Insolvency: Bankruptcy, Imprisonment for Debt, and Company Winding-Up in Nineteenth Century England* (Oxford: Oxford University Press, 1995).

2. Drew R. McCoy, *The Elusive Republic: Political Economy in Jeffersonian America*, 179 (Chapel Hill: University of North Carolina Press, 1980).

3. McCoy, *The Elusive Republic*, 181–82 (quoting Ford, ed., *Writings of Jefferson*, 6:145).

4. 31 *Congressional Record* 2358 (1898) (statement of Senator Stewart of Nevada).

5. England first introduced the discharge in 1705. For a discussion and additional historical overview, see Charles J. Tabb, "The Historical Evolution of the Bankruptcy Discharge," 65 *American Bankruptcy Law Journal* 325 (1991).

6. The complete explanation is slightly more elaborate. Willful and malicious torts cannot be discharged in Chapter 7 cases, but they are dischargeable if the debtor files under Chapter 13 instead. (The distinctions between Chapter 7 and Chapter 13 are described in the text that follows this note). If Simpson could file for Chapter 13, he could therefore discharge the judgment. Only debtors who have less than $871,550 in secured obligations and less than $290,525 in unsecured debts can file for Chapter 13, however, and the judgment by itself far exceeds these requirements.

7. Under current law, the exemptions are set forth in Bankruptcy Code, sec. 522.

8. In contrast to the dearth of literature from a more theoretical perspective, there is a large literature explaining bankruptcy doctrine for the benefit of practitioners. Since early in the twentieth century, the leading treatise has been *Collier on Bankruptcy*. The most recent edition is *Collier on Bankruptcy* (Lawrence P. King ed. 15th ed. 1996).

9. Charles Warren, *Bankruptcy in United States History* (Cambridge: Harvard University Press, 1935).

10. James A. McLaughlin, "Book Review," 49 *Harvard Law Review* 861, 862 (1936) (reviewing Charles Warren, *Bankruptcy in United States History* (1935)).

11. In addition to *Bankruptcy in United States History*, two other, very different, books from the first half of the twentieth century also warrant brief mention. An earlier book by F. Regis Noel provides a slightly more theoretical review of nineteenth-century bankruptcy legislation. Noel's principal concern is to demonstrate the need for federal bankruptcy legislation and the problems with leaving insolvency law to the states. F. Regis Noel, *A History of the Bankruptcy Clause of the Constitution of the United States of America* (Gettysburg, Pa., 1918). A second book, by ardent New Dealer Max Lowenthal, is a case study of the St. Paul railroad reorganization and thus has a much more limited focus. Max Lowenthal, *The Investor Pays* (New York: Knopf, 1933). *The Investor Pays* is an exposé of the role of Wall Street banks and lawyers in railroad reorganization, very much in the spirit of Louis Brandeis's populist attacks on big business.

Louis D. Brandeis, *Other People's Money* (1914). Several books on current U.S. bankruptcy law have taken a somewhat similar approach, as described in the notes below.

12. Peter J. Coleman, *Debtors and Creditors in America: Insolvency, Imprisonment for Debt, and Bankruptcy, 1607–1900* (Madison: State Historical Society of Wisconsin, 1974). The other book from this era that warrants mention is Edward I. Altman, *Corporate Financial Distress and Bankruptcy*.

13. Thomas H. Jackson, *The Logic and Limits of Bankruptcy* (Cambridge: Harvard University Press, 1986).

14. Theresa Sullivan, Elizabeth Warren, and Jay L. Westbrook, *As We Forgive Our Debtors: Bankruptcy and Consumer Credit in America* (Oxford: Oxford University Press, 1989).

15. David T. Stanley and Marjorie Girth, *Bankruptcy: Problem, Process, Reform* (Washington, D.C.: Brookings Institution, 1971). The Brookings study had an enormous influence on the debates that led to the 1978 Bankruptcy Code.

16. Teresa A. Sullivan, Elizabeth Warren, and Jay L. Westbrook, *The Fragile Middle Class: Americans in Debt* (New Haven: Yale University Press, 2000).

17. A more recent book by Karen Gross is similarly policy oriented in focus, arguing for a communitarian approach to bankruptcy. Karen Gross, *Failure and Forgiveness* (New Haven: Yale University Press, 1997).

18. Eric A. Posner, "The Political Economy of the Bankruptcy Reform Act of 1978," 96 *Michigan Law Review* 47 (1997). Another scholar has recently written a political account focusing on the 1984 amendments to the Bankruptcy Code. Susan Block-Lieb, "Congress's Temptation to Defect: A Political and Economic Theory of Legislative Resolutions to Financial Common Pool Problems," 39 *Arizona Law Review* 801 (1997).

19. Bruce G. Carruthers and Terence C. Halliday, *Rescuing Business: The Making of Corporate Bankruptcy Law in England and the United States* (Oxford: Clarendon Press, 1998).

20. Gordon Tullock, "Public Choice," in John Eatwell, Murray Millgate, and Peter Newman, eds., 3 *The New Palgrave: A Dictionary of Economics*, 1040, 1040 (New York: Stockton Press, 1987). For a much more extensive overview of the public choice literature with relevant citations, see David A. Skeel Jr., "Public Choice and the Future of Public Choice–Influenced Legal Scholarship, 50 *Vanderbilt Law Review* 647 (1998).

21. Mark J. Roe, *Strong Managers, Weak Owners* (Princeton: Princeton University Press, 1996).

CHAPTER 1
THE PATH TO PERMANENCE IN 1898

1. Warren, *Bankruptcy in United States History*, 4–5.

2. *The Federalist* No. 42, 271 (James Madison) (Clinton Rossiter ed., 1961).

3. In an important new article, Erik Berglof and Howard Rosenthal explore the ideological basis of nineteenth-century bankruptcy legislation and point out that each of the nineteenth-century bankruptcy laws followed a financial panic and came at a time when the conservatives controlled both Congress and the presidency. Erik Berglof

and Howard Rosenthal, "The Political Economy of American Bankruptcy: The Evidence from Roll Call Voting, 1800–1978" (unpublished manuscript, 1999).

4. In the academic literature, Warren is best known for emphasizing the bust-and-boom pattern. Warren, *Bankruptcy in United States History*. This observation was long a commonplace in the legislative debates on bankruptcy. Opponents of bankruptcy pointed to the pattern as evidence that the nation did not need a permanent bankruptcy law, and bankruptcy advocates contended that lawmakers simply needed to fix the problems of the earlier laws.

5. Act of April 4, 1800, chap. 19, 2 Stat. 19 (repealed 1803); Act of December 19, 1803, chap. 6, 2 Stat. 248 (repealing 1800 act). The other three nineteenth-century bankruptcy acts were the 1841 act, Act of August 19, 1841, chap. 9, 5 Stat. 440 (repealed 1843); the 1867 act, Act of March 2, 1867, chap. 176, 14 Stat. 517 (repealed 1878); and the 1898 act, Bankruptcy Act of 1898, chap. 541, 30 Stat. 544 (repealed 1978).

6. The best study of early state insolvency law is Coleman, *Debtors and Creditors*.

7. Coleman, *Debtors and Creditors*, 31–36; *Ogden v. Saunders*, 12 Wheaton 213 (1827) (inability to bind out-of-state creditors).

8. Quoted in Warren, *Bankruptcy in United States History*, 56.

9. Ann Fabian, "Speculation on Distress: The Popular Discourse of the Panics of 1837 and 1857," 3 *Yale Journal of Criticism* 127 (1989). Reverend Parker is quoted at 131; metaphors of weather are described at 133.

10. Quoted in Warren, *Bankruptcy in United States History*, 58.

11. Quoted in Warren, *Bankruptcy in United States History*, 68.

12. McLaughlin, "Book Review," 862.

13. The tension between northeastern lawmakers and their colleagues in the South and West is the central theme of Warren's bankruptcy history, and it is a division that lawmakers repeatedly noted themselves in the nineteenth-century debates. At the end of the century, bankruptcy advocates tried to recharacterize the debate by insisting that everyone except large, northeastern commercial houses favored bankruptcy legislation. During the debates on the Bankruptcy Act of 1898, for instance, Representative Grosvenor of Ohio excoriated Marshall Field & Co., the "merchant prince," for opposing the bankruptcy legislation and warned that honest debtors needed the protection of a bankruptcy law. 31 *Congressional Record* 1902 (1998)(Congressman Grosvenor).

14. See, for example, *Sturges v. Crowninshield*, 4 Wheaton 122 (1819) (rejecting the distinction between "bankruptcy" and "insolvency" laws). Supreme Court pronouncements in cases such as *Sturges* did not end the constitutional debate altogether. Even after the opinion, some lawmakers continued to argue that the Bankruptcy Clause prohibited Congress from enacting a general bankruptcy law. See, for example, *Congressional Globe*, 26th Cong., 1st sess., app. 461 (1840) (remarks of Senator Wall) (contending that the 1841 act was unconstitutional because it was an insolvency law rather than just a bankruptcy bill).

15. *Sturges v. Crowninshield*, 17 U.S. (4 Wheat.) 122, 195 (1819).

16. For a recent description of the federal courts' role in promoting the expansion of commerce generally, see Charles Sellers, *The Market Revolution: Jacksonian America, 1815–1846*, 55–59 (New York: Oxford University Press, 1991).

17. See, for example, Berglof and Rosenthal, "Political Economy of Bankruptcy," 15.

18. During the debates on the 1841 act, Clay moved to strike the involuntary provision from the bankruptcy bill. The failure of Clay's motion was one of several defining moments in the debates. For a discussion of the motion and Clay's insistence that only voluntary bankruptcy be included, see Warren, *Bankruptcy in United States History*, 62–63.

19. In *Social Choice and Individual Values* (New York: John Wiley & Sons, 1951), Arrow demonstrated with his "Impossibility Theorem" that it is impossible to guarantee that a collective decision-making process will both satisfy a short list of fairness requirements and maintain rationality, which Arrow defined as the ability to aggregate the preference rankings of three or more voters in a transitive fashion. "Transitivity," for the purposes of Arrow's rationality requirement, means that if X defeats Y, and Y defeats Z, X must also defeat Z.

The most important of the "fairness" requirements are "range" and "independence of irrelevant alternatives." The range postulate requires that no possible individual preference ranking be off-limits. Independence requires that each decision maker adhere to her actual ranking of the alternatives, rather than, for example, altering her choice for strategic reasons, such as the desire to affect a subsequent vote. Thus, logrolling of the sort described below with the 1841 act violates the independence requirement. Social choice theory is discussed in more detail in David A. Skeel Jr., "The Unanimity Rule in Delaware Corporate Law," 83 *Virginia Law Review* 127 (1997).

The text that follows, which applies these insights to nineteenth century bankruptcy legislation, elaborates on David A. Skeel, Jr., "Bankruptcy Lawyers and the Shape of American Bankruptcy Law," 67 *Fordham Law Review* 497, 500–503 (1998)

20. To give the most obvious possibility, if all of the lawmakers agreed that Complete Bankruptcy was the most "conservative" position, Voluntary Only was the "moderate" view, and No Bankruptcy was the "liberal" choice, their preferences would be fully consistent—even if they vigorously disputed which choice was best. In social choice terms, these preferences are *unipeaked*, and cycling arises only if lawmakers' preferences are *multipeaked*. With unipeaked preferences, the views of the median voter generally prevail. (I discuss these terms in more detail in Skeel, "The Unanimity Rule.")

Although many issues do align along this conservative-to-liberal spectrum, the bankruptcy debates clearly were more complicated. As the illustration in the text suggests, many lawmakers did not view Voluntary Only as an intermediate choice. Some conservative lawmakers saw Voluntary Only as worse than No Bankruptcy, whereas others viewed it as better, and liberal lawmakers were equally divided.

21. In terms of the requirements of Arrow's theorem, as described in note 19, the expansive interpretation of the Constitution eliminated possible restrictions on lawmakers' range.

22. The theorists most prominently associated with these insights have been Kenneth Shepsle and Barry Weingast. See, for example, Kenneth A. Shepsle, "Institutional Arrangements and Equilibrium in Multidimensional Voting Models," 23 *American Journal of Political Science* 27 (1979); Kenneth A. Shepsle and Barry R. Weingast, "Uncovered Sets and Sophisticated Voting Outcomes with Implications for Agenda Institutions," 28 *American Journal of Political Science* 49 (1984). A useful overview is Gary J. Miller, "The Impact of Economics on Contemporary Political Science," 35 *Journal of Economic Literature* 1173, 1183–89 (1997).

23. For a careful analysis of the repeal of the 1841 act, see Berglof and Rosenthal, "Political Economy of Bankruptcy," 36–39.

24. Warren, *Bankruptcy in United States History*, 104. Warren discusses the debates on the 1867 bankruptcy act and its subsequent amendments at 95–127.

25. Warren, *Bankruptcy in United States History*, 104 (quoting Paine).

26. 28 *Congressional Record* 4534 (1896).

27. This bill, the "Nelson bill," did provide for involuntary bankruptcy but sharply limited its scope—generally to debtors who acted fraudulently.

28. *House Report No. 67*, 53d Cong., 1st sess., 1 (1893).

29. *House Report No. 206*, 53d Cong., 2d sess., 1–2 (1894).

30. Representative Bailey of Texas, who proposed a Voluntary Only bill that passed the House in 1894, claimed that the Judiciary Committee had voted in favor of a Complete bill only because several committee members were absent at the time of the vote. 25 *Congressional Record* 2813 (1893).

31. Lawrence Friedman, *A History of American Law*, 308 (New York: Simon and Schuster, 2d ed. 1985).

32. Edward J. Balleisen, "Vulture Capitalism in Antebellum America: The 1841 Federal Bankruptcy Act and the Exploitation of Financial Distress," 70 *Business History Review* 473, 487 (1996). On the nature of antebellum legal practice, Balleisen cites Friedman, *History of American Law*, 306–11.

33. Balleisen, "Vulture Capitalism," 487.

34. Bradley Hansen, "Commercial Associations and the Creation of a National Economy: The Demand for Federal Bankruptcy Law," 72 *Business History Review* 86 (1998).

35. 13 *Congressional Record* 5134 (1886) (statement of Senator Brown).

36. For a helpful overview of the legislative history of the 1898 act, with particular emphasis on the efforts to resolve the differences between the House (Henderson) and Senate bills, see Charles J. Tabb, "A Century of Regress or Progress? A Political History of Bankruptcy Legislation in 1898 and 1998," 15 *Bankruptcy Developments Journal* 343 (1999).

37. Many of these memorials can be found in a large collection of materials submitted by business groups shortly before Congress finally enacted the 1898 act. Memorials, Press Clippings, and Documents on Torrey Bankruptcy Bill, S. Doc. 237, 54th Cong., 1st sess. (1896).

38. 25 *Congressional Record* 2815 (1894) (Congressman Oates), 2814 (Congressman Bryan).

39. Money center banks may also have played a role, although, as I note in n.46 below, they were rarely visible in the legislative process. The influence of creditors groups can be seen as supporting Mancur Olson's theory in *The Rise and Decline of Nations* that interest group activity is directly related to the duration of a nation's political stability. Whether U.S. bankruptcy law is beset by increasing inefficiencies, as Olson's argument would predict, is less clear.

40. The analysis that follows borrows from David A. Skeel Jr., "The Genius of the 1898 Bankruptcy Act," 15 *Bankruptcy Developments Journal* 321, 327–28 (1999). For a good discussion of the politics of nineteenth-century English bankruptcy legislation, see Lester, *Victorian Insolvency*. For an overview of the features of English bankruptcy law that I describe below, as manifested in more recent cases, see Douglas G. Boshkoff,

"Limited, Conditional, and Suspended Discharges in Anglo-American Bankruptcy Proceedings," 131 *University of Pennsylvania Law Review* 69 (1982).

41. The best history of American populism is still Richard Hofstadter, *The Age of Reform: From Bryan to F.D.R.* (New York: Random House, 1955).

42. Gerald Berk, *Alternative Tracks: The Constitution of American Industrial Order, 1865–1917*, 78, 79 (Baltimore: Johns Hopkins University Press, 1994).

43. For discussion, see Todd J. Zywicki, "Senators and Special Interests: A Public Choice Analysis of the Seventeenth Amendment," 73 *Oregon Law Review* 1007 (1994).

44. On the overrepresentation of rural interests, see Hofstadter, *The Age of Reform*, 116–17.

45. 31 *Congressional Record* 2358 (1898) (statement of Senator Stewart). The comments of Congressman Sibley quoted at the end of the paragraph in the text are from 25 *Congressional Record* 2805 (1893).

46. One group that did not play as visible a role as one might expect was banks. It is possible that regional banks did exert an influence. Berglof and Rosenthal find a correlation between banking centers and voting on the 1898 act. Berglof and Rosenthal, "Political Economy of Bankruptcy," 44–49. Although local banks have often proven influential in American politics, they were surprisingly quiet on bankruptcy, perhaps because they were able to protect their interests under state law. See, for example, Skeel, "Genius of 1898 Act," 333.

47. The best historical evidence concerning these administrative costs can be found in an 1874 report filed by the attorney general. Letter from Attorney General in Compliance with Senate Resolution of February 23, 1873, Senate Executive Doc. No. 19, 43d Cong., 1st sess. (1874).

48. 21 *Congressional Record* 7617 (1890) (statement of Congressman Abbott).

49. Although historians have traditionally focused on the role of midwestern lawmakers, the most solid support seems to have come from the South. Keith T. Poole and Howard Rosenthal, "The Enduring Nineteenth-Century Battle for Economic Regulation: The Interstate Commerce Act Revisited," 36 *Journal of Law and Economics* 837 (1993).

50. See 13 *Congressional Record* 43 (1882) (Lowell bill, as amended to include specific salaries in section 20).

51. 13 *Congressional Record* 145 (1882) (criticizing Senator Ingalls's voluntary bill for its fee-based approach).

52. 13 *Congressional Record* 42 (1882) (statement of Senator Ingalls). Senator Ingalls had introduced a very different bankruptcy bill, the "Equity bill," several years earlier. Ingalls's bill proposed to authorize the federal courts to handle bankruptcy under their equity power and included few specific details as to how bankruptcy should work.

53. Almost the only serious discussion of the issue in the legislative record came in a memorial that included the minutes of a meeting of the National Organization of Members of Commercial Bodies. Asked by a creditor representative why the Torrey bill let state lawmakers control exemptions, Jay Torrey conceded his displeasure with this provision, but assured the questioner that state control was a political necessity. *Proceedings of National Association of Credit Men*, S. Doc. No. 156, 55th Cong., 1st sess. 15 (1898).

54. For discussion, see Tabb, "Century of Regress," 374–76.

55. James Olmstead spoke for these critics when he scoffed at the new legislation as little more than a "Hebrew Jubilee," a debtor relief measure unprecedented in Western civilization. James Olmstead, "Bankruptcy: A Commercial Regulation," 15 *Harvard Law Review* 829 (1902).

56. *Hanover National Bank v. Moyses*, 186 U.S. 181 (1902).

57. 6 *Bulletin* 2 (1902) (unsigned editorial commentary).

58. Edwin Brandenburg was similarly important and published another influential early treatise. Edwin C. Brandenburg, *Brandenburg on Bankruptcy* (1905).

59. William Niskanen is most closely identified with this view. Niskanen argued that agencies use their informational advantage to maximize the agency's budget. William A. Niskanen, *Bureaucracy and Representative Government* (Chicago: Aldine, Anderson, 1971). Niskanen's work prompted a vigorous debate. For an argument that Congress can control agency discretion in a variety of ways, see Barry R. Weingast and Mark J. Moran, "Bureaucratic Discretion or Congressional Control? Regulatory Policymaking by the Federal Trade Commission," 91 *Journal of Political Economy* 765 (1983).

CHAPTER 2
RAILROAD RECEIVERSHIP AND THE ELITE REORGANIZATION BAR

1. The classic account is Alfred D. Chandler Jr., *The Visible Hand: The Managerial Revolution in American Business* (Cambridge: Harvard University Press, 1978).

2. Friedman, *History of American Law*, 180–81.

3. I have discussed the early development of corporate law in more detail in other work. David A. Skeel Jr., "Rethinking the Line between Corporate Law and Corporate Bankruptcy," 72 *Texas Law Review* 471, 482–87 (1994).

4. Alfred D. Chandler Jr., *The Railroads: The Nation's First Big Business*, 3 (New York: Harcourt, Brace and World 1965).

5. Many of the details that follow can be found in Chandler, *The Railroads*.

6. John Steele Gordon, *The Scarlet Woman of Wall Street: Jay Gould, Jim Fisk, Cornelius Vanderbilt, the Erie Railway Wars, and the Birth of Wall Street*, 100–101 (New York: Weidenfeld and Nicolson, 1988). The quotations appear on p. 100.

7. William Cronon, *Nature's Metropolis: Chicago and the Great West*, 325, 326 (New York: W. W. Norton, 1992).

8. Cronon, *Nature's Metropolis*, 84–85. The quotation appears on p. 84.

9. The details of the description that follows come from Charles Adams's famous contemporary account of the Erie battle. Charles Francis Adams Jr., "A Chapter of Erie," *North American Review*, July 1869, reprinted in Charles Francis Adams Jr. and Henry Adams, *Chapters of Erie and Other Essays* (New York, 1871), and excerpted in Chandler, *The Railroads*, 71–88.

10. Chandler, *The Railroads*, 85.

11. Berk, *Alternative Tracks*, 77.

12. Albro Martin, "Railroads and the Equity Receivership: An Essay on Institutional Change," 34 *Journal of Economic History* 685, 688 (citing Henry Swain, *Economic Aspects of Railroad Receiverships*, vol. 3, no. 2 of *Proceedings of the American Economic Association*, 68 (New York, 1898)).

13. See generally Martin, "Railroads and Equity Receivership," 707 (describing Parliament control of railway charters).

14. Skeel, "Rethinking the Line," 481 (quoting 1840 speech by Senator Clay).

15. 30 *Congressional Record* 788 (1897).

16. U.S. Const. art. I, sec. 8. The Commerce Clause and the Bankruptcy Clause are closely connected, as their joint origins in Article I, section 8 of the Constitution suggest.

17. Robert T. Swaine, *The Cravath Firm and Its Successors*, 2 vols. (New York: Ad Press, 1946, 1948), 1:485 (Ohio & Mississippi), 1:511 (Norfolk & Western).

18. See, for example, Oscar Lasdon, "The Evolution of Railroad Reorganization," 88 *Banking Law Journal* 3, 6 (1971).

19. As quoted in Gerrard Glenn, "The Basis of Federal Receivership," 25 *Columbia Law Review* 434, 442 (1925). See also Bradley Hansen, "The Wabash Receivership and the Public Interest Origins of Corporate Reorganization," 74 *Business History Review* 377 (2000) (quoting *Munroe*).

20. Jerome N. Frank, "Some Realistic Reflections on Some Aspects of Corporate Reorganization," 19 *Virginia Law Review* 541, 543 (1933) (part 1 of two-part article).

21. For a widely cited overview by a leading twentieth-century reorganizer, see Paul D. Cravath, "Reorganization of Corporations: Certain Developments of the Last Decade," in 1 *Some Legal Phases of Corporate Financing, Reorganization, and Regulation*, 153 (New York: McMillan, 1917). A helpful historical treatment is Stuart Daggett, *Railroad Reorganization* (Cambridge: Harvard University Press, 1908).

22. Unlike the current automatic stay, 11 U.S.C., sec. 362, the receivership bill did not freeze all obligations. Under established case law, the railroad was required to continue paying its obligations under any mortgage superior in priority to that of the mortgage holders who had petitioned for foreclosure. James Byrne, "The Foreclosure of Railroad Mortgages in the United States Courts," in *Some Legal Phases*, 77, 98.

23. Peter Tufano, "Business Failure, Judicial Intervention, and Financial Innovation: Restructuring U.S. Railroads in the Nineteenth Century, 71 *Business History Review* 1, 15 (citing W. Hastings Lyon, *Corporation Finance*, 275–87).

24. Cravath, "Reorganization of Corporations," 204–5.

25. I follow the Tufano's useful analysis in my characterization of these issues. "Business Failure," 6–14.

26. The classic explication of over- and underinvestment problems is Stewart C. Myers, "Determinants of Corporate Borrowing," 5 *Journal of Financial Economics* 147 (1977).

27. Tufano, "Business Failure," 12 (citing Joseph Weiner, "Conflicting Functions of the Upset Price in a Corporate Reorganization," 27 *Columbia Law Review* 135–36 (1927)).

28. Weiner, "Conflicting Functions," 145.

29. Berk, *Alternative Tracks*, 58.

30. On the attitudinal model, see Harold J. Spaeth, "The Attitudinal Model," in *Contemplating Courts*, 296 (Washington, D.C.: Congressional Quarterly Press, Lee Epstein ed., 1995); Frank B. Cross, "Political Science and the New Legal Realism: A Case of Unfortunate Interdisciplinary Ignorance," 92 *Northwestern University Law Review* 251, 265–311 (1997) (describing and analyzing the attitudinal model).

31. Quoted in Glenn, "Basis of Federal Receivership," 442.

32. Thomas H. Jackson and Robert E. Scott give a good overview of these tensions in "On the Nature of Bankruptcy: An Essay on Bankruptcy, Sharing, and the Creditors' Bargain," 75 *Virginia Law Review* 155, 187–89 (1989).

33. Martin, "Railroads and Equity Receivership," 699.

34. Oliver E. Williamson, "Credible Commitments: Using Hostages to Support Exchange," 73 *American Economic Review* 519 (1983).

35. *Central Trust Co. v. Wabash*, 29 Fed. 618, 626 (E.D. Mo. 1886).

36. For one overview of the often-told story of the Wabash receivership, see Martin, "Railroads and Equity Receivership," 697–701. Brad Hansen has recently challenged the traditional view that the Wabash receivership transformed receivership practice. Hansen argues that the ostensible innovations of the Wabash receivership, such as its initiation by Wabash's managers, actually predated the Wabash case. Hansen, "The Wabash Receivership."

37. The most strident critic was probably D. H. Chamberlain, who had unsuccessfully represented dissenting creditors in the receivership and later put his complaints in print in the pages of the *Harvard Law Review*. D. H. Chamberlain, "New-Fangled Receiverships," 10 *Harvard Law Review* 19 (1896). For a defense in doctrinal terms of the process that emerged, see Glenn, "Basis of Federal Receivership."

38. Henry Swaine, 3 *Economic Studies of the American Economic Association* 71, 77 (1898) (cited in Hansen, "The Wabash Receivership," 18).

39. The disadvantages of state court receivership are described in Cravath, "Reorganization of Corporations," 159.

40. Frank Buckley has argued that federal judges were motivated by the prestige of large receiverships. Frank Buckley, "The American Stay," 3 *University of Southern California Interdisciplinary Journal* 733 (1994).

41. Ron Chernow, *The House of Morgan: An American Banking Dynasty and the Rise of Modern Finance*, 29–45 (New York: Simon and Schuster, 1991). Recent empirical studies suggest that the involvement of J. P. Morgan and other Wall Street banks in the 1920s increased a firm's value overall; it is quite plausible that bankers had a similarly beneficial effect in receivership. See, for example, Bradford DeLong, "Did J. P. Morgan's Men Add Value? An Economist's Perspective on Financial Capitalism," in *Inside the Business Enterprise: Historical Perspectives on the Use of Information*, 205 (Chicago: University of Chicago Press, Peter Temin ed., 1991).

42. 228 U.S. 482 (1913).

43. Robert Gordon has attributed the contractualization trend to ideological shifts in American political life. On Gordon's view, the use of contract reflected the leavening of Federalist and Whig conceptions of an enlightened judiciary by more democratic, Jacksonian values. In reorganization, this meant a shift from focusing on fiduciary obligations to a greater emphasis on free contract. Robert Gordon, "Legal Thought and Legal Practice in the Age of American Enterprise, 1870–1920," in *Professions and Professional Ideologies in America* 70, 101–10 (Chapel Hill: University of North Carolina Press, ed. Gerald L. Geison, 1983).

44. Cravath, "Reorganization of Corporations," 177.

45. Swaine, *Cravath Firm*, 1:248.

46. Cravath, "Reorganization of Corporations," 178.

47. The absolute priority rule prohibits a reorganization plan from paying a class of lower-priority creditors or shareholders before higher-priority classes are paid in full. Under current bankruptcy law, proponents of a reorganization plan are required to honor the absolute priority rule only with respect to classes that vote against the plan. 11 U.S.C., sec. 1129(b).

48. For a good discussion, see Douglas G. Baird and Thomas H. Jackson, "Bargaining after the Fall and the Contours of the Absolute Priority Rule," 55 *University of Chicago Law Review* 738 (1988).

49. Cravath, "Reorganization of Corporations," 197.

50. Swaine, *Cravath Firm*, 1:172.

51. Swaine, *Cravath Firm*, 1:173.

52. Swaine, *Cravath Firm*, 1:183 (Missouri Pacific); see also 1:186 (*Boyd* technique used in Missouri, Kansas, and Texas reorganization).

53. On the elite bar's dominance, see, for example, "Introductory Note," in *Some Legal Phases*, viii ("[A] limited number of law firms, mostly in New York . . . became expert in reorganization practice and were retained in one role or another in nearly every railroad receivership").

54. For a discussion of the Delaware legal culture and the Delaware Supreme Court's penchant for reaching unanimous results, even on highly contested corporate law issues, see Skeel, "Unanimity Norm."

55. Cravath, "Reorganization of Corporations," 208–9.

56. Swaine, *Cravath Firm*, 2:12 (five partners), 2:319 (thirteen partners, forty-six staff).

57. Swaine, *Cravath Firm*, 1:1–2 (Blatchford), 1:111–14 (Seward).

CHAPTER 3
ESCAPING THE NEW DEAL: THE BANKRUPTCY BAR IN THE 1930S

1. *Strengthening of Procedure in the Judicial System: The Report of the Attorney General on Bankruptcy Law and Practice*, Senate Document No. 72-65 (1932); *Report on the Administration of Bankruptcy Estates*, 71st Cong. (Committee Print 1931).

2. *Joint Hearings on S.3866 before the Subcommittees on the Judiciary*, 72d Cong., 1st sess. (1932) (hereinafter, *1932 Hearings*).

3. Act of March 3, 1933, chap. 204, sec. 77, 47 Stat. 1474 (1933); Act of June 7, 1934, chap. 424, sec. 77B, 48 Stat. 912 (1934).

4. Public Law No. 75-696, 52 Stat. 840 (1938) (codified prior to repeal at 11 U.S.C. (1938)) (hereinafter, Chandler Act).

5. Hunt's most frequently cited article is a legislative update on the deliberations on the Chandler bill. Reuben G. Hunt, "The Progress of the Chandler Bill," 42 *Commercial Law Journal* 195 (1937).

6. Colonel William J. Donovan, "The Proposed Revision of the National Bankruptcy Act," *Credit Monthly*, April 1930, 17. The subsequent quote appears at 17.

7. F. B. McComas, "The Donovan Plan for Bankruptcy Reform as Interpreted in the West," *Credit Monthly*, September 1930, 26.

8. *Strengthening of Procedure*, 1. President Hoover's announcement is quoted and the details of the Thacher investigation are described at 1.

9. *Strengthening of Procedure*, 33.

10. See, for example, Paul G. Mahoney, "The Exchange as Regulator," 83 *Virginia Law Review* 1453, 1472–73 (1997).

11. W. Randolph Montgomery, "The Donovan Plan for Bankruptcy Reform Answers Its Critics," *Credit Monthly*, August 1930, 11, 12.

12. *Strengthening of Procedure*, 104.

13. *Strengthening of Procedure*, 118.

14. *Strengthening of Procedure*, 25.

15. The best account of Progressivism and populism is still Hofstadter, *The Age of Reform*.

16. David A. Skeel Jr., "Vern Countryman and the Path of Progressive (and Populist) Bankruptcy Scholarship," 113 *Harvard Law Review* 1075, 1084–87 (2000).

17. I have described the public choice literature in more detail in other work. Skeel, "Public Choice." The analysis that follows elaborates on this article and Skeel, "Bankruptcy Lawyers."

18. The pioneering influence in the collective action literature, which contrasts the influence of large and small groups, was Mancur Olson, *The Logic of Collective Action* (Cambridge: Harvard University Press, 1971). Russell Hardin added the important qualification that the size of the group is not necessarily determinative. Rather, the question is whether some subset of the group has enough at stake to justify engaging in collective action. Russell Hardin, *Collective Action* (Baltimore: Johns Hopkins University Press, 1982).

19. Joseph P. Kalt and Mark A. Zupan, "Capture and Ideology in the Economic Theory of Politics," 74 *American Economic Review* 279 (1984) (analyzing voting on the Surface Mining Control and Reclamation Act).

20. *Hearing on H.R. 1670, etc., 5009, before the House Committee on the Judiciary*, 73d Cong., 1st sess., 207 (1933) (Representative Shannon of Missouri reads telegram).

21. For a discussion of the desperate conditions and agitation for federal action, see Arthur M. Schlesinger, *The Crisis of the Old Order, 1919–1933*, 166–76 (Boston: Houghton Mifflin, 1957).

22. *1932 Hearings*, 822 (American Paint and Varnish), 585 (Cromton Co).

23. The competing interests of banks and finance companies are explored in Posner, "Political Economy"; Peter V. Letsou, "The Political Economy of Consumer Credit Regulation," 44 *Emory Law Journal* 587, 631–36 (1995).

24. For a useful discussion in the banking law context, see Jonathan R. Macey, "The Political Science of Regulating Bank Risk," 49 *Ohio State Law Journal* 1277, 1288–90 (1989).

25. *Hearing before the Committee on the Judiciary, House of Representatives, on H.R. 6439*, 75th Cong., 1st sess. (1937) (hereinafter, *1937 House Hearings*). The speakers mentioned in the text appear at 17 (statement of Referee Watson Adair, National Bankruptcy Conference and National Association of Referees), 28 (statement of Randolph Montgomery, National Association of Credit Men), 28 (statement of Jacob Weinstein, National Bankruptcy Conference), 8, 120 (statement of Professor James McLaughlin, Harvard Law School and National Bankruptcy Conference).

26. Examples of the classic pluralist view include Earl Latham, *The Group Basis of Politics* (Ithaca, N.Y.: Cornell University Press, 1952); David B. Truman, *The Governmental Process* (New York: Knopf, 2d ed. 1971).

27. *1932 Hearings*, 743.

28. *1932 Hearings*, 734.

29. *1932 Hearings*, 484–84 (statement of Jacob Lashly, American Bar Association).

30. *1932 Hearings*, 456 ff.

31. *1932 Hearings*, 463 ff. (statement of M. R. Sturtevant, vice president, First National Bank, St. Louis, for American Bankers Association).

32. Montgomery, "Donovan Plan for Reform," 11. The quotation comes from 12.

33. McComas, "Donovan Plan for Reform," 50–51.

34. *1932 Hearings*, 362 (statement of Orville Livingston, secretary-manager, St. Louis Association of Credit Men).

35. See, for example, *Revision of the National Bankruptcy Act, House Report No. 1409*, 75th Cong., 1st sess., 2 (1937) (hereinafter, *1937 House Report*).

36. See, for example, *Hearing before Subcommittee No. 1 of Committee on the Judiciary on H.R. 18694*, 61st Cong., 2d sess. 31–32 (1910) (statement of Harold Remington) (describing expansion of jurisdiction as giving creditors equivalent rights under federal bankruptcy law as under state law).

37. A similar issue, though it does not seem to have been a pressing concern in the early twentieth century, was bankruptcy waiver. McLaughlin recommended a provision specifically invalidating such waivers. James A. McLaughlin, "Amendment of the Bankruptcy Act," 40 *Harvard Law Review* 583, 591–92 (1927) (part 2 of two-part article).

38. In 1903, for instance, Congress excluded fraudulent conveyances from the requirement that bankruptcy litigation be brought in state court and gave concurrent jurisdiction to the bankruptcy court. Bankruptcy Act, sec. 23(b), 32 Stat. 798 (1903). The same amendments expanded the preference provision, Bankruptcy Act, sec. 60a, 32 Stat. 799 (1903), and the 1910 amendments added further adjustments. Bankruptcy Act, sec. 60a, 32 Stat. 842 (1910).

39. Strengthening the trustee's avoidance powers also benefits bankruptcy lawyers, though in a slightly more subtle way. By invalidating a property interest, the trustee frees up assets that would otherwise be unavailable. The power to retrieve assets for the estate gives the trustee, and thus his lawyer and the other lawyers involved in the case, appreciably more flexibility than they would have if the assets were encumbered. In corporate bankruptcy cases, the funds can be used to facilitate the reorganization effort.

40. *1932 Hearings*, 11.

41. *1937 House Report*, 2 (describing amendment to sec. 34a).

42. The Chandler Act also made clear that the trustee could assert title to the debtor's property from the moment the debtor filed for bankruptcy, rather than waiting until the court authorized the case to proceed (ibid., 34 (describing amendment to sec. 70)). In addition, the Chandler Act increased the dominance of bankruptcy over nonbankruptcy law by giving the bankruptcy precedence over any state law receivership that had been set up prior to bankruptcy. Finally, the Chandler Act continued to expand the reach of bankruptcy's preference and fraudulent conveyance provisions. Among other things, the reform adopted a substantially broader test for the kinds of prebankruptcy "transfers" that the trustee could retrieve from creditors and add to the assets of the bankruptcy case (ibid., 20 (describing amendment to sec. 2a)).

43. Ibid., 25 (describing amendment to sec. 7a(8)).

44. *1937 House Hearings*, 280–281 (statement of Edwin Sunderland), 303–4 (statement of John Gerdes).

45. *1937 House Hearings*, 205.

46. *1932 Hearings*, 743.

47. *1937 House Hearings*, 250 (statement of Valentine Nesbit); for Nesbit's insistence that debtors wished to pay, see ibid., 263 ("I think the success we have had . . . was because the creditors are being paid reasonably promptly, the debtor wants to pay and does pay, and you cannot have a one-sided agreement").

48. *1937 House Hearings*, 388.

CHAPTER 4

WILLIAM DOUGLAS AND THE RISE OF THE SECURITIES AND
EXCHANGE COMMISSION

1. A brief, helpful overview of the development of the corporate reorganization bar is Leonard M. Rosen and Jane Lee Vris, "A History of the Bankruptcy Bar in the Second Circuit," in *The Development of the Bankruptcy Bar in the Second Circuit,* 155 (1995).

2. Swaine, *Cravath Firm*, 2:7. The quote in the text that follows appears at 2:8.

3. Swaine, *Cravath Firm*, 2:164.

4. Lowenthal, *The Investor Pays*. The reformers' anger was fueled by a Supreme Court decision upholding the Wall Street bankers' and lawyers' fee requests over an objection by the Interstate Commerce Commission. *United States v. Chicago, Milwaukee, St. Paul & Pacific Railway Company*, 282 U.S. 311 (1931).

5. Chester McLain to William O. Douglas, January 11, 1929, William O. Douglas Papers, Library of Congress (hereinafter, WOD Papers), Container No. 4.

6. Douglas to McLain, October 30, 1929, WOD Papers, Container No. 4.

7. Douglas to Felix Frankfurter, December 8, 1933, WOD Papers, Container No. 4.

8. Robert T. Swaine, "Corporate Reorganization Under the Bankruptcy Power," 19 *Virginia Law Review* 317, 317–18 (1933); see also Robert T. Swaine, "Federal Legislation for Corporate Reorganization: An Affirmative View," 19 *American Bar Association Journal* 698 (1933) (reprinting speech).

9. Robert T. Swaine, "Corporate Reorganization" 331.

10. Swaine, *Cravath Firm*, 2:431.

11. *Harkin v. Brundage*, 276 U.S. 36, 52 (1928); *Shapiro v. Wilgus*, 287 U.S. 348, 356 (1932). The Supreme Court sounded this theme once again two years later, when Justice Brandeis noted, "All the cases in which this Court appears to have [upheld the use of the equity receivership device] . . . dealt with railroads or other public utilities where continued operation of the property . . . seemed to be required in the public interest." *First National Bank v. Flershem*, 290 U.S. 504, 515 n. 7 (1934). See also Henry Friendly, "Some Comments on the Corporate Reorganizations Act," 48 *Harvard Law Review* 39, 42–45 (1934) (describing the uncertainty created by the cases).

12. *1932 Hearings*, 519.

13. *1932 Hearings*, 790.

14. Act of March 3, 1933, chap. 204, 47 Stat. 1474 (1933) (codified prior to repeal at 11 U.S.C., sec. 204).

15. For a good illustration of reorganizers' confidence that the new reforms would not undermine existing practice, see Churchill Rodgers and Littleton Groom, "Reorganization of Railroad Corporations under Section 77 of the Bankruptcy Act," 33 *Columbia Law Review* 571, 587 (1933). Written by two prominent reorganization lawyers, the article suggests that reorganizers could limit ICC oversight of their fee arrangements by providing for the fees by contract.

Congress amended the railroad reorganization provisions and strengthened ICC oversight somewhat in 1935. Bankruptcy Act of 1898 Amendments, Public Law No. 74-381, 49 Stat. 911 (1935) (amending 11 U.S.C., sec. 205 (1935)).

16. *Hearing on H.R. 1670, etc, 5009, before the House Committee on the Judiciary,* 73d Cong., 1st sess. (1933). The Long Island Lumber Telegram appears at 207, and the quote from Representative McKeown appears at 185.

17. George G. Battle, "The Enactment of the New Bankruptcy Law Will Check the Tendency toward Currency Inflation," 19 *Virginia Law Review* 340 (1933).

18. William Douglas to E. Merrick Dodd, January 29, 1934, WOD Papers, Container No. 5.

19. Securities Exchange Act of 1934, Public Law No. 73-291, sec. 211, 48 Stat. 881, 909 (1934).

20. For an interesting discussion of the New Dealers' divide-and-conquer strategy, see Ralph F. DeBedts, *The New Deal's SEC: The Formative Years,* 82 (New York: Columbia University Press, 1964).

21. Yale University News Statement, WOD Papers, Container No. 32.

22. Douglas's equity receivership study is analyzed in William O. Douglas and J. H. Weir, "Equity Receiverships in the United States District Court for Connecticut, 1920–1929, 4 *Connecticut Bar Journal* 1 (1930). For examples of his work on the securities acts, see William O. Douglas and G. E. Bates, "Some Effects of the Securities Act upon Investment Banking," 1 *University of Chicago Law Review* 283 (1933); William O. Douglas and G. E. Bates, "Stock 'Brokers' as Agents and Dealers," 43 *Yale Law Journal* 46 (1933).

23. I discuss Douglas's corporate and bankruptcy scholarship in detail elsewhere. Skeel, "Vern Countryman."

24. Douglas to A. A. Berle Jr., January 3, 1933, WOD Papers, Container No. 2.

25. James Allen, introduction to William O. Douglas, *Democracy and Finance,* x (New Haven: Yale University Press, 1940).

26. James F. Simon, *Independent Journey: The Life of William O. Douglas,* 141 (New York: Harper and Row, 1980).

27. Simon, *Independent Journey,* 145–47 (Dulles and Untermyer questioning), 144 (Swaine questioning). Douglas's account of the Swaine questioning is in William O. Douglas, *Go East, Young Man,* 260 (New York: Random House, 1971).

28. 1 *Securities and Exchange Commission Report on the Study and Investigation of the Work, Activities, Personnel, and Functions of Protective and Reorganization Committees* (1937) (hereinafter, *SEC Report*). The criticisms of the existing receivership process are summarized at 863–96; see especially 863–68.

29. *SEC Report,* 1:6–64. Fortington's role is described at 1:8, and the quotation in the text below comes from 1:64.

30. *SEC Report,* 1:865, 867.

31. Abe Fortas to William Douglas, May 20, 1937, WOD Papers, Container No. 6.

32. *1937 House Hearings*, 199.

33. DeLong, "J. P. Morgan's Men," 205. DeLong notes that the added value could have come either from improved performance or from monopoly rents obtained by businesses that Morgan participated in.

34. W. Braddock Hickman, *Corporate Bond Quality and Investor Experience*, 22 (Princeton: Princeton University Press, 1958).

35. A recent study by Randy Kroszner may support this conclusion. Kroszner determined that the Supreme Court's 1935 decision upholding congressional legislation that invalidated the gold indexation clauses in corporate bonds—a decision that would be expected to devalue the bonds, since Congress had removed an important price protection—actually increased the bonds' value. Kroszner speculates that the increase in value may have stemmed from the benefits of reducing debt overhang, avoiding bankruptcy, or some combination of the two. If avoiding bankruptcy was a major reason for the increase in value, this would suggest that the reorganization process was quite costly during this era. Bankers' and lawyers' fees were, of course, an important component of this cost. Randall S. Kroszner, "Is It Better to Forgive Than to Receive? Repudiation of the Gold Indexation Clause in Long-Term Debt during the Great Depression" (unpublished manuscript, 1999).

36. *New York World Telegram*, September 27, 1934, WOD Papers, Container No. 29.

37. Abe Fortas to William Douglas, September 29, 1934, WOD Papers, Container No. 6.

38. The Sabath bill is included and described in the hearings held on the bill in 1937. *Conservator in Bankruptcy, Hearings before the Committee on the Judiciary, House of Representatives, on H.R. 9 and H.R. 6963*, 75th Cong., 1st sess. (1937).

39. The Lea bill is introduced and described in the hearings held on the bill in 1936 and 1937. *To Amend the Securities Act of 1933, Hearing before the Committee on Interstate and Foreign Commerce, House of Representatives, on H.R. 6968*, 75th Cong., 2d sess. (1937) (hereinafter, *Lea Hearings*). The bill also is usefully discussed in Cloyd LaPorte, Note, "Changes in Corporate Reorganization Procedure Proposed by the Chandler and Lea Bills," 51 *Harvard Law Review* 672 (1938).

40. In the 1930s, Senator Fletcher insisted that the Banking Committee (which he chaired) have jurisdiction over securities legislation, because the Banking Committee had overseen the lengthy securities investigation that arguably spawned the securities reforms. DeBebts, *The New Deal's SEC*, 34.

41. Douglas to Sabath, October 6, 1934, WOD Papers, Container No. 29; Joseph Kennedy to Adolph Sabath, October 19, 1934, WOD Papers, Container No. 29.

42. Interview between Mr. Boland and Mr. Comer, January 10, 1935, WOD Papers, Container No. 29.

43. Abe Fortas, Memorandum to William Douglas, October 7, 1935, WOD Papers, Container No. 6 (emphasis deleted).

44. *1937 House Hearings*, 364–65 (statement of John Gerdes, appearing on behalf of Trade and Commerce Bar Association). Gerdes was also a member of the NBC.

45. Hunt, "Progress of Chandler Bill," 197.

46. *Lea Hearings*, 132 ff. (statement of Orrin G. Wood, Investment Bankers Association of America).

47. In her fascinating biography of Abe Fortas, Douglas's principal assistant at the SEC, Laura Kalman attributes the demise of the Lea bill to opposition by Adolph Sabath, who resented the SEC's competition with his bill. Laura Kalman, *Abe Fortas: A Biography* (New Haven: Yale University Press, 1990). Sabath did criticize the Lea bill at the Lea bill hearings as overlapping with his own bill, but it seems unlikely that this alone thwarted the Lea bill. Moreover, his opposition could have been neutralized if the SEC had made its bill less sweeping, and thus more modest in scope than the Sabath bill. Interestingly, Sabath offered extravagant praise for the Chapter X of the Chandler bill during the brief congressional debates on the bill before it passed. "Because of the deep understanding of the subject by the author of this bill [Representative Chandler]," Sabath said, "he incorporated in it a great many of the objectives which I have been striving for. Since my bill undoubtedly will die with this Congress, I am happy that the Chandler bill will afford a great deal of relief to holders of defaulted securities." 83 *Congressional Record* 9483 (1937).

48. WOD to Adolf Berle, December 29, 1933, WOD Papers, Container No. 2.

49. Jacob Weinstein of the National Bankruptcy Conference suggested that the SEC agreed to limit itself to an advisory role in Chapter X as a concession to the NBC. *1937 House Hearings*, 146 ("The SEC wanted broad powers, and we said no, it was not advisable. The court ought to retain . . . control").

In the Trust Indenture Act hearings, Douglas and the SEC adjusted the conflict-of-interest requirements and the trustee liability provisions slightly but insisted on retaining the general framework.

50. 83 *Congressional Record* 8711 (1937).

51. Chandler Act, sec. 189 (trustee runs business), sec. 169 (trustee develops plan).

52. Chandler Act, secs. 157, 158. In addition to the provisions quoted in the text, section 158 also included a catchall clause excluding any one who "appears" due to a "direct or indirect relationship to . . . the debtor or such underwriter . . [to have] an interest materially adverse to" the creditors or stockholders. Chandler Act, sec. 158(4).

53. Robert T. Swaine, " 'Democratization' of Corporate Reorganizations," 38 *Columbia Law Review* 256 (1938).

54. Chandler Act, sec. 165. In the hearings on the Trust Indenture Act of 1939, which included a similar provision, bankers claimed that they actually did not have the lists, since depository institutions tended to hold securities on investors' behalf. Most observers assumed the banks did have the lists, however, and there was general agreement that access to the lists should not be restricted. Swaine, "Democratization of Corporate Reorganizations," 266 (leading reorganization lawyer concedes virtues of the change).

55. Chandler Act, sec. 176 (no preapproval solicitation). Section 212 authorized the court to invalidate the terms of any deposit agreement.

56. For a discussion of this problem, see Frank, "Some Realistic Reflections."

57. R. G. Page, chairman, Committee on Mortgage Trusteeships, American Bankers Association, to William O. Douglas, August 4, 1937, SEC Files, Douglas Box No. 15 (enclosing untitled speech). The quoted material is p. 15 of the speech. The SEC continued to insist that the voting prohibition was necessary to prevent bankers and other insiders from commandeering the voting process. For a summary of the SEC's arguments, see *SEC Report*, 6:143–56.

58. For an excellent discussion of the background of the voting prohibition and its contemporary significance, see Mark J. Roe, "The Voting Prohibition in Bond Workouts," 97 *Yale Law Journal* 232 (1987).

59. Chandler Act, sec. 208 (party in interest); secs. 172–73 (report on reorganization plan, discussed in text following). Further, Chandler Act, sec. 265(2) authorized the SEC to fix compensation, based on its powers under section 4(b) of the Securities Exchange Act of 1934.

60. William O. Douglas, "Protective Committees in Railroad Reorganizations," 47 *Harvard Law Review* 565 (1934); Max Lowenthal, "The Railroad Reorganization," 47 *Harvard Law Review* 18 (1933).

61. Jerome Frank to Douglas, January 19, 1934, WOD Papers, Container No. 6.

62. Douglas to Felix Frankfurter, February 19, 1934, WOD Papers, Container No. 6. The quoted portions are taken from p. 1 and p. 3 of the letter.

63. William Douglas to Franklin D. Roosevelt, July 7, 1936, Franklin D. Roosevelt Papers, quoted in Simon, *Independent Journey*, 156.

64. *Case v. Los Angeles Lumber Products*, 308 U.S. 106 (1939); *Consolidated Rock Products v. DuBois*, 312 U.S. 510 (1941).

65. William Douglas, Diary, 12, WOD Papers, Container No. 1780 (entry for November 4, 1939).

66. Swaine surveyed the state of railroad receivership law in an article written near the end of the Roosevelt era. Robert T. Swaine, "A Decade of Railroad Reorganizations under Section 77 of the Bankruptcy Act," 56 *Harvard Law Review* 1037, 1193 (1943) (two-part article).

CHAPTER 5
RAISING THE BAR WITH THE 1978 BANKRUPTCY CODE

1. Stanley and Girth, *Bankruptcy*, 105.

2. Charles Elihu Nadler, "Solicitation in Bankruptcy Matters," 55 *Commercial Law Journal* 229 (1950). The quotations in this paragraph appear on p. 229.

3. Nadler, "Solicitation in Bankruptcy Matters," 234. The other quotations in this paragraph also appear on p. 234.

4. Editors, "Interim Report: Committee on Bankruptcy," 56 *Commercial Law Journal* 97 (1951).

5. Stanley and Girth, *Bankruptcy*, 78.

6. Frank R. Kennedy, "Oral History" (unpublished manuscript, 1989).

7. For a thoughtful political history of the rise of the consumer protection movement, see Mark V. Nadel, *The Politics of Consumer Protection* (Indianapolis: Bobbs-Merrill, 1971).

8. George M. Treister, "Bankruptcy Jurisdiction: Is it Too Summary?" 39 *Southern California Law Review* 78 (1966).

9. Vern Countryman, "Improvident Credit Extension: A New Legal Concept Aborning," 27 *Maine Law Review* 1, 1 (1975) (citing *Fed Res. Bul.* A52, A54 (Dec. 1970), A44, A47 (July 1974)).

10. As a first step, the Supreme Court was authorized to issue bankruptcy rules that would override existing statutory law in the event of a conflict. Drafted by bankruptcy experts such as Larry King and Frank Kennedy, the new rules foreshadowed many of

the changes that eventually made their way into the 1978 Code. See Lawrence P. King, "The History and Development of the Bankruptcy Rules," 70 *American Bankruptcy Law Journal* 217 (1996).

11. The legislative history of the 1978 Code is outlined in detail in the following sources: Carruthers and Halliday, *Rescuing Business*, 78–86; Posner, "Political Economy," 67–74; Kenneth N. Klee, "Legislative History of the New Bankruptcy Code," 54 *American Bankruptcy Law Journal* 275 (1980).

12. *Commission to Study Bankruptcy Laws, 1968: Hearings on S.J. Res. 100 before the Subcommittee on Bankruptcy of the Senate Committee on the Judiciary*, 90th Cong., 1st sess. (1968); *Bankruptcy: Hearings on S.J. Res. 88, H.R. 6665, and H.R. 12250 before Subcommittee No. 4 of the House Committee on the Judiciary*, 91st Cong., 1st sess. (1969) (hereinafter, *1969 Hearings*).

13. *Report of the Commission on the Bankruptcy Laws of the United States*, H.R. Doc. No. 93–137 (1973). The principal recommendations of the 1973 commission report are outlined in the first chapter, 1–31.

14. *Bankruptcy Act Revision: Hearings on H.R. 31 and H.R. 32 before the Subcommittee on Civil and Constitutional Rights of the House Committee on the Judiciary*, 94th Cong., 1st sess. (1975–76) (hereinafter, *1975–76 House Hearings*); *Hearings before the Subcommittee on Improvements in Judiciary Machinery of the Committee on the Judiciary on S. 235 and S 236*, 94th Cong., 1st sess. (1975) (hereinafter, *1975 Senate Hearings*).

15. Interview with J. Ronald Trost, June 30, 2000. Additional hearings were held in both the House and the Senate in 1977. *Bankruptcy Court Revision: Hearings on H.R. 8200 before the Subcommittee on Civil and Constitutional Rights of the House Committee on the Judiciary*, 95th Cong., 1st sess. (1977); *Bankruptcy Reform Act of 1978: Hearings on S. 2266 and H.R. 8200 before the Subcommittee on Improvements in Judicial Machinery of the Senate Committee on the Judiciary*, 95th Cong., 1st sess. (1978) (hereinafter, *1977 Senate Hearings*) (hearings took place on November 28–29 and December 1, 1977).

16. Stanley and Girth, *Bankruptcy*.

17. Stanley and Girth, *Bankruptcy*, 200.

18. *Commission on Bankruptcy Laws*, 8.

19. *1975–76 House Hearings*, 255.

20. *1975 Senate Hearings*, 7 (statement of National Bankruptcy Review Commission).

21. *1975–76 House Hearings*, 593.

22. *1975 Senate Hearings*, 553.

23. *1975–76 House Hearings*, 1269, 1270 (statement of George Ritner); Posner, "Political Economy," 83–84.

24. For the credit industry perspective, see *1975 Senate Hearings*, 124, 126 (statement of Walter W. Vaughan, American Bankers Association and Consumer Bankers Association), 185, 193 (statement of Linn K. Twinem, special counsel, Beneficial Finance System). The quotation in the text is at p. 193.

25. *1975 Senate Hearings*, 305, 307 (statement of Richard A. Hesse, professor, Franklin Pierce Law Center, and National Consumer Law Center).

26. *Commission on Bankruptcy Laws*, 124.

27. *1977 Senate Hearings*, 488–89.

28. *1977 Senate Hearings*, 612 (statement of Robert B. Chatz, president, Commercial Law League).

29. Not least of the oddities of this arrangement was courts' assumption that the parties could "consent" to jurisdiction if they wished. As House Judiciary Committee attorney Ken Klee noted in the 1975 Senate hearings, jurisdictional infirmities have not traditionally been waivable. *1975–76 House Hearings*, 144.

30. *Commission on Bankruptcy Laws*, 21, 101.

31. See, for example, Michelle J. White, "Legal Complexity and Lawyers' Benefit from Litigation," 12 *International Review of Law and Economics* 381 (1992).

32. The only reference to exemptions in the hearings on the Chandler Act was a letter submitted by Jacob Weinstein on behalf of the National Bankruptcy Conference. The letter indicates that the conference considered uniform federal exemptions but concluded that exemptions policy is local in nature and farm state lawmakers would oppose federalization. *1937 House Hearings*, 387. The failure to federalize exemptions is consistent with Stephen Gardbaum's argument in a recent article that despite the common perception that states lost power during the New Deal, they actually retained and even expanded their authority in many respects. In Gardbaum's view, the principal effect of the New Deal was to restrain the courts, and to leave more room for legislative creativity. Stephen Gardbaum, "New Deal Constitutionalism and the Unshackling of the States," 64 *University of Chicago Law Review* 483 (1997).

33. Vern Countryman, "For a New Exemption Policy in Bankruptcy," 14 *Rutgers Law Review* 678 (1960). Frank Kennedy initially defended the long-standing approach of deferring to the states. Frank Kennedy, "Limitation of Exemptions in Bankruptcy," 45 *Iowa Law Review* 445 (1960).

34. For a fascinating political history of one of these reforms, the Truth-in-Lending Act, see Edward L. Rubin, "Legislative Methodology: Some Lessons from the Truth-in-Lending Act," 80 *Georgetown Law Journal* 233 (1991).

35. Posner, "Political Economy," 94–108.

36. *1975 Senate Hearings*, 630 (written statement of American Life Insurance Association).

37. *1975–76 House Hearings*, 938 (Consumer Law Center), 977 (National Bankruptcy Conference).

38. *1975 Senate Hearings*, 537 (written statement of Commercial Law League); *1975–76 House Hearings*, 1658 (statement of L. E. Creel III, Dallas Bar Association).

39. *Commission on Bankruptcy Laws*, 159.

40. *1975 Senate Hearings*, 143 (statement of Alvin O. Wiese Jr., chair, Bankruptcy Subcommittee, National Consumer Finance Association).

41. *Commission on Bankruptcy Laws*, 176.

42. *1975 Senate Hearings*, 144 (statement of Alvin O. Wiese Jr., chair, Bankruptcy Subcommittee, National Consumer Finance Association).

43. *1975 Senate Hearings*, 142 (statement of Alvin O. Wiese Jr., chair, Bankruptcy Subcommittee, National Consumer Finance Association).

44. *1975–76 House Hearings*, 940–41 (statement of Ernest L. Sarason Jr., staff attorney, National Consumer Law Center).

45. Conversation with author, September 16, 1999.

46. Posner, "Political Economy," 90–91.

47. 458 U.S. 50 (1982).

CHAPTER 6
REPUDIATING THE NEW DEAL WITH CHAPTER 11 OF THE BANKRUPTCY CODE

1. *1975 Senate Hearings*, 383 (statement of Charles Seligson).

2. A superb early discussion is Eugene V. Rostow and Lloyd N. Cutler, "Competing Systems of Corporate Reorganization: Chapters X and XI of the Bankruptcy Act," 48 *Yale Law Journal* 1334, 1362 (1949). Section 130(7) required firms to show that they could not obtain adequate relief under Chapter XI as a prerequisite to using Chapter X.

3. *1975 Senate Hearings*, 367 (statement of Larry King).

4. *SEC v. United States Reality & Improvement Co.*, 310 U.S. 434 (1940).

5. *House Report No. 2372*, 76th Cong., 2d sess., 2 (1940).

6. Benjamin Weintraub and Harris Levin, "A Sequel to Chapter X or Chapter XI: Coexistence for the Middle-Sized Corporation," 26 *Fordham Law Review* 292 (1957); Benjamin Weintraub et al., "Chapter X or Chapter XI: Coexistence for the Middle-Sized Corporation," 24 *Fordham Law Review* 616 (1956).

7. *General Stores Corp. v. Shlensky*, 350 U.S. 462 (1956).

8. *SEC v. Canandaigua Enterprises*, 339 F.2d 14, 21 (2d Cir. 1964). Here, as in many of the cases, the lower court had rejected the SEC's demand for a transfer.

9. The discussion that follows is based on interviews by the author with an SEC official in June and July 1999.

10. Simon, *Independent Journey*.

11. William O. Douglas, Memorandum, No. 796, Securities and Exchange Commission v. U.S. Reality & Improvement Company, WOD Papers, Container No. 50 (undated).

12. *General Stores Corp. v. Shlensky*, 472 (Justice Frankfurter, dissenting).

13. The bankruptcy court's recommendations on whether to move a case out of Chapter XI were automatically reviewed by the district court, so the SEC was not solely at the mercy of the bankruptcy judge. But the district courts did not have any significant incentive to wrest the case from the bankruptcy judge. Taking the case meant dealing with the cumbersome apparatus of Chapter X, for instance, and reorganization cases were less likely to be an improvement on the district court's docket than they were for bankruptcy judges.

14. A good illustration of the SEC's recognition of this dilemma is Allen F. Corotto and Irving H. Picard, "Business Reorganization under the Bankruptcy Reform Act of 1978—a New Approach to Investor Protection and the Role of the SEC," 28 *DePaul Law Review* 961, 965 n. 19 (1979), which was written by two SEC officials.

15. Joel Seligman, *The Transformation of Wall Street A History of the Securities and Exchange Commission and Modern Corporate Finance*, 77 (Boston: Northeastern University Press, rev. ed. 1995).

16. Jonathan R. Macey, "Administrative Agency Obsolescence and Interest Group Formation: A Case Study of the SEC at Sixty," 15 *Cardozo Law Review* 909 (1994).

17. Seligman, *Transformation of Wall Street*, 265.

18. *1977 Senate Hearings*, 490 (Marsh), 630 (SEC Commissioner Philip Loomis).

19. *1977 Senate Hearings*, 646 (statement of SEC official); *1975–76 House Hearings*, 613 (comments of Congressman Edwards).

20. My thanks to Professors Frank Partnoy and Thomas Smith for suggesting and discussing the line of reasoning I describe in the text of this paragraph.

21. Franco Modigliani and Merton H. Miller, "The Cost of Capital, Corporation Finance, and the Theory of Investment," 48 *American Economic Review* 261 (1958).

22. James Cox and Matthew D. McCubbins, *Legislative Leviathan: Party Leadership in the House* (1993). Cox and McCubbins contend that political parties act as legislative cartels, employing congressional processes to further party goals.

23. Weingast and Marshall are perhaps best known for emphasizing the importance of a committee's ability to determine whether legislation is revisited. Barry R. Weingast and William J. Marshall, "The Industrial Organization of Congress; or, Why Legislatures, Like Firms, Are Not Organized as Markets," 96 *Journal of Political Economy* 132 (1988). For discussion of committee control over the decision whether to revisit an issue, see Kenneth A. Shepsle and Barry R. Weingast, "The Institutional Foundations of Committee Power," 81 *American Political Science Review* 85 (1987) (emphasizing that the committee's "ex post veto" is crucial since, if committees' influence were limited to the decision whether to consider legislation, they would lose control once they let legislation go forward). Commentators who emphasize committee independence also point to factors such as the seniority system, which operated in the past, and to some extent still operates, as a norm that committee leadership will be chosen based on length of service.

Still another view of committees suggests that the principal role of committees is to generate information for Congress. The principal proponent of the informational theory of committees is Keith Krehbiel. Keith Krehbiel, *Information and Legislative Organization* (Ann Arbor: University of Michigan Press, 1991). The discussion in the text below can be seen as incorporating the informational perspective.

24. *1969 Hearings*, 64.

25. Kennedy, "Oral History," 26.

26. *1975–76 House Hearings*, 329.

27. The discussions between the National Bankruptcy Conference and the SEC, and the NBC's disapproval of the proposed legislation, are described in an NBC memo. Sydney Krause to Benjamin Wham et al., "Memorandum," March 16, 1959, SEC Files (memorandum describing proposed legislation and meeting between National Bankruptcy Conference and SEC).

28. Richard V. Bandler et al. to Frederick Zazove, Chief Counsel, SEC Division of Corporate Regulation, "SEC Office Memorandum," February 13, 1959, SEC Files.

29. Posner, "Political Economy," 114.

30. *1975 Senate Hearings*, 709.

31. *1975 Senate Hearings*, 650 (written statement of John J. Creedon, American Life Insurance Association), 672 (oral statement).

32. Roberta Romano has chronicled managers' role in state enactment of antitakeover legislation. Roberta Romano, "The Political Economy of Takeover Statutes," 73 *Virginia Law Review* 111 (1987).

33. *1975–76 House Hearings*, 596–97 (statement of George Triester).

34. Trost, interview. Another prominent attorney told me that there was a simple explanation for Marsh's aversion to the SEC: the SEC had the audacity to challenge Marsh's fee request in an important Chapter X case in which Marsh represented the trustee.

35. *1975–76 House Hearings*, 596.
36. Carruthers and Halliday, *Rescuing Business*, 206.
37. *1977 Senate Hearings*, 669 (statement of Judge Herbert Katz).
38. Aaron Levy to Robert E. Feidler, September 26, 1977, 2–3, SEC Files.
39. See, e.g., Aaron Levy to Robert E. Feidler, October 17, 1977, SEC Files (including eleven pages of proposed adjustments to the Senate bill).
40. Aaron Levy to Robert E. Feidler, May 1, 1978, SEC Files.
41. See, for example, *1975–76 House Hearings*, 1747 ff. (statement of American Bankers Association) (raising each of the concerns discussed in the text that follows).
42. Carruthers and Halliday, *Rescuing Business*, 181–86.

CHAPTER 7
CREDIT CARDS AND THE RETURN OF IDEOLOGY
IN CONSUMER BANKRUPTCY

1. Lendol Calder, *Financing the American Dream: A Cultural History of Consumer Credit*, 263 (Princeton: Princeton University Press, 1999).
2. National Bankruptcy Review Commission, *Bankruptcy: The Next Twenty Years* (1997) (hereinafter, *1997 Commission Report*), preface, 1–2.
3. The 1973 commission report notes, for instance, that the legislation establishing the commission listed "the increase in the number of bankruptcies by more than 1000 per cent in the preceding twenty years" as the first of four reasons for undertaking a bankruptcy study. *Commission on Bankruptcy Laws*, 1.
4. *Bankruptcy Reform Act of 1978 (Future Earnings): Hearing before the Subcommittee on Courts of the Committee on the Judiciary, United States Senate*, 97th Cong., 1st sess. 13 (1981) (hereinafter, *1981 Hearings*) (statement of James C. Barr, executive vice president, Credit Union National Association).
5. *1975–76 House Hearings*, 1360 (statement of Alvin O. Wiese Jr., National Consumer Finance Association).
6. Michael Pertschuk, *Revolt against Regulation: The Rise and Pause of the Consumer Movement* (Berkeley and Los Angeles: University of California Press, 1982).
7. William C. Whitford, "The Ideal of Individualized Justice: Consumer Bankruptcy as Consumer Protection, and Consumer Protection in Bankruptcy," 68 *American Bankruptcy Law Journal* 397 (1994).
8. E-mail correspondence from Henry Sommer to David Skeel, July 18, 2000.
9. Henry Sommer, "The New Law of Bankruptcy: A Fresh Start for Legal Services Lawyers," *Clearinghouse Review*, May 1979, 1.
10. *1981 Hearings*, 72, 73.
11. *1981 Hearings*, 144.
12. Vern Countryman, "The Bankruptcy Boom," 77 *Harvard Law Review* 1452, 1460 (1964). The quotation in the text that follows comes from Vern Countryman, "Bankruptcy and the Individual Debtor—and a Modest Proposal to Return to the Seventeenth Century," 32 *Catholic University Law Review* 809, 821 (1983).
13. *1981 Hearings*, 78 (statement of Phillip Shuchman and Thomas Rhorer). Countryman's testimony appears at *1981 Hearings*, 74.
14. Teresa A. Sullivan, Elizabeth Warren, and Jay Lawrence Westbrook, "Limiting Access to Bankruptcy Discharge: An Analysis of the Creditors' Data," 1983 *Wisconsin Law Review* 1091, 1145.

15. 11 U.S.C., sec. 707(b).

16. "I cannot tell you strongly enough," Metzenbaum gushed in his remarks on the compromise bill, "how pleased I am that, after continuous battle, day in and day out, pressure, pressure, pressure to let the bill go with the future income mortgaging provision in it, we have successfully worked out with the author of this amendment the total elimination of the future income language. And for that I want to express my personal appreciation to him." 130 *Congressional Record* S5387–S5388 (daily ed. April 27, 1983) (quoted in Susan Block-Lieb, "Using Legislative History to Interpret Bankruptcy Statutes," in *Bankruptcy Practice and Strategy* (Alan N. Resnick ed., 1987), par. 2.02[7], 2–45 n. 244).

17. Quoted in *1997 Commission Report*, preface, 1.

18. The vote to approve Warren as reporter was unanimous, which is somewhat surprising given the ideological battle that developed on the commission. The unanimity no doubt reflected a desire to begin in consensus, as well as deference to the decision made by the gravely ill Chairman Synar.

19. Although the commission majority was led by the Democrat-appointed chairman, Brad Williamson, and the two most vocal dissenters (Jones and Jim Shepard) were Republican appointees, both blocs included appointees of both parties.

20. Berglof and Rosenthal, "Political Economy of Bankruptcy," 52.

21. Elizabeth Warren, "Reducing Bankruptcy Protection for Consumers: A Response," 72 *Georgetown Law Journal* 1333, 1343 (1984).

22. *1997 Commission Report*, preface, 4.

23. See generally Douglass C. North, *Institutions, Institutional Change, and Economic Performance* (Cambridge: Cambridge University Press, 1990).

24. Elizabeth Warren, "The New Women's Issue: Bankruptcy Law," *Christian Science Monitor*, September 10, 1999.

25. *In re Anastas*, 94 F.3d 1280 (9th Cir. 1996).

26. Warren, "The New Women's Issue."

27. Donald L. Barlett and James B. Steele, "Soaked by Congress," *Time*, May 15, 2000, 64.

28. "A Gift for the Credit Card Industry," *New York Times*, May 30, 2000, 22.

29. Advocates of reform responded to the renewed uproar about lavish homestead exemptions—and the complaint that the rich would prosper at the expense of the poor—by attempting to target only the states with unlimited homestead exemptions. Although the bill passed by the House in early 2001 did not impose significant, new limitations, the Senate Bill limits the homestead exemption to $125,000.

30. William C. Whitford, "Has the Time Come for Repeal of Chapter 13," 65 *Indiana Law Review* 85 (1989).

CHAPTER 8
BANKRUPTCY AS A BUSINESS ADDRESS: THE
GROWTH OF CHAPTER 11 IN PRACTICE AND THEORY

1. LoPucki and Whitford analyzed the results of their study, which includes all "megabankruptcies" filed after the 1978 Code was enacted and reorganized as of March 1988, in a series of law review articles. The most extensive analysis is in Lynn M. LoPucki and William C. Whitford, "Corporate Governance in the Bankruptcy

Reorganization of Large, Publicly Held Companies," 141 *University of Pennsylvania Law Review* 669 (1993).

2. I have explored the connection in great detail in other work. David A. Skeel Jr., "An Evolutionary Theory of Corporate Law and Corporate Bankruptcy," 51 *Vanderbilt Law Review* 1325 (1998); Skeel, "Rethinking the Line."

3. For a discussion, and empirical evidence that Federated gained value as a result of its Chapter 11 reorganization, see Steven N. Kaplan, ""Federated's Acquisition and Bankruptcy: Lessons and Implications," 72 *Washington University Law Quarterly* 1103 (1994).

4. Roe, *Strong Owners, Weak Managers.*

5. These cases are discussed in Robert K. Rasmussen and David A. Skeel Jr., "The Economic Analysis of Corporate Bankruptcy Law," 3 *American Bankruptcy Institute Law Journal* 85 (1995).

6. Theodore Eisenberg and Lynn M. LoPucki, "Shopping for Judges: An Empirical Analysis of Venue Choice in Large Chapter 11 Reorganizations," 84 *Cornell Law Review* 967, 979 (1999).

7. The quotations and much of the information in this paragraph come from Kevin J. Delaney, *Strategic Bankruptcy: How Corporations and Creditors Use Chapter 11 to Their Advantage*, 60–61 (Berkeley and Los Angeles: University of California Press, 1992).

8. Richard B. Sobol, *Bending the Law: The Story of the Dalkon Shield Bankruptcy* (Chicago: University of Chicago Press, 1991).

9. The argument described in this paragraph was made by Thomas C. Smith in "A Capital Markets Approach to Mass Tort Bankruptcy," 104 *Yale Law Journal* 367 (1993).

10. The use of bankruptcy to address mass tort problems has generated a large and still growing literature. Prominent contributions include Edith H. Jones, "Rough Justice in Mass Future Claims: Should Bankruptcy Courts Direct Tort Reform?" 76 *Texas Law Review* 1695 (1998) (criticizing bankruptcy as running roughshod over the concerns implicated by Rule 23 outside of bankruptcy); John C. Coffee Jr., "Class Wars: The Dilemma of the Mass Tort Class Action," 95 *Columbia Law Review* (1995) (describing conflict between attorney's and plaintiffs interests but taking sympathetic view on use of bankruptcy); Mark J. Roe, "Bankruptcy and Mass Tort," 84 *Columbia Law Review* 846 (1984) (defending bankruptcy forum and proposing administrative approach to tort claims).

11. 11 U.S.C., sec. 524(g).

12. For a critical discussion of the commission's proposals (by a dissenting member of the commission), see Jones, "Rough Justice," 1702–22.

13. 117 S. Ct. 2231 (1997).

14. "Profiting from the Failures of Others," *National Law Journal*, April 2, 1990, 1, 29.

15. "Profiting from Failures."

16. Rosen and Vris, "History of Bankruptcy Bar," 155.

17. See, for example, Jonathan D. Glater, "For Lawyers, Is Boom Near in Insolvency," *New York Times*, December 26, 2000, C1.

18. Elizabeth Warren, "Bankruptcy Policy," 54 *University of Chicago Law Review* 775, 792–93 (1987).

19. Skeel, "Vern Countryman."

20. See, for example, Jackson, *Logic and Limits*; Douglas G. Baird and Thomas H. Jackson, "Corporate Reorganizations and the Treatment of Diverse Ownership Interests: A Comment on Adequate Protection of Secured Creditors in Bankruptcy," 51 *University of Chicago Law Review* 97 (1984).

21. Borrowed from the economics literature, the common pool metaphor suggests that the fishermen who fish at a single "pool" may fish too much and deplete the pool if they cannot bargain with each other to limit their activity. Each fisherman has an incentive to overfish for fear that others will do the same, even though there would be more fish for everyone, and a healthy pond, if all limited their fishing. Behavior that is rational for each individual turns out to be irrational for the group, or collective.

22. One of the first articles to make this point was Randal C. Picker, "Security Interests, Misbehavior, and Common Pools," 59 *University of Chicago Law Review* 645 (1992).

23. Michael Bradley and Michael Rosenzweig, "The Untenable Case for Chapter 11," 101 *Yale Law Journal* 1043 (1992). Adler's proposal differs in several significant details, as he points out in Barry E. Adler, "Financial and Political Theories of American Corporate Bankruptcy," 45 *Stanford Law Review* 311 (1993).

24. Lynn M. LoPucki, "Strange Visions in a Strange World: A Reply to Professors Bradley and Rosenzweig," 91 *Michigan Law Review* 79 (1992).

25. Douglas Baird considered the possibilities of a straight auction. Douglas G. Baird, "The Uneasy Case for Corporate Reorganizations," 15 *Journal of Legal Studies* 127 (1986); Douglas G. Baird, "Revisiting Auctions in Chapter 11," 36 *Journal of Law and Economics* 633 (1993). Lucian Bebchuk proposed the first options-based auction, and his proposal was subsequently embellished by several prominent economists. Lucian A. Bebchuk, "A New Approach to Corporate Reorganizations," 101 *Harvard Law Review* 775 (1988); Philippe Aghion, Oliver Hart, and John Moore, "The Economics of Bankruptcy Reform," 8 *Journal of Law, Economics, and Organization* 523 (1993). The menu approach described in the text that follows came from Robert K. Rasmussen, "Debtor's Choice: A Menu Approach to Corporate Bankruptcy," 71 *Texas Law Review* 51 (1992).

26. Alan Schwartz, "A Contract Theory Approach to Business Bankruptcy," 107 *Yale Law Journal* 1807 (1998). Schwartz has subsequently defended his analysis in an exchange with Lynn LoPucki. Lynn M. LoPucki, "Contract Bankruptcy: A Reply to Alan Schwartz," 109 *Yale Law Journal* 317 (1999); Alan Schwartz, "Bankruptcy Contracting Revisited," 109 *Yale Law Journal* 343 (1999).

27. On stay waivers, see Marshall E. Tracht, "Contractual Bankruptcy Waivers: Reconciling Theory, Practice, and Law, 82 *Cornell Law Review* 301 (1997); on prepackaged bankruptcy, see Elizabeth Tashjian et al., "Prepacks: An Empirical Analysis of Prepackaged Bankruptcies," 40 *Journal of Financial Economics* 135 (1996).

28. *1975–76 House Hearings*, 1893 (statement of Harvey Miller, National Bankruptcy Conference) (defending prebankruptcy solicitations); *1975 Senate Hearings*, 398 (statement of Benjamin Weintraub, Levin & Weintraub) (describing prebankruptcy solicitations in Chapter XI cases and arguing they should be permitted).

29. 28 U.S.C., sec. 1408.

30. Robert K. Rasmussen and Randall S. Thomas, "Timing Matters: Promoting Forum Shopping by Insolvent Corporations," 94 *Northwestern University Law Review* 1357, 1373 (2000).

31. The discussion that follows is drawn in part from David A. Skeel Jr., "What's So Bad about Delaware?" 54 *Vanderbilt Law Review* 309 (2001). This paper responds to an article by Lynn LoPucki and Sarah D. Kalin, "The Failure of Public Company Bankruptcies in Delaware and New York: Empirical Evidence of a 'Race to the Bottom,'" 54 *Vanderbilt Law Review* 231 (2001), which reports on their study showing that Delaware firms are more likely to require a second bankruptcy filing and concludes that Delaware's bankruptcy judges do not adequately scrutinize the reorganization plans they confirm. Following up on earlier work such as David A. Skeel Jr., "Bankruptcy Judges and Bankruptcy Venue: Some Thoughts on Delaware," 1 *Delaware Law Review* 1(1998), my reply defends Delaware and argues that, rather than removing state of incorporation as a venue option, the Bankruptcy Code should *require* that firms file in their state of incorporation. In another reply, Bob Rasmussen and Randall Thomas defend Delaware's handling of prepackaged bankruptcy cases but express more skepticism about Delaware oversight of traditional Chapter 11 cases. Robert K. Rasmussen and Randall S. Thomas, "Whither the Race: A Comment on the Effects of the Delawarization of Corporate Reorganizations," 54 *Vanderbilt Law Review* 283 (2001).

32. 77 *Congressional Record* 7890 (May 2, 1934).

33. I describe the debate in some detail in Skeel, "Rethinking the Line."

34. "Houston, We Know We Have a Problem (but We're Working on It!)," 35 *Bankruptcy Court Decisions: News and Comment* A1 (February 8, 2000).

35. Trost, interview.

36. This language dates back to a 1939 decision by Justice Douglas, *Case v. Los Angeles Lumber Products*, 308 U.S. 106 (1939).

37. The best history of the new value rule is Douglas G. Baird and Robert K. Rasmussen, "Boyd's Legacy and Blackstone's Ghost," 1999 *Supreme Court Review* 393 (2000). In equity receiverships, shareholders (and often other security holders) were permitted to retain their equity interest if they paid a cash "assessment" when the corporation was reorganized. For discussion, see Tufano, "Business Failure." This was not simply a special perk for shareholders. Reorganizers believed that current security holders were the best source of desperately needed cash, and the assessments were viewed as the only way to finance a successful reorganization. Although William Douglas and the reformers acknowledged the need for assessments, they worried that, since the firm's managers were generally significant shareholders, the managers would strike a deal with the firm's senior creditors that benefited senior creditors and shareholders at the expense of junior creditors. In his early years on the Supreme Court, Douglas reconciled these concerns in *Case v. Los Angeles Lumber Products*, by recognizing, but sharply limiting, the right of shareholders or managers to retain their interest. Managers' promise to continue managing the business in the future did not qualify, because its value was too intangible—not "money or money's worth."

38. *Norwest Bank Worthington v. Ahlers*, 485 U.S. 197 (1988).

39. *Bank of America National Trust Savings Association v. 203 North LaSalle Street Partnership*, 119 S. Ct. 1411 (1999).

40. 11 U.S.C., sec. 362(d)(3).

41. For a discussion of the various viewpoints, and a defense of "modified territoriality," see Lynn M. LoPucki, "Cooperation in International Bankruptcy: A Post-Universalist Approach," 84 *Cornell Law Review* 696 (1999).

EPILOGUE
GLOBALIZATION AND U.S. BANKRUPTCY LAW

1. Jay Lawrence Westbrook, "Local Legal Culture and the Fear of Abuse," 6 *American Bankruptcy Institute Law Review* 25, 32–33 (1998) (citing Hans Peter Graver, "Consumer Bankruptcy: A Right or a Privilege? The Role of the Courts in Establishing Moral Standards of Economic Conduct," 20 *Journal of Consumer Policy* 161 (1997)).

2. North, *Institutions, Institutional Change*, 87.

3. Christopher Rhoads, "New Tax Law Will Transform Germany, Inc.," *Wall Street Journal*, July 17, 2000, A29.

4. Editorial, "The Big Bankruptcy," *Wall Street Journal*, July 17, 2000, A34.

5. For a useful discussion of the new law, see Klaus Kamlah, "The New German Insolvency Act: *Insolvenzordnang*," 70 *American Bankruptcy Law Journal* 417 (1996).

6. For a discussion, see Elspeth Guild, "How Can Social Protection Survive EMU? A United Kingdom Perspective," 24 *European Law Review* 22 (1999).

7. Sullivan, Warren, and Westbrook, *The Fragile Middle Class*. The unemployment findings are summarized at p. 105, and medical issues at p. 144.

8. Sullivan, Warren, and Westbrook, *The Fragile Middle Class*, 5.

9. For a discussion, see Johanna Niemi-Kiesilainen, "Changing Directions in Consumer Bankruptcy Law and Practice in Europe and the USA," 20 *Journal of Consumer Policy* 133 (1997).

INDEX

A. H. Robins, 20, 217–18, 219
ABA. *See* American Bar Association
Abe Fortas: A Biography (Kalman), 259n.47
abortion amendment, 209
absolute priority rule, 10, 67, 124–25, 162, 233–35, 253n.47
Adair, Watson, 87
Adler, Barry, 226, 269n.23
administrative reform proposals: in commission report (1973), 139, 141, 142–47; in Hastings-Michener bill, 74, 80, 90, 91; opponents of, 90–93, 143–45; in Sabath bill, 113–14; supporters of, 91–92, 145; in Thacher report, 79
administrative structure, minimalist, 40, 90
Aghion, Philippe, 269n.25
agrarian movements, 3, 38–39
alimony, 206–7
Allegheny International, 216
allowable claim, 148
Amchem Products, Inc. v. Windsor, 220
American Bankers Association, 85, 118, 121–22
American Bar Association (ABA), 45, 75, 76, 91
American Lawyer, 221
American Life Insurance Association, 178
American Paint and Varnish Manufacturers Association, 83
American Trial Lawyers Association (ATLA), 220
ancillary receivership, 104, 105, 107
Antibankruptcy Law Association, 82–83
apathy, rational, 80
Arlan's Department Stores, 166
Arnold, Thurmond, 122
arrangement (reorganization process), 9
Arrow, Kenneth, 28–29
Arrow's Theorem, 30, 248n.19
As We Forgive Our Debtors (Warren, Westbrook, and Sullivan), 13, 195
Association of the Bar of the City of New York, 77
ATLA. *See* American Trial Lawyers Association
attitudinal model, 61

auctions, 226
automatic stay, 10–11, 98, 225, 228–29

Bailey, Joseph, Representative, 27, 39
Bailey bill, 37, 249n.30
Baird, Douglas, 12, 200, 201, 224, 225, 269n.25
Balick, Helen, 229
Balleisen, Edward, 34, 249n.32
bankruptcy: involuntary, 8, 32, 42–43; prepackaged, 228–29, 232; voluntary, 3, 8, 28, 32
Bankruptcy Act (1800), 25, 31, 90
Bankruptcy Act (1841), 25, 31–32, 90; debates on, 248n.18
Bankruptcy Act (1867), 25, 90; and administrative costs, 40; Civil War and, 32; corporate bankruptcy in, 54; state exemptions in, 41–42
Bankruptcy Act (1898), vii, 6; corporate bankruptcy in, 9; debate on, 247n.13; enactment of, 32–33, 37, 43; limitations on jurisdiction of bankruptcy court in, 94; minimalist administrative structure in, 40, 90; party politics and, 23–24, 43–44, 239; personal bankruptcy in, 7; railroads excluded from, 54
Bankruptcy Act, England (1869), 36, 37–38, 90
Bankruptcy Act, England (1883), 38
bankruptcy agency. *See* administrative reform proposals
bankruptcy bar: demography of, 76, 134; effect of Chandler Act on, 80, 131, 132–33; emergence of, 44–46; investigation of, 77–80, 111; vs. reorganization bar, 69–70, 73; and SEC, 97, 116–17, 118
Bankruptcy Clause (of U.S. Constitution), 23, 27, 31, 52–54, 251n.16
Bankruptcy Code (1978), vii, 4, 6; 1984 amendment to, 196–97; 1994 amendment to, 197–202; Brookings study and, 246n.15; commission report (1973) and, 139–57; *See also* Chapter 7; Chapter 11; Chapter 13
Bankruptcy Committee, 45, 91, 134
Bankruptcy in United States History (Warren), 12, 238, 245n.9, 247n.4